T0388032

Digital Transformation in Accounting

Digital Transformation in Accounting is a critical guidebook for accountancy and digital business students and practitioners to navigate the effects of digital technology advancements, digital disruption, and digital transformation on the accounting profession.

Drawing on the latest research, this book:

- Unpacks dozens of digital technology advancements, explaining what they are and how they could be used to improve accounting practice.
- Discusses the impact of digital disruption and digital transformation on different accounting functions, roles, and activities.
- Integrates traditional accounting information systems concepts and contemporary digital business and digital transformation concepts.
- Includes a rich array of real-world case studies, simulated problems, quizzes, group and individual exercises, as well as supplementary electronic resources.
- Provides a framework and a set of tools to prepare the future accounting workforce for the era of digital disruption.

This book is an invaluable resource for students on accounting, accounting information systems, and digital business courses, as well as for accountants, accounting educators, and accreditation / advocacy bodies.

Richard Busulwa is a Lecturer and Researcher in the Business School at Swinburne University of Technology, Australia.

Nina Evans is Associate Professor of STEM at the University of South Australia.

Business and Digital Transformation

Digital technologies are transforming societies across the globe, the effects of which are yet to be fully understood. In the business world, technological disruption brings an array of challenges and opportunities for organizations, management and the workplace.

This series of textbooks provides a student-centred library to analyse, explore and critique the evolutionary effects of technology on the business world. Each book in the series takes the perspective of a key business discipline and examines the transformational potential of digital technology, aided by real world cases and examples.

With contributions from expert scholars across the globe, the books in this series enable critical thinking students to excel in their studies of the new digital business environment.

Strategic Digital Transformation
A Results-Driven Approach
Edited by Alex Fenton, Gordon Fletcher and Marie Griffiths

Hospitality Management and Digital Transformation
Balancing Efficiency, Agility and Guest Experience in the Era of Disruption
Richard Busulwa, Nina Evans, Aaron Oh and Moon Kang

Digital Transformation in Accounting
Richard Busulwa and Nina Evans

For more information about this series, please visit www.routledge.com/Routledge-New-Directions-in-Public-Relations--Communication-Research/book-series/BAD

Digital Transformation in Accounting

Richard Busulwa and Nina Evans

LONDON AND NEW YORK

First published 2021
by Routledge
2 Park Square, Milton Park, Abingdon, Oxon OX14 4RN

and by Routledge
52 Vanderbilt Avenue, New York, NY 10017

Routledge is an imprint of the Taylor & Francis Group, an informa business

© 2021 Richard Busulwa and Nina Evans

The right of Richard Busulwa and Nina Evans to be identified as authors of this work has been asserted by them in accordance with sections 77 and 78 of the Copyright, Designs and Patents Act 1988.

All rights reserved. No part of this book may be reprinted or reproduced or utilised in any form or by any electronic, mechanical, or other means, now known or hereafter invented, including photocopying and recording, or in any information storage or retrieval system, without permission in writing from the publishers.

Trademark notice: Product or corporate names may be trademarks or registered trademarks, and are used only for identification and explanation without intent to infringe.

British Library Cataloguing-in-Publication Data
A catalogue record for this book is available from the British Library

Library of Congress Cataloging-in-Publication Data
Names: Busulwa, Richard, 1980– author. | Evans, Nina, author.
Title: Digital transformation in accounting / Richard Busulwa and Nina Evans.
Description: Abingdon, Oxon ; New York, NY : Routledge, 2021. | Series: Business & digital transformation | Includes bibliographical references and index.
Identifiers: LCCN 2020051665 (print) | LCCN 2020051666 (ebook) | ISBN 9780367362065 (hardback) | ISBN 9780367362096 (paperback) | ISBN 9780429344589 (ebook)
Subjects: LCSH: Accounting—Data processing. | Accounting—Computer programs. | Computer software—Accounting. | Information storage and retrieval systems—Accounting.
Classification: LCC HF5679 .B838 2021 (print) | LCC HF5679 (ebook) | DDC 657.0285—dc23
LC record available at https://lccn.loc.gov/2020051665
LC ebook record available at https://lccn.loc.gov/2020051666

ISBN: 978-0-367-36206-5 (hbk)
ISBN: 978-0-367-36209-6 (pbk)
ISBN: 978-0-429-34458-9 (ebk)

Typeset in Bembo MT Pro
by Apex CoVantage, LLC

Access the Support Material: www.routledge.com/9780367362096

 Printed in the United Kingdom by Henry Ling Limited

Contents

List of figures x
List of tables xii
Acknowledgments xiv

PART I
Digital technology advancements, digital disruption, and digital business transformation 1

1 **Introduction and need for this book** 3

   Introduction 3
   Need for this book 4
   Research for this book 5
   How to use this book 7

2 **IT, information systems, strategic information systems, and digital technologies** 10

   Introduction 10
   Information systems 10
   Information technology and information communications technology 14
   Strategic information systems and digital technologies 15
   Implications for accountants 16

3 **Digital technology advancements and digital disruption: game-changing opportunities and existential threats** 19

   Introduction 19
   Digital technology advancements and digital disruption 19
   Unpacking digital disruption 21
   Existential threats and game-changing opportunities 23
   Implications for accountants 26

4 Digital business, the digital business imperative, and digital business transformation   29

Introduction 29
Digital business 29
The digital business imperative 33
Digital business transformation 33
Implications for accountants 35

PART II
Digital disruption and digital transformation of accounting   41

5 Digital disruption and digital transformation of accounting   43

Introduction 43
Digital disruption of accounting 43
Disruption and transformation of the accounting value proposition 50
Disruption and transformation of accounting functions 52
Digital technology advancements anticipated to have a profound direct impact on accounting 63
Implications for accountants 72

6 Impact of digital disruption and digital transformation on accountants   77

Introduction 77
Impact of digital disruption and digital transformation on accountants 77
New or enhanced roles and activities required of accountants 78
IFAC future-fit accounting roles 81
ACCA future career zones 85
New or enhanced digital technology competencies required of accountants 87
An organizing framework for accounting technology competencies 96

PART III
Leveraging digital technologies to thrive in the digital era: roles of accountants in organization digital business capabilities   109

7 The role of accountants in digital transformation strategy, digital business strategy, digital innovation, digital learning, adaptability, and agility   111

Introduction 111
The role of accountants in digital business strategy and digital transformation strategy 111
The role of accountants in digital innovation 115
The role of accountants in organizational digital learning 117
The role of accountants in organizational adaptability, agility, and ambidexterity 119

Contents vii

8 The role of accountants in digital customer engagement, digital stakeholder engagement, and digital customer experience — 125

Introduction 125
Required accounting roles and competencies for digital customer engagement and digital stakeholder engagement 125
Required accounting roles and competencies for digital customer experience 129

9 The role of accountants in enterprise architecture, technology sourcing, data analytics, data science, and data management — 133

Introduction 133
Required accounting roles and competencies for enterprise architecture management 133
Required accounting roles and competencies for technology sourcing 138
Required accounting roles and competencies for data management, data science, and data analytics 139

10 The role of accountants in cybersecurity, information privacy, and digital ethics — 144

Introduction 144
Required accounting roles and competencies for cybersecurity 144
Required accounting roles and competencies for information privacy and other digital ethics issues 148

11 The role of accountants in digital leadership, accelerated change and transformation, digital risk management, and digital governance — 154

Introduction 154
Required accounting roles and competencies for digital leadership 154
Required accounting roles and competencies for accelerated change and transformation 158
Required accounting roles and competencies for digital risk management and governance 159

PART IV
Keeping up with digital technology advancements — 165

12 Keeping up with digital technologies — 167

Introduction 167
Importance and challenge of keeping up with digital technologies 167
Common strategies and practices for keeping up with digital technologies 168
Strategies and practices from the research on technological knowledge renewal effectiveness 168
Strategies and practices from practitioners 170
Implications for accountants 177

PART V
Digital technologies deep dive — 181

13 Data, data management, data analytics, and data science technologies — 183

Introduction 183
Data 184
Big data 186
Data management 188
Business intelligence and business analytics 188
Data analytics and data science 189
Data visualization 191

14 Internet of things (IoT) technologies — 197

Introduction 197
The internet of things and the internet of everything 198
Smart buildings, smart workspaces, and smart homes 203
Smart infrastructure, smart cities, and smart government 205
Risks and other issues 207

15 Artificial intelligence technologies — 211

Introduction 211
Artificial intelligence and machine learning 212
Knowledge graphs, neural networks, and deep learning 214
Natural language processing, speech recognition, and computer vision 216
Common AI issues and risks 218

16 Video analytics, computer vision, and virtual reality technologies — 221

Introduction 221
Video analytics and computer vision 221
Virtual reality, augmented reality, and mixed reality 224
Business value of VR, AR, and MR 226

17 Robotics, drones, and 3D / 4D printing technologies — 232

Introduction 232
Robots and robotics 232
Drones 236
3D and 4D printing 240
Issues and challenges 243

18 Network and connectivity technologies — 251

Introduction 251
6G, 5G, 4G, LTE, and other cellular networks 251

GPS III, GPS Block III, and low earth orbit (LEO) satellites 254
NBIoT, LTE Cat-M1, LoRaWAN and other low-power wide-area network technologies 256
NFC, Smart Bluetooth, iBeacon, and other communication protocols 258

19 Blockchain and other distributed ledger technologies   265

Introduction 265
Distributed ledger technology (DLT) 266
Blockchain 267
Types of blockchain 269
Blockchain applications and use cases 270
Blockchain use cases in accounting 273
Risks and issues 275

Index   279

Figures

2.1	Components of an information system	11
2.2	Types of information systems, including example systems and example users	14
3.1	Digital technology advancements cause digital disruption but can be leveraged to respond to disruption and recreate value offerings and capabilities	20
3.2	Kodak failed to effectively respond to disruption from digital cameras and smartphones, despite creating the technology behind them	24
4.1	Digital business maturity models, like this one, attempt to map where an organization is along various digital business capabilities or outcome areas	32
4.2	Digital business transformation is not just about using digital technologies; it is also about changing organization structures, overcoming change barriers, and managing both digital risks and change risks	35
5.1	Some researchers are proposing the inclusion of an accounting information systems course or unit in undergraduate accounting degrees focusing on these identified AIS competency areas	49
5.2	AI and cognitive technologies, drones / robotics, and PPA / RPA can be combined to give robots / drones the human-like ability to do inventory counts / verifications	53
5.3	Data mining methods and tools offer new and potentially more efficient / effective ways to do both retrospective and prospective analysis and reporting	55
5.4	Data analytics and data science methods and techniques now being applied to different audit procedures / activities	59
5.5	Cloud computing service models and example vendors	64
6.1	ACCA future career zones	85
6.2	Digital technology competencies within the AAA and IMA accounting competency framework	88
6.3	The design thinking process and some of each stage's objectives, artefacts, and outputs	91
6.4	The Cynefin framework is one of several frameworks that can be used by individuals and organizations to make sense of information and events in complex settings	95
6.5	Accounting digital technology competencies	97
7.1	Digital business requires new organizational capabilities or digital enhancements of traditional capabilities to achieve the same or enhanced aims to traditional business	112

8.1	Traditional customer engagement vs. digital customer engagement	126
8.2	A research-derived taxonomy of digital customer engagement practices	127
9.1	Example enterprise architecture governance model	137
10.1	NIST cybersecurity capability functions and practices	147
11.1	Results of a survey of 3,300 *MIT Sloan Management Review* readers, Deloitte Dbriefs webcast subscribers, and other interested parties, regarding what is different about working in a digital business environment	155
11.2	Results of a survey of 3,300 *MIT Sloan Management Review* readers, Deloitte Dbriefs webcast subscribers, and other interested parties, regarding the most important skill leaders need to succeed in a digital workplace	156
11.3	Having working knowledge of accelerated change and transformation methodologies like the Change Acceleration Process can be an invaluable tool in digital leaders' rapid change and transformation tool arsenal	158
13.1	An example of different types of data	185
13.2	Example of sources of big data	187
13.3	Data management, business intelligence, business analytics, and data science overlaps	190
14.1	The internet of everything extends the internet of things by connecting people, processes, data, and things	199
14.2	Edge computing brings computation and data storage to the locations where they are needed, instead of requiring sensor data to be sent to the cloud and waiting for the cloud to send the results of computation back to the location	201
15.1	Part of a knowledge graph showing information about key figures in US politics at a point in time	215
15.2	A simple neural network vs. a deep learning neural network	216
15.3	Computer vision can enable self-driving cars to "see" better than humans	217
16.1	An example of VCA / computer vision software developed by Voxel51	222
16.2	An example of VCA / computer vision software recognizing both people and actions/events	223
16.3	Using a HoloLens 2 headset	226
17.1	Components of a drone	237
17.2	NASA's proposed space for drone operation: below aircraft space and above suburban infrastructure and dwellings	239
17.3	Anatomy of a basic 3D printer	241
18.1	How cellular phones work	252
18.2	Low earth orbit (LEO), medium earth orbit (MEO), and highly elliptical orbit (HEO)	255
18.3	An NFC-enabled phone sets up a current, the NFC tag receives the "induced current", and, recognizing it is a valid signal, offers connection to the phone and begins data transfer	258
19.1	Each blockchain block contains some data, the hash of the block, and the hash of the previous block	267
19.2	A chain of blocks, with each block other than the genesis block having the hash of the previous block	267
19.3	The funds transfer process in a traditional digital ledger vs. in a blockchain network	273

Tables

1.1	Key literatures reviewed at each research stage for this book and the focus of each literature review	6
5.1	Example digital technology tools used to automate audit tasks	48
5.2	Example applications of RPA in the finance function	69
5.3	Current AI applications as reported by the big four accounting firms	70
6.1	Examples of different corporate accelerator models and their structures, objectives, and characteristics	93
7.1	Impact of digital technology advancements on digital innovation and examples of opportunities that can be leveraged	116
7.2	Google and reflect	121
8.1	Google and reflect	131
9.1	Example enterprise architecture management activities, tasks, and artefacts	135
9.2	Benefits of effective enterprise architecture management	136
9.3	Google and reflect	141
10.1	Ten messages for global leaders from the 2019 World Economic Forum annual meeting on cybersecurity	146
11.1	Google and reflect	161
12.1	Top learning tools sorted alphabetically by learning tool type and their change in ranking from year to year – part 1	171
12.2	Top learning tools sorted alphabetically by learning tool type and their change in ranking from year to year – part 2	172
12.3	Top learning tools sorted alphabetically by learning tool type and their change in ranking from year to year – part 3	172
13.1	Data-related roles and type of expertise	190
13.2	Google and reflect	191
13.3	Example tools and vendors	192
14.1	Cities around the world and their smart city maturity (e.g. if they have a smart city roadmap or smart city department, and the presence of key smart city domains or application areas)	206
15.1	Types of AI, their capabilities, and implications for human beings	213
16.1	Google and reflect	228
17.1	Google and reflect	244
17.2	Example tools and vendors	244
17.3	Discussion questions	245
18.1	Types of satellite or orbit, and what they are used for	256

18.2	Google and reflect	260
18.3	Example tools and vendors	260
18.4	Discussion questions	261
19.1	Blockchain opportunities and challenges for auditing	274

Acknowledgments

We are thankful to Associate Professor Mary Dunkley and Professor Keryn Chalmers from Swinburne University of Technology for the support provided in the research and writing of this book. We are thankful to Kristina Abbots and Christiana Mandizha at Routledge for providing us with the opportunity to research and write the book; as well as for being easy to work with. And we are thankful to Natalie Tomlinson and Chloe James at Routledge for their support with the final editing and production process.

Part I
Digital technology advancements, digital disruption, and digital business transformation

1 Introduction and need for this book

Introduction

Digital technology advancements such as cloud computing, the internet of things, blockchain, and artificial intelligence are driving disruptions at organization, society, and industry level[1]. These digital technology-related disruptions are commonly referred to as digital disruption or digital disruptions. At organization level, digital disruption typically manifests itself as changes in competing products and services, changes in customer expectation and behaviors, changes in data availability, changes in competing business models, changes in the competitive landscape, and changes in the bases of competition (or sources of competitive advantage)[2]. Irrespective of which of these changes are most pronounced for a particular organization or industry, digital disruption can render much of existing approaches to value creation, existing business models, existing approaches to competition, and / or existing business processes and workflows obsolete. Faced with growing obsolescence in many of their activities and workflows, organizations can deny / ignore the occurrence of digital disruption. Or they can accept the occurrence of digital disruption but not the urgent need to respond to it. Alternatively, they can accept the occurrence of digital disruption, accept the urgent need to respond to digital disruption, and undertake digital business transformation to recreate themselves in order to be able to adapt to digital disruption and to leverage digital technology advancements as a source of competitive advantage, adaptability, and agility. This process of organizations recreating themselves to adapt to digital disruption, and to leverage digital technologies for competitive advantage, adaptability, and agility is most accurately referred to as digital business transformation; even though it is more commonly referred to as digital transformation. The term digital transformation is often used as a broad reference to digitization, digitalization, and digital business transformation. Notwithstanding this loose use of the term, we hereon use both terms interchangeably, since digital transformation is a more common term to readers. But, each time we use the term digital transformation, we strictly mean digital business transformation (we clarify the exact differences and implications of the differences in chapter 4).

In disrupting organizations' product / service offerings, as well as the underlying business processes and workflows facilitating delivery of those products / services, digital disruption, in turn, disrupts the professions. That is, it renders significant aspects of the existing roles and activities performed by particular professions obsolete – thus requiring them to perform new roles and activities in order to remain relevant. Like organizations, professions faced with growing obsolescence in existing roles and activities can deny / ignore digital disruption and the urgency of responding to it, or they can act quickly to recreate themselves in order to adapt to digital disruption in a timely manner, and to leverage digital technologies to offer new or significantly enhanced value. As one of these professions, the accounting profession is not immune to digital disruption. In fact, compelling arguments have been made that accounting tops lists of professions most at risk of digital disruption[3,4,5]. And institutions, such as the International Federation of Accountants (IFAC), accounting associations, accounting professional bodies, and accounting professional service firms, are calling for changes to accounting roles, activities, and competencies in order for accountants to be able to adapt to disruption and reshape their value proposition. Notwithstanding contentions of accounting being at high risk of losing relevance due to digital disruption, researchers, governance bodies, and futurists are converging on the view that digital technology advancement and digital business transformation actually make accountants much more important than ever. This is because digital business transformation and digital business come with significant financial, technological, and strategic risks. Accountants need to play critical roles in helping organizations to safely undertake digital business transformation, to optimally leverage digital technology advancements, and to realize the full benefits of becoming a digital business. But playing these critical roles requires changes in the roles, activities, and competencies of accountants. And it requires accountants to understand key digital technologies and their implications for organizations, to understand digital transformation and digital business capabilities and practices, and to understand how digital technologies and digital business capabilities impact accounting value creation and practice.

Need for this book

Although interdisciplinary, digital transformation and digital business have strong roots in the disciplines of information systems, information technology, computer science, computer engineering, and software engineering. These disciplines are notorious for their specialized terminology, jargon, acronyms, and abbreviations – which can often get in the way of understanding critical digital technology issues and their implications. This challenge is compounded by the proliferation in digital technologies, and the pace with which innovations in these technologies are occurring. Even IT professionals can easily get overwhelmed by the slippery terminology, concepts, and issues. But while in the past accountants could get away with relegating such digital technology issues to the "techies" in order to focus on accounting specific activities, they now need to make sense of the specialized terminology, and to understand critical digital technology issues and their implications. They then need to be able to draw on this understanding to effectively leverage digital technologies to deliver on the evolving accounting value proposition. Unfortunately, in our review of more than 250 undergraduate and postgraduate accounting degrees and courses around the world, we found that, at best, most degrees and courses tended to only cover traditional information systems and IT concepts (e.g. hardware, software, networks, operating systems, ERP systems, databases, decision support systems, etc.), with little mention of emerging technologies or of digital transformation and digital business concepts and issues. In doing so, we contend that they miss opportunities to help accountants make sense of the slippery terminology related to digital transformation and digital business, to understand the different digital technologies and their implications for digital business transformation and digital business, to understand how all of this impacts accounting value creation and practice, and to build future accountants' ability to keep up with accelerating digital technology advancements. Seizing these missed opportunities is critical to ensuring accountants are optimally positioned to effectively participate in their organizations' digital transformation and digital business efforts. This, in turn, is critical to ensuring accountants remain invaluable to maximizing their organizations' long-term survival.

Filling these gaps is the focus of this book. That is, the book explores digital technology advancements and digital disruption from the perspective of the accounting profession. It explains the concepts of digitalization, digital business, and digital transformation; and how these concepts interact with different digital technologies to impact the role of accountants and the accounting value proposition. As a part of this, the book unpacks more than 36 key digital technology advancements (e.g. internet of things, artificial intelligence, robotics, blockchain, augmented reality). It explains how they work, their implications for organizational strategy and operational processes, and their implication for accounting value creation. The book then explains the role accountants can play in undertaking digital business transformation and leveraging digital technology advancements to enable their organizations to simultaneously pursue efficiency, agility, and customer experience – so as to gain competitive edge today and guard against disruption tomorrow. To conclude, a framework is provided that accountants can use to effectively develop required digital technology competencies and to keep up with accelerating digital technology advancements.

Research for this book

The research for this book consisted of six stages. In stage 1, we undertook a review of the relevant and seminal information systems research on digital technology advancements, digital disruption, digital transformation, and digital business. The purpose of this stage was to understand the implications of these concepts for organizations and for the professions. In stage 2, we undertook a review of the accounting and accounting information systems research on the implications of digital technology advancements and digital business transformation for accounting. The aim of this stage was to understand accounting researchers' perspectives on how digital technology advancements and digital business transformation were changing the accounting value proposition and, therefore, what the implications were for accounting roles and competencies. In stage 3, we reviewed research reports by key accounting professional institutions / stakeholders investigating the implications of digital transformation and digital technologies for the accounting profession. These stakeholder reports included reports by institutions such as the International Federation of Accountants, accounting associations, accounting professional bodies, accounting professional service firms, and accounting recruitment firms. The aim of this stage was to understand these different stakeholders' perspectives on how digital technologies were changing the accounting value proposition and the required technology competencies of accountants. In stage 4, we sought out industry case studies of accountants performing the changed accounting roles and activities, of accountants leveraging emerging digital technologies to deliver enhanced value, of accountants leveraging their new or enhanced digital technology competencies, and of organizations benefiting from the new or enhanced value created by accountants. The aim of this stage was to find practical examples of accountants effectively participating in their organizations' digital transformation and digital business capabilities. In stage 5, we reviewed relevant academic and non-academic literature on digital technology competencies required of accountants in order to play a sufficient role in digital business transformation and digital business. The aim of this stage was to identify key competencies and propose a framework for their development. Finally, in stage 6, we reviewed more than 250 accounting degrees and courses / units to explore the degree and nature of digital technology competencies embedded within those degrees and units. The aim of this stage was to understand the breadth and depth of digital technology, digital transformation, and digital business-related competencies within accounting degrees and courses / units. See Table 1.1 for a summary of the research activities undertaken at each stage of the research process.

Table 1.1 Key literatures reviewed at each research stage for this book and the focus of each literature review

Research stage	Research activity
Stage 1	Review of the *information systems academic research* for discussions of:
	• The relationship between traditional information systems concepts and contemporary digital business concepts
	• The link between digital technology advancements and digital disruption
	• The need for digital transformation and digital business
	• The capabilities required for digital transformation and digital business
	• The accounting roles and competencies required for digital transformation and digital business
Stage 2	Review of the *accounting and accounting information systems research* discussing:
	• Technology and information systems competencies required by accountants
	• Digital technology advancements
	• Digital transformation and digital business
	• Digital transformation and digital business capabilities
	• Impact of digital technology advancements, digital transformation, and digital business on the roles of accountants
	• Impact of digital technology advancements, digital transformation, and digital business on the required competencies of accountants
Stage 3	Review of the *key accounting professional bodies / institution research reports* discussing:
	• Implications of digital technology advancements, digital transformation, and digital business for accounting value creation
	• Implications of digital technology advancements, digital transformation, and digital business for accounting roles and competencies
	• Key digital technology advancements impacting accounting value creation
	• Example use cases of different digital technologies in accounting value creation
	Example professional bodies / institutions included the International Federation of Accountants (IFAC), accounting associations, accounting professional bodies, accounting professional service firms, and accounting recruitment firms
Stage 4	Review of *industry case studies* focusing on:
	• Digital transformation initiatives and the roles of accountants in these initiatives
	• Approaches to building digital business capabilities and the roles of accountants in these approaches
	• Digital business and digital technology roles and competencies required of accountants
	• Digital transformation and digital business challenges, benefits, and lessons learned
Stage 5	Review of *academic and non-academic literature* discussing:
	• Digital technology competencies required of accountants in order to play a sufficient role in digital business transformation and digital business.
	• The rationale for each required digital technology competency
Stage 6	Review of *accounting IT / IS / technology degrees and courses around the world* for:
	• Key topics taught
	• Presence and approach to teaching contemporary digital technology concepts and tools
	• Presence approach to teaching digital disruption concepts / issues
	• Presence and approach to teaching digital transformation concepts / issues
	• Presence and approach to teaching digital business concepts / issues
	• Presence and approach to teaching digital business capabilities concepts and issues
	• Presence and approach to teaching required accounting digital technology competencies

How to use this book

This book is organized into five parts. Part I provides an overview of key digital technology concepts and their implications for accountants. In this part we unpack, delineate, and accurately contextualize key digital technology, digital business, and digital transformation-related terms that accountants and other accounting profession stakeholders will be repeatedly exposed to. Having a clear understanding of these terms is crucial to understanding digital business transformation, digital business, and the implications of different digital technology advancements for accountants. Part II discusses the effects of digital disruption on accounting value creation and on the roles and activities facilitating this value creation. It explains the implications of digital disruption for the accounting value proposition, for accounting functions (e.g. financial accounting, management accounting, audit, tax), for accounting roles, and for accounting competency requirements. An organizing framework is provided for making sense of digital technology competencies required of accountants. Part III introduces accountants to key organizational digital business capabilities and discusses the roles of accountants in helping organizations to build and sustain these digital capabilities. It also discusses examples of the key technology-related competencies accountants require for each particular capability. Part IV discusses the challenges of keeping up with digital technologies, and also discusses strategies and practices accountants can leverage to keep up with digital technology and digital business advancements. Finally, part V unpacks more than 36 different digital technologies and explains what they mean, how they work, their implications for accountants and for the accounting value proposition, how they might evolve in future, and what accountants should look out for as these technologies evolve. At the end of each chapter are interactive and reflection activities and exercises that include a *Google and reflect* section, a *discussion questions* section, and an *example tools and vendors* section. The Google and reflect section provides common terminology or language for each discussed topic and encourages students to use a search engine to find their meaning. The discussion questions section provides questions to test or extend understanding and to stimulate reflection. And the example tools and vendors section identifies some common vendors of different technology platforms and tools to enable readers to look further into particular platforms and tools. Below, we briefly discuss how the different anticipated users of this book can use it.

Accountants

Each chapter of this book is able to be read as a stand-alone chapter. Thus, accountants wanting to understand foundational digital technology, digital transformation, and digital business-related terminology can go straight to part I; or to the specific chapter or term. Accountants already having this background and wanting to better understand the implications of digital disruption, digital transformation, and digital business for the accounting value proposition and for accounting roles and activities can go straight to part II; or to a specific discussion in part II as outlined in the table of contents. Accountants only interested understanding their role in helping their organization to build or sustain a specific digital business capability can go straight to the chapter on that capability. Accountants only interested in what digital technology competencies are required of them or how to develop them can go straight to chapter 6 and chapter 12. And accountants wanting a quick introduction to, or overview of, a particular digital technology can look for the relevant chapter on that technology in part V. Readers should notice that we have unpacked each part and chapter extensively in the table of contents and index to enable them to go straight to the information they need (e.g. a specific terminology, a specific technology, a specific accounting function, a specific competency).

Accounting instructors

Accounting instructors can use this book as the principal book for courses or units focusing on the impact of and role of technology in accounting. For example, each chapter can form a topic to be covered over a 12-week semester. Used this way, the book will provide future accountants with a comprehensive and integrated understanding of key digital technologies, their interrelationships with digital transformation and digital business concepts, how they can optimally be leveraged by organizations, the role of accountants in enabling this, the competencies required to do so, and how to cultivate those competencies. We strongly suggest that every accounting program needs such a course / unit. Alternatively, instructors can use the book as a supplementary text in any accounting course / unit; particularly for modules / topics discussing the implications of particular digital technologies for an accounting issue / practice or the types of tools and use cases applying to an accounting issue / practice (e.g. in a financial accounting unit, instructors may direct students to the discussions on the impact of digital technology advancements and digital disruption on financial accounting practice; as well as to the sections of the book introducing students to the digital technologies of particular relevance to financial accounting). Used this way, the book can enable instructors to direct students to a particular digital technology implication (e.g. need to provide interactive / layered / customizable financial reports), or to direct them to a use case related to that implication (e.g. leveraging XBRL to provide interactive / layered / customizable financial reports), or to direct them to an explanation of how a relevant digital technology works (e.g. how XBRL works).

Accounting students

Students investigating a particular digital technology, a particular digital transformation or digital business concept / issue, or the implications of a particular digital technology or digital business issue for accounting will find this book invaluable. The book aims to explain digital technology, digital business / digital transformation concepts, and their application to accounting in simple terms. Students can also use the book as a credible reference resource for digital technology-related assessment activities. For more proactive students, a cover-to-cover read of the book would provide an invaluable lens for understanding digital technology advancements, digital business transformation, and digital business. We anticipate this lens would enable such students to optimally position themselves for career success, and to have an "unfair" competitive advantage.

Researchers

Accounting researchers interested in undertaking research at the intersection of digital business transformation or digital technology advancements and accounting may find this book an invaluable starting point for an overview of key terminology, concepts, issues, and implications.

Notes

1 Vial, G. (2019). Understanding digital transformation: A review and a research agenda. The Journal of Strategic Information Systems, 28(2), 118–144.
2 Vial, G. (2019). Understanding digital transformation: A review and a research agenda. The Journal of Strategic Information Systems, 28(2), 118–144.
3 Nagarajah, E. (2016). Hi robot: What does automation mean for the accounting profession?. Accountants Today, 34–37. Retrieved November 29, 2019, from https://www.pwc.com/my/en/assets/press/1608-accountants-today-automation-impact-on-accounting-profession.pdf
4 Halal, W., Kolber, J., Davies, O., & Global, T. (2017). Forecasts of AI and future jobs in 2030: Muddling through likely, with two alternative scenarios. Journal of Futures Studies, 21(2), 83–96.
5 Jensen, B., & Koch, M. (2015). Man and machine: Robots on the rise? The impact of automation on the Swiss job market. Deloitte. Retrieved from https://www2.deloitte.com/content/dam/Deloitte/ch/Documents/innovation/ch-en-innovation-automation-report.pdf

2 IT, information systems, strategic information systems, and digital technologies

Introduction

Although they differ significantly and have important interrelationships, the terms information technology (IT), information systems (IS), and digital technology are often used interchangeably as umbrella terms for computer / software-related products and solutions. This can result in misunderstandings, trivialization of the importance of one or more terms, and feelings of overwhelm for some stakeholders outside of the IT / IS profession when it comes to use of the term or of related terms. It is this type of misunderstanding of slippery and overlapping IT / IS-related terms that leads to some accountants underestimating or only seeing a part of the importance and value of digital technologies and digital business concepts for business management and accounting practice. This misunderstanding can lead them to also misunderstand their role in IS and digital technology issues; and to see such issues as ones that can be relegated to the IT / IS function. This misunderstanding, and resultant attitudes and actions, can be a risk to accountants' careers, and even to the fates of their organizations (e.g. if it results in businesses underestimating key business risks or threats). In this chapter we unpack these terms, delineate the boundaries between them, explain how they interrelate and interact, and explain their significance. We finish the chapter by explaining the important and growing role of accountants in information systems and digital technology-related issues.

Information systems

An *information system* is a collection of interrelated components (hardware, software, networks, data, processes, and people) that work together to perform a specific role for an organization (the collection, storage, organization, and transformation of data into information and knowledge; as well as the distribution of that information and knowledge throughout the organization)[1]. The distributed information and knowledge play a crucial role in the operations and strategy of an organization (e.g. supporting decision-making, coordination, and control at all levels and in all parts of the organization)[2].

Components of an information system

Regarding the components of an information system (i.e. hardware, software, networks, data, processes, and people – see Figure 2.1), hardware includes all the physical components used by an organization for collecting, storing, organizing, transforming, and distributing data and information. For example, hardware includes physical computers

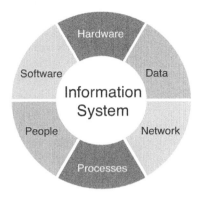

Figure 2.1 Components of an information system

and computer components, smart phones, servers and server components, sensors, physical robots, drones, and more. The software component of information systems refers to sets of instructions or software algorithms or code for controlling or telling the hardware what to do. Software includes systems software (which operates the hardware and coordinates instructions between application software and the hardware – e.g. operating system software, utilities software, compilers, assemblers, debuggers, and drivers). Popular operating systems software includes Microsoft Windows operating systems, Mac operating systems, Linux operating systems, and Android operating systems. The software component also includes application software (the software most people are familiar with and interact with to perform tasks or work e.g. word processing software, spreadsheets, and other apps). The data component of information systems refers to what data is collected (e.g. text, videos, images, etc.), how that data is stored (e.g. in what systems / databases, what locations, etc.), how it is organized, how it is transformed into information, how it is presented for understandability, and how it is distributed throughout the organization. For more information, see chapter 13 on data, data management, big data, business intelligence, data analytics, and data science. The network component of information systems refers to the technology that enables devices within an information system to communicate with each other, and for communication between different information systems to occur. The network component includes networking hardware and software (e.g. servers, coaxial cables, network interface cards, hubs, routers, LAN cables, network operating systems etc.).

Although many people tend to focus on the technology aspects of information systems (i.e. hardware, software, data, and network technology), the process and people components are important aspects of information systems that shouldn't be overlooked. Regarding the process component, organizations have a range of processes for getting organizational work done and meeting organizational objectives (e.g. product development processes, procurement processes, customer acquisition processes, customer support processes, accounting processes, marketing processes, HR processes, strategy-making processes, governance processes, and more). Technology is increasingly becoming integrated into these processes and used to design, facilitate, manage, and optimize them. For example, hardware and software are used to detect when particular processes have not occurred or to trigger particular processes to occur (e.g. sensors can detect an unsafe change in temperature and initiate a building evacuation; or video monitoring hardware and software may spot vandalism and automatically request security or police attendance), to provide data used to perform many processes (e.g. data-driven operational decisions), to alert people to events that have occurred or not occurred (e.g. patients missed during ward rounds), to orchestrate or perform processes (e.g. driving vehicles), to provide platforms on which people perform processes (e.g. workflow management platforms), to automate processes (e.g. robotic process automation or workflow automation), and more. Used in the right processes and in the right ways, both software and hardware can optimize process efficiency (e.g. speed and cost), effectiveness (e.g. customer satisfaction, stakeholder satisfaction, and competitive advantage), adaptability (e.g. ability to adapt processes to unexpected internal and external changes), and agility (e.g. capacity for flexibility and speed in sensing and responding to external changes).

Regarding the people component of information systems, it is people who are creators of information systems (e.g. imagining, designing, developing information systems), are operators of information systems (e.g. implement, troubleshoot, maintain, train users, support users), are administrators of information systems (e.g. specific systems upkeep, configuration, database maintenance), and are managers of information systems (e.g. governance, performance management, risk management, project management). And it is people who are users of information systems, who experience the benefits or challenges of using information systems, and who are ultimately served by the outputs of information systems. Thus, the people aspect of information systems is typically concerned with the different formal and informal roles involved in the creation, operation / administration, management, use, and value of information systems. Examples of information systems creation roles include systems analysts, systems architects, systems engineers, programmers, software engineers, hardware engineers, and network engineers. Examples of systems operators include hardware technicians, helpdesk analysts, security analysts / engineers, IS product managers, and IS trainers. Examples of information systems administration roles include systems administrators, database administrators and network administrators. Examples of managers of information systems include chief information officer (CIO), chief technology officer (CTO), chief digital officer (CDO), and IS functional or specialist managers (e.g. application managers, network services managers, desktop support managers, systems design and development managers, enterprise resource planning (ERP) managers, IS security managers, IS project managers). As we noted earlier, the people component of information systems is also concerned with users of information systems. A focus of this aspect is how users adopt new information systems. Frameworks such as Everett Rogers's Diffusion of Innovations categorizes user adoption behavior into innovators, early adopters, early majority, late majority, and laggard approaches or adoption behaviors. Understanding the different types of adopters, adoption approaches, or adoption behaviors is often leveraged to improve the speed and effectiveness with which information systems are implemented.

Roles of information systems

Information systems play three key roles in organizations. First, as we noted earlier, the components of an information system work together to capture data, store it, organize it, transform it into information, and organize that information into organizational knowledge. Second, the information and knowledge produced by information systems is distributed throughout the organization to support decision-making (e.g. day-to-day operational decisions and more long-term strategic decisions). Operational decisions include decisions such as how much inventory to buy and from whom, who to put on what shifts, which customers to serve and when. Strategic decisions include decisions such as what business models and revenue models to use, what technology infrastructure to use, and how to combine business models and technology infrastructure to optimize competitiveness, adaptability, and agility. Third, and finally, information systems facilitate operational and strategic processes (e.g. enabling a range of organizational processes and workflows such as product development, procurement, customer acquisition, customer support, accounting, marketing, HR, strategy-making, risk management, and governance). Almost all organizational work is informed, facilitated, and consumed by information systems.

Types of information systems

The term information systems is often combined with other terms to refer to subsets of information systems, or to particular types of information systems. These subsets, or typologies, are usually based on which technologies are used or not used, on which processes those information systems subsets focus on, on the stakeholders the specific information systems subsets serve in an organization, or on the specific organizational functions or processes the information systems subsets focus on. Subsets, or types of information systems, focusing on the technologies used or not used include computer-based information systems, and manual-based information systems. Computer-based information systems are information systems that use computer hardware and software to capture data, store it, organize it, transform it into information, organize that information into organizational knowledge, and disseminate it throughout the organization. In contrast, manual-based information systems are information systems that perform the role of information systems without computer hardware and software (e.g. using paper, filing cabinets, people's memories etc.). Types of information systems focusing on stakeholders in the organization hierarchy include transaction processing systems (e.g. those used by operational level employees to serve customers), management information systems and decision support systems (e.g. those used by middle managers and senior managers to monitor and manage performance), and executive information systems (those used by the top management team or executive team to monitor organization-wide performance and risk and to inform strategic decision-making). Types of information systems focusing on specific organizational processes / activities include data warehousing systems, enterprise resource planning systems, and office automation systems. Types of information systems focusing on specific organizational functions include hospitality information systems, property management systems, customer relationship management systems, marketing information systems, accounting information systems, HR information systems, procurement systems and more (see Figure 2.2).

Information systems specialists typically study degrees in information systems that focus on systems design and development methodologies, enterprise information management, enterprise architecture and governance, database systems and information modelling, business process management, project and change management, IS Security, and IS strategy and governance. They often specialize in areas such as IS infrastructure management, IS project and change management, business analysis, business analytics, and functional IS areas (e.g. accounting information systems, HR information systems). IS specialists enter careers such as business systems analysts, solution architects, data and analytics managers, data engineers,

14 *Digital technology advancements*

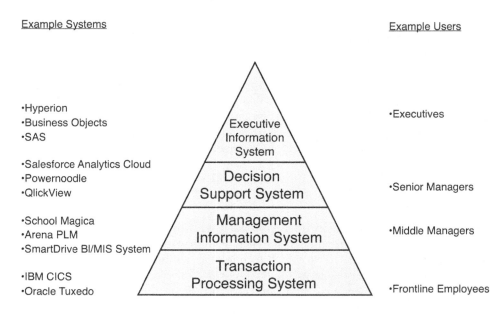

Figure 2.2 Types of information systems, including example systems and example users

IS project managers, consultants, and functional system managers (e.g. finance systems managers, HR information systems managers, property information systems managers).

Information technology and information communications technology

Although people use the terms IT and Information systems interchangeably, *information technology* is actually a subset of information systems. As a subset, it typically only focuses on the technology component of information systems (i.e. the hardware, software, networks, and data capture and transformation components). IT specialists focus on ensuring the organization has the right hardware and software products, installing them, customizing them, integrating them with existing products, maintaining them, supporting users to use them, and ensuring that the security, availability, and accessibility of each product, and of the information system as a whole is optimized. IT specialists typically require degrees in information technology or computer science and, within such degrees, they often specialize in hardware and / or software areas such as network design, hardware design, software design, software development, cybersecurity, artificial intelligence, and the internet of things. And they enter careers such as network architects, software developers, IT systems analysts, security analysts, web developers, systems administrators, software product managers, and IT managers.

The term *information communications technology* (ICT) is sometimes used interchangeably with IT. It refers to the convergence or integration of IT with audiovisual technologies and telephone networks (e.g. media broadcasting technologies, audio and video transmission, and telephony). Thus, the term ICT can be thought of as an extended synonym for the term IT.

Strategic information systems and digital technologies

Strategic information systems

Strategic information systems are information systems that can significantly transform the strategic position of an organization in its external environment. Such transformation can be in the form of breakthroughs in efficiency, differentiation, innovation, adaptability, and agility. Efficiency breakthroughs include dramatically speeding up or enabling cost leadership in processes such as product and service delivery processes, customer engagement and support processes, and strategy execution processes. For example, in its early days, Dell Technologies leveraged internet technology to be able to offer custom built-to-order computers to customers at a cost of 10% of its revenue[3]. In contrast, competitors such as Hewlett-Packard, Gateway, and Cisco could only do this at a cost of 20% to 50% of their revenue[4]. This improved Dell's strategic position in the personal computer industry, enabling it to grow into an industry leader. Differentiation breakthroughs include being able to offer products and services that, relative to competitors, have a uniqueness that is important to customers. For example, Apple has leveraged a closed technology ecosystem and greater investment in product design to differentiate its products from competitors. As a result, Apple is able to charge much more for its products and enjoys greater customer loyalty. Innovation breakthroughs relate breakthroughs in the rate at which new and better products / services are created and delivered. For example, Amazon's first product was an online bookstore platform but it has since leveraged its information systems (technology infrastructure, processes, and people) to globally deliver a consistent stream of new products including Kindle, Amazon Web Services, Amazon Prime, Amazon Publishing, and Amazon Robotics. These innovation breakthroughs have propelled Amazon to become a dominant leader in a range of industries. Adaptability refers to an organization's ability to adapt its operations to surprising events in its external environment (e.g. financial crises, pandemics, disruptive competition), and agility refers to an organization's capacity for flexibility and speed in sensing and responding to external changes. Companies such as Google and Intel configure their information systems to enable them to maximize their adaptability and agility. For example, Google uses its sophisticated information systems to sense changes in its external environment (e.g. collect and interpret data on search patterns and online advert performance) and then uses the insights to drive operational responses to external events[5]. And both Google and Intel use investment arms such as Google Ventures and Intel Capital to discover and profit first from breakthrough products and market innovations[6,7]. Thus, designed or configured appropriately, information systems (different combinations of technology, networks, people, and business processes) can be very powerful strategic weapons capable of transforming the fortunes of organizations.

Digital technologies

The term *digital technologies* refers to combinations of information (or data), computing (or computation), communication, and connectivity technologies[8]. Digital technologies include all types of electronic hardware and software that use information in the form of binary code (i.e. represented by strings of 0's and 1's). Digital technologies include electronic tools, systems, devices, and other things (e.g. personal computers, calculators, traffic light controllers, mobile telephones, satellite technology, high-definition televisions, the internet and other networks, software applications, email, mobile apps, etc.). Digital technologies generate, receive, store, process, transmit, and even act on data. Increasingly, digital technologies are enabling all manner of things (e.g. people, organizations, physical products, physical infrastructure, software, etc.) to capture data within and around them, to communicate that data with other things locally or globally, to receive information from other things, to use sophisticated computation / algorithms to gain insights from that information (e.g. spot patterns, understand instructions), and to use combinations of algorithms and robotics capabilities to act on that information in the same way that a person can (e.g. call the police on capturing or receiving information that a known fugitive is nearby).

We noted earlier that, used the right way, information systems can become very powerful strategic weapons capable of conferring often insurmountable strategic advantages. The right digital technologies can supercharge this strategic power of information systems by drastically enhancing how efficiently and effectively such information systems function. For example, the right combination of digital technologies can speed up the rate at which data flows between hardware, software, networks, business processes, and people – making it near instant. The right combination of digital technologies can transform all of an organization's infrastructure (buildings, machinery, furniture, cars, stationery, etc.) into smart things capable of collecting data, communicating data, acting on data insights, and doing all of these things autonomously. The right combination of digital technologies can enable an organization's employees to work from anywhere in the world, to collaborate with any of the organization's infrastructure and other physical things, and to serve large numbers of customers globally in real time irrespective of their location. The right combination of digital technologies can enhance the efficiency and effectiveness of interactions between people, technology, and processes. These examples only touch on the surface of the power of digital technologies to supercharge the strategic power of information systems. Microsoft, Google, Amazon, and other global giants are leveraging combinations of digital technologies and breakthroughs in these digital technologies to create strategic information systems that enable them to efficiently and effectively serve billions of people globally per day. Doing so has conferred significant wealth and global influence to the owners and employees of these organizations.

Implications for accountants

So far, we have unpacked the terms IT, information systems, strategic information systems, and digital technologies. We have delineated the overlaps and boundaries between them. We have also explained the importance of digital technologies to information systems and how they can supercharge the efficiency, effectiveness, and strategic value of information systems. Ensuring the effective design, implementation, operation, maintenance, and optimization of information systems is not just the responsibility of the IT / IS or similar function, but a shared responsibility of managers and leaders at all levels. For example, managers can play an important role in ensuring that the right digital technologies are used, that the right operational and strategic processes are in place, that these processes leverage digital technologies for optimal efficiency and effectiveness, that the right job roles exist with the right capabilities to ensure information systems function optimally, that the right strategic partnerships are in place to optimize the strategic value of IS, and that employees throughout the organization continuously upgrade their technology skills and keep up with digital technologies. In their role as trusted advisors and business partners to managers and leaders, accountants share this responsibility. To deliver trustworthy advice and effective business partnering in relation to efficient and effective use of IS, accountants have to first be able to make sense of the slippery terminology and acronyms related to information systems and digital technologies. Doing so positions them to make clear sense of what they read and hear about different digital technologies and the implications for their organizations' information systems, and to constructively engage in conversations with stakeholders about digital technology and information systems issues (e.g. conversations with stakeholders such as strategic leaders, employees, IT / IS professionals, IT / IS consultants, IT / IS vendors, IT / IS auditors, and strategic partners of the organization). Being able to make sense of what they read and hear, and to engage constructively with relevant stakeholders on IS issues will, in turn, put them in a position where they are able to leverage informed insights to spot opportunities for improving their organization's information systems, and to effectively participate in and play a leadership role in necessary IS-related changes.

Google and reflect

chief information officer (CIO), chief technology officer (CTO), chief digital officer (CDO), IT manager, IS manager, digital strategist, business systems analyst, ERP system, IT strategy, information systems strategy, information systems governance, information systems assurance, information systems security, digital technology device, digital technology platform, digital convergence

Discussion questions

1. What is the difference between IT and ICT?
2. What is the difference between IT and information systems?
3. Are information systems part of IT or is IT a part of information systems? Does it matter which is a part of which?
4. What is the best metaphor you can think of to explain the interrelationship between digital technologies and information systems?
5. Are digital technologies a part of IT or is IT a part of digital technologies?
6. What is the role of digital technologies in information systems?
7. What are five different types of digital technologies?
8. Assuming that an organization is not already using the digital technologies you identified above, how could using them improve each component of an information system?
9. Assuming that an organization is not already using the digital technologies you identified above, how could using them improve the functioning of its information systems? (E.g. how would using them impact efficiency, effectiveness, strategic position?)
10. What are strategic information systems? How can they transform the strategic positioning of an organization? (Identify five ways they can transform it)
11. Identify two organizations that are exemplar users of information systems as powerful strategic weapons.
12. What is the role of accountants in the efficient and effective functioning of information systems?
13. What is the role of accounting and finance managers in the efficient and effective functioning of information systems?

14 Identify five actions that accountants can take to improve the effectiveness and efficiency of information systems in their organization.
15 Identify five actions that accounting and finance managers can take to improve the efficiency and effectiveness of information systems in their organization.

Notes

1 Bourgeois, D. (2014). Information systems for business and beyond. The Saylor Foundation.
2 Laudon, K.C., & Laudon, J.P. (2019). Management information systems: Managing the digital firm. Pearson.
3 The power of virtual integration: An interview with Dell Computer's Michael Dell. (1998, March). Harvard Business Review. Retrieved April 21, 2020, from: https://hbr.org/1998/03/the-power-of-virtual-integration-an-interview-with-dell-computers-michael-dell
4 What you don't know about Dell. (2003, November 3). Bloomberg. Retrieved April 21, 2020, from: https://www.bloomberg.com/news/articles/2003-11-02/what-you-dont-know-about-dell
5 Adaptability: The new competitive advantage. (2011, July). Harvard Business Review. Retrieved April 21, 2020, from: https://hbr.org/2011/07/adaptability-the-new-competitive-advantage
6 Rowley, J. (2018, February 17). A peek inside Alphabet's investing universe. Retrieved April 21, 2020, from: https://techcrunch.com/2018/02/17/a-peek-inside-alphabets-investing-universe/
7 Burgelman, R.A., & Grove, A.S. (2007). Let chaos reign, then rein in chaos – repeatedly: Managing strategic dynamics for corporate longevity. Strategic Management Journal, 28(10), 965–979.
8 Bharadwaj, A., El Sawy, O., Pavlou, P., & Venkatraman, N. (2013). Digital business strategy: Toward a next generation of insights. MIS Quarterly, 37(2), 471–482.

3 Digital technology advancements and digital disruption

Game-changing opportunities and existential threats

Introduction

Although organizations are affected at different times and to different degrees by digital disruption, sooner or later digital disruption becomes a serious existential issue for most organizations. Digital disruption manifests itself as gradual or sudden loss of customers, falling prices, diminished availability of product / service input suppliers, loss of talented staff, challenges accessing funding, and more. Whether it occurs seemingly slowly or suddenly, it ultimately poses existential threats for most organizations. To guard against digital disruption, managers need to understand how digital disruption happens and the nature of the existential threats it creates. Digital disruption is driven by digital technology advancements. But as well as driving digital disruption, digital technology advancements present game-changing opportunities for organizations that can leverage them effectively. Thus, managers need to understand the game-changing opportunities digital technologies present. It follows then that, in their roles as trusted advisors and strategic business partners, accountants must also understand both the existential threat of digital disruption, and also the game-changing opportunities presented by digital technologies. Aside from the trusted advisor and strategic business partner imperative, digital technology advancements are also disrupting the accounting profession, the accounting value proposition, and the nature of accounting work. In this chapter, we explain how digital technology advancements cause digital disruption, the types of disruption created, the threats of not responding to this disruption in a timely manner, the types of game-changing opportunities presented by digital technology advancements, and how organizations can leverage digital technology advancements to both adapt to disruption and to seize the game-changing opportunities digital technology advancements present. The inability to guard against disruption paves the way to the fates of disrupted organizations like Kodak[1], Blockbuster[2] Video, and Borders bookstores[3]. The ability to adapt to and to seize the opportunities offered by digital technologies paves the way to the fates of organizations like Netflix, Caterpillar, Walmart, and Disney who have leveraged digital technologies to thrive in the face of disruption.

Digital technology advancements and digital disruption

Digital technology advancements

In the preceding chapter, we defined digital technologies as technologies that combine information (or data), computing (or computation), communication, and connectivity technologies. Digital technologies include social, mobile, analytics, cloud, internet, internet of things (IoT), software, platform, artificial intelligence, robotics, drones, satellites, blockchain, and

20 *Digital technology advancements*

other technologies[4]. Innovations in these technologies have been advancing and continue to advance at an exponential rate. *Digital technology advancements* include ongoing breakthroughs in processing speeds, memory capacity, number and size of pixels in digital cameras, computational capacity, network capacity, and software sophistication[5]. Advancements also include the introduction and commercial adoption of technologies like blockchain, edge computing, 5 and 6G technology, brain-computer interfaces, 4D printing, neuromorphic hardware, exoskeletons, and quantum computing. Consider that all these advancements, and more, have occurred in just over 40 years since the introduction of the IBM PC. Thus, when we refer to advances in digital technologies or digital technology innovations, we are referring to the introduction of new digital technologies, or to breakthroughs in the capacity of existing digital technologies. For instance, the introduction of new digital technologies like 3D printing and 5G; or significant improvements in existing technologies like computational power, cloud computing capacity, or artificial intelligence capabilities.

Digital technology advancements as a source of digital disruption

The term disruption refers to preventing something (e.g. routines, processes, events) from continuing as usual, or as expected. Put another way, it refers to interrupting the normal course of action, or throwing the status quo into disorder. *Digital disruption*, then, refers to digital technology-induced disruption. Digital disruption is often discussed from the perspective of incumbent organizations that are heavily invested in established ways of doing things, and whose established way of operating is interrupted or made irrelevant[6]. But digital disruption can also occur at an industry, sector, and / or society level[7]. That is, the established way of doing things in a whole industry, sector, or society can be disrupted. For example, the introduction of electronic health records can render hospitals' and medical clinics' prior processes for storing, retrieving, and transmitting patient information obsolete (an industry level disruption). And the introduction of, and improvements in, telehealth can increase the availability and quality of healthcare services to rural and emerging economies, reduce the need for travel for some patients, and reduce the cost of certain types of care (an industry and society level disruption). Figure 3.1 shows how use of digital technology innovations fuels digital disruptions, which then requires organizational strategic responses to adapt to the disruptions. Effecting these strategic responses,

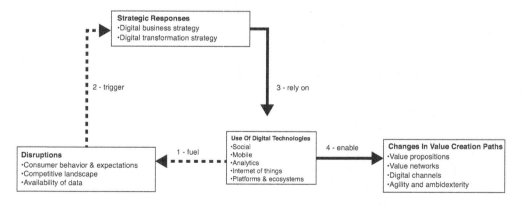

Figure 3.1 Digital technology advancements cause digital disruption but can be leveraged to respond to disruption and recreate value offerings and capabilities[8]

in turn, relies on using digital technology innovations to achieve new breakthroughs in customer value, in efficiency, and in adaptability and ambidexterity.

Unpacking digital disruption

The introduction of new digital technologies or breakthroughs in existing digital technologies results in three types of disruptions: disruption of consumer or customer expectations and behaviors, disruption of the competitive landscape, and disruption of available data[9]. We unpack each of these disruptions in more detail below.

Disruption of customer expectations and behaviors

Businesses make money and are able to continue their existence if they cost-effectively provide products and / or services that customers want and choose to buy from them. Customers typically want and choose to buy products that they expect to provide the best cost-benefit proposition (e.g. most accessible, best quality, best brand image, most compatible with other products, and best suited for the particular job the customer is trying to get done, at a particular price). Using search engines, social media, data analytics, artificial intelligence, and other digital technologies, consumers have access to an unprecedented amount of information about available product and service options, and the differences in benefits and costs of these options. For example, at the push of a button, they can see almost all available options for a particular product or service and compare their benefits and costs. In addition, consumers can easily access information on what accessibility, convenience, and other benefits are possible from substitute products / services. For example, when it comes to banking services, most consumers can easily check whether online banking, mobile banking, blockchain-based payment, email-based payment, and cardless cash withdrawal services are possible. The easy access to product / service information and options, as well as knowledge of what is possible, shapes consumer expectations and behavior. Continuing with the banking services example, banks that are either not competitive on price and / or don't provide online banking, mobile banking, blockchain-based payment, email-based payment, and cardless cash withdrawal services (for example), may gradually find themselves unable to attract new customers, and also find their existing customers choosing to go with banks that live up to these consumer expectations. Thus, digital technology advancements (the introduction of new digital technologies, or improvements in existing ones) change consumer expectations[10]. They also change consumer behaviors, either due to changed expectations or changes in consumer routines and habits[11]. For example, the introduction of driverless cars (a digital technology advancement) may significantly reduce consumer driving, car purchasing, car parts purchasing, and other related consumer routines. This may disrupt operations of organizations providing products and services used in those consumer routines.

Disruption of the competitor field and bases of competition

The introduction of new digital technologies or improvements in existing digital technologies can lower barriers to entry into an industry, allowing new startups to enter that industry as competitors, as well as allowing existing organizations in different industries to enter the industry. For example, digital technology advancements enabled startups like Spotify (in 2006), Soundcloud (in 2007), and Tidal (in 2014) to enter and become dominant players in the music industry. And such advancements enabled Apple (iTunes / Apple Music), Google (YouTube Music), and Amazon (Amazon Music) to leverage the digital platforms used in different industries (e.g. cloud infrastructure, search, and device platforms) to become dominant players in the music industry. Digital technology advances lower barriers to new competitors entering an industry by lowering the cost to produce and distribute products, as well as to acquire customers, support them, and manage relationships with them. For example, by leveraging cloud infrastructure to record and stream music, new entrants in the music industry were able to offer music to customers instantly (instead of waiting for physical CD delivery), to offer it at a better price (since cost was low), and to offer it to almost everyone with an internet connection (significantly expanded distribution). Thus, they were able to have significantly greater margins, as digital technologies enabled them to circumvent costly activities traditionally associated with music production and distribution (e.g. signing artists, managing artists, operating recording venues, promoting artists, setting up and managing live shows, producing CDs, packaging, marketing, and distributing artists' music, and manually managing intellectual property rights).

Digital technologies also disrupt incumbent organizations' bases, or sources, of competitive advantage[12,13]. For example, over a long period of time, incumbent organizations dominating the music industry had established competitive advantages such as locking in key strategic partners (e.g. companies doing artist scouting, recording, live venue management, packaging, marketing, and distribution), cost leadership (e.g. from using their size to negotiate the lowest fees for artists, recording, packaging, marketing, and distribution), and brand differentiation (e.g. being more attractive to top artists due to their brands being more recognized, better financed, and having greater album sales capability). Digital technology advancements removed the potency of these advantages by making them much less relevant to music sales. By leveraging digital technology infrastructure, new competitors could circumvent the need for traditional strategic partners (e.g. companies providing recording, packaging, marketing, and distribution services), they could also reach anyone around the world with an internet connection (minimizing the need to rely on the established sales infrastructure of traditional record labels). New competitors then leveraged search engine optimization (SEO), social media, artificial intelligence, mobile, and other digital technologies to acquire customers, provide them with the songs they wanted instantly, and do all this at a fraction of the cost that traditional record labels provided their music for. The bases or sources of competition then evolved to include, for example, the quality and availability of digital music platforms, the number of consumers active on those platforms, and the ease with which artists could get their music onto those platforms.

Disruption of data availability

Organizations that leverage new or improved digital technologies are able to capture and have access to more data (e.g. data about consumers and consumption experiences, data about processes for creating and providing products / services, and data about the market dynamics of their industries)[14]. This data provides them with additional strategic advantages. For example, they can monetize it by selling it to third parties (e.g. Facebook and Google monetize their user data by selling user-targeted advertising; and Amazon uses its data for targeted adverts as well as dynamic product pricing). Outside such monetization, organizations can employ sophisticated analytics to optimize consumer experience, to optimize operational efficiency and effectiveness, and for strategic sensing of market and other external environment trends. They can also use collected data, in combination with sophisticated artificial intelligence algorithms, to provide automated consumer experiences. For example, Google and Apple leverage their data, along with sophisticated artificial intelligence, to offer chatbots and virtual assistants like Siri and Google Assistant. In the hotel industry, organizations like Hilton augment their customer service with robots like Connie, the robot concierge. The data available from digital technologies includes data captured by the organization, as well as data captured by external organizations (e.g. governments, suppliers, platform organizations, etc.). Savvy competitors can clean, store, organize, and integrate external and internal data, then leverage it for real-time operational insights, as well as for strategic insights. By doing so, they have an additional basis of competitive advantage. The additional data availability digital technologies enables disrupts existing ways of doing things by necessitating that organizations change what data they are capturing themselves, what data they are pulling in from external sources, how they integrate this data, and how they optimize the insights available to operational and strategy processes. That is, organizations can't continue as they have been, as they risk losing competitive positioning.

Existential threats and game-changing opportunities

The introduction of new digital technologies, and / or improvements in existing digital technologies, creates existential threats for organizations; but it also offers game-changing opportunities[15]. In the paragraphs that follow, we unpack the nature of the existential threats, and the game-changing opportunities for alert and proactive organizations.

Existential threats

By disrupting customer expectations and behaviors, disrupting the competitive landscape and bases of competition, and disrupting the data available to be used, digital technology advancements create an "adapt or risk your survival" ultimatum for incumbent organizations in an industry. This survival risk is the existential threat created by digital technology advancements. If organizations continue to do what they have always done (or only make tokenistic changes), and don't adapt their product and service offerings to changed customer expectations and behaviors, existing customers will start going to other organizations with better value or more convenience. In addition, organizations that continue to operate the way they always have will struggle to attract new customers. In less extreme cases, the effect of disruption may play out as gradual customer attrition, gradual price erosion, gradual decline in revenue, decreasing margins, and loss of profitability, until a point at which it is no longer worth sustaining the business. In more extreme cases, the effect of disruption can manifest itself much more rapidly, resulting in sudden and significant financial losses that bring about heavy layoffs, fire sale acquisition, or even insolvency. This can occur for particular organizations, it can occur for an industry, or it can occur for a whole sector or geography. For example, digital technology advancements brought about the slow, but eventual, demise of Kodak (Figure 3.2 shows how Kodak failed to effectively respond to disruption from digital cameras and smartphones, despite creating the technology behind them – Kodak invented the first digital camera in 1975)[16]. In contrast, digital disruption brought about the sudden demise of many organizations in the taxi industry[17]. Organizations can ignore or deny the existential threat created by digital technology advancements, or they can leverage digital technologies to reconfigure their product and service offerings, to redesign their operational processes, and to reform their medium and long-term strategies for continuous adaptation to certain future disruption. For example, Walmart has managed to adapt to the disruption of retail by leveraging digital technologies to transform both its products / services, its distribution approach, and its customer relationships and experiences[18]. Other retailers, such as Borders[19], either ignored, denied, or were not quick enough to understand and leverage the power of digital technologies to adapt to the disruption of retail[20,21,22].

Game-changing opportunities

Proactive organizations can leverage new digital technologies or improvements in existing digital technologies to seize three common types of game-changing opportunities. Effectively seizing one or more of these opportunities can safeguard their market position for a period or enable them to leapfrog competitors to become a market leader. The first type of game-changing opportunity is leveraging digital technologies to introduce new or significantly enhanced products and services that meet or exceed customer expectations[23]. Netflix's business model was originally based on renting out movies stored on physical media (e.g. VHS, DVDs, Blu-ray). The company recognized the game-changing opportunities in internet and cloud computing digital technologies. Netflix leveraged these digital technologies to transform its product offering into a video streaming service. Blockbuster Video, the industry leader with more than 10,000 retail stores and a turnover of more than US$5 billion, clung onto its established business model until it was

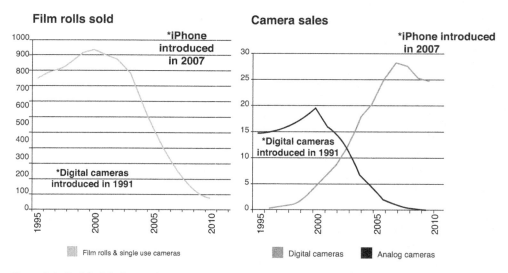

Figure 3.2 Kodak failed to effectively respond to disruption from digital cameras and smartphones, despite creating the technology behind them[24]

untenable. It eventually attempted to leverage digital technologies to revamp its offering, but by then it was too late. In 2010, the industry leader declared bankruptcy and now no longer exists. Netflix, in the meantime, has gone from strength to strength, continuing to embrace digital technologies such as mobile streaming, artificial intelligence-based personalized recommendation algorithms, set-top boxes, smart TVs, Xbox / PlayStation / Wii consoles, and virtual private networks. Netflix also leveraged the data collected from different digital technologies to better understand what consumers like to watch, when they like to watch it, and how they like to watch it. This, in turn, continuously feeds its programming and service delivery. Today Netflix has a turnover of more than US$20 billion and annual income / profit of more than US$2 billion.

Other proactive organizations are leveraging digital technologies to transition from product to platform organizations. That is, rather than just being sellers of products, they are providing the infrastructure that other entities (e.g. businesses, contractors, consumers) can use to create, market, sell, or enhance their products and customer experiences more conveniently and at lower cost. For example, Caterpillar, the heavy equipment manufacturer, leveraged digital technologies to offer a vehicle management platform that users of its equipment can draw on for vehicle utilization, health, location, servicing and longevity insights[25]. In addition to quality equipment, such a platform makes it difficult for customers to switch from Caterpillar in the absence of breakthrough competitor offerings.

The second type of game-changing opportunity available to proactive organizations is leveraging digital technologies to bypass intermediaries and interact directly with consumers[26,27], to enhance collaboration and coordination between strategic partners in the value chain[28], or to create and manage an ecosystem-based business model[29,30]. Microsoft had traditionally distributed its hardware and software through resellers but has recently started to also sell direct to consumers its surface hardware and cloud services[31,32,33]. This direct interaction with customers enables greater understanding of the customer, greater control of the customer experience, and greater customer engagement opportunities[34]. Organizations can also leverage digital technologies for more effective and faster collaboration and coordination with strategic value chain partners[35]. For instance, organizations can integrate aspects of their information systems with those of strategic partners and have shared systems for collaboration and coordination that draw on the data from both sets of systems. This can improve data visibility, workflow visibility, engagement, incentives, and more. Organizations can also leverage digital technologies to create and manage an ecosystem of suppliers, consumers, and other stakeholders[36]. For example, Uber continues to build and manage an evolving ecosystem for transportation made up of self-employed drivers, restaurants, hospitals and medical clinics, end consumers, certifiers, and other stakeholders.

Digital technologies expand the number of possible consumer engagement channels from traditional physical mail, phones, and email to online live chat, social media, mobile, mobile apps, IoT devices, and more. These expanded engagement channels bring about opportunities to engage with customers via their dominant or preferred engagement channels. And improved engagement can lead to better customer acquisition and retention.

Finally, the third type of game-changing opportunity available to organizations is leveraging digital technologies to improve their adaptability, agility, and ambidexterity. We defined adaptability in the previous chapter as the ability to reconfigure routines, processes, and practices to suit the demands of unexpected internal and external changes. For example, reconfiguring an organization's product development and delivery processes to suit changes in customer expectations and behaviors as Netflix did. And we defined agility as the capacity for flexibility and speed in sensing and responding to external changes. For example, through sophisticated data analytics as well as their Google Ventures and Intel Capital arms, Google and Intel are highly agile organizations able to continuously adapt and thrive in industries characterized by an extraordinary rate of change, unpredictability, growing convergence, and an assault on technology standards[37,38,39]. In contrast to adaptability and agility, ambidexterity is concerned with having processes to ensure existing process efficiency in parallel with processes to undertake exploratory activities so as to discover new products and services. For example, for a long time, Intel has operated both efficiency and exploratory processes. Efficiency activities have enabled it to maximize revenue and profitability from its existing products and processes. At the same time, exploratory activities have enabled Intel to discover breakthrough products prior to the decline of their existing core products[40,41]. Organizations can leverage digital technologies to configure their operations and strategy for optimal adaptability, agility, and ambidexterity.

Implications for accountants

Depending on the specific industries they work in, accountants may have already started to experience the effects of industry level and organization level digital disruption. Depending on the specific accounting work they are involved in, accountants may have already started experiencing the effects of digital disruption in the accounting profession and in their accounting work. Either way, the digital disruption to date is just the beginning, in the same way that early digital disruption of the video rental, taxi, and photography industries were just the beginning for those industries. Accelerating digital technology advancements will continue to raise customer expectations and change customer behaviors, to introduce new competitors and raise the capabilities of existing competitors, and to change the bases of competition. This will, in turn, continue to change what support strategic leaders and managers require of accountants – thus changing the nature of accounting work and how that work is done. To ensure their continued value to strategic leaders and managers, accountants must keep up with evolving digital technologies and find ways to both best support their organizations to leverage them to thrive, as well as for accountants themselves to leverage digital technology advancements to improve the efficiency and effectiveness of accounting value creation.

Google and reflect

business ecosystem, disruptive technology, disruptive innovation, digital disruption, digital innovation, digital platform, digital technology infrastructure, cloud infrastructure, bimodal IT, operational backbone, digital backbone, SEO, adaptability, agility, ambidexterity, online travel agency (OTA)

Discussion questions

1 What is the difference between the terms digital disruption, disruptive technology, and disruptive innovation?
2 How do digital technology advancements cause disruption?
3 What are the three types of disruption caused by the introduction of new digital technologies or breakthroughs in existing ones?
4 What are the different ways digital disruption manifests itself in an organization's financial performance?

5 Which digital technology advancement has had the most disruptive impact on the accounting profession in the last ten years?
6 Which digital technology trend is likely to have the most disruptive impact on the accounting profession in the next ten years?
7 What are the three common types of game-changing opportunities that can be seized by leveraging digital technology advancements?
8 What is the difference between adaptability, agility, and ambidexterity?
9 How can an organization use digital technologies to enhance its adaptability?
10 How can an organization use digital technologies to enhance its agility?
11 How can an organization use digital technologies to enhance its ambidexterity?
12 What is the role of accountants in guarding against digital disruption in their organizations?
13 In an entry level role, what can an accounting graduate do to contribute to the adaptability, agility, and ambidexterity of their organization?

Notes

1 Satell, G. (2018). How Blockbuster, Kodak and Xerox really failed (It's not what you think). Retrieved April 25, 2020, from: https://www.inc.com/greg-satell/pundits-love-to-tell-these-three-famous-innovation-stories-none-of-them-are-true.html
2 Downes, L., & Nunes, P. (2013). Blockbuster becomes a casualty of big bang disruption. Retrieved April 26, 2020, from: https://hbr.org/2013/11/blockbuster-becomes-a-casualty-of-big-bang-disruption
3 Frazier, M. (2011). The three lessons of the Borders bankruptcy. Forbes. Retrieved April 25, 2020, from: https://www.forbes.com/sites/myafrazier/2011/02/16/the-three-lessons-of-the-borders-bankruptcy/#3c1218242a1a
4 Vial, G. (2019). Understanding digital transformation: A review and a research agenda. The Journal of Strategic Information Systems, 28(2), 118–144.
5 Roser, M., & Ritchie, H. (2013). Technological progress. Our World in Data. Retrieved April 23, 2020, from: https://ourworldindata.org/technological-progress
6 Skog, D. A., Wimelius, H., & Sandberg, J. (2018). Digital disruption. Business & Information Systems Engineering, 60(5), 431–437. https://doi.org/10.1007/s12599-018-0550-4
7 Skog, D. A., Wimelius, H., & Sandberg, J. (2018). Digital disruption. Business & Information Systems Engineering, 60(5), 431–437. https://doi.org/10.1007/s12599-018-0550-4
8 Vial, G. (2019). Understanding digital transformation: A review and a research agenda. The Journal of Strategic Information Systems, 28(2), 118–144.
9 Vial, G. (2019). Understanding digital transformation: A review and a research agenda. The Journal of Strategic Information Systems, 28(2), 118–144.
10 Vial, G. (2019). Understanding digital transformation: A review and a research agenda. The Journal of Strategic Information Systems, 28(2), 118–144.
11 Vial, G. (2019). Understanding digital transformation: A review and a research agenda. The Journal of Strategic Information Systems, 28(2), 118–144.
12 Vial, G. (2019). Understanding digital transformation: A review and a research agenda. The Journal of Strategic Information Systems, 28(2), 118–144.
13 Reeves, M., & Deimler, M. (2009). New bases of competitive advantage. Retrieved April 26, 2020, from: https://www.bcg.com website: https://www.bcg.com/en-au/publications/2009/business-unit-strategy-new-bases-of-competitive-advantage.aspx
14 Vial, G. (2019). Understanding digital transformation: A review and a research agenda. The Journal of Strategic Information Systems, 28(2), 118–144.
15 Vial, G. (2019). Understanding digital transformation: A review and a research agenda. The Journal of Strategic Information Systems, 28(2), 118–144.
16 Satell, G. (2018). How Blockbuster, Kodak and Xerox really failed (It's not what you think). Retrieved April 25, 2020, from: https://www.inc.com/greg-satell/pundits-love-to-tell-these-three-famous-innovation-stories-none-of-them-are-true.html

17 Goldstein, M. (2018). Dislocation and its discontents: Ride-sharing's impact on the taxi industry. Forbes. Retrieved from: https://www.forbes.com/sites/michaelgoldstein/2018/06/08/uber-lyft-taxi-drivers/#6a5415559f0d
18 Danziger, P.N. (2018). Walmart doubles down on its transformation into a technology company. Forbes. Retrieved from: https://www.forbes.com/sites/pamdanziger/2018/10/22/walmart-doubles-down-on-its-transformation-into-a-technology-company/#408a349b404c
19 Frazier, M. (2011). The three lessons of the Borders bankruptcy. Forbes. Retrieved April 25, 2020, from: https://www.forbes.com/sites/myafrazier/2011/02/16/the-three-lessons-of-the-borders-bankruptcy/#3c1218242a1a
20 Frazier, M. (2011). The three lessons of the Borders bankruptcy. Forbes. Retrieved April 25, 2020, from: https://www.forbes.com/sites/myafrazier/2011/02/16/the-three-lessons-of-the-borders-bankruptcy/#3c1218242a1a
21 Streitfeld, D. (2017). Bookstore chains, long in decline, are undergoing a final shakeout. The New York Times. Retrieved April 25, 2020, from: https://www.nytimes.com/2017/12/28/technology/bookstores-final-shakeout.html
22 Abramovich, G. (2017). 5 ways Amazon has disrupted retail – so far. (2020). Retrieved April 25, 2020, from: https://cmo.adobe.com/articles/2017/10/two-ways-amazon-is-disrupting-retail-and-advice-for-the-way-forward.html#gs.4zgb8m
23 Vial, G. (2019). Understanding digital transformation: A review and a research agenda. The Journal of Strategic Information Systems, 28(2), 118–144.
24 Alley. (2011). You press the button. Kodak used to do the rest. Retrieved June 18, 2020, from: https://www.technologyreview.com/2011/12/09/189254/you-press-the-button-kodak-used-to-do-the-rest/
25 Vial, G. (2019). Understanding digital transformation: A review and a research agenda. The Journal of Strategic Information Systems, 28(2), 118–144.
26 Calder, N., Parvarandeh, S., & Brady, M. (2018). Harvard Business Review. Building a direct-to-consumer strategy without alienating your distributors. Retrieved April 26, 2020, from: https://hbr.org/2018/12/building-a-direct-to-consumer-strategy-without-alienating-your-distributors
27 Vial, G. (2019). Understanding digital transformation: A review and a research agenda. The Journal of Strategic Information Systems, 28(2), 118–144.
28 Vial, G. (2019). Understanding digital transformation: A review and a research agenda. The Journal of Strategic Information Systems, 28(2), 118–144.
29 Vial, G. (2019). Understanding digital transformation: A review and a research agenda. The Journal of Strategic Information Systems, 28(2), 118–144.
30 Ref, R. (2019). How ecosystems create value for their members. Accenture. Retrieved April 26, 2020, from: https://www.accenture.com/au-en/insights/strategy/how-ecosystems-create-value-members
31 Foley, M. (2019). Microsoft to start selling more Azure services directly starting in March. ZDNet. Retrieved April 25, 2020, from: https://www.zdnet.com/article/microsoft-to-start-selling-more-azure-services-directly-starting-in-march/
32 Warren, T. (2013). Microsoft is now selling its Surface tablets direct to businesses. Retrieved April 25, 2020, from: https://www.theverge.com/2013/3/19/4124400/microsoft-surface-business-order-site
33 Burke, S. (2013). Microsoft partners fuming at Surface slight. CRN Australia. Retrieved April 25, 2020, from: https://www.crn.com.au/news/microsoft-partners-fuming-at-surface-slight-348654
34 Calder, N., Parvarandeh, S., & Brady, M. (2018). Building a direct-to-consumer strategy without alienating your distributors. Harvard Business Review. Retrieved April 26, 2020, from: https://hbr.org/2018/12/building-a-direct-to-consumer-strategy-without-alienating-your-distributors
35 Andal-Ancion, A., Cartwright, P.A., & Yip, G.S. (2003). The digital transformation of traditional business. MIT Sloan Management Review. Retrieved April 26, 2020, from: https://sloanreview.mit.edu/article/the-digital-transformation-of-traditional-business/
36 Ref, R. (2019). How ecosystems create value for their members. Accenture. Retrieved April 26, 2020, from: https://www.accenture.com/au-en/insights/strategy/how-ecosystems-create-value-members
37 Eisenhardt, K.M., & Sull, D.N. (2001). Strategy as simple rules. Harvard Business Review, 79(1), 107–116.
38 Davis, J., Eisenhardt, K.M, & Bingham, C.B. (2009) Optimal structure, market dynamism, and the strategy of simple rules. Administrative Science Quarterly, 54, pp 413–452.
39 Davis, J., Eisenhardt, K.M, & Bingham, C.B. (2009) Optimal structure, market dynamism, and the strategy of simple rules. Administrative Science Quarterly, 54, pp 413–452.
40 Burgelman, R.A., & Grove, A.S. (2007). Let chaos reign, then rein in chaos – repeatedly: Managing strategic dynamics for corporate longevity. Strategic Management Journal, 28(10), 965–979.
41 Busulwa, R., Tice, M., & Gurd, B. (2018). Strategy execution and complexity: Thriving in the era of disruption. Routledge.

4 Digital business, the digital business imperative, and digital business transformation

Introduction

We noted earlier how digital technology advancements disrupt customer expectations and behaviors, disrupt the competitive field and bases of competition, and disrupt data availability. In chapter 3, we discussed the existential threats and game-changing opportunities created by such disruption. Digital business offers organizations the opportunity to guard against and adapt to disruption, as well as the opportunity to become disruptors themselves. But realizing the promise and benefits of digital business comes with significant challenges and risks. Accountants can play a critical role in supporting managers to safely navigate these challenges and risks. Doing so requires accountants to understand the promise of digital business, the nature of the business transformation required to realize that promise, the risks associated with such transformation, and how such transformation can be undertaken successfully and safely. In this chapter, we unpack the nature, characteristics, and promise of digital business. We then explain the imperative for organizations to become digital businesses. We discuss digital business transformation and the challenges and risks associated with the journey to becoming a digital business. Finally, we discuss the implications for accountants – that is, the unique role they can play in accelerating and enhancing the success rate of digital business transformation efforts. On completion of this chapter, we expect current and prospective accountants to understand what they can do now and in the future to build their digital business and digital transformation knowledge and competencies, how they can leverage those knowledge and competencies to effectively lead or support digital transformation efforts, and how they can leverage their newfound knowledge, competencies, and digital leadership experiences to supercharge their career development.

Digital business

Pinning down a slippery term

World-leading IT research firm Gartner defines *digital business* as the creation of new business designs by blurring the digital and physical worlds[1]. Forrester, another leading technology research firm, defines digital business as the use of digital assets and ecosystems to continually improve customer outcomes while, at the same time, continuously increasing operational agility. Yet another IT research firm, Aragon Research, defines a digital business as an organization with business models that enable it to proactively reach, serve, and support their customers and partners from their contextual perspective (i.e. from each customer's unique setting or environment, device, timing, etc.), rather than restricting them to what is defined by the business's traditional infrastructure[2]. Digital business has also been defined more simply as the use of digital technologies to enable major business improvements, such as enhancement of customer experience, operations optimization, and creation of new business models[3].

Gartner's Jorge Lopez proposes that what makes digital business different from prior terms such as e-business, for example, is the presence and integration of connected and intelligent things with business processes and people[4]. He adds that once objects ("things") start to negotiate amongst themselves, as well as communicate with business processes and people, an entirely new world of potential becomes possible[5]. In the past, people were required to be proxies for objects at certain stages (e.g. turn them on, sense for them, transfer data to / from them, perform actions that required intelligence); but, increasingly, human proxies are required less and less, as things become more intelligent (e.g. using data analytics, artificial intelligence), become better able to sense (e.g. using a vast array of sensors) and become better able to communicate (e.g. exchange information with other things, processes, and people via the cloud). In addition, things are also becoming better able to take physical action (e.g. using robotic and drone capabilities); and becoming more autonomous (e.g. aware of themselves and others, aware of the environment around them, and able to independently determine the optimal actions to take)[6].

Karel Dörner, a Senior Partner at McKinsey & Company, proposes that the promise of digital business is a universe of applications and digitized assets that almost automatically work together to deliver value and yield competitive advantage[7]. He adds that this promise requires companies to understand where the new frontiers of value are, and to be open to reexamining their entire way of doing business[8]. Forrester's Nigel Fenwick puts it another way, saying that companies must think of their businesses as being part of a dynamic ecosystem that connects digital resources inside and outside the firm to create value for customers[9]. That is, not as a set of products and services, but as a personal value ecosystem that customers can assemble to suit their unique needs and desires. And that companies create greater value by increasing their role and value in customers' personal value ecosystems[10]. Either way, Karel Dörner adds that being a digital business, and realizing the promise of digital business, requires sophisticated engineering, integration, and orchestration capabilities[11].

Digital business as a future state

Digital business is often described as a future state (i.e. how a business should function once it becomes a digital business and what characteristics or capabilities it should have in order to function this way). Such characteristics and capabilities discussed to date include having a frictionless operating system (e.g. one that delivers easy communication / interaction / engagement and collaboration across the value chain and between internal and external stakeholders)[12]. They also include having a competitive digital platform strategy[13,14] (e.g. one that enables rapid value delivery, enables other stakeholders' technologies or platforms to integrate / interact with the organization's digital platform in a simple "plug and play" manner, enables easy self-service access to data insights, enables stakeholders to run value creation improvement experiments safely, and ensures consistent / dependable customer experience). They further include designing products and customer experiences based on value as defined by the customer (e.g. leveraging technology to be where customers are, to do things with them, to walk in their shoes, and to understand their preferences and habits). The characteristics and capabilities of a digital business include intelligence-driven decision-making or weaponization of data for competitive advantage (e.g. collecting, storing, cleaning, curating, featurizing, modeling, productionalizing, and leveraging data to support operational and strategic execution). An increasingly discussed characteristic or capability of digital businesses is combining technical excellence and an engineering culture that gets things done / delivered (e.g. upgrading engineering skills and capabilities to world class level and cultivating an engineering culture that enables engineering to be more integrated into the business).

Digital business as a change journey or change process

Digital business has also been described as a journey or process of change (i.e. what activities a business should undertake, and in what sequence, in order to become a digital business, to realize the promise of digital business, or to avert the dangers of not becoming a digital business). Discussion of required changes has included digitalizing stakeholder interactions / communications, business processes, business functions, and business models (i.e. turning them into more digital ones). Then connecting and integrating them internally and externally, as well as with digitalized things internal and external to the organization.

It has also included enhancing the sensing (e.g. sensors), computational capacity (e.g. computation speed, sophistication), connectivity (e.g. connection speed, strength, distance, reliability), intelligence (e.g. data analytics, data science, artificial intelligence), autonomy (e.g. applications and things that can sense, make decisions, and take corresponding action independently – without human intervention), and scalability of business models / processes / technology platforms (e.g. being able to serve many more customers around the world quickly and at acceptable cost and risk). More recently, it has included activities such as enhancing customer engagement across a range of platforms and channels (e.g. desktop, mobile, social, video, internet of things / IoT, video), and building the digital strategy and digital innovation capability to be able to better sense, adapt to, and capitalize on new customer expectations and preferences.

Whether viewed as a future state or a change process, most organizations' digital business capability, functioning, or change journey exist across a digital business maturity continuum. At one end are digital natives like Google, Amazon, Microsoft, and Apple, who are very advanced in their digital business capabilities and functioning. At the other end of the continuum are businesses either turning a blind eye to advancing digital disruption or realizing the need for change but moving too glacially to digitize their records let alone digitalizing most of their processes. The first category of organizations typically grow rapidly from strength to strength, entering new markets, disrupting dominant incumbents, making outsized profits, and expanding their influence and power. Of the second category of organizations, some are lucky enough to survive disruption when it eventually reaches them, and others experience a slow loss of relevance before, finally, death or sudden collapse. Most organizations are somewhere between these two extremes. A range of models exist for measuring or mapping an organization's digital business maturity, such as the one in Figure 4.1.

Benefits of being a digital business

Organizations that undertake the journey to become digital businesses and compete effectively as digital businesses open themselves up to a range of benefits. From a customer perspective, they expand their ability to engage with their customers, have an expanded understanding of customer needs and preferences, offer them better value, and be able to enter

32 Digital technology advancements

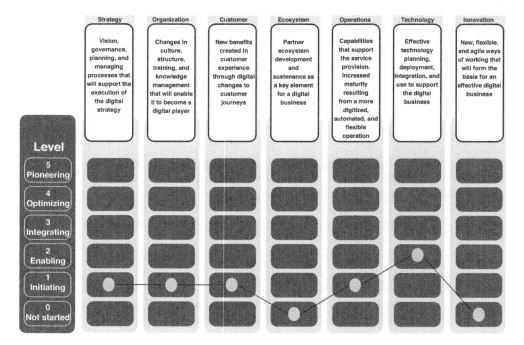

Figure 4.1 Digital business maturity models, like this one[15], attempt to map where an organization is along various digital business capabilities or outcome areas

other markets to acquire new customers. From a product perspective, digital businesses are better able to identify and act on new product / service / value delivery opportunities or to digitally enhance existing products / services. From an operations perspective, digital businesses can realize efficiency and effectiveness breakthroughs that nondigital businesses can't dream of (e.g. a nondigital business couldn't dream of the speed to market, employee productivity, process efficiency, or asset utilization of, say, Amazon or Google).

From a strategy perspective, digital businesses are able to employ novel, highly agile, and highly scalable business models (e.g. marketplaces, ecosystem platforms), are able to unbundle offerings to offer customization / remove non-value-adding aspects of a product (e.g. so customers can buy the one song they like for US$2 instead of a whole album they partially listen to for US$30), and are able to unconstrain supply (e.g. have access to all suppliers rather just a few). From a decision-making perspective, digital businesses are able to access massive amounts of data from within and outside of the firm, they are able to optimally manage and use this data to make better and faster decisions (e.g. through access to real-time insights). In doing so, they weaponize data and make it a strong competitive capability. From a technology infrastructure perspective, digital businesses are able to assemble and integrate hardware, things, networks, software, and platforms to enable them to function optimally as a digital business. Finally, from a people perspective, digital businesses have enough people in the organization with the right digital mindsets (attitudes and behaviors) and skills (e.g. digital technology, digital business, and communication / influence skills) to effect a digital business culture (or the collective appreciation of the importance and urgency of becoming a digital business).

The digital business imperative

In chapter 3, on digital disruption, we explained how digital technology advancements disrupt customer expectations and behaviors, disrupt the competitive field and bases of competition, and disrupt data availability. We noted that this disruption creates existential threats for organizations not able to guard against it or adapt to it in a timely manner. We pointed to examples of disrupted organizations and industries such as Kodak, Blockbuster Video, Borders bookstores, the taxi industry, and the newspaper industry. We also explained the game-changing opportunities presented by digital technology advancements, which are essentially the promise of or actual opportunities available to digital businesses. We propose that the *digital business imperative* is a four-pronged ultimatum for businesses. The first such ultimatum is to guard against and have the capacity to adapt to disruption (e.g. like Intel, Disney, and Caterpillar) or face certain death[16,17,18]. The second is to become a digital business, and realize the promise of digital business, or become sidelined by competitors who do so (ultimately leading to certain death)[19,20,21]. The third is to continuously and sufficiently upgrade and leverage digital business capabilities to become the disruptor, or still risk disruption from companies with superior digital business capabilities[22,23,24]. This is in spite of having become a digital business. Finally, even though businesses may initiate efforts to guard against disruption, to build their capacity to adapt to disruption, to become digital businesses, and to leverage their digital business capabilities in order to become a disruptor, if they can't do it fast enough (relative to the speed of technology changes and / or the speed of existing competitors and new entrants), they may still risk disruption and death[25,26].

Digital business transformation

Defining digital business transformation

Like digital business, the term *digital business transformation*, often used interchangeably with digital transformation, is also a term that is difficult to define. Gartner defines it as:

> The process of exploiting digital technologies and supporting capabilities to create a robust new business model[27].

Synthesizing the extant definitions of digital business transformation, University of Montreal Assistant Professor Gregory Vial defined it as:

> A process that aims to improve an entity by triggering significant changes to its properties through combinations of information, computing, communication, and connectivity technologies[28].

Michael Wade, Professor of Innovation and Strategy as well as Cisco Chair in Digital Business Transformation at IMD business school, and Donald Marchand, Professor of Strategy Execution and Information Management, offer a simpler definition of digital business transformation as:

> Organizational change through the use of digital technologies to materially improve performance[29].

ZDNet's Mark Samuels adds that although the idea is to use digital technologies to make processes more efficient and effective, it's not just replicating those processes into digital form, rather, it is transforming them and, in turn, transforming the product / service the business is offering into something significantly better[30]. Salesforce, a leading cloud customer relationship management (CRM) platform, proposes this definition of digital transformation:

> Digital transformation is the process of using digital technologies to create new – or modify existing – business processes, culture, and customer experiences to meet changing business and market requirements. This reimagining of business in the digital age is digital transformation[31].

Digital business transformation is not just about digital technologies

Bringing together the different definitions above, as well as the earlier definition of digital business, we put it yet another way and propose that digital business transformation is the process of transforming to or becoming a digital business – thus realizing the promise of being a digital business. Digital transformation researchers and practitioners point out that the transformation to a digital business is not just about changes to the digital technologies used. It is also about changes to an organization's strategy (e.g. business models, bases of competition, strategy execution, adaptability and agility), changes to its structure (e.g. organization hierarchy, business functions, roles and responsibilities), changes to its processes (e.g. operational, functional, and strategic processes), changes to its workforce at all levels (e.g. hiring and retention choices, roles and responsibilities, cultivating appropriate competencies, attitudes, and behaviors), and changes to its culture (e.g. collective attitudes and behaviors)[32].

Challenges and risks of digital business transformation

In general, such all-encompassing change and transformation efforts have a low success rate, with management consultancy firm Mckinsey estimating it at about 30%. This means up to 70% of such change and transformation efforts fail to deliver. McKinsey further points out that the success rate of digital transformation efforts is even lower, at about 16%. A range of potential causes for this low success rate have been discussed. These include unspoken disagreement among senior managers about the goals for and approach to digital transformation[33], organizations not having the supporting digital capabilities to support the transformation (e.g. appropriately skilled people, technology infrastructure)[34], lack of a clear strategy and CEO sponsorship of it[35], falling into the "let's wait and see" trap, not understanding what needs to change and how to go about it, challenges getting the right technology and / or the right talent to operate it, employee resistance to change or efforts to undermine the change, obsession with technology tools that don't meaningfully improve customer value, not changing fast enough, challenges sourcing top talent (e.g. technology leaders, digital strategists, designers, DevOps engineers, data scientists, artificial intelligence specialists, etc.)[36], and not dealing with employees' fears of being replaced[37].

Successful digital transformation is the barrier between the existential threats of disruption and the promise or benefits of being a digital business. Thus, in spite of the low success rate, organizations invest in digital business transformation and navigate the obstacles

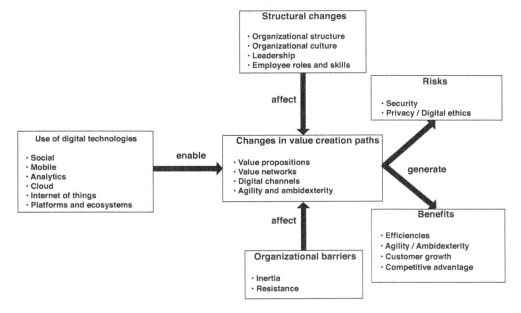

Figure 4.2 Digital business transformation is not just about using digital technologies; it is also about changing organization structures, overcoming change barriers, and managing both digital risks and change risks

and challenges because the alternative, digital disruption, has little upside. Figure 4.2 (adapted from Gregory Vial – see footnote 28) summarizes how use of digital technologies combines with structural changes to overcome organizational barriers to digital business transformation and enable changes in value creation paths. It also shows examples of the benefits and risks associated with these changes.

Implications for accountants

Accountants can play a critical business partnering role in digital business transformation and digital business. For example, they can ensure that the best decisions are made based on relevant and credible data, they can ensure that smart investments in enabling technologies and digital tools are made, they can ensure that safe business model changes and process redesigns occur, and they can ensure that the growing transformation (or lack of transformation) risks are managed effectively. This is part of their emerging roles as copilots (e.g. change facilitators and strategy execution facilitators), navigators (e.g. strategic foresight, agility, and sustainable profitability enablers), brand protectors (e.g. risk managers and stewards), storytellers (e.g. helping managers understand the story behind the data), trusted professionals (e.g. ensuring ethical and responsible risk-taking), process control experts (e.g. supporting effective process and workflow redesign), and digital business and digital technology enablers (e.g. enabling digital technology adoption and digital business transformation)[38]. Given this vital position they occupy and the roles they can play, they are critical to the success of digital transformation efforts. Through their actions (or lack of action) they can significantly enhance the chance of success or significantly derail digital business transformation efforts.

To leverage their important role to significantly enhance the chance of success of digital transformation efforts, accountants can develop their digital business / digital transformation competencies and then leverage these competencies to support digital transformation efforts. To develop these competencies, accountants can undertake ongoing groundwork to understand and keep up with digital technologies (e.g. cloud, IoT, Ai, blockchain, robotics, drones, LPWAN, LEO satellites, etc.), to understand and keep up with digital business and digital transformation concepts and practices (e.g. digital business characteristics, digital business strategy, digital business models, digital innovation practices, successful digital transformation approaches and cases, digital transformation leadership roles and responsibilities, etc.), and to understand relevant change and transformation methodologies (e.g. agile, lean, change acceleration methods). They can then build on this understanding with increasingly important accounting specific competencies such as data skills, strategic technology skills, digital leadership skills, strategic thinking skills, and cross functional leadership and change management skills. Further, they can build informal networks vertically and across the organization that are important for accelerating strategy execution and change / transformation efforts.

Having done the ongoing groundwork to develop the aforementioned digital technology, digital business, and digital transformation competencies, accountants can then leverage these competencies to accelerate and improve the odds of success for digital transformation efforts. For example, they can use their digital transformation and digital business knowledge and skills to support managers to cultivate the digital business and digital transformation competencies of their direct reports; and of other people across the organization. They can support managers to shape appropriate digital business and digital transformation attitudes and behaviors, thus helping nurture the digital culture to support digital business transformation efforts. They can support managers to ensure the hiring of direct reports and other employees with appropriate digital business and digital transformation attitudes and skills. They can leverage their digital business and digital transformation knowledge / skills to take on and successfully carry out one or more key digital transformation leadership roles (e.g. chief digital officer, project / program manager, operating model lead, customer engagement lead, digital product manager, ethics compliance lead, UX designer, change and transformation specialist, digital risk manager, etc.)[39]. Or they can support such leaders to ensure they successfully fulfil those roles. They can leverage their informal networks to accelerate implementation of transformation initiatives, and to encourage functional and frontline staff to understand and accept transformation-related changes. Finally, they can leverage their technology and data skills to work hand in hand with technologists, operational and functional leaders, and senior executives to accelerate transformation efforts while limiting the associated risks.

The alternative to building and leveraging the digital business and digital transformation knowledge and skills / abilities we've described above is for accountants to become one more of the bottlenecks or barriers to digital business transformation efforts. For example, lacking the digital business and digital transformation knowledge and skills / abilities, accountants are likely to find themselves disrupted by those with that knowledge and skills / abilities.

Google and reflect

digitization, digitalization, digital business, digital business transformation, digital transformation, digital business capabilities, digital business competencies, digital platforms, digital strategy, omnichannel strategy, scalability, digital customer engagement, digital customer experience, agile methodologies, lean methodologies, digital accelerator, user story, customer touch point, digital business imperative, digital transformation imperative, user-centered design

Discussion questions

1. What is the difference between the terms digital transformation and digital business transformation?
2. Which of the definitions of digital business transformation provided above makes the most sense to you? Why?
3. What does the common assertion that "digital transformation is not about technology" mean?
4. Are any businesses you know of fully digital businesses? If not, what can make them fully digital businesses?
5. Once an organization becomes a digital business, does it have any need for digital transformation?
6. What is meant by the assertion that digital business is "a change process or a journey"?
7. What is meant by the assertion that digital business is "a future state"?
8. What are the top four benefits of being a digital business? Why are these more important than other benefits?
9. What is the digital business imperative?
10. People often talk about the digital business imperative and the digital transformation imperative. Are these the same or different?
11. What are some challenges and risks of digital business transformation?
12. What is the success rate for transformation efforts in general? What is the success rate for digital transformation efforts? Why is the success rate for digital transformation efforts much worse?
13. What are two important implications of digital business and digital business transformation for accountants?
14. What are five things accountants can do to maximize their organizations' chances of succeeding at digital transformation?

Notes

1. Gartner Inc. (2014). Digital business. Retrieved April 28, 2020, from: https://www.gartner.com/en/information-technology/glossary/digital-business
2. Aragon Research. (2020). Defining digital business – Business and IT glossary. Retrieved May 20, 2020, from: https://aragonresearch.com/glossary-digital-business/
3. Chaffey, D. (2015). Digital business and e-commerce management: Strategy, implementation and practice, 6th edn. Financial Times Prentice Hall, Harlow.
4. Lopez, J. (2014). Digital business is everyone's business. Forbes. Retrieved from: https://www.forbes.com/sites/gartnergroup/2014/05/07/digital-business-is-everyones-business/#636bd0da7f82
5. Lopez, J. (2014). Digital business is everyone's business. Forbes. Retrieved from: https://www.forbes.com/sites/gartnergroup/2014/05/07/digital-business-is-everyones-business/#636bd0da7f82
6. Lopez, J. (2014). Digital business is everyone's business. Forbes. Retrieved from: https://www.forbes.com/sites/gartnergroup/2014/05/07/digital-business-is-everyones-business/#636bd0da7f82
7. Dörner, K., & Edelman, D. (2015). What "digital" really means. McKinsey & Company. Retrieved April 28, 2020, from: https://www.mckinsey.com/industries/technology-media-and-telecommunications/our-insights/what-digital-really-means

8 Dörner, K., & Edelman, D. (2015). What "digital" really means. Retrieved April 28, 2020, from: https://www.mckinsey.com/industries/technology-media-and-telecommunications/our-insights/what-digital-really-means
9 Sacolick, I. (2017). Driving digital: The leader's guide to business transformation through technology. Amacom.
10 Fenwick, N. (2015). Unleash your digital predator. Retrieved May 22, 2020, from: https://go.forrester.com/blogs/15-12-09-unleash_your_digital_predator/
11 Dörner, K., & Edelman, D. (2015). What "digital" really means. Retrieved April 28, 2020, from: https://www.mckinsey.com/industries/technology-media-and-telecommunications/our-insights/what-digital-really-means
12 Swords, J. (2020). Becoming a modern digital business in 2020. Thoughtworks. Retrieved May 22, 2020, from: https://www.thoughtworks.com/perspectives/edition8-modern-digital-business-article
13 Swords, J. (2020). Becoming a modern digital business in 2020. Thoughtworks. Retrieved May 22, 2020, from: https://www.thoughtworks.com/perspectives/edition8-modern-digital-business-article
14 Gupta, S. (2018). Driving digital strategy: A guide to reimagining your business. Harvard Business Press.
15 Valdez-de-Leon, O. (2016). A digital maturity model for telecommunications service providers. Technology Innovation Management Review, 6(8).
16 Stanek, R. (2018). Council post: Why it's important to make your company the disruptor, not the disrupted. Forbes. Retrieved from: https://www.forbes.com/sites/forbestechcouncil/2018/06/04/why-its-important-to-make-your-company-the-disruptor-not-the-disrupted/#4ddb3e8331a6
17 Vial, G. (2019). Understanding digital transformation: A review and a research agenda. The Journal of Strategic Information Systems, 28(2), 118–144.
18 Schadler, T., & Fenwick, N. (2017). The digital business imperative. Forrester. Retrieved May 22, 2020, from: https://www.forrester.com/report/The+Digital+Business+Imperative/-/E-RES115784
19 Schadler, T., & Fenwick, N. (2017). The digital business imperative. Forrester. Retrieved May 22, 2020, from: https://www.forrester.com/report/The+Digital+Business+Imperative/-/E-RES115784
20 Stanek, R. (2018). Council post: Why it's important to make your company the disruptor, not the disrupted. Forbes. Retrieved from: https://www.forbes.com/sites/forbestechcouncil/2018/06/04/why-its-important-to-make-your-company-the-disruptor-not-the-disrupted/#4ddb3e8331a6
21 Vial, G. (2019). Understanding digital transformation: A review and a research agenda. The Journal of Strategic Information Systems, 28(2), 118–144.
22 Stanek, R. (2018). Council post: Why it's important to make your company the disruptor, not the disrupted. Forbes. Retrieved from: https://www.forbes.com/sites/forbestechcouncil/2018/06/04/why-its-important-to-make-your-company-the-disruptor-not-the-disrupted/#4ddb3e8331a6
23 Fenwick, N. (2015). Unleash your digital predator. Retrieved May 22, 2020, from: https://go.forrester.com/blogs/15-12-09-unleash_your_digital_predator/
24 Stanek, R. (2018). Council post: Why it's important to make your company the disruptor, not the disrupted. Forbes. Retrieved from: https://www.forbes.com/sites/forbestechcouncil/2018/06/04/why-its-important-to-make-your-company-the-disruptor-not-the-disrupted/#4ddb3e8331a6
25 Ross, J. (2018). Digital is about speed – but it takes a long time. MIT Sloan Management Review. Retrieved May 22, 2020, from: https://sloanreview.mit.edu/article/digital-is-about-speed-but-it-takes-a-long-time/
26 Brown, S. (2020). Strategy at the speed of digital. McKinsey & Company. Retrieved May 22, 2020, from: https://www.mckinsey.com/business-functions/strategy-and-corporate-finance/our-insights/strategy-at-the-speed-of-digital
27 Gartner. (2018). Gartner glossary: Digital business transformation. Retrieved May 22, 2020, from: https://www.gartner.com/en/information-technology/glossary/digital-business-transformation
28 Vial, G. (2019). Understanding digital transformation: A review and a research agenda. The Journal of Strategic Information Systems, 28(2), 118–144.
29 Marchand, D.A., & Wade, M.R. (2014). Digital business transformation: IMD Business School. Where is your company on the journey. Retrieved May 22, 2020, from: https://www.imd.org/research-knowledge/articles/digital-business-transformation-where--is-your-company-on-the-journey/
30 Samuels, M. (2018). What is digital transformation? Everything you need to know about how technology is reshaping business. ZDNet. Retrieved May 22, 2020, from: https://www.zdnet.com/article/what-is-digital-transformation-everything-you-need-to-know-about-how-technology-is-reshaping/

31 Salesforce. (2018). What is digital transformation? A definition by Salesforce. Retrieved May 22, 2020, from: https://www.salesforce.com/products/platform/what-is-digital-transformation/
32 Vial, G. (2019). Understanding digital transformation: A review and a research agenda. The Journal of Strategic Information Systems, 28(2), 118–144.
33 Sutcliff, M., Narsalay, R., & Sen, A. (2019). The two big reasons that digital transformations fail. Harvard Business Review. Retrieved May 22, 2020, from: https://hbr.org/2019/10/the-two-big-reasons-that-digital-transformations-fail
34 Sutcliff, M., Narsalay, R., & Sen, A. (2019). The two big reasons that digital transformations fail. Harvard Business Review. Retrieved May 22, 2020, from: https://hbr.org/2019/10/the-two-big-reasons-that-digital-transformations-fail
35 Boulton, C. (2019). 12 reasons why digital transformations fail. CIO. Retrieved May 22, 2020, from: https://www.cio.com/article/3248946/12-reasons-why-digital-transformations-fail.html
36 Boulton, C. (2019). 12 reasons why digital transformations fail. CIO. Retrieved May 22, 2020, from: https://www.cio.com/article/3248946/12-reasons-why-digital-transformations-fail.html
37 Tabrizi, B., Lam, E., Girard, K. & Irvin, V. (2019). Digital transformation is not about technology. Harvard Business Review. Retrieved May 22, 2020, from: https://hbr.org/2019/03/digital-transformation-is-not-about-technology
38 IFAC. (2019). Future-fit accountants: Roles for the next decade. Retrieved 18 December 2019, from: https://www.ifac.org/knowledge-gateway/preparing-future-ready-professionals/discussion/future-fit-accountants-roles-next
39 Boulton, C. (2018). 8 essential roles for a successful digital transformation. CIO. Retrieved May 22, 2020, from: https://www.cio.com/article/3258767/8-essential-roles-for-a-successful-digital-transformation.html

Part II
Digital disruption and digital transformation of accounting

5 Digital disruption and digital transformation of accounting

Introduction

As digital technologies advance, they are driving a range of disruptions in accounting work (e.g. disrupting the data available for accounting work, disrupting the tools used to perform accounting work, disrupting how accounting processes and procedures can best be performed, and disrupting what roles and activities accountants are able to perform). In this chapter, we explore these different disruptions and discuss how they change accounting work. We then discuss the impact and implications of these disruptions on the accounting value proposition and on accounting functions (e.g. financial accounting, management accounting, audit, tax, accounting information systems, and business partnering / advisory. Finally, we discuss the key digital technology advancements anticipated to have or to continue having a profound direct impact on accounting work (e.g. cloud computing, XBRL, data analytics / data science, artificial intelligence (AI), robotic process automation (RPA) / intelligent process automation (IPA), the internet of things (IoT), blockchain), and we identify the specific accounting functions and activities each digital technology is anticipated to have the greatest impact on. Current and future accountants may find themselves using new digital technology tools to perform accounting work, auditing new digital technology tools used by organizations, devising policies to safeguard organizations from new digital risks, advising on information systems architecture decisions, managing or working with big data, configuring robotic process automation or intelligent process automation processes, advising on strategic technology investments, and supporting strategic leaders and business managers to lead digital transformation and build digital business capabilities. In these types of situations, accountants need to understand how digital technology advancements disrupt accounting work and the roles of accountants, the new capabilities required across accounting functions, the digital leadership / strategic technology / technical technology competencies required of accountants, and how accountants can cultivate these competencies in order to continue to deliver on the evolving accounting value proposition. We expect that current and future accountants will apply the digital disruption and digital transformation lens provided in this chapter to consider the impact of digital technology advancements on their future work / career prospects, and to position themselves to seize the numerous career opportunities that digital technology advancements present for the prepared accountant.

Digital disruption of accounting

In earlier chapters, we defined disruption as the process or effect of preventing something from happening as usual, or throwing the normal course of action into disorder. For example, disruption may prevent routines, processes, activities, or events from occurring as they have previously occurred. We also referred to digital disruption as digital technology-induced disruption. That is, as the introduction of new digital technologies, or advancements in existing ones, subsequently bring about the process or effect of preventing routines, processes, activities, or events from occurring as they have previously occurred. We noted that digital disruption is typically discussed in the context of disruptions at organization level, but that disruptions can also occur at industry, sector, institution, society, or profession level. Both direct and indirect forces drive digital disruption of the accounting profession, as we discuss in the paragraphs that follow.

Indirect disruption

Indirectly, the digital disruption of accounting is being driven by the digital disruption of organizations and, thus, the resultant changes in stakeholder expectations of accountants (e.g. stakeholders such as business managers, governance teams, regulators, and communities). We previously outlined how, at an organization level, digital technology innovations result in disruptions of customer expectations and behaviors, disruption of the competitive field and bases of competition, and disruption of data availability. These disruptions, in turn, prevent organizations that want to maximize their longevity from continuing to operate as they have always done. Continuing to do so puts their long-term survival at risk, thus requiring them to adapt to digital disruption. Adapting to digital disruption requires organizations to undertake digital business transformation, and to effectively compete as digital businesses. That is, adapting to digital disruption requires them to reconfigure their infrastructure, strategic processes, business models, and operational processes so as to deliver significant efficiency breakthroughs (in line with or better than new industry entrants or digitally adapted traditional competitors), to deliver innovative new products, to deliver significant breakthroughs in customer experience and value, and to redesign their businesses for adaptability and agility. However, undertaking digital business transformation and effectively competing as a digital business is challenging and comes with significant risks. These risks are compounded by parallel challenges faced by organizations, such as growing complexity and uncertainty, unprecedented levels of regulation and growth in compliance requirements, shifting talent and capability requirements, and growing community expectations for inclusive capitalism and corporate responsibility[1]. In light of the digital business transformation and digital business change imperative, as well as the associated transformation challenges and risks, accounting profession stakeholders' expectations of accountants are changing. For example, business managers increasingly expect accountants to play a greater role in anticipating or detecting disruptive threats and competitive advantage opportunities, to play a greater role in enabling digital business transformation, to play a greater role in process control and process redesign, and to play a greater role in facilitating change and strategy execution[2]. Similarly, top management and governance teams increasingly expect accountants to play a greater role in effectively protecting organizations from emerging cybersecurity, digital ethics, and corporate responsibility risks[3]. In addition, communities and societies increasingly expect accountants to play an important role in ensuring responsible risk-taking, ethical conduct, and transparent communication by their organizations[4].

These new and / or expanded stakeholder expectations disrupt accounting practice in three ways. First, they change which existing accounting roles and activities are of most value. For example, some traditional accounting roles and activities such as transaction recording, month end reconciliations, and financial report preparation are increasingly able to be performed by sophisticated artificial intelligence, data analytics, and data visualization algorithms – requiring significantly less or no accountant input. In contrast, assurance and business partnering roles and activities become more valuable with advancements in digital technologies. Second, an increase in stakeholder expectations requires accountants to perform new roles and activities in order to live up to these changed stakeholder expectations. Examples of these new accounting roles and activities include combining accounting and digital technology know-how to help organizations navigate the new digital risk landscape, to help organizations make smart investments in digital business transformation enabling digital technologies, and to help organizations shift processes and business models to digital. Third, changes in accounting roles result in changes in the competencies required to fulfill these roles. For example, new or enhanced accounting roles in digital transformation and digital business require accountants to have new digital technology competencies (e.g. XBRL, data analytics, data science, and blockchain knowledge and skills), to have new digital transformation and digital business competencies (e.g. knowledge of digital business strategy, knowledge of digital business models, knowledge of information systems architecture), and to have new accelerated change and transformation methodology competencies for change and strategy execution roles (e.g. competencies such as knowledge of agile, lean, and design thinking methodologies).

Direct disruption

Directly, the digital disruption of accounting occurs through five key disruptions or changes. These include disruption of the data available to accountants, disruption of tools available to perform accounting work, disruption of the type of value accountants are able to create, disruption of the optimal ways to perform accounting work, and disruption of the competencies required for accounting work. We discuss each of these in more detail below.

Disruption of data availability

Providing information useful for decision-making has been a central part of the accounting value proposition even before Luca Pacioli's time, in the late 1400s and early 1500s. To this end, accountants have always sought to leverage the best data possible (e.g. quality and quantity) to inform the usefulness, completeness, and reliability of the information provided. Over time, the data sources have evolved from paper-based systems, to digitized transaction recording applications, to enterprise resource planning systems, to integrated digital platforms and ecosystems. These evolutions gradually increased the amount of available data and / or the extent to which available data could be leveraged in decision-making, until an inflection point was reached – when there was an exponential growth in the amount of data available, the variety of available data, the available sources of data and the democratization of access to data. The exact time at which this inflection point occurred can be debated, but the forces that drove it include the advent, convergence, and wide-scale adoption of internet and network connectivity, cloud computing, IoT, and artificial intelligence technologies. Examples of the explosion and exponential growth in sources of available data include internal organizational data from hundreds or even thousands of organizational systems, applications, and devices (e.g. mobile apps, desktop apps, ERP systems, cryptocurrency payment platforms, IoT devices, social media apps), partner ecosystem data (e.g. data from thousands of vendor or business partners' systems, applications, and devices), and data from external entities (e.g. data from an almost unlimited number of online platforms, government institutions / agencies, big data aggregators, and more).

Examples of the explosion in data variety or data types include the availability of large and growing volumes of structured data, unstructured data, machine data, open data, dark data, real-time data, spatiotemporal data, unverified data, outdated data, video data, social media data, cryptocurrency data, image data, sound data, email data, and more. More than 90% of the world's data have been created in the last two years alone[5]. Examples of the growth in available data include more than 188 million emails being currently sent every minute[6], more than 500 million tweets being sent per day, more than four petabytes of Facebook data being added each day[7], more than five billion search engine searches being made per day[8], and the evolution of data scales from kilobytes / megabytes / gigabytes / terabytes to petabytes / zettabytes / yottabytes[9]. Much of this explosion in data has occurred with just over 50% of the world's population being online[10]. It has occurred prior to the pending explosion of data that will be created by billions, and perhaps even trillions, of additional IoT devices coming online and starting to communicate with each other. And it has occurred prior to the wide-scale integration between people, things, and processes / routines. Examples of the democratization of data include easy access to sophisticated data analytics tools, and easy access to data by most people within and even outside an organization (e.g. consider the array of open source tools and open source data being used by a diverse range of stakeholders around the world to create and disseminate trustworthy Covid-19 data insights). In many organizations, data that was once the exclusive domain of select functional employees, such as accountants, are now becoming available across functions, and even available organization wide. This empowers a wider and more diverse audience to analyze this data using the organization's available internal analytics tools, or using free and source tools, to spot insights and to verify insights derived by others.

The growth in the amount of data available, the variety of available data, the available sources of data, and the accessibility of data creates a range of threats, opportunities, and challenges for accountants. Accountants have the opportunity to significantly improve the breadth, completeness, reliability, and usefulness of the information used for decision-making. To do so, they face challenges. For example, they need to understand different types of data, and the value of the data to organizations. They need to be able to integrate disparate datasets in order to draw out deeper and more meaningful insights. They need to be able to analyze the different types of data (e.g. structured data, unstructured data, machine data, video and image data). They need to be able to leverage all this data for real-time prescriptive and predictive insights. And they need to be able to communicate insights from such voluminous and diverse data to a variety of stakeholders (e.g. discussing it, visualizing it, making it engaging, making it interactive, making it customizable).

The disruption of data availability also creates threats for accountants. For example, broader availability of data introduces competitors to accounting roles relating to the provision of useful information for decision-making. Competitors may be functional or cross-functional data scientists, data analysts outside the accounting function, data management experts within IT/ IS / technology functions, data analytics service providers outside of the organization, or new intelligent and autonomous data analytics products (e.g. AI-based digital analyst algorithms). To remain competitive, accountants must continuously improve the scope of the information they provide, and the efficiency and effectiveness with which they provide information for decision-making. As well as facing competition to provide the best information for decision-making, the information provided by accountants can increasingly be checked or audited for relevance, completeness, reliability, and usefulness by other stakeholders. This is due to those stakeholders also having access to the same data, and the same sophisticated data analytics tools available to accountants. If accounting information lacks sufficient relevance, completeness, reliability, and usefulness, the increased ability of stakeholders to cross-check accounting work poses a threat to accountants' credibility and legitimacy. This creates pressures for accountants to ensure the information they provide can stand up to scrutiny, both in appearance and in substance.

Disruption of the tools used to perform accounting work

Digital technology advancements introduce new tools and / or enhance existing tools that can be used to perform accounting work (e.g. see table 5.1 identifying some digital technology tools used to automate audit tasks). These new tools typically offer more efficient and effective ways of performing accounting work. For example, the introduction of cloud computing and mobile computing enabled the use of cloud accounting platforms and mobile apps, which have become highly effective tools for performing accounting work. Through their use, transaction recording can occur from anywhere with an internet connection. It can occur once (as opposed to needing duplicate transaction recording and / or data entry), it can be analyzed closer to real time (as opposed to waiting long periods for access to the data), and it can be automatically analyzed and reported (as opposed to waiting for manual data analysis to occur). The introduction of artificial intelligence enabled the use of artificial intelligence algorithms to automatically extract transactions from bank statements and to enter them into the accounting system, or to use phone cameras to take photos of receipts and have artificial intelligence algorithms read the images and automatically enter relevant transactions into accounting systems. The introduction of data visualization technologies enabled accountants to use tools such as Tableau, SAS, and Power BI to better present data insights. Furthermore, advancements in digital technologies such as the internet of things (IoT), robotic process automation, robotics, and drones provide new tools for accountants to improve a range of accounting practices. For example, shifting to automatic and real-time inventory monitoring through use of intelligent robots and drones that leverage IoT sensors and computer vision, using RPA to automate structured and repetitive accounting tasks, implementing continuous audits, or establishing immutable records. Thus, digital technology advancements result in the introduction of new or improved work tools that disrupt how accounting activities can be carried out, and who or what can carry out particular accounting activities. For example, if smart devices can capture transactions and sophisticated algorithms can analyze and report on those transactions, then accountants may not need to be involved in transaction reporting; but they may instead play more of an oversight / troubleshooting and advisory role. Digital technology advancements disrupt how efficiently accounting activities can be carried out (e.g. recording and reporting on transactions may be able to occur in real time); and they also disrupt how effectively the activities can occur (e.g. smart algorithms can be used for continuous monitoring to spot issues or predict issues and prompt their early resolution). Remaining competent in evolving accounting work requires that accountants are able to use an expanding range of digital technologies and tools relevant to different accounting activities. Examples of these new or enhanced tools for auditors include robotic process automation tools like Blue Prism and Pega, audit analytics software like IDEA, and process mining software like QPR ProcessAnalyzer. Examples of these new or

Table 5.1 Example digital technology tools used to automate audit tasks[11]

A comparison between automation tools for audit tasks

Tools	Tool execution	Audit task
Excel Macros	Rules-Based Functions	Reconciliations
IDEA	Calculations	Analytical Procedures
		Internal Control Testing
		Detail Testing (Attribute Match)
Python	Rules-Based Functions	Reconciliations
R	Calculations	Analytical Procedures
	Web Scraping	Internal Control Testing
RPA Vendor Tools, such as	Importing Data	Detail Testing (Attribute Match)
UiPath and Blue Prism	Exporting Data	Input: Collection of Data
		Output: Compilation of Audit Test Results

enhanced tools for financial accountants and management accountants include the Xero, SAP S/4HANA, Tableau, XBRL, SAS, and idaciti tools or platforms.

Disruption of the type of value accountants are able to create

Digital technology advancements expand the roles and activities accountants can perform. First, new or enhanced digital technology tools enable accountants to perform traditional accounting activities much faster – thus freeing up value creation capacity. Accountants can leverage this free value creation capacity to create more and better value for their stakeholders. For example, an accountant in a mining organization can leverage drone, video analytics, and computer vision digital technologies to automatically count inventory levels like mineral stockpiles in real time and with greater accuracy[12]. This can save weeks' worth of time (e.g. time visiting the site, time making / adjusting / validating estimates, etc.). This saved time can be utilized to address other critical stakeholder challenges (e.g. digital risk management, strategic sensing, change facilitation, digital transformation enablement, etc.). As accountants help stakeholders solve these challenges, accounting stakeholder expectations of the roles accountants are able to play in these challenges expands, as does their reliance on accountants to play such roles. Through this ongoing process, the type of value accountants can create, and the reliance on accountants to create such value, expands across a range of digital transformation and digital business challenges. For example, owing to this process playing out, accountants are increasingly involved in cybersecurity risk management, process digitalization, data management, digital ethics, and strategy execution issues. Accountants who don't effectively leverage digital technologies to expand their efficiency and the type of value they are able to create are likely to find themselves under-delivering on stakeholder expectations and, thus, losing relevance.

Disruption of the optimal ways to perform accounting work

By offering new or enhanced ways to perform accounting activities, digital technology advancements expand the repertoire of approaches that can be used to perform accounting work. For example, decision-making information can be presented in the standardized reports built into cloud accounting platforms, or it can be extracted and presented in custom Excel reports, or it can be automatically pushed into user customizable and interactive data visualization applications. The information can be presented on a monthly basis or it can be made available to provide real-time predictions and prescriptions. As another example, auditors can leverage digital technologies such as machine learning to review full populations of data for fraud instances, instead of just reviewing a sample. They can leverage natural language processing technology to read all of an organization's legal contracts, invoices, quotes, and emails. And they can leverage sophisticated knowledge graphs and neural network or deep learning tools to discover facts and patterns that are impossible for the human mind to discover without the use of technology. As these reporting and auditing examples illustrate, digital technologies expand the number of ways it is possible to perform accounting work. In doing so, they disrupt what constitutes the optimal or best practice ways of performing accounting work. Thus, in order to remain at a competitive level of practice, accountants and accounting function leaders have to remain alert to digital technology advancements and continuously monitor the new or enhanced ways of performing accounting work that they enable. By continuously identifying and adopting optimal approaches to carrying out accounting work, accountants and accounting functions can maximize their efficiency and effectiveness.

Disruption of competencies required by accountants

Digital technologies disrupt the competencies required to effectively perform accounting work. They do this by requiring new digital technology competencies (e.g. so that accountants can use new or enhanced digital technology tools for traditional accounting work), and by requiring new or enhanced competencies to carry out new or enhanced accounting roles and activities. For example, in the information provision example we provided earlier, accountants would need data management, data analytics, and data visualization competencies. And in the audit example we provided earlier, auditors would need knowledge and skills in big data analytics, machine learning, robotic process automation, natural language processing, knowledge graphs, neural networks, and deep learning technologies. Figure 5.1 shows a proposal for digital technology topics to include *accounting information systems* (AIS) courses / units within undergraduate accounting degrees[13].

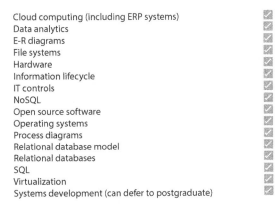

Figure 5.1 Some researchers are proposing the inclusion of an accounting information systems course or unit in undergraduate accounting degrees focusing on these identified AIS competency areas[14]

As well as proficiency with new digital technology tools, accountants have to understand the strategic implications of digital technologies in order to play critical roles in digital business transformation and digital business (e.g. roles such as effective business partnering in the reconfiguration of business models and infrastructure for adaptability and agility). This means that accountants face parallel pressures to develop their accounting competencies, their digital technology competencies, and their strategic change and transformation competencies. Neglecting any one of these groups of competencies puts them at risk of losing relevance or being sidelined by competitors.

Disruption and transformation of the accounting value proposition

At a high level, the *accounting value proposition* refers to the capacity to provide accurate, relevant, reliable, timely, and useful information to suit the conscious and unconscious information needs of a range of decision makers. Examples of these decision makers can include governance teams, internal managers, regulatory bodies, investors, lenders, and the general public. Examples of the decisions being made include what to invest or not invest in, to whom and how much money to lend, how to configure operational processes for optimal efficiency, how to best enhance a firm's long-term prospects, how to best roster staff to minimize costs without undermining employee engagement, whether to keep a particular management team in place, and how to manage the social and environmental activities of an organization. Accounting stakeholders, or users of accounting information, place trust and confidence in accountants to ensure the right information is provided, to the right stakeholders, for the right decisions, at the right time, and in the right place.

Digital technology advancements disrupt the accounting value proposition in four main ways. First, they influence or change accounting stakeholders' perceptions of the role and value of the accounting value proposition, and of the role of accountants in this value proposition. For example, digital technology tools like the Xero cloud accounting platform and associated apps marketplace provide small and medium-sized business managers with the ability to record business transactions and generate financial and operating performance reports by themselves. Some of these stakeholders, whilst still acknowledging the decision usefulness of accounting information, may see limited value in the role of accountants in the accounting value proposition. They may reason that they can leverage digital technology tools to realize the aspects of the accounting value proposition of importance to them without the help of accountants. In contrast, other small and medium-sized business managers may reason that while the accounting value proposition is still of importance to them, the value of accountants in this value proposition is in designing, configuring, or overseeing automated decision support tools. That is, they may reason there is less value in recording transactions and generating reports as digital technology tools can do this. Yet other stakeholders, enterprise level accounting stakeholders for example, may see the accounting value proposition as being more important than ever for ensuring data integrity in a world of data proliferation (e.g. for providing assurance that data generated by internet of things devices or AI algorithms can be trusted to be accurate, without bias, and acquired and used ethically). As these three different examples illustrate, while digital technology advancements may not diminish the value of accounting information, they shift stakeholders' perceptions of the roles and activities accountants need to play in its provision, and their perceptions of the extent to which accountants are actually playing these roles to enable full realization of the accounting value proposition.

Second, digital technology advancements influence or change accountants' ability to fully deliver on the accounting value proposition or aspects of it. They do this by constantly shifting stakeholders' information needs and expectations of accountants (e.g. expectations for more information, better information, better communicated information) and constantly shifting the tools required to provide accounting information (e.g. cloud accounting platforms and app marketplaces, artificial intelligence tools, unstructured data analysis tools, XBRL, and blockchain technologies).

Third, digital technology advancements introduce new challenges for realizing the accounting value proposition. For example, growing risk exposures as well as growing data volume, velocity, and variety create information assurance challenges for accountants. And growth in the number and diversity of internal and external apps, devices, platforms, sub-systems, ecosystems, and network connectivity sources that integrate to facilitate organizational workflows create significant complexity. This complexity can make acquiring, deciphering, and using the resultant data to deliver on the accounting value proposition much more challenging.

Finally, digital technology advancements change accountants' value creation capacity (i.e. they equip accountants with the ability to create more and better value for accounting stakeholders). In doing this, digital technologies enable accountants to expand the scope and impact of the accounting value proposition. For example, digital technologies significantly expand volume of data, variety of data, velocity of data, and veracity of data available to accountants. And they expand the tools available for carrying out accounting work. Accountants able to leverage these tools and data can provide decision-making information that both lives up to and exceeds stakeholders' expectations. For example, they can move beyond provision of financial information to deliver on the promise of integrated reporting and the multi-capitals perspective. Furthermore, accountants can leverage digital technologies to provide early warnings of pending strategic disruptions, or of fraud events about to happen, thereby becoming increasingly critical linchpins in strategy formation and execution. For example, accountants can leverage AI tools to provide real-time predictive and prescriptive strategic adaptation insights from analysis of big data being generated in real-time online. Accountants can also leverage digital technologies to improve communication of accounting information. For example, instead of traditional static reports, accountants can better communicate information through interactive visualizations, multi-layered / drill-down / slice and dice / self-customization-enabled reports, and machine readable financial reports).

In addition to the earlier discussed disruptions of the accounting value proposition's realization, digital technologies such as process facilitation platforms, applications, devices, and device ecosystems are increasingly inserted between accountants and their stakeholders[15]. As a result, as well as proficiency in accounting-specific digital technologies and tools, accountants also need working knowledge of key business platforms, applications, and devices. They also need working knowledge of key digital business capabilities and related technologies / tools in order to report and advise on those capabilities. The requirement for such knowledge and proficiency means that digital technologies moderate who can provide accounting information (e.g. accountants who are able to use accounting-specific technologies as well as the particular organization's digital technology tools), how they can provide it (e.g. using accounting-specific technologies or using the organization's unique tools), where they can provide it (e.g. anywhere in the world or just at the office), and when they can provide it (e.g. anytime or just during business hours). Based on these varied examples of the impact of technology on the realization of the accounting value proposition, we contend that that not only does accounting have a strong competitor in digital technologies for the mantle of "language of business", digital technologies are also becoming both the language of accounting work and non-optional tools for effectively delivering on the accounting value proposition.

Disruption and transformation of accounting functions

The accounting value proposition is delivered through the main accounting functions of financial accounting, management accounting, audit, tax, business partnering / advisory, and accounting information systems. In the remainder of this chapter, we discuss the impact of digital technology advancements on these functions.

Financial accounting

The financial accounting function focuses on effectively identifying, measuring, recording, and summarizing business transactions and events, then translating the resultant data into financial statements or reports, typically for external users. Financial accounting's outputs (financial statements or reports) are guided and / or governed by accounting frameworks and principles (such as the Conceptual Framework and the GAAP), by national or international accounting standards (e.g. IFRS), and by national and international regulatory bodies (e.g. IASB, AASB, US SEC). The reports must be prepared to a set routine schedule (e.g. to meet quarterly and annual reporting requirements), and are used by a diverse range of external users for investment, resource allocation, compliance, and social and environmental responsibility assurance decisions.

Digital technology advancements disrupt financial accounting in six key ways. First, they change how business transactions can be identified. AI-based algorithms can monitor business processes and business bank statements to automatically identify business events or transactions that need recording (e.g. the Xero cloud accounting platform integrates into a business's bank account information and automatically identifies bank transactions that need to be recorded). In a similar way, AI-based algorithms can monitor business processes and identify events or activities that may require recording and reporting (e.g. an AI-based algorithm can be designed to read a legal letter and identify a potential contingent liability for the financial accounting team to further investigate). Second, digital technology advancements disrupt the recording of financial transactions (e.g. the Xero cloud accounting platform discussed earlier automatically prepares the corresponding journal entries so accountants need only approve or modify the journal entries). And, again, as an example, AI-based algorithms can also be designed to further investigate and prepare draft reporting of the contingent liabilities they identify. Third, digital technology advancements disrupt measurement of the elements of financial statements. They do this by providing complementary or better, and therefore more reliable, measurement approaches. For example, inventory can now be specifically measured and tracked in real time using sensors and internet connectivity, or large inventory stockpiles can be more accurately measured using drones and computer vision. This may render LIFO (last in, first out) and FIFO (first in, first out) approaches to measurement / valuation to increasingly become irrelevant [16]. Figure 5.2 shows how artificial intelligence and cognitive technologies, drones / robotics, and privileged process automation (PPA) / robotic

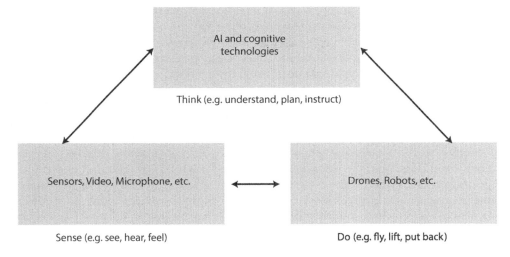

Figure 5.2 AI and cognitive technologies, drones / robotics, and PPA / RPA can be combined to give robots / drones the human-like ability to do inventory counts / verifications[17]

process automation can be combined to automate inventory counts / verifications using robots / drones (e.g. like a human being, robots / drones enabled to see, feel, hear, and act – meaning they can see inventory, understand what is happening in the inventory environment, move inventory to see behind it, lift inventory to check weights, and more).

Similarly, receivables measurement / valuation can be improved through algorithms that assess in real time the likelihood receivables going bad and thus their true value[18], as opposed to applying less credible annual rates / averages. Assets can be peer valued or better compared through tagging or through use of big data[19]. And the availability of voluminous, diverse, rapidly growing, and more reliable datasets mean that more reliable measurement / valuation is not only possible for accountants but also for users of accounting information. As a result, the relationship between accounting reports and market valuation of entities can diverge greatly where the available data is not leveraged by financial accountants[20]. Fourth, digital technologies dramatically expand the amount of information and the type of information that can be contained in financial reports or integrated reports. For example, through XBRL-based reports, financial statement information can be layered and embedded with metadata (data about data) to enable diverse financial report or integrated report users to roll up, drill down, slice and dice reported information to suit their custom decision-making needs[21]. Various other types of information can be provided as metadata, and the information can be provided in human readable and machine readable formats. Digital technologies can also ease the breadth and depth of integrated reporting information provision and use of the multi-capitals perspective. Fifth, digital technology advancements disrupt the usability and engagement of financial statements. For example, we discussed earlier the benefits of XBRL-based reports for expanding the amount of information that can be provided. XBRL-based reports also enhance the usability of reports by enabling report users to interact with the reports (e.g. to drill down, roll up, slice and dice, and benchmark reported information or to transfer that information to different accounting applications or different data visualization applications). In doing so, they shift financial reporting from static reports to active engagement tools. Finally, digital technology advancements disrupt financial or integrated report assurance. They do this by enabling report preparers and auditors to better verify the integrity of the information provided, and to even provide user verifiable integrity checks (e.g. as information layers or metadata within XBRL-based reports). Leveraged this way, digital technologies can improve the credibility of reported information, the comfort / confidence that users have in the reported information, and the functioning of capital markets and societies.

Management accounting

In contrast to the financial accounting function, which focuses on external users of accounting information, the management function focuses on internal users of accounting information. Typically, these users are strategic leaders, operating managers, functional managers, and change leaders. Examples of the type of accounting information provided to them includes information about cost behavior, process efficiency and effectiveness, performance of the organization / business units / teams / individuals, resource allocation requirements, strategy foresight and execution effectiveness, the implications of day-to-day decisions. Management accountants play critical roles in strategy, change management, performance management, and internal control. Playing such roles requires identifying the information needs of decision makers, sourcing of relevant data, analyzing data, presenting analysis insights, engaging with and influencing stakeholders, and partnering with a range of stakeholders across hierarchies and value chains to effect change and business transformation.

Digital technology advancements disrupt management accounting in four main ways.

First, they disrupt the information needs and expectations of management accounting stakeholders. Owing to the digital transformation and digital business imperatives driven by digital technology advancements, management accounting stakeholders (organization leaders and managers) require expanded information to effectively undertake digital business transformation and effectively operate as a digital business. For example, they require information about digital disruption opportunities and threats, effective digital business model designs, effective digital process configurations, digital transformation effectiveness, digital risk exposures, and effectiveness of digital business capabilities such as digital stakeholder engagement, digital customer service, digital innovation, and organizational agility. Management accounting stakeholders expect management accountants to play a greater role in meeting these expanded information needs. Owing to these expanded information needs and expectations, digital technology advancements also disrupt management accounting roles. For example, management accountants are expected to play a greater role in change facilitation / strategy execution (e.g. planning, measuring, monitoring change initiatives), to play a greater role in strategy formation (e.g. strategic sensing, evaluating business model design), to play a greater role in brand protection (e.g. identifying risk exposures, assessing the effectiveness of risk management efforts, evaluating digital risks), to play a greater role in data management (e.g. data capture, data storage, data integration, data governance), to play a greater role in identifying and evaluating digital technology investment and technology architecture options, and to play a greater role in the process / workflow redesigns necessary to enable digital transformation.

Second, digital technology advancements disrupt management accountants' data analysis activities. They do this by expanding the data available to management accountants (i.e. volume, variety, velocity of data), the methods available / required to analyze data (e.g. data science and machine learning methods), and the tools available / required to manage and analyze data (e.g. data management tools like Oracle Data Management Suite, data analytics tools like R programming language, and data mining tools like RapidMiner). Figure 5.3 shows applications of data mining methods and tools for accounting reporting that have been identified by various accounting researchers[22]. As can be seen, data mining methods and tools can be leveraged for data mining-driven activity based costing analysis (e.g. calculating real-time overhead rates and profit targets), for predicting bankruptcies (e.g. finding and comparing changes in payables / receivables and cash in / cash out to identify when bankruptcy indicators are met / exceeded), for fraud detection (e.g. finding payment anomalies for in-depth investigation), for cost prediction (e.g. using historical cost data and planned demand to predict future costs), and for comparing financial performance as per numerical information vs. as per text or narrative information[23]. The expansion of available data, analysis methods, and analysis tools requires management accountants to adopt data analysis approaches that leverage these data, methods, and tools to optimize the efficiency and effectiveness of data analysis activities.

Third, digital technology advancements disrupt the way management accountants present and communicate information. They do this by introducing new information presentation and communication tools (e.g. data visualization tools, data translation tools, data transfer tools). These tools increasingly enable anywhere, anytime, real-time, automated, customizable and omnichannel communication / presentation of information.

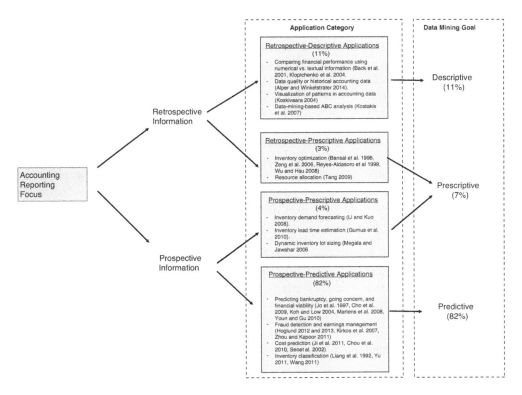

Figure 5.3 Data mining methods and tools offer new and potentially more efficient / effective ways to do both retrospective and prospective analysis and reporting[24]

In doing so, they require management accountants to leverage the tools to provide their stakeholders with increasingly greater information accessibility, customization, and understandability.

Finally, through use of new digital tools, management accountants can also improve stakeholder engagement through greater responsiveness to stakeholder information needs, greater ability of stakeholders to interact with data provided by management accountants, and greater customization of information provided by management accountants to the digital channel / device / sensory preferences of stakeholders.

Tax

The tax function of accounting is typically responsible for management or oversight of tax planning, income tax preparation and lodgement, tax compliance, tax policies and procedures, and tax-related risk[25]. Examples of tax planning activities include anticipating and planning for the management of the different types and amounts of tax payable in different scenarios, and under different jurisdictions (e.g. VAT, GST, property tax, payroll tax, and income tax payable in different states and countries)[26]. Examples of income tax preparation and lodgement activities include drafting proforma income tax returns, doing tax account reconciliations, and doing income tax return reviews[27]. Examples of tax compliance activities include monitoring GST / VAT / property / income tax compliance requirements, interacting with tax authorities, and reviewing submittable tax information for compliance[28]. Examples of tax policies and procedures activities include drafting / reviewing / approving tax policies, monitoring compliance with these policies and procedures, and ensuring these policies and procedures will bring about compliance with regulatory requirements[29]. Furthermore, tax risk management activities include assessing and managing compliance risks and reputational risks associated with tax affairs[30].

Digital technology advancements disrupt the tax function in three key ways. First, they introduce new or enhanced tools that can be used to carry out tax function activities. These tools enable tax function activities to be carried out much more efficiently and effectively. For example, data analytics tools can be used to carry out tax payable calculations, to perform tax account reconciliations, and to perform income tax reviews much faster than a human can. Predictive analytics and data visualization tools can be used in tax planning to automatically show tax payable under different scenarios and thus highlight optimal tax strategies. And machine learning tools can be used to identify non-compliant or fraudulent tax information prior to submission to authorities. As well as the tax function being able to use new digital technology tools, regulators are also able to leverage these tools to better check tax information submitted by organizations. For example, they can match an organization's submitted data to all similar organizations within and outside of an industry and for current and past years. Or they can match an organization's submitted tax information to corresponding information submitted by the organization's vendors and customers. This enhances the need for tax accountants to leverage digital technology advancements in order to ensure their submissions are free from omissions, errors, and fraudulent behavior.

Second, digital technology advancements disrupt tax compliance processes. As regulators leverage digital technologies to improve the efficiency and effectiveness of their compliance enforcement activities, they end up redesigning / reconfiguring compliance processes. They may redesign compliance processes to take advantage of the improved process automation, systems integration, record immutability, and accountability benefits digital technologies enable. With regard to process automation, a number of tax authorities have shifted or are shifting to automated data acquisition from taxpayers. For example, the SAF-T (Standard Audit File for Tax), an attachment to the corporate income tax return, is increasingly being adopted by tax authorities in many countries as a way of allowing them to automatically perform advanced data analytics on an organization's tax data in case of a tax audit[31]. In disrupting tax compliance processes, digital technology advancements require tax accountants to ensure that their organizations' accounting and other systems can integrate with regulators' platforms and enable automated compliance checks.

Third, digital technology advancements disrupt the tax function by expanding tax accountant stakeholder expectations. Given the availability of sophisticated digital technology tools, tax accountants' stakeholders increasingly expect more. For example, they expect tax accountants to be able to anticipate tax law changes and their implications for tax payable (e.g. by mining web content or tax law-related datasets and spotting emerging tax law issues and proposed legislation), to identify compliant / optimal / sustainable tax strategies, to leverage real-time internal and external data to shape realization of tax policies / plans / strategies, to perform tax function activities much more efficiently and effectively (e.g. perform routine tax calculations and reconciliations much faster and more accurately, provide a greater and more efficient tax payable and tax compliance forecasting capability), to ease compliance with any regulatory audit requirements, and to minimize organizational risk associated with tax compliance[32,33].

Audit

The audit function of accounting undertakes a range of activities to enable it to inform users of accounting information, and those charged with organizational governance, of the extent to which the reported information complies with applicable accounting standards and laws, and can be trusted to be true and fair (i.e. free from risks of material misstatements and omissions). The audit function of accounting has external audit, internal audit, and government audit aspects. As their name suggests, external audits are performed by an external entity independent of the organization. For organizations legally required to provide audited financial statements (e.g. stock exchange listed organizations or other organizations with stakeholders depending on such statements), external auditors undertake a range of activities and tests to assess that the statements comply with applicable laws / standards and are true and fair representations of the organization's position and performance. These activities involve collecting and assessing information on the infrastructure, systems, and processes enabling the production of the financial statements (e.g. software systems, transaction recording procedures, measurement approaches). The outcome of external audit activities is the expression of an opinion from external auditors as to the extent to which external users of the financial statements of an organization can have confidence in the accuracy and completeness of those statements, and why / why not. In contrast to external audits, internal audits often performed by the internal employees of an organization for the organization's management team or other leaders. The aims of internal audits can include undertaking an audit of financial statements to enable resolution of any issues prior to external audits occurring, and reviewing the organization's infrastructure / policies and procedures / processes and workflows for risk exposures and performance improvement opportunities. Finally, the government audits deal with government-initiated audits. That is, preparing for them, facilitating provision of necessary information, verifying the accuracy of the outcomes of these audits, and accepting or contesting the outcomes of the audits.

Digital technology advancements disrupt the auditing function in six key ways. First, they disrupt the data available to auditors. They do this by enabling access to new data (e.g. big data, IoT data, search engine data, social media data), as well as better access to existing data (e.g. enabling automated analysis of text data within legal contracts or of email conversations and video recordings). Auditors can leverage this expanded internal and external data to improve their analysis and testing activities, and therefore the issues / risks they are able to discover and the level of assurance they are able to provide. For example, an external auditor may use big data to compare elements of an organization's financial statements or measurement approaches to industry peers. Or she may perform checks on client applications of big data to test for application accuracy. And an internal auditor may leverage expanded data access to spot fraud (e.g. by accessing email data, video data, and IoT device data). The increase in data availability makes it possible for auditors to undertake better tests and to offer better levels of assurance. In doing so, it puts pressure on auditors to expand the amount and type of information collected and used in audits.

Second, digital technology advancements introduce more sophisticated or powerful methods (e.g. see Figure 5.4) and tools for carrying out audit activities. For example, they introduce robotic process automation and intelligent automation tools that can be used to automate structured and routine auditing tasks (e.g. collecting data, filling in planning worksheets, sending follow up reminders to relevant stakeholders to forward required information, simulating the actual execution of tasks for observation[34], doing physical inventory checks using drones / IoT devices / AI algorithms)[35]. And process mining tools can be used to analyze business processes for internal control effectiveness (e.g. analyzing event logs to check for segregation of duties, sequencing of events, personnel involved, and any event omissions). Leveraging AI algorithms, it is possible to evaluate all of an organization's event logs to gather complete evidence and provide higher levels of assurance regarding process compliance and accuracy of process outputs. Machine learning and AI-based analytics tools can be used to review full datasets to detect fraud or to spot patterns only machines are capable of discovering. Natural language processing technologies can be used by auditors to review all of an organization's invoices, contracts, emails, or transcribed virtual meeting recordings. Computer vision and drone / robotic technologies can be used to inspect assets and sites. And chatbots and digital assistants can be used to engage with all stakeholders. Use of these different digital technologies may enable full identification of risks of material misstatement in financial statement information. In fact, the tools may be leveraged to enable real-time continuous audit and assurance. As a result, the availability of such tools puts pressure on auditors to change their practices in order to realize the full benefits of these tools.

Third, digital technology advancements disrupt the audit process and corresponding audit activities by changing the roles and activities auditors have to perform and how they perform them. We've previously described how one way they do this is by taking over certain auditing activities and doing them better (e.g. with robotic process automation taking over structured, routine, and repetitive tasks). By taking over such activities or tasks, digital technologies enable auditors to focus on more value-added roles and activities that they previously may not have had time for. Another way digital technology advancements disrupt the audit process is by requiring it to occur at the speed of change. That is, requiring auditors' stakeholder engagement, data collection, analysis and testing, and reporting processes or procedures to adapt with the external and internal dynamism

Predictive	Engagement	Planning	Testing	Review	Opinion	Continuous activities	Descriptive	Engagement	Planning	Testing	Review	Opinion	Continuous activities
Analytical Hierarchy Processes (AHP)	✓	✓					Clustering Models	✓	✓	✓	✓	✓	✓
Artificial Neural Networks (ANN)		✓		✓	✓	✓	Descriptive Statistics	✓	✓	✓	✓		✓
Auto Regressive Integrated moving average (ARIMA)						✓	Process Mining; Process Discovery Models						✓
Bagging and Boosting models	✓	✓		✓	✓	✓	Ratio Analysis	✓	✓	✓	✓		✓
Bayesian Theory / Bayesian Belief Networks (BBN)	✓				✓	✓	Spearman Rank Correlation Measurement	✓	✓	✓	✓	✓	✓
Benford's Law		✓ ✓		✓ ✓	✓ ✓	✓ ✓	Text Mining Models						✓
C4.5 Statistical Classifiers						✓	Visualization						✓
Dempster-Shafer Theory Models	✓					✓	**Prescriptive**	Engagement	Planning	Testing	Review	Opinion	Continuous activities
Expert Systems Decision Aids		✓ ✓	✓	✓ ✓	✓	✓ ✓	Artificial Neural Networks (ANN)	✓	✓	✓	✓	✓	✓
Genetic Algorithms		✓ ✓ ✓ ✓				✓ ✓ ✓ ✓	Auto Regressive Integrated Moving Average (ARIMA)		✓	✓	✓	✓	✓
Hypothesis Evaluations	✓	✓	✓	✓	✓	✓	Expert Systems/Decision Aids	✓	✓	✓	✓	✓	✓
Linear Regression	✓	✓		✓ ✓ ✓	✓ ✓ ✓	✓ ✓ ✓	Genetic Algorithms	✓ ✓	✓	✓	✓	✓	✓
Log Regression	✓			✓	✓	✓	Linear Regression	✓	✓	✓	✓	✓	✓
Monte Carlo Study / Simulation						✓	Log Regression		✓	✓	✓	✓	✓
Multi-criteria Decision Aid	✓ ✓				✓	✓	Monte Carlo Study/Simulation		✓	✓	✓	✓	✓
Probability Theory Models	✓ ✓				✓ ✓	✓	Time Series Regression		✓	✓	✓	✓	✓
Process Mining; Process Optimizations		✓			✓	✓	Univariate and Multivariate Regression Analysis		✓	✓	✓	✓	✓
Structural Models	✓	✓		✓		✓							
Support Vector Machines (SVM)						✓ ✓							
Time Series Regression					✓	✓							
Univariate and Multivariate Regression Analysis					✓	✓							

Figure 5.4 Data analytics and data science methods and techniques now being applied to different audit procedures / activities[36]

of the organization. This requires audit teams to adopt accelerated change and transformation methodologies like agile, design thinking, and lean to enable faster, more flexible auditing practices[37]. The scale and speed of technological advancements and the growing need for integrability between digital technology platforms or tools, information systems, datasets, and interorganizational ecosystems means that carrying out or facilitating auditing processes increasingly has an information systems architecture aspect to it. That is, carrying out or facilitating auditing processes requires auditors to work with technology teams to ensure that digital technology-based audit tools can integrate into organizations' information systems infrastructure to access and consume required data from the business, and that business processes and controls are configured in such a way as to enable RPA and IPA testing (e.g. that they are configured to enable appropriate capturing of all required event log data). For example, auditors can ensure that they have direct access to enterprise data lakes to be able to leverage machine learning tools for continuous audit and real-time risk identification and mitigation[38].

Fourth, digital technology advancements disrupt the risk landscape within and outside of organizations. They do this by introducing new or more severe cybersecurity, information privacy, and digital ethics risks[39,40,41]. In doing so, they make it more challenging for auditors to assess the risks of material misstatement. For example, how do auditors assess the risk that financial statements are incorrect due to hacking, or due to bias in AI models used by the organization, or due to unethical collection and use of data by the organization? As a core value of the auditing function is the assessment of risks and controls, auditors need to have a deep understanding of the new or expanded risks brought about by different digital technologies, how these risks can best be assessed, the types of controls necessary to mitigate these risks, and the impact on financial statements of escalations of those risks or of different types of lapses in controls of those risks.

Fifth, digital technology advancements expand the auditing function's work by requiring auditors to audit new digital technology tools and / or their use in organizations. For example, internal auditors may have to audit high-stakes AI decision models and tools for errors or bias[42,43]. Or auditors may have to audit IoT devices, platforms, and associated workflows for compliance with information privacy and digital ethics policies. Alternatively, auditors may have to audit cryptographic assets[44].

Finally, digital technology advancements expand assurance possibilities and the value it is possible for auditors to create. By leveraging time freed up by digital technologies taking over necessary but low value-added tasks, as well as leveraging the expanded power of digital technology tools, auditors can focus on higher value-added tasks and create more impactful value. For example, auditors can better prepare organizations' stakeholders to spot and prevent emerging risks (e.g. by giving them access to and teaching them how to use the same digital technology tools used by auditors or providing them with chatbots to help deal with risk-related issues)[45]. Auditors can establish real-time automated and continuous risk detection, alert, and correction accountability systems[46]. As these examples illustrate, by leveraging freed-up time and expanded digital technology capabilities, auditors can raise the confidence of stakeholders in financial statements to higher levels in spite of growing complexity and uncertainty.

Business partnering / advisory

The business partnering or advisory function of accounting involves partnering or working closely alongside other areas of the business to improve their decision-making and effectiveness in the pursuit of organizational objectives[47,48]. This includes advising managers and leaders on strategic and operational decision options and implications, interpreting and explaining the meaning and implications of performance data as well as external environment data, advising them on key business planning assumptions and tradeoffs, and supporting them with strategy execution[49].

Digital technology advancements disrupt business partnering and advice in four key ways. First, they change the nature of the challenges faced by managers and leaders. Owing to digital transformation and digital business imperatives, the new or additional challenges for managers relate to effectively undertaking digital business transformation, building and optimizing digital business capabilities, and effectively competing as a digital business. As a result, the strategic insight, decision-making, planning, change, and strategy execution support they need from accounting business partners relate to these digital transformation and digital business related challenges. For examples, managers and leaders require support understanding digital disruption opportunities and threats, safely and effectively undertaking digital business transformation, identifying effective digital business model designs, effecting and optimizing process digitization, effectively building and optimizing digital business capabilities (e.g. digital customer engagement, digital innovation, agility, and ambidexterity), and identifying and mitigating digital risk exposures. Thus, this shift in managerial and leadership challenges shifts both the partnering and advisory expectations managers and leaders have of accountants as well as how the business partnering / advisory function can most contribute value to the organization. The business partnering / advisory function can expand its value creation by supporting managers to see and understand opportunities and risks, helping them to source and use the right digital technologies and tools, helping them understand the risk and implications of different IS architectures, helping them understand how they can safely be both fast and adaptive, helping them automate and optimize business processes, helping them identify and control cybersecurity and digital ethics risks, and helping them sustain and optimize digital capabilities.

Second, digital technology advancements change the data available to business partnering and advisory teams and the tools available to make the most of this data. This enables these teams to offer better data-driven insights. For example, business partnering and advisory teams can leverage greater access to internal data, greater volumes of big data, and sophisticated digital technology tools to offer data-driven support (e.g. combining big data, search engine data, and internal data to provide effective strategic sensing dashboards that provide early warnings of emerging strategic risks and opportunities). The expansion of data availability and data analytics tools also enables business partnering / advisory teams to help leaders and managers understand what data is available and how to make the most of it. For example, they can help risk managers tap into the right big data and organizational data lakes, to leverage the right digital technology tools suited to risk analytics, and to integrate and automate risk analytics.

Third, digital technology advancements disrupt the analysis techniques and implementation frameworks used by advisory teams. They do this by amplifying the number, scope, and speed of disruptions. As a result of more, bigger, and faster disruptions, organizations have to work increasingly rapidly in order to both adapt to disruption and maintain competitiveness. This need for speed in change, transformation, and strategy execution efforts requires accelerated change and transformation techniques and methodologies. Examples of these methodologies and techniques include design thinking, agile innovation, lean thinking, sense making, and agile strategy execution. Thus, to maintain or enhance their effectiveness in supporting managers and leaders, business partnering and advisory teams need to be able to understand and use these frameworks and their associated analysis techniques. The accelerated change and transformation frameworks and associated analysis techniques (e.g. empathy maps, complexity analysis tools, value stream mapping, user personas) complement traditional analytical techniques and frameworks such as activity-based costing, shareholder value analysis, SWOT, Porter's Five Forces, Root Cause Analysis, and Profit Pools[50].

Finally, digital technology advancements introduce new business partnering / advice competitors like internal and external data scientists, futurists, specific accelerated change and transformation methodology service providers, and AI algorithms. As a result, to remain relevant, business partnering and advisory teams need to maintain their digital technology competencies, their accelerated change / transformation competencies, and the resultant value they create at a competitive level.

Accounting information systems

The accounting information systems function plays a critical leadership role in the acquisition, design, implementation, operation and maintenance, effectiveness, and improvement of the systems that work together to collect, store, manage, process, and retrieve the data used in accounting information. This function of accounting ensures that the right data or information is available for use across the accounting functions of financial accounting, management accounting, tax, audit, and business partnering / advisory. Accounting information systems function roles can include finance systems managers, finance systems implementation leads, finance systems administrators, finance systems designers, finance systems analysts, and systems accountants. Through these different roles, the accounting information systems function may carry out or advise on finance systems acquisition activities (e.g. business cases, system / vendor evaluation, service level agreement negotiation), finance systems design and / or modification activities, finance systems integration activities, data management activities (e.g. data coming into and going out of finance systems and tools), implementation of systems controls, designing standardized reports, automating finance processes, and more.

Digital technology advancements disrupt the accounting information systems function in four key ways. First, they disrupt data availability and stakeholder expectations. Since far more internal and external data is available and / or able to be captured, there is the opportunity, and stakeholder expectation, that this data is able to be used in accounting roles, activities, and outputs (e.g. via accounting information systems applications such as data visualization tools, and via data stores and data lakes accessible by accounting information systems).

Second, digital technology advancements disrupt the accounting information systems function by dramatically increasing the number and types of internal and external applications that require integration with accounting information systems. For example, software and hardware tools used by operations or by different value chain functions may need real-time access to AIS data; and AIS may need access to data within those applications. Examples of these applications and tools may include mobile apps, data science apps, timesheet apps, executive and operational dashboard apps, IoT apps, and AI apps. The expansion in the number of hardware and software tools needing to interface with accounting information systems expands the AIS function's involvement in organization-wide systems integration, data management, and systems architecture activities.

Third, digital technology advancements disrupt the exposure of AIS to digital risks. We discussed earlier the evolving digital risk landscape and the dramatically increased exposure of organizations' information systems to cybersecurity, information privacy, and digital ethics risks. This extends to AIS, expanding the importance of the AIS team's responsibility and requirement to ensure that cybersecurity, information privacy, and digital ethics risks associated with AIS are identified, mitigated through effective controls, and their negative impacts minimized.

Finally, digital technology advancements disrupt the need for adaptability and agility of AIS. Owing to more frequent and larger scale digitally-driven as well as non-digital disruptions (e.g. the GFC, Covid-19), organizations need to be able to rapidly reconfigure their processes to adapt to disruptions. This requires information systems that can rapidly be scaled, integrated, made available in different settings (e.g. at work, at home, globally, online, offline), reconfigured to fit different architectures, and more. Since AIS are no exception to this, the AIS function needs to ensure that AIS choices evolve with digital technology advancements to optimize their adaptability and agility. Not effectively doing so can impede the delivery of all other accounting functions and put the organization's longevity at risk.

Digital technology advancements anticipated to have a profound direct impact on accounting

We discussed earlier the direct and indirect disruptive forces digital technologies are having on accounting. While almost all digital technology advancements have a degree of impact on accounting work, some have more profound disruptive or transformative effects. In this section, we discuss some of the digital technologies either currently having a profound direct disruptive and transformative impact on accounting work or that are poised to do so. The list of technologies that make up this category is likely to continuously change with further advancements in digital technologies. Nevertheless, we discuss the current list to illustrate the point that although accountants need to keep an eye on all digital technology advancements, they also need to be more proactive with particular digital technology advancements (i.e. understand their implications early, prepare for their impact, develop competencies in them early, advocate for their adoption and use, etc.).

Cloud computing

Cloud computing refers to the use of software and data that is hosted on external organizations' servers, as opposed to on-premise servers or computers / devices. As a result of this external storage, cloud-based software platforms or applications can be made available over the internet and accessed via internet connected devices. Cloud-based systems, platforms, or applications can be owned by the organization using them or provided via software as a service models where the vendor maintains and keeps the software up to date. Cloud hosting services are typically offered on usage-based subscription models. Figure 5.5 provides examples of different types of cloud service models or offerings (e.g. software as a service or SaaS, function as a service or FaaS, data as a service or DaaS, platform as a service or PaaS, storage as a service or STaaS, infrastructure as a service or IaaS, desktop as a service, data center as a service), and examples of different vendors within each cloud service model or offering. Cloud accounting platforms offer a range of accounting and accounting-related software on a subscription fee basis, meaning that cloud accounting platform users pay a monthly or annual fee to have access to the latest version of the software. This fee can be based on the number of software users, on the number of software features used, on the amount of data storage used, on a fixed fee, or on some

64 *Digital disruption and transformation*

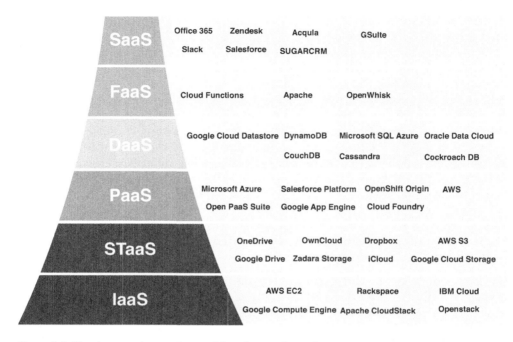

Figure 5.5 Cloud computing service models and example vendors

other basis. The platform provider then takes responsibility for continuously evolving the cloud accounting platform to changes in digital technology advancements, changes in user requirements, changes in statutory requirements, and changes in competing offerings. Cloud accounting platforms require minimal user maintenance, are automatically backed up, enable work from anywhere and on any device with an internet connection and browser or apps, provide near real-time access to information, are typically more secure, expand internal and external collaboration opportunities (e.g. through easier integration, data sharing, and process sharing), are elastic (meaning the required capacity and cost scales with the user requirements), often automatically have the latest technology advances and best practices built in, and typically offer an ecosystem or marketplace of integrating platforms and applications. These integrations enable cloud accounting platform users to leverage a broad range of accounting-related digital technologies to support accounting value creation. For example, Xero users have access to a marketplace of systems and applications that integrate with Xero to allow them to port their data into thousands of external applictions or to port data from those external applications into Xero. So accountants can, for example, integrate and leverage data visualization apps to improve presentation of information provided (e.g. Power BI, Futrli, Fathom), data cleaning and transformation apps (e.g. JetConvert), chatbot and digital assistant apps (e.g. Aider, Zave), and artificial intelligence audit and process automation apps (e.g. XBert). Enterprise level platforms like Oracle and SAP have similar integrating system and application marketplaces. In summary, cloud accounting can have a profound impact on how accounting processes and activities can be performed and thus on the efficiency and effectiveness of accounting value creation.

XBRL

XBRL (Extensible Business Reporting Language) is an electronic markup language that converts financial and non-financial information into machine readable and human readable formats[51,52]. XBRL is part of the markup language family that also includes HTML (Hypertext Markup Language) and XML (Extensible Markup Language). Markup languages differ from programming languages like C and Java that are used to develop software applications. Instead, markup languages simply add tags to data items. These tags provide additional meaning and context to the data (e.g. for an inventory value of US$100,000 in a financial report, a tag may provide additional context and meaning such as: the definition of inventory, the reporting time frame, the relevant reporting standard, the relevant inventory valuation method, etc.). This additional meaning and context is referred to as metadata (data about data or information about data). XBRL is actually a derivative of XML (Extensible Markup Language), a universal standard for structuring documents and data on the web. The "eXtensible" in XML means that the language can have many derivative languages unique to different industries or purposes. For example, ebXML is a derivative for e-business transaction language, chemXML is a derivative for the chemical industry language, and XBRL is a derivative for business reporting language. And the "ML" or "Markup Language" refers to the use of tagging to add meaning and context (or metadata) to the data. Tags usually consist of an opening tag in the format <.......> and a closing tag in the format </.......>. Below is an example of XBRL tag syntax for a financial statement data element[53]:

<ifrs-gp:Inventories contextRef="Current_AsOf" uniRef="U-Euros" decimals ="0"> 100000</ifrs-gp:Inventories>

The opening tag is <ifrs-gp:Inventories contextRef="Current_AsOf" uniRef="U-Euros" decimals ="0">. And the closing tag is </ifrs-gp:Inventories>. The syntax tells us that the IFRS-GP taxonomy is being used ("ifrs-gp"), that an inventory balance is being reported ("ifrs-gp:Inventories"), that the reported inventory balance is current as of the specified date in the report ("contextRef="Current_AsOf""), that the unit of reference or the balance is being reported in Euros ("uniref="U-Euros""), and that the inventory balance is 100,000 euros to zero decimal places ("decimals="0">100000<"). Not only is this XBRL tag syntax able to be read and understood by different accounting and non-accounting software algorithms, it also provides much more context and meaning behind the 100,000 inventory balance.

There are a range of underlying components that make XBRL possible, efficient, and effective for different types of reporting, as well as amenable to wide adoption by different stakeholders. These components include XBRL specifications, XBRL taxonomies, XBRL instance documents, XBRL elements, and XBRL linkbases. XBRL specifications set out the standards, rules, and formatting to guide the creation of XBRL data tags. For example, when tagging an element of the balance sheet, the specification requires XBRL data tag creators to identify the element name, identify the parent element it rolls up into, and identify whether it is a monetary or share type element. As a result, a user may create a metadata tag or XBRL tag such as:

<element name= "CurrentAsset. CashandCashEquivalents" type= "xbrl:monetary"/>

XBRL taxonomies are hierarchical dictionaries that define the specific XBRL tags that can be used for individual items of data (e.g. items like "Net Income", "Non-Current Assets", "Net Assets"), as well as their attributes, and interrelationship with other individual data items. But the reporting requirements and meaning of a data item like "Net Income" can differ significantly across stakeholders (e.g. regulators, management teams, general purpose users) and across accounting standards and principles (e.g. IFRS, AASB, Japanese GAAP). As a result, there are different taxonomies that can be used (e.g. IFRS taxonomy, US GAAP taxonomy, GRI taxonomy, XBRL global ledger taxonomy, organization-specific taxonomies). Instance documents are XBRL-coded or tagged reports (e.g. an XBRL-tagged balance sheet or an XBRL-tagged debt covenant report). XBRL instance documents (or XBRL-tagged reports) contain the XBRL specification version ID as well as the name and location of the XBRL taxonomy. XBRL elements (also referred to as XBRL concepts) are the different types of data and metadata (information about data). They include the data elements (the numeric elements such as 100,000 and the non-numeric elements such as that the number represents inventory), the context elements (e.g. that the inventory balance is as of date specified), the unit elements (e.g. that the unit of measurements is Euros), the period elements (e.g. that the reporting year is 2020), the entity elements (e.g. that the reporting entity is Alibaba Group Holding Limited), and the identifier elements (such as unique account number identifiers). Finally, XBRL linkbases define the relationships between data or elements or concepts. They include definition links (e.g. that Zip Code is the postal code used in the United States), calculation links (e.g. that assets = liabilities + stockholders' equity), presentation links (defining how elements are to be presented), label links (defining the labels to be used in the document), and reference links (defining the relationships between elements and the relevant standards).

XBRL is license free, provides structure and rich metadata in machine and human readable formats, is software and hardware agnostic, and enables provision of multiple levels of detail. The result is that the data becomes intelligent, interactive, discoverable, portable, reusable, and cost-efficient to collect / store / analyze / transform. XBRL can be used to integrate financial and non-financial data and is therefore well suited for developments in integrated reporting's multiple capital model. It can also be leveraged for more efficient and effective delivery of audit, management accounting, risk management, and governance functions. XBRL is already being used by millions of organizations around the world and becoming the de facto reporting standard required by a lot of regulatory bodies. It is likely that the positive impacts it has had on financial reporting so far are just the tip of the iceberg and it holds potential for much greater impact on all forms of reporting (e.g. resolving "single source of truth", stakeholder engagement, and customization issues).

Big data, data analytics, and data science technologies

Big data refers to datasets that are so voluminous, so complex, and being created so fast, that traditional data processing software and approaches can't handle them. And *data analytics* is an umbrella term referring to any form of analysis of data to uncover trends, patterns, and anomalies, or simply to measure performance[54,55,56]. Data analytics can also refer to one or more approaches, methodologies, and tools used to achieve the objectives of data analytics. Related to data analytics, *data science* is a method for drawing insights from large datasets of structured and unstructured data[57] using techniques and theories across disciplines such as mathematics, statistics, computer science, and information science.

In combination with the disruption of data availability, big data, data analytics, and data science technologies significantly impact the roles and activities performed by accountants. In their evolving roles as data stewards, data analysts, systems designers, assurance providers, cyber risk managers, strategic risk navigators, brand protectors, storytellers, trusted professionals, process and control experts, co-pilots, and digital and technology enablers[58,59,60], accountants depend on these digital technologies to discover critical insights from the large treasure troves of internal and external data now available. Within these evolving roles, accountants may find themselves needing to explain the financial value of different data and data management activities, being involved in leading or participating in data management activities, preparing / reviewing / approving business cases for big data / data analytics / data science projects, advising managers at all levels on data analytics and data science requirements, building big data / data analytics / data science products or tools, using big data / data analytics / data science products or tools, auditing big data / data analytics / data science-related products and activities (e.g. the logic and outputs of high-stakes AI algorithms), and more. As can be seen, key disruptive and transformative impacts of this set of digital technologies include expansion of accountants' information analysis and provision roles, expansion of accountants' roles in data management, expansion of accountants' roles in the development of analytics and decision tools, expansion of accountants' dependency on these digital technology tools to effectively perform accounting work, and expansion of the competencies required in these digital technologies and their related tools in order to effectively perform traditional, new, and emerging accounting roles. For accountants who understand the disruptive and transformative impact of these digital technologies, and who develop the necessary proficiency in them, these digital technologies offer vastly expanded reporting, compliance, business partnering, and other organizational value creation opportunities. For accountants underestimating them or not developing the necessary proficiency in them, these digital technologies are likely to shrink the roles of these accountants (as aspects of these roles are taken over by other professionals or external entities), and to diminish their credibility and influence with key stakeholders.

Data visualization technologies

Data visualization technologies offer new and enhanced ways of presenting information to decision makers. In place of static reports such as PDFs and spreadsheets, data visualization enables presentation of information via interactive dashboards, infographics, heat maps, network diagrams, cartograms, word clouds, videos, and more. Data visualization enables near instant conversion of visualizations, enabling customization of data presentation formats (e.g. a manager who prefers interactive dashboards can receive data in that format with a click of a button; and a manager who better understands heat maps can receive the same data but in that preferred format). Data visualization expands the repertoire of approaches and tools for communicating insights and thus the level of user engagement that can be achieved. Data visualization tools can both supercharge the level of engagement and the efficiency with which decision-making information can be presented. As a result, they enable accountants to move from passive presentation to active stakeholder engagement. Accountants not leveraging data visualization technologies are likely to both offer mostly passive presentation of information and also be far less efficient and effective in their information presentation roles.

Cognitive computing, artificial intelligence, and robotic process automation technologies

Collectively, cognitive computing and artificial intelligence technologies attempt to replicate, augment, and even exceed human sensing, thinking, and action. They bring together related technologies such as computer vision, machine learning, deep learning, natural language processing, and neural networks. In the collection of digital technology deep dive chapters (part V) we unpack the meaning, applications, and implications of key cognitive computing and artificial intelligence technologies and concepts in more detail. Robotic process automation is the use of virtual robots to perform routine accounting tasks (e.g. an RPA program may observe the sequence of actions an accountant goes through to log into an ERP system, review an invoice, check that an authorized person at the organization incurred the expense, check that it is the right amount and from the right organization, then approve it or send it through a range of acceptable approval processes until it is approved and paid. The RPA program can then carry out this sequence of activities automatically as per relevant triggers). Together, cognitive computing, artificial intelligence, and RPA technologies present great efficiency, effectiveness, and value creation opportunities for accountants. Efficiency wise, these technologies significantly expand process or workflow automation, data integration, and data analytics possibilities. For example, they can automate the creation, reviewing, approval, and routing of documents in purchasing, invoicing, purchase ordering, expense reporting, accounts payable, and accounts receivable processes. Or they can automate the reviewing of all of an organization's legal contracts for fraud, compliance, and other risks. They can greatly enhance data analytics and data management technologies by enabling them to scour vast structured and unstructured data sets in and outside the organization with real-time diagnostic, predictive, and prescriptive insights. They can automate the preparation of standardized financial reports as well as custom management reports (e.g. natural language processing algorithms can understand the requests of operating managers, can understand what information is available within internal financial and other systems, can understand all the reporting formats currently possible, and can leverage all this understanding to prepare relevant reports for managers). And they can collect usage data to improve the design and usefulness of these reports. Table 5.2 shows some examples of different RPA applications or use cases within the accounting and finance function.

Cognitive computing and artificial intelligence technologies can sift through the organization's different data stores, clean data, integrate it, and provide single source of truth datasets. They can then perform analyses and glean insights that the human mind can't (e.g. AI algorithms can undertake continuous Twitter sentiment analysis, continuous online news content analysis, continuous competitor information analysis, and continuous strategy execution progress analysis to provide previously impossible levels of strategic sensing and execution monitoring). As a result, their adoption and use in accounting activities enables accountants to significantly improve the scope, efficiency, and effectiveness of their information provision activities. Cognitive computing and artificial intelligence technologies can also enhance the extent and effectiveness with which accountants can engage stakeholders. For example, accountants can leverage AI-based chatbots to expand the number of stakeholders whose questions they are able to answer (e.g. by integrating digital analysts and chatbots into financial information system data, accountants can enable almost every authorized stakeholder to query this information in natural language and receive answers in natural language). Stakeholders can receive responses to their questions in near real

Table 5.2 Example applications of RPA in the finance function[61]

Application	What it can do	Examples
DATA ASSEMBLY	RPA can automatically and routinely stich vast amounts of data across fragmented systems	Data stiching across ERP systems, databases, custom built cross-departmental systems
BASIC ANALYTICS	RPA can perform basic analytical tasks on vast amounts of structured - and in some cases - unstructured data	Account comparisons, error, and anomaly flagging
AUTOMATING BASIC OPERATIONS	RPA can carry out repetitive daily operations automatically to replace otherwise slow and error-prone labor-intensive processes	Transaction processing, invoice and expense collection and organization, payment execution, and other accounts receivable and payable support
AUTOMATING COMPLIANCE TASKS	RPA can assist with basic human-facing interaction automation such as simple auto-email and chatbot deployment	Basic query handling, complaint responses, expense / billings training for workforce
	Many repetitive manual tasks associated with compliance are ripe for allocation to an RPA system	Data entry, taxation filing
	The assembly and analysis of data makes for a clear, reliable, and automated account of all sources and destinations of payment	To produce an audit trail, conduct due diligence data gathering
	More complex RPA systems can trigger a response to compliance	Block actions or transactions that do not meet compliance standards

time, thus improving their engagement with financial information. Cognitive computing and artificial intelligence technologies can also enable accountants to better spot, mitigate, and limit risk impacts (e.g. AI-based algorithms can undertake continuous monitoring of every digitalized process in the organization to identify risks exposures and sources, prescribe preventative or impact limiting measures, and even action these measures – all in real time). The scope of accounting activities and value creation that cognitive computing, artificial intelligence, and robotic process automation technologies enable is still in its infancy but evolving rapidly with advances in this set of digital technologies. Table 5.3 shows some of the current artificial intelligence applications in accounting, as reported by the big four accounting firms.

Internet of things, internet of everything, and network connectivity technologies

Internet of things (IoT) and internet of everything (IoE) technologies are technologies that enable all manner of things to be able to transfer data or communicate with each other, as well as with processes and with people – usually without requiring the input or intervention of a human being[62]. The "things" can range from buildings, furniture, and home appliances to infrastructure, body implants, and even living things (such as trees or wildlife). The various things are usually embedded or fitted with a diverse range of sensors that can collect data from the thing or the thing's environment (e.g. motion sensors, voice sensors, proximity sensors, touch sensors, temperature sensors, light sensors, smoke

Table 5.3 Current AI applications as reported by the big four accounting firms[63]

AI type	Current AI applications as reported by big 4 accounting firms
Machine Learning	• Classifier (tax transaction, contract) • Fraud detection • Review full population for outliers
Big AI / Smart Analytics	• Large-scale data analysis • Discover facts and relationships that are difficult for the human mind to discover
Natural Language Processing	• Synthesis of text (e.g. review of contracts, vendor invoices, emails, transcribed conversation)
Machine Vision	• OCR + machine learning to extract data from images • Drones + IoT to perform inventory inspection
Intelligent RPA	• Test of transactions • Document work papers • GL review • Bank confirmation
Speech Recognition	• Decode conversation • Chatbots • Digital assistants

sensors, time sensors). The things can then share this data with other things over a network (e.g. the internet). If fitted with computation, the things can analyze the data they collect and receive, becoming "smart". *Network connectivity technologies* are digital technologies that enable a network to be established between and with things. Network connectivity technologies have advanced to enable easier, stronger, broader, long-distance, and more accessible network connections to be established among and with things. In the collection of digital technology deep dive chapters (part V) we unpack the meaning, applications, and implications of key IoT, IoE, and network connectivity technologies and concepts in more detail.

For accountants, growth in the adoption of IoT, IoE, and network connectivity technologies dramatically expand value creation possibilities and risk of obsolescence of many existing accounting processes. For example, this set of digital technologies dramatically expands process and asset visibility. This can enable accountants to better understand process and workflow bottlenecks and to better understand the real-time condition and location of assets (e.g. inventory or non-current assets). Currently, process and asset visibility is limited to the data stored in business information systems or data captured from physical observation of processes and assets, or the opinions of process owners and participants. But once these processes and assets are connected to the internet, data about them and around them can be configured to automatically flow into accounting systems and tools. This, for example, is likely to make aspects of existing stocktaking, inventory valuation, and asset valuation activities obsolete. For accountants to make the most of the process and asset visibility, they have to understand the kind of data being collected by the various things, how they combine with other data to become even more meaningful, and how the data can be used for improved decision-making[64]. And accountants have to be able to deal with and leverage the dramatic increase in data availability that will come with growth in pervasiveness of IoT, IoE, and network connectivity technologies. This may require that accountants redesign their recording, reporting, and information communication systems and practices[65]. To better understand the growth in data availability and the possibilities that come with this data availability, imagine the amount of data that becomes available if every single physical object in your home is suddenly equipped with sensing, computation, internet connectivity, and the ability to interact with all other objects within and outside of your house; as well as with people and processes outside of your house. And imagine the value creation possibilities that come with that data if you can understand and use it all (e.g. you could understand the condition and location of anything in and surrounding your house, you could control the action and autonomy of everything in and perhaps surrounding your house, you could configure processes occurring in your home for optimal autonomy, efficiency, and effectiveness).

As well as expanding the visibility of assets and processes, IoT, IoE, and network connectivity technologies dramatically expand the integrability of assets and processes with other assets and processes within and outside the organization, as well as with people within and outside of the organization. This, in turn, greatly expands the collaboration potential between things, processes, and people. This greatly expanded integration and collaboration capacity opens up new efficiency possibilities. For example, employees could remotely control assets and remotely carry out business processes that previously required physical presence. Or algorithms could be used to orchestrate all business processes and asset management processes. Alternatively, sophisticated computation can be integrated to make assets and processes highly intelligent and able to take autonomous actions (e.g. make and action energy efficiency decisions, interact with customers, manufacture goods, etc.). Accountants can play an important business partnering role in helping management teams understand the business case, financial value, and strategic / operational process implications of internet of things and internet of everything (IoE) technologies.

The rapid expansion in the number of organizational things, processes, and people connected to the internet dramatically expands the organization's risk exposure. For example, any one of these things, processes, or people can be targeted as an access point by cybercriminals locally or around the world. In addition to this risk, there may be information privacy issues associated with the data collected by things, how that data is stored, and how it is used. For example, in collecting information about their surroundings, things may inadvertently collect information that they are not authorized to collect. AI-based algorithms may then use that data in ways that are not legal or socially acceptable (e.g. inadvertently identifying the location of people in witness protection or compromising people's right to privacy without their authorization). As key actors in organization's risk management efforts, accountants need a good understanding of the different risks associated with IoT, IoE, and network connectivity technologies, as well as how these risks can best be mitigated or their impact minimized.

Blockchain and other distributed ledger technologies

Part V of this book contains a chapter dedicated to blockchain and distributed ledger technologies. The chapter explains the functioning and benefits of blockchain and other distributed ledger technologies, including discussions of the functioning and benefits of smart contracts and cryptocurrency. Blockchain and other distributed ledger technologies offer new tamper-proof ways to verify identity and ownership, to make near instant payments without the need for the involvement of third parties, to store value (e.g. through cryptocurrency), to facilitate peer to peer fundraising and lending (e.g. ICOs and STOs), to automate the execution of contractual agreements and related workflows (e.g. via smart contracts), to improve auditability, to distribute data storage, and to do all of this more securely and at a lower cost[66,67]. The transformative impact of blockchain technologies has been equated to the advent of the internet[68].

Accounting strategic leaders have contended that blockchain technology is fundamentally an accounting technology[69], given its role in facilitating accounting-related workflows like measuring and reporting financial information, ascertaining asset ownership and value, accounting for asset ownership transfer, accounting for transaction payments, recording transactions, verifying and authorizing transactions, auditing transactions, and quantifying and mitigating risk. The accounting profession's blend of technical accounting and business knowledge positions accountants well for supporting leaders and managers to understand the business value and financial implications of adopting blockchain technology, to work with blockchain specialists to effectively implement blockchain technologies and platforms, to work with strategic leaders in identifying effective blockchain-based business models, to work with blockchain consortiums and policymakers to set effective standards, and to advise on blockchain-related investment and risk management decisions[70]. Using blockchain for accounting functions can provide greater transparency, improve efficiency, and indisputable certainty about the nature and history of transactions and asset ownership. Although blockchain applications, use cases, and impacts on the accounting profession are still in their early stages, they are advancing rapidly with increasing growth in blockchain technology adoption.

Implications for accountants

As we have discussed, digital technology advancements have direct and indirect disruptive effects on accounting value creation, on accounting functions, and on the work performed by accountants. Current and future accountants need to understand these disruptive effects, the new capabilities required across accounting functions, as well as the new roles and activities required of accountants. They then need to understand the required digital leadership competencies, strategic technology competencies, and technical technology competencies required to effectively perform evolving accounting roles and activities. Armed with this understanding, they will be well positioned to cultivate the required competencies to thrive in transforming accounting functions.

Google and reflect

XML, XBRL, XBRL specifications, XBRL taxonomies, XBRL instance documents, XBRL elements, XBRL linkbases, metadata, US GAAP taxonomy, GRI taxonomy, XBRL global ledger taxonomy, robotic process automation (RPA), intelligent process automation (IPA), privileged process automation (PPA), cryptographic asset, distributed ledger, immutable record, cognitive computing, high-stakes AI decision, network connectivity technologies, data steward, systems designer, cyber risk manager, information systems architecture, systems integration, process automation, autonomous process.

Discussion questions

1 How do digital technology advancements indirectly disrupt accounting work?
2 What are the different ways digital technology advancements directly disrupt accounting work?

3 What are the different ways digital technology advancements disrupt the accounting value proposition?
4 What are the different ways digital technology advancements disrupt the management accounting function?
5 What are the different ways digital technology advancements disrupt the financial accounting function?
6 What are the different ways digital technology advancements disrupt the tax function?
7 What are the different ways digital technology advancements disrupt the audit function?
8 What are the different ways digital technology advancements disrupt the AIS function?
9 What are the different ways digital technology advancements disrupt the business partnering or advisory function of accounting?
10 How can digital technology transform financial reporting from static information provision to active engagement?
11 What is a future fit accountant according to the International Federation of Accountants (IFAC)?
12 Identify four changed accounting roles and activities as a result of digital technology advancements.
13 Explain what outcomes each of IFAC's seven future fit accounting roles focus on delivering (i.e. the Co-Pilot, the Navigator, the Brand Protector, the Storyteller, the Trusted Professional, the Process and Control Expert, the Digital and Technology Enabler).
14 How do digital technology advancements disrupt data availability? How does this disruption of data availability create competitive threats and loss of relevance risks for the accounting profession?
15 Identify three or more approaches accountants and accounting leaders have taken to adapt to digital disruption.
16 Do you believe accountants and the accounting profession have been successful at adapting to digital disruption, undertaking digital business transformation, and operating in digital business settings?
17 Is there or can there be an end to digital technology advancements?
18 Is there or can there be an end to digital business transformation?

Notes

1 IFAC. (2017a). Developing a future ready profession. Retrieved from: https://www.ifac.org/system/files/publications/files/Developing-a-Future-Ready-Profession.pdf
2 International Federation of Accountants (2019). Future-fit accountants: CFO and finance function roles for the next decade. (n.d.). Retrieved from: https://www.ifac.org/system/files/publications/files/IFAC-Future-Fit-Accountant-ROLES-V5-Singles.pdf
3 International Federation of Accountants (2019). Future-fit accountants: CFO and finance function roles for the next decade. (n.d.). Retrieved from: https://www.ifac.org/system/files/publications/files/IFAC-Future-Fit-Accountant-ROLES-V5-Singles.pdf
4 International Federation of Accountants (2019). Future-fit accountants: CFO and finance function roles for the next decade. (n.d.). Retrieved from: https://www.ifac.org/system/files/publications/files/IFAC-Future-Fit-Accountant-ROLES-V5-Singles.pdf
5 Marr, B. (2019, September 5). How much data do we create every day? The mind-blowing stats everyone should read. Forbes. Retrieved from: https://www.forbes.com/sites/bernardmarr/2018/05/21/how-much-data-do-we-create-every-day-the-mind-blowing-stats-everyone-should-read/#292e039e60ba
6 Desjardins, J. (2019, March 13). What happens in an internet minute in 2019? Retrieved July 20, 2020, from: https://www.visualcapitalist.com/what-happens-in-an-internet-minute-in-2019/

7 Desjardins, J. (2019, April 17). How much data is generated each day? Retrieved July 20, 2020, from: https://www.weforum.org/agenda/2019/04/how-much-data-is-generated-each-day-cf4bddf29f/
8 Marr, B. (2019, September 5). How much data do we create every day? The mind-blowing stats everyone should read. Forbes. Retrieved from: https://www.forbes.com/sites/bernardmarr/2018/05/21/how-much-data-do-we-create-every-day-the-mind-blowing-stats-everyone-should-read/#292e039e60ba
9 Desjardins, J. (2019, April 17). How much data is generated each day? World Economic Forum. Retrieved July 20, 2020, from: https://www.weforum.org/agenda/2019/04/how-much-data-is-generated-each-day-cf4bddf29f/
10 Individuals using the internet (% of population) | Data. (2020). World Bank. Retrieved July 20, 2020, from: https://data.worldbank.org/indicator/IT.NET.USER.ZS
11 Moffitt, K.C., Rozario, A.M., & Vasarhelyi, M.A. (2018). Robotic process automation for auditing. Journal of Emerging Technologies in Accounting, 15(1): 1–10.
12 ASEAN Federation of Accountants (2019). Impact of technology to the accounting profession. Retrieved from: http://www.afa-accountants.org/files/AFA_Connect_03_-_June_2019_(A5)_-_16_Juli_2019.pdf
13 Coyne, J.G., Coyne, E.M., & Walker, K.B. (2016). A model to update accounting curricula for emerging technologies. Journal of Emerging Technologies in Accounting, 13(1): 161–169.
14 Coyne, J.G., Coyne, E.M., & Walker, K.B. (2016). A model to update accounting curricula for emerging technologies. Journal of Emerging Technologies in Accounting, 13(1), 161–169.
15 IFAC. (2017a). Developing a future ready profession. Retrieved from Retrieved from https://www.ifac.org/system/files/publications/files/Developing-a-Future-Ready-Profession.pdf
16 Cong, Y., Du, H., & Vasarhelyi, M.A. (2018). Technological disruption in accounting and auditing. Journal of Emerging Technologies in Accounting, 15(2), 1–10. https://doi.org/10.2308/jeta-10640
17 Adapted from Vasarhelyi, M. (2019). Audit's new frontier: Data analytics, AI and automation. CPA Australia presentation, Australia.
18 Cong, Y., Du, H., & Vasarhelyi, M.A. (2018). Technological disruption in accounting and auditing. Journal of Emerging Technologies in Accounting, 15(2), 1–10. https://doi.org/10.2308/jeta-10640
19 Cong, Y., Du, H., & Vasarhelyi, M.A. (2018). Technological disruption in accounting and auditing. Journal of Emerging Technologies in Accounting, 15(2), 1–10. https://doi.org/10.2308/jeta-10640
20 Cong, Y., Du, H., & Vasarhelyi, M.A. (2018). Technological disruption in accounting and auditing. Journal of Emerging Technologies in Accounting, 15(2), 1–10. https://doi.org/10.2308/jeta-10640
21 Zhang, L., Pei, D., & Vasarhelyi, M. A. (2017). Toward a new business reporting model. Journal of Emerging Technologies in Accounting, 14(2), 1–15.
22 Amani, F.A., & Fadlalla, A.M. (2017). Data mining applications in accounting: A review of the literature and organizing framework. International Journal of Accounting Information Systems, 24, 32–58. mindshift_emergingtech.pdf?sfvrsn=2
23 Amani, F.A., & Fadlalla, A.M. (2017). Data mining applications in accounting: A review of the literature and organizing framework. International Journal of Accounting Information Systems, 24, 32–58. mindshift_emergingtech.pdf?sfvrsn=2
24 Amani, F.A., & Fadlalla, A.M. (2017). Data mining applications in accounting: A review of the literature and organizing framework. International Journal of Accounting Information Systems, 24, 32–58. mindshift_emergingtech.pdf?sfvrsn=2
25 PWC. (2018). Tax function of the future spotlight on: Tax organization design: Options to manage global tax in a post-tax reform world. (n.d.). Retrieved from: https://www.pwc.com.au/tax/assets/global-tax/tax-function-of-the-future-organisational-design.pdf
26 PWC. (2018). Tax function of the future spotlight on: Tax organization design: Options to manage global tax in a post-tax reform world. (n.d.). Retrieved from: https://www.pwc.com.au/tax/assets/global-tax/tax-function-of-the-future-organisational-design.pdf
27 PWC. (2018). Tax function of the future spotlight on: Tax organization design: Options to manage global tax in a post-tax reform world. (n.d.). Retrieved from: https://www.pwc.com.au/tax/assets/global-tax/tax-function-of-the-future-organisational-design.pdf
28 PWC. (2018). Tax function of the future spotlight on: Tax organization design: Options to manage global tax in a post-tax reform world. (n.d.). Retrieved from: https://www.pwc.com.au/tax/assets/global-tax/tax-function-of-the-future-organisational-design.pdf
29 PWC. (2018). Tax function of the future spotlight on: Tax organization design: Options to manage global tax in a post-tax reform world. (n.d.). Retrieved from: https://www.pwc.com.au/tax/assets/global-tax/tax-function-of-the-future-organisational-design.pdf

30 PWC. (2018). Tax function of the future spotlight on: Tax organization design: Options to manage global tax in a post-tax reform world. (n.d.). Retrieved from: https://www.pwc.com.au/tax/assets/global-tax/tax-function-of-the-future-organisational-design.pdf
31 Deloitte. (2017). Effect of changes in technology on tax compliance. (n.d.). Retrieved from: https://www2.deloitte.com/content/dam/Deloitte/global/Documents/Tax/gx-effect-of-changes-in-technology-on-tax-compliance.pdf
32 PWC. (2018). Tax function of the future spotlight on: Tax organization design: Options to manage global tax in a post-tax reform world. (n.d.). Retrieved from: https://www.pwc.com.au/tax/assets/global-tax/tax-function-of-the-future-organisational-design.pdf
33 Thomson Reuters Tax & Accounting. (2015, October 7). How digital technology is transforming tax and finance – Thomson Reuters Tax & Accounting – ANZ. Retrieved August 10, 2020, from: https://tax.thomsonreuters.com.au/blog/how-digital-technology-is-transforming-tax-and-finance
34 Protiviti. (2018). Going digital: The future auditor in action. Retrieved August 13, 2020, from: https://www.protiviti.com/US-en/insights/newsletter-bulletin-v7i6-digital-future-auditor
35 Moffitt, K.C., Rozario, A.M., & Vasarhelyi, M.A. (2018). Robotic process automation for auditing. Journal of Emerging Technologies in Accounting, 15(1), 1–10.
36 Vasarhelyi, M. (2019). Audit's New Frontier: Data Analytics, AI and Automation. CPA Australia presentation, Australia.
37 Protiviti. (2018). Going digital: The future auditor in action. Retrieved August 13, 2020, from: https://www.protiviti.com/US-en/insights/newsletter-bulletin-v7i6-digital-future-auditor
38 Protiviti. (2018). Going digital: The future auditor in action. Retrieved August 13, 2020, from: https://www.protiviti.com/US-en/insights/newsletter-bulletin-v7i6-digital-future-auditor
39 IFAC. (2017a). Developing a future ready profession. Retrieved from: https://www.ifac.org/system/files/publications/files/Developing-a-Future-Ready-Profession.pdf
40 Doutt, A., Ide, C., Julie Bell Lindsay, Doutt, A., Ide, C., & Bell Lindsay, J. (2019). Emerging technologies, risk, and the auditor's focus. The Harvard Law School Forum on Corporate Governance. Retrieved from: https://corpgov.law.harvard.edu/2019/07/08/emerging-technologies-risk-and-the-auditors-focus/
41 Cong, Y., Du, H., & Vasarhelyi, M.A. (2018). Technological disruption in accounting and auditing. Journal of Emerging Technologies in Accounting, 15(2), 1–10. https://doi.org/10.2308/jeta-10640
42 Guszcza, J., Rahwan, I., Bible, W., Cebrian, M., & Katyal, V. (2018). Why we need to audit algorithms. Harvard Business Review. Retrieved from: https://hbr.org/2018/11/why-we-need-to-audit-algorithms
43 The Institute of Internal Auditors. (2018). The IIA's artificial intelligence auditing framework special edition. (n.d.). Retrieved from: https://na.theiia.org/periodicals/Public%20Documents/GPI-Artificial-Intelligence-Part-III.pdf
44 Chartered Professional Accountants Canada (2020). Audit considerations related to cryptocurrency assets and transactions. Retrieved August 13, 2020, from: https://www.iasplus.com/en-ca/publications/cpa-canada/audit-considerations-related-to-cryptocurrency-assets-and-transactions
45 Cong, Y., Du, H., & Vasarhelyi, M.A. (2018). Technological disruption in accounting and auditing. Journal of Emerging Technologies in Accounting, 15(2), 1–10. https://doi.org/10.2308/jeta-10640
46 Cong, Y., Du, H., & Vasarhelyi, M.A. (2018). Technological disruption in accounting and auditing. Journal of Emerging Technologies in Accounting, 15(2), 1–10. https://doi.org/10.2308/jeta-10640
47 IFAC. (2017a). Developing a future ready profession. Retrieved from: https://www.ifac.org/system/files/publications/files/Developing-a-Future-Ready-Profession.pdf
48 Osmer, S., & Donaldson, G. (2011). Mastering finance business partnering. (n.d.). Retrieved from: https://www.cimaglobal.com/Documents/Thought_leadership_docs/2011-03-21-KPMG%20CIMA%20business%20partnering%20white%20paper%20280111.pdf
49 Osmer, S., & Donaldson, G. (2011). Mastering finance business partnering. (n.d.). Retrieved from: https://www.cimaglobal.com/Documents/Thought_leadership_docs/2011-03-21-KPMG%20CIMA%20business%20partnering%20white%20paper%20280111.pdf
50 Osmer, S., & Donaldson, G. (2011). Mastering finance business partnering. (n.d.). Retrieved from: https://www.cimaglobal.com/Documents/Thought_leadership_docs/2011-03-21-KPMG%20CIMA%20business%20partnering%20white%20paper%20280111.pdf
51 Hoffman, C., & Watson, L. (2009). XBRL for dummies. John Wiley & Sons.
52 Australian Taxation Office Standard Business Reporting Initiative. (2018). XBRL fundamentals. Standard Business Reporting. Retrieved July 23, 2020, from: https://www.sbr.gov.au/

76 *Digital disruption and transformation*

about-sbr/publications-and-resources/learning-modules/xbrl-fundamentals#:~:text=XBRL%20 (eXtensible%20Business%20Reporting%20Language,(%20XML%20Schema%2C%20XLink).

53 Example adapted from Hoffman, C., & Watson, L. (2009). XBRL for dummies. John Wiley & Sons.
54 Comparing business intelligence, business analytics and data analytics. (2019). Tableau software. Retrieved December 16, 2019, from: https://www.tableau.com/learn/articles/business-intelligence/bi-business-analytics
55 Business analytics: everything you need to know. (2019). MicroStrategy. Retrieved December 16, 2019, from: https://www.microstrategy.com/us/resources/introductory-guides/business-analytics-everything-you-need-to-know
56 Boulton, C. (2019). Data analytics examples: An inside look at 6 success stories. CIO. Retrieved December 17, 2019, from: https://www.cio.com/article/3221621/6-data-analytics-success-stories-an-inside-look.html
57 Olavsrud, T. (2019). What is data science? Transforming data into value. CIO. Retrieved December 16, 2019, from: https://www.cio.com/article/3285108/what-is-data-science-a-method-for-turning-data-into-value.html
58 Sledgianowski, D., Gomaa, M., & Tan, C. (2017). Toward integration of big data, technology and information systems competencies into the accounting curriculum. Journal of Accounting Education, 38, 81–93.
59 Vasarhelyi, M. (2019). Audit's new frontier: Data analytics, AI and automation. CPA Australia presentation, Australia.
60 IFAC. (2019). Future-fit accountants: roles for the next decade. Retrieved December 18, 2019, from: https://www.ifac.org/knowledge-gateway/preparing-future-ready-professionals/discussion/future-fit-accountants-roles-next
61 AFP. (2017). Emerging technologies and the finance function. Retrieved from: https://www.afponline.org/docs/default-source/default-document-library/pub/afp-mindshift_emergingtech.pdf?sfvrsn=2
62 Frangoul, A. (2017). The internet of things: Why it matters. CNBC. Retrieved December 23, 2019, from https://www.cnbc.com/2017/10/23/the-internet-of-things-why-it-matters.html
63 Vasarhelyi, M. (2019). Audit's new frontier: Data analytics, AI and automation. CPA Australia presentation, Australia.
64 Chandi, N. (2018). Council post: The internet of things for accountants. Forbes. Retrieved from: https://www.forbes.com/sites/forbestechcouncil/2017/03/27/the-internet-of-things-for-accountants/#7e59e37b445b
65 Chandi, N. (2018). Council post: The internet of things for accountants. Forbes. Retrieved from: https://www.forbes.com/sites/forbestechcouncil/2017/03/27/the-internet-of-things-for-accountants/#7e59e37b445b
66 Finley, K. & Barber, G. (2019). Blockchain: The complete guide. Wired. Retrieved January 22, 2020, from: https://www.wired.com/story/guide-blockchain/
67 Mearian, L. (2020). What is blockchain? The complete guide. Computerworld. Retrieved January 22, 2020, from: https://www.computerworld.com/article/3191077/what-is-blockchain-the-complete-guide.html?page=2
68 Tapscott, D & Kirkland, R. (2016). How blockchains could change the world. (2020). McKinsey & Company. Retrieved January 22, 2020, from: https://www.mckinsey.com/industries/technology-media-and-telecommunications/our-insights/how-blockchains-could-change-the-world
69 Institute of Chartered Accountants in England and Wales (2018). Blockchain and the future of accountancy. Retrieved January 22, 2020, from: https://www.icaew.com/-/media/corporate/files/technical/information-technology/thought-leadership/blockchain-and-the-future-of-accountancy.ashx
70 Institute of Chartered Accountants in England and Wales (2018). Blockchain and the future of accountancy. Retrieved January 22, 2020, from: https://www.icaew.com/-/media/corporate/files/technical/information-technology/thought-leadership/blockchain-and-the-future-of-accountancy.ashx

6 Impact of digital disruption and digital transformation on accountants

Introduction

In this chapter, we turn from the impact of digital disruption and digital business transformation on accounting practice, to its impact on accountants, the people doing accounting work. The impact of digital disruption and digital business transformation on accountants manifests itself as required changes in the roles / activities that accountants perform, and as changes in the competencies required by accountants to perform these changed roles / activities. Or, put another way, owing to digital disruption and digital business transformation, accountants are required to perform new or enhanced accounting roles / activities; and, in order to effectively perform these new or enhanced roles and activities, accountants need to cultivate new or enhanced accounting competencies. In this chapter, we review the extant accounting research to identify and explain the different new or enhanced roles accountants are required to perform, as well as the new or enhanced competencies accountants are required to have in order to perform them. We discuss each new or enhanced accounting role and competency in detail. We then provide an organizing framework to help accountants, accounting educators, and accreditation / advocacy bodies to make sense of the nature of the different new or enhanced roles and competencies required, to understand their interrelationships with each other, and to understand their interrelationships with existing accounting competency requirements. Understanding the new or enhanced roles and competencies required of accountants is critical to effectively cultivating the necessary competencies and, in turn, being able to effectively perform the new or enhanced accounting roles required. Effectively delivering on the new or enhanced roles required of accountants is critical to keeping up with accounting stakeholder expectations; which is, in turn, critical to maintaining and enhancing relevance of the accounting profession and the value of accountants.

Impact of digital disruption and digital transformation on accountants

In the preceding chapter, we discussed how digital disruption and digital transformation disrupt accounting practice by disrupting stakeholders' expectations of accountants, disrupting the data available to accountants, disrupting the tools used to perform accounting work, disrupting the type of value accountants are able to create, disrupting what constitutes optimal ways to perform accounting work, and disrupting the competencies required to perform accounting work. Effectively adapting to these disruptions requires transforming accounting practice in order to enable accountants to perform new or enhanced accounting roles and activities. In turn, performing these new or enhanced accounting roles and activities requires new or enhanced accounting competencies. Thus, digital disruption and digital transformation have a strong direct and indirect impacts on accountants by requiring them to perform these new or enhanced accounting roles and activities, as well as requiring them to have new or enhanced accounting competencies in order to perform these roles and activities. In the remainder of this chapter, we explore discussions of these new and enhanced accounting roles and competencies within the academic accounting research, within accounting professional service firm research reports, and within the research reports of key accreditation, strategic leadership, governance, and advocacy bodies of the accounting profession. For both new or enhanced accounting roles and competencies, we synthesize the discussions by diverse stakeholders into a clear set of roles and competencies. We then discuss the meaning and value of each role and competency.

New or enhanced roles and activities required of accountants

Since the advent of the personal computer and the internet, accounting scholars, professional services firms, accounting professional bodies, and key accreditation and governance bodies have discussed the new or enhanced roles required of accountants due to digital technology advancements. Over time, they have identified a range of new or enhanced roles and activities required of accountants. These new or enhanced accounting roles and activities have often emerged and evolved iteratively, in line with digital technology advancements and the disruptions induced by digital technology advancements. We discuss the most commonly cited and more recent roles below.

Enablers of organization-wide exploration, investment in, and effective leveraging of new or enhanced digital technologies and related tools

One commonly discussed role is the need for accountants to be proactive enablers of organization-wide exploration, investment in, and effective leveraging of new or enhanced digital technologies and related tools. For example, the International Federation of Accountants (IFAC), has proposed that accountants need to actively participate in technology investment decisions to ensure investments in the right technologies and tools are made, that technology adoption projects are implemented rapidly and effectively, and that optimal value is realized from these digital technology investments[1]. As a part of this role, IFAC proposes that accountants need to raise awareness of the strategic value of different digital technologies and tools[2], and to partner with CIOs and CTOs to make sure that digital technology investments drive business value[3].

Ensurers of the effective leveraging of data to optimize organization-wide decision-making

A second commonly discussed new or enhanced role is the need for accountants to play a key leadership role in enabling the harnessing of vast internal and external datasets to optimize organization-wide decision-making. In relation to this, the Association of Chartered Certified Accountants (ACCA) has proposed that accountants need to ensure the effective use of these datasets to optimize the delivery of decision insights throughout the organization (e.g. ensure delivery of deeper, more real-time, more forward looking, and more prescriptive insights)[4]. Similarly, researchers exploring the long-term career competency requirements of all accountants, have proposed that board members, CEOs, and other strategic leaders are increasingly turning to accountants to help organizations cut through complexity, make sense of vast amounts of data, and ensure the right information is made available for effective decision-making in all parts and at all levels of the organization[5]. CPA Canada notes that accountants need to use these vast datasets to build new decision and governance models beyond the traditional financial and management accounting models[6]. IFAC adds that accountants need to deliver insights that anticipate customer needs, drive operational efficiency, innovation, and adaptability[7]. CPA Canada further adds that accountants need to use this vast data to measure value creation beyond financials and capture social and environmental impact[8].

Handlers of sophisticated digital technology demands within accounting services and activities / Power users of sophisticated technology tools

A third commonly discussed new or enhanced role is the need for accountants to be handlers of sophisticated digital technology demands in accounting services and activities[9]. Such demands can include being experts in key digital technologies relevant to the accounting function (e.g. cloud accounting platforms, data management technologies, robotic process automation or RPA, intelligent process automation or IPA, XBRL, blockchain technologies), playing leadership or facilitation roles in systems design and development activities[10] (e.g. systems analysis, systems design, systems development of accounting and non-accounting information systems), playing evaluation and advisory roles in enterprise architecture decisions (e.g. evaluating the impact of current and proposed architectures), and being designers or evaluators of control practices to minimize digital technology-related risks[11]. This role is closely related to a fourth commonly discussed role which focuses on accountants being power users of advanced data analytics and reporting technologies and tools[12]. As power users of such technologies and tools, accountants can perform related roles such as ERP systems managers or administrators[13,14], big data analytics specialists[15], advanced querying and data mining specialists[16], XBRL facilitators[17], and RPA / IPA specialists.

Ensurers of the effective management of cyber risk and other digital and ethics risks

A fifth commonly discussed new or enhanced role required of accountants is playing a leadership role in the management of cyber risk. The expanded number of potential cyberattack points (e.g. IoT devices, mobile devices, cloud platforms, digital ecosystems) and the growing sophistication of cyberattacks makes intrusion an even more significant threat to organizations than it has been in the past. Accounting scholars have proposed that accountants need to play proactive leadership and support roles in cyber risk management activities. Such activities include establishing adequate cyber risk management policies and processes, cyber risk identification and evaluation, intrusion detection, and risk mitigation activities[18]. Other scholars have proposed that accountants also need to play key roles in fraud prosecution cases undertaken by or against an organization[19]. Examples of such roles and activities may include analysis of evidence within digital assets or tools, presentation of findings as an expert witness, or contestation of other expert witness assertions[20]. Related to this cybersecurity role, IFAC has proposed that accountants need to broaden their risk management role beyond financial controls and reporting to ensure that all forms of organizational risks (e.g. other digital risks, ethics risks, uncertainty risks) are adequately controlled and managed[21].

Data integrity, ethics, and public trust stewards

With such voluminous, diverse, and exponentially growing data available for decision-making, a key risk organizations face is using poor data for decisions or using good data but for the wrong decisions. In addition to this data-related risk, there is growing information privacy and digital ethics issues associated with the use of data. Without due care, organizations can find themselves having access to so much data but little trust in the data. Or they may find themselves using their data, only to violate ethics norms and lose public trust. As a result of these issues and risks, a range of accounting professional, accreditation, and advocacy bodies have called for accountants to play key data integrity, ethics, and public trust stewardship roles[22,23,24,25]. That is, to ensure that data acquisition, integration, and management activities are undertaken in such a way that data can be trusted in decision-making (e.g. the data is of good quality, free from alteration due to cyberattacks, free from bias). And to ensure that data use is governed in such a way that data use does not breach ethical norms and public expectations (e.g. violation of consumer privacy, use of data for activities the general public would not condone, failure to protect or safely dispose of sensitive information after use).

Enablers / facilitators of strategy-making, change, and process redesign

Finally, accounting scholars and professional bodies have proposed that accountants need to play a greater role in supporting strategy, change, and process redesign. Although such roles may not at first appear related to digital technologies, the need for such roles is largely driven by growing digital disruption and digital transformation of business. These disruptions and transformations are making strategy and change much more challenging for organizations, notwithstanding that this disruption and transformation is in conjunction with parallel issues such as growing complexity and volatility, growing regulation and compliance requirements, growing public expectations, and a growing shift in what constitutes good organizational performance are also key contributors. As a result, accounting scholars and professional bodies have called for accountants to play proactive facilitation and support roles in strategy-making processes (e.g. in strategy foresight, strategy formation, execution planning, execution monitoring, execution performance management), in change processes (e.g. assessing current and proposed future state benefits and risks, measuring progress), and in process redesign initiatives (e.g. process analysis, process design, process digitization, process automation, process optimization). For example, a joint taskforce of the Institute of Management Accountants (IMA) and the Management Accounting Section (MAS) of the American Accounting Association (AAA) proposed that accountants needed to play coordination roles in strategy formation and analysis, strategic planning, and strategy execution[26,27]. And, in relation to change management, IFAC has proposed that accountants need to play change facilitation and change leadership roles[28]. Further, CPA Canada has added that accountants need to be at the forefront of driving organizational agility and innovation[29], which are shaped by an organization's strategy-making and change capabilities[30]. In relation to process redesign, IFAC has proposed that accountants need to play key roles in ensuring that their organization has optimal business processes and workflows in place (e.g. by documenting business processes, evaluating processes for efficiency and risk, facilitating process redesign)[31,32].

Strategic leadership, accreditation, and professional membership bodies have started to synthesize the various new or enhanced accounting roles and activities into integrated frameworks identifying and explaining important emerging accounting roles and career focus areas. For example, IFAC has identified and explains seven new or enhanced accounting value creation roles for the next decade[33]. And ACCA has identified five "career zones", or value creation focus areas for accountants wanting to enhance their value and career prospects[34]. Notwithstanding that the identified roles and career focus areas may continue to evolve, these frameworks provide meaningful integration of the extant discussions regarding the impact of digital technology advancements on the roles of accountants. We discuss IFAC's and ACCA's frameworks in more detail below and explain the role of digital technology advancements in shaping and continuing to shape each role. Understanding these roles and how they are shaped by digital technology advancements can help accountants to hone their abilities in particular roles and, therefore, position themselves for greater career success. We discuss them further below.

IFAC future-fit accounting roles[35]

Acknowledging that the nature of organizational work and the nature of accounting work was rapidly evolving due to digital technology advancements, in combination with other disruptive trends, IFAC tapped into the experiences of business and finance leaders on its Professional Accountants Business Committee, as well as the experiences of key accounting stakeholders (e.g. boards, CEOs, executive and operating management teams), to identify the key accounting roles required for the next decade. The seven "future-fit" roles identified by IFAC included the *co-pilot*, the *navigator*, the *brand protector*, the *storyteller*, the *trusted professional*, the *process and control expert*, and the *digital technology enabler*. IFAC proposes that the seven roles are not mutually exclusive. That is, that an accountant may perform one or more roles, or even all roles, depending on the characteristics of their organization (e.g. organization type, finance team size, and finance team skill sets)[36]. Also, accountants may perform different roles to different degrees depending on their position in the finance function and or in the organization's hierarchy, or depending on the degree to which each role is of value to their organization. We discuss each specific role in more detail below, as well as how digital technology advancements shape and will continue to shape each role.

The co-pilot

This accounting role focuses on partnering with and supporting strategic leaders and managers in the organization in strategy-making, strategy execution, and change facilitation / realization decisions and activities[37]. This role is typically taken on by a senior person in the accounting and finance team (e.g. CFO, Finance Director / vice president, finance-based or originated strategy manager) to ensure the occupant has the relevant strategic mindset, can inspire and lead others within and outside the finance function, can align business and finance strategy, and can identify or understand and facilitate the execution of key strategic and change initiatives[38]. We anticipate that the co-pilot may rise from a management accounting, business services / advisory, accounting information systems, or other relevant function of accounting that hones the competencies required for the role. The co-pilot creates value for organizations by ensuring strategy-making and change processes are effectively supported (e.g. that they draw on the right insights, are aligned with relevant governance and operational processes); and that finance processes (e.g. resource allocation, policies and controls, performance management) and other business processes work together to accelerate strategy-making, strategy execution, and change efforts. Strategy-making, execution, and change efforts are increasingly focused on effectively undertaking digital business transformation, building competitive digital business capabilities, and leveraging these digital capabilities to enhance competitiveness, adaptability, and agility. Even where these efforts are focused elsewhere, strategy-making, execution and change are increasingly enabled and managed by digital technology tools (e.g. strategy making and execution platforms, data analytics and strategic sensing platforms, performance management platforms). As a result, proficiency with digital technology advancements plays a critical role in shaping the ability of accountants to effectively fulfil the co-pilot role.

The navigator

Growing velocity, complicatedness, complexity, and disruptive events in business environments make sustained profitability and longevity a significant challenge for organizations[39]. It requires having the right product offerings and delivering on customer value expectations, doing this efficiently, and, at the same time, preparing for and adapting to disruptions (e.g. technology or social change-driven disruptions, as well as surprise events like the global financial crisis (GFC) and the Covid-19 pandemic)[40]. In the navigator role, accountants can play a critical role in ensuring strategic leaders accurately anticipate changes or disruptions on the horizon, that they understand the opportunities and threats these disruptions or changes present, and that they have the optimal information to make the right tradeoffs[41]. Playing such a role may require proficiency with big data, predictive analytics, artificial intelligence and data science-based modeling, and scenario planning. And it may require integrated analysis of external environments, markets, customers, products, suppliers, ecosystems, technology trends, workforces, assets, and internal processes. Thus, to effectively fulfill the navigator role, accountants need to leverage digital technology advancements such as data analytics and data science tools and models, artificial intelligence tools and models, data visualization tools, big data and other dataset management tools, scenario planning and predictive modeling tools, and more. They also need to understand how key digital technology advancements disrupt and shape social dynamics, market and industry dynamics, competitive dynamics, business capabilities, and product offerings. Such understandings will help with foresight, adaptability / agility, and sustained profitability deliverables that are essential to the navigator role.

The brand protector

In the chapter on digital risk management, we discussed how digital technology advancements, digital transformation, and digital business bring about new risks that may not have been encountered before and also add complexity to existing risks – thus significantly changing the risk landscape (e.g. types of risks, potential attack points, and severity of impacts). We provided examples of new risk exposures such as inappropriate employee behaviors on social media, employees inadvertently clicking on suspect links in emails / online, employees divulging sensitive corporate information, artificial intelligence product / tool algorithm-related risks (e.g. biased data, unsuitable modeling techniques, algorithmic bias), the expanded number of cyberattack points due to expansion of IoT devices / platforms / networks integrating with an organization's infrastructure, the expanded number of cyber criminals online who increasingly have access to more sophisticated attack tools, and the growth of misinformation risks (e.g. cyber criminals / nation states / competitors or other troublemakers using sophisticated digital editing and imitation technologies like machine learning, bots, and natural language generation to spread false information, incite adverse reactions, delegitimize leaders and influencers, and damage brands). In addition to these expanded digital risk exposures, there are also additional and more severe risks associated with growing velocity, complicatedness, complexity, and disruptive events in business environments (e.g. the Covid-19 pandemic); as well as expanded social and environmental responsibility expectations. Taken together, the expanded risk exposures pose significant risks to an organization's tangible and intangible assets, now and in the future. In the brand protector role, accountants undertake stewardship activities to protect an organization's tangible assets (e.g. financial assets, non-financial assets, data) and intangible assets (e.g. brand promise / reputation). These activities can include ensuring effective governance and control, ensuring there is organization-wide respect of key stakeholder expectations and the organization's license to operate in different communities, and leading the cultivation of sustainability, risk conscious, and ethical attitudes and practices at all levels of the organization. Fully comprehending and safeguarding the organization from these different risks requires an understanding of digital technologies, digital transformation, and digital business. This understanding, in turn, enables accountants to understand the related risk exposures and how to safeguard against them. In addition, understanding and being proficient with a range of digital technology tools can significantly enhance the ability of accountants to effectively identify and manage risks (e.g. artificial intelligence tools can read contractual agreements and emails to spot fraud risks, or real-time monitoring of networks / event logs / data can enable real-time or predictive identification of cyberattacks).

The storyteller

With so much data now available, so many stakeholders involved in decision-making, and so many perspectives or ways of seeing the world at play, ensuring diverse stakeholders' understanding of the organization's narrative can be a challenge. But understanding this narrative is important to ensuring varied stakeholders are engaged, take required actions, and don't engage in actions that impede or harm the organization. In the storyteller role, accountants leverage their storytelling and communication skills to enlighten internal and external stakeholders. That is, to ensure they clearly understand the organization's purpose for existing, how the organization creates value and its effectiveness in doing so, the organization's evolving opportunities and challenges, the organization's position in the external environment, the organization's internal environment, and the stakeholder attitudes / behaviors / actions that enhance or hurt the organization's prospects. Although effective storytelling and communication is an important aspect of all roles, it is particularly important to senior finance leaders, accountants working in advisory / decision support roles, or accountants working in particular specialist areas (e.g. integrated reporting, tax planning, internal audit). Accountants may need to use sophisticated data analytics, data visualization, and stakeholder engagement technology tools to both build their own understanding of the organization's narrative and to use these tools in enlightening others.

The trusted professional

An established body of research links organizational trust (trust of and within an organization) with organizational performance (e.g. it speeds up decision-making, accelerates strategy execution, enhances or safeguards employee morale)[42]. However, the ever-growing challenges of building and maintaining organizational trust are also well documented[43]. For example, growing data availability and sophistication of analytics tools are making it easier and easier for organization stakeholders to discover untrustworthy behaviors and intentions (e.g. unethical leadership, irresponsible behaviors, exploitative business practices, lies, etc.). The negative impacts of lost trust are only growing (e.g. an instantaneous ability to let the whole world know about trust breaches, greater potential for customer and community outrage, greater potential for legal liability, growing government intervention, and more). In the trusted professional role, accountants can help their organizations to build and safeguard trust by ensuring ethical leadership, responsible business practices, and ethical attitudes and behaviors. Doing so may involve activities such as effectively assessing or reporting on the extent to which an organization is living up to its mission and values, constructively challenging business decisions and attitudes to ensure objectivity / unbiased consideration of all relevant information, building strong relationships with stakeholders across the organization to ensure effective communication and political support of key stakeholders, positively influencing others' behaviors (e.g. towards ethical and responsible conduct), and ensuring effective policies and processes are in place to safeguard against the enemies of trust (e.g. fraud, corruption, misdemeanors, hypocrisy / cynicism, lack of empathy / psychopathy). Accountants may need to rely on sophisticated data analytics, stakeholder engagement, and workflow management technologies and tools to support them in carrying out the aforementioned activities.

The process and control expert

Digital technology advancements, digital disruption, digital business, and new or enhanced digital business capabilities often require processes and workflows to be redesigned or reconfigured to reflect new automation, integration, intelligence, autonomy, and optimization possibilities. In the process and control expert role, accountants can support strategic leaders and managers to ensure that efficient and effective end-to-end processes are in place. This can include activities such as process analysis / mining, process design, process modeling, process integration, process automation, process monitoring, implementing process controls, identifying non-value-added activities within processes, implementing process autonomy, and more. Through these different activities, accountants can ensure that organizations have efficient, effective, adaptable, and agile processes that are optimized for both today's needs and tomorrow's opportunities and threats. To effectively fulfil the process and control expert role, accountants need to be proficient with relevant digital technologies and tools (e.g. process mining tools, process design tools, digitalized process control tools, process automation tools, process integration tools, etc.). They also need to have sufficient knowledge of digital disruption, digital transformation, digital business, and digital business capabilities to understand how different process configurations can impact digital transformation, digital capabilities, and the ability to sustainably compete as a digital business.

The digital and technology enabler

Undertaking digital business transformation, having the right digital technology infrastructure in place, having it optimally configured, building and continuously improving digital business capabilities, and effectively competing as a digital business all come with significant challenges and risks. In the digital and technology enabler role, accountants can play a critical role in enabling organizations to efficiently, effectively, and safely undertake this change agenda. This can include activities such as evaluating existing and potential technology investments, collaborating with technology teams to optimize architecture management, working with technology / process improvement / operations teams to maximize business process enablement, enabling a data-driven culture, and leveraging digital technologies to enhance adaptability / ambidexterity / agility. Effectively carrying out the digital and technology enabler role requires deep knowledge of digital technologies and tools, deep knowledge of digital transformation, deep knowledge of digital business capabilities, and deep knowledge of business practices and opportunities.

ACCA future career zones[44]

Similarly acknowledging the existential threats and game-changing opportunities facing organizations, ACCA called for accountancy to be reimagined as a profession able to play a critical role in supporting / enabling the building and leveraging of organizational capabilities for effectively competing in the digital age[45]. Bringing together its various research initiatives over three years that explored the forces disrupting or shaping the future of the profession, ACCA identified five new or enhanced accounting roles or career zones (e.g. the relevant research initiatives involved thousands of surveys, interviews, global roundtables, and third-party research on particular issues). These new or enhanced accounting roles included the *assurance advocate*, the *business transformer*, the *data navigator*, and the *digital playmaker* (see Figure 6.1). We discuss each of these roles and how they are shaped by digital technology advancements below.

The assurance advocate
The assurance advocate brings new levels of trust and integrity to organizational operations. They may focus on enterprise risk, helping **drive transparency and understanding of emerging issues affecting business performance**, or be at the forefront of shaping future forward-looking audit practices as the capabilities of digital and technologies expand. They could be driving best practices in emerging control frameworks or helping organizations meet ever-growing regulatory demands or managing complex tax issues. They may even be auditing algorithms in the future. They are essential to the strong stewardship of sustainable organisations for the future.

The business transformer
The business transformer is the architect of organizational change. They could be driving major business change initiatives or transforming finance operations. They may be leading innovative smaller accountancy firms that transform client businesses. They could be exploring growing careers in external advisory services driven by innovation and economic growth. Or they may be leading smaller enterprises as digital platforms open the door to new commercial opportunities. They are critical to creating change, driving the strategies of organizations, and supporting sustainable organizations for the future.

The data navigator
The data navigator is a true business partner. They see extraordinary opportunities from the expansion of data and use emerging tech and analytical tools to drive insights that deliver business outcomes and **sound financial management of the organisation**. They champion ever-growing multi-rich data sets and use smart data to generate brilliant forward-looking analysis to support decision making. This could be exploring new geographic market opportunities or building the case for investment. They understand that the currency of good information is at the heart of building sustainable future organizations.

The digital playmaker
The digital playmaker is a technology evangelist. They see remarkable possibilities for emerging digital tools in transforming the organizations in which they work. They are champions of technology adoption and data governance within the organization. They look to connect across teams and functions to leverage the power of technology. They may focus on digital implementation programs or have specialized **expertise in particular finance and business technologies**. They understand that digital transformation in today's global economy is the lifeblood of future sustainable organizations.

The sustainability trailblazer
The sustainability trailblazer is at the heart of management in the organization. They play a key role in establishing frameworks that capture, evaluate and report on the activities that truly drive value and in ways that are much more transparent and meaningful to the outside world. They **will transform management accounting fit for a multi-capital world and see emerging opportunities with better external disclosures to ever-growing stakeholder groups**. They understand that aligning the pursuit of profit with the pursuit of purpose is integral to building sustainable future businesses.

Figure 6.1 ACCA future career zones[46]

The assurance advocate

Citing growing disruption, increasingly complex and uncertain business environments, growing connectivity and interconnectedness, and growing stakeholder expectations and scrutiny, ACCA proposes that effective risk management, audit, and assurance activities are more important than ever[47]. As a result, there are greater demands for risk management, audit, and integrated assurance activities to evolve so as to provide accounting stakeholders (boards, management teams, oversight and regulatory bodies, communities) with confidence in reported business performance and conditions[48]. This is the focus of the assurance advocate role. New or enhanced activities within this role include enterprise risk management, driving business transparency, leveraging digital technologies to drive the effectiveness of audit practices, driving effective use of best practice control frameworks, helping organizations to meet regulatory and tax compliance obligations, and auditing algorithms[49]. To be sure, accountants have always performed these activities, but the way they can now be performed, and need to be performed, is changing rapidly. For example, there are more efficient and effective technology tools that can be used, and assurance requirements are broadening to encompass the whole enterprise, as well as business, product, and digital ecosystems. There are overlaps of this role with aspects of IFAC's brand protector and trusted professional roles. To effectively perform the assurance advocate role, accountants need to understand and be able to leverage digital technology advancements related to audit / assurance and related to risk management (e.g. data analytics and data science technologies, data management technologies, artificial intelligence and machine learning technologies, and blockchain technologies). They also need to understand the specific risks posed by digital technology advancements, digital business transformation, and competing as a digital business.

The business transformer

Similar to aspects of IFAC's co-pilot and navigator roles, in ACCA's business transformer role, accountants focus on supporting strategic leaders to undertake strategy, change, and business transformation[50]. This role can involve provision of external and internal advisory services such as helping organizations to identify and implement new business models, access new markets, create new digitally enabled products and platforms, and architect and drive major business transformation initiatives[51]. Since a large aspect of business change and transformation initiatives is focused on digital transformation and digital business capabilities, or is enabled by digital technologies, the business transformer role requires accountants to have sufficient knowledge of relevant digital technologies, and of relevant digital transformation and digital business concepts, strategies, and practices.

The data navigator

In the data navigator role, accountants grasping the power of data and the extraordinary opportunities it offers can play critical data acquisition, data management, and data leveraging roles to enhance organizational efficiency, effectiveness, adaptability, and agility. This role may involve activities such as finding and championing the acquisition of valuable datasets, leading the cleaning and integration of datasets, formatting datasets for use by a range of different internal and external stakeholders, championing the acquisition / implementation / utilization of powerful data science and data analytics tools, and providing powerful decision insights[52]. Effectively performing this role requires accountants to understand and be able to leverage a range of different digital technologies and tools (e.g. machine learning and AI tools, data management tools, IoT tools, cloud computing tools). In addition, accountants need to understand digital transformation, digital business, digital business capabilities, and digital business processes. This understanding enables them to target the power of data on key digital transformation, digital business, digital business capability, and digital business initiatives / processes / issues.

The digital playmaker

In the digital playmaker role, accountants are digital evangelists who see the game-changing opportunities digital technology advancements offer to transform business value creation[53], competitiveness, adaptability, and agility. In this evangelical role, they may champion experimentation with and adoption of emerging technologies. They may support technology adoption, digital business transformation, and digital capability building initiatives[54]. They may help organizations connect digital technology infrastructure, business processes, and customer value creation, so as to drive breakthroughs in competitiveness, adaptability, and agility. For this role, accountants need deep understanding of different technologies, the new possibilities they offer, their implementation and utilization practices, and the adoption and utilization realities.

The sustainability trailblazer

ACCA proposes that organizations of all sizes and in all sectors face growing expectations and pressures from communities, regulators, investors, and customers to transparently account for value creation activities and their impacts on communities and environments[55]. In the sustainability trailblazer role, accountants are at the heart of efforts to fully measure, evaluate, and report on these activities and their impacts[56]. As a result, they may lead the transformation of accounting practices to fit the multi-capitals perspective, and the alignment of the pursuit of profit with the sustainability agenda[57]. Accountants can leverage digital technologies to effectively deliver on this role. For example, a number of researchers and practitioners have proposed that effective integrated reporting relies on interactive digital technologies that move beyond passive online presentation / reception to active engagement[58].

New or enhanced digital technology competencies required of accountants

Effectively performing the new or enhanced accounting roles driven by digital technology advancements requires accountants to have new or enhanced digital technology competencies. Accounting scholars, professional services firms, accounting professional bodies, and key accreditation and governance bodies have explored the specific new or enhanced digital technology competencies (knowledge, skills, abilities) required by accountants. To this end, an abundance of digital technology competencies have been identified, some new and some extensions of existing competency requirements. In general, the identified digital technology competencies fall into one of three categories: foundational technology competencies, accounting information systems competencies, and emerging technology competencies. In the remainder of this chapter, we discuss each of these in more detail below. We also identify some competency gaps, and propose

88 *Digital disruption and transformation*

additional competencies, and competency categories. Finally, we finish by reconceptualizing the competency categories into a digital technology competency framework to provide more specific guidance to accountants' competency development efforts.

Foundational technology competencies

The joint taskforce of the Institute of Management Accountants, and the American Accounting Association, proposed a competency framework identifying 16 accounting competency categories. These competency categories were further grouped into three interconnected components or higher level categories: foundational competencies, broad management competencies, and accounting competencies (see Figure 6.2)[59]. From a technology competency perspective, the framework identified the need for *technological* competencies as one of the foundational competencies. It also identified *information systems* as one of the accounting competencies[60]. The foundational technological competencies identified included the ability to use different software, knowledge of the purpose and design of information systems (IS), knowledge of systems architecture, knowledge of processing modes, knowledge of network types, knowledge of hardware components (including mobile devices), knowledge of operating and application software (including cloud computing), knowledge of systems security, and knowledge of IS continuity[61]. While not specifically pointing to it as a foundational competency, researchers and advocacy / accreditation bodies have also pointed to the need for accountants to have data and data management competencies (e.g. data creation or acquisition, data sharing, data analytics, data mining, data reporting, and data storage within and across organizations)[62,63].

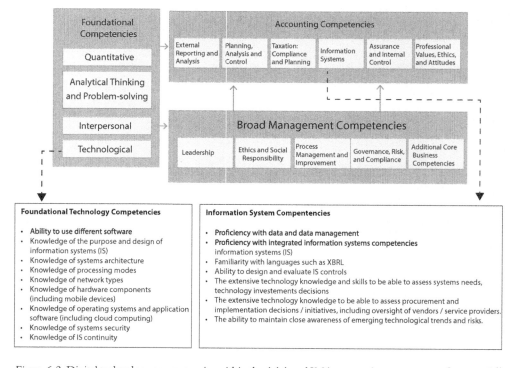

Figure 6.2 Digital technology competencies within the AAA and IMA accounting competency framework[64]

Information systems competencies

Within the AAA and IMA-proposed accounting competency framework (see Figure 6.2), the identified information systems competencies include proficiency with data and data management (e.g. data gathering, data validation, data analysis, data organization and access, database management), proficiency with integrated information systems (e.g. specialized software / reporting systems with decision support, enterprise resource planning (ERP) systems, business intelligence systems / applications, enterprise analytics systems / applications, information search and retrieval systems / applications, and data mining systems / applications), familiarity with languages such as XBRL, ability to design and evaluate IS controls, ability to manage IS risks and compliance (e.g. overseeing fraud prevention, privacy safeguards, data integrity), ability to leverage extensive technology knowledge and skills to assess system needs and technology investment decisions, ability to leverage extensive technology knowledge to assess procurement and implementation decisions / initiatives (including oversight of vendors / service providers), and ability to maintain close awareness of emerging technological trends and risks.

Accounting researchers and professional and accreditation bodies have expanded on particular AAA and IMA framework information system competency areas and also introduced additional competency areas. To date, the expanded or added competency areas have included data and data management, querying or programming languages, and data analytics. For example, data and data management competencies have been expanded to include information lifecycle management[65], data warehousing[66,67], and virtualization[68,69]. Data analytics competencies have been expanded to include knowledge of and proficiency with different data analytics methodologies (e.g. descriptive analytics, diagnostic analytics, predictive analytics, prescriptive analytics)[70]. And competencies relating to familiarity with querying or programming languages have been extended beyond XBRL to include VBA[71], SQL[72], NoSQL[73], Python[74], and R[75]. New competency areas include systems design, development, implementation, and maintenance[76,77] (e.g. knowledge or proficiency with entity relationship diagrams, data flow diagrams, REA diagrams, relational databases, and relational database models)[78]. Other new competency areas to date include knowledge / proficiency with file systems[79], knowledge / proficiency with open source software[80], knowledge / proficiency with cloud service levels[81], the ability to collaborate with technology experts effectively[82,83], the ability to enable a data-driven culture[84,85], and the ability to redesign / reconfigure digital processes for optimal performance (e.g. knowledge / proficiency with process analysis, process design, process control, process automation)[86,87].

Emerging digital technology competencies

A range of studies and discussions have occurred regarding the anticipated impact of key emerging digital technologies on the accounting profession, and on accounting work[88]. A subset of these discussions and studies have focused on the corresponding emerging technology competencies required by accountants[89]. Largely, these discussions and studies have focused on identifying the emerging digital technologies accountants need to have working knowledge of, on identifying the specific digital technology tools accountants need to be proficient in, and on identifying the methods / practices related to these technologies / tools that accountants need to be proficient in. In relation to emerging digital technologies that accountants need to have working knowledge of, the commonly identified digital technologies to date include big data and data analytics[90], artificial intelligence (including robotic process automation and intelligent process automation, bots / chatbots and intelligent assistants, knowledge graphs / artificial neural networks and deep learning, and machine learning)[91,92], the internet of things (including smart workspaces and smart homes, smart government, smart infrastructure and smart cities, and Industrie 4.0)[93,94], video analytics and computer vision[95,96], virtual / mixed / augmented reality[97], robotics and drones[98], 3D and 4D printing[99], network and connectivity technologies (e.g. 5G and 6G, GPS III and LEO satellites, LPWA and LPWAN, NFC, Bluetooth Smart and Beacon protocols)[100], blockchain and other distributed ledger technologies[101], neurotechnologies (e.g. smart drugs, neural imaging, brain computer interfaces)[102], and new computing technologies (e.g. quantum computing, biological computing, neural network processing)[103]. Some discussions and studies have added that accountants need to understand digital technology infrastructure and architecture[104] (e.g. how these different digital technologies can optimally be integrated and work together), as well as APIs and modularization[105]. Needless to say, no study proposes that every accountant needs to be an expert in every digital technology identified. Indeed, professional bodies emphasize different digital technology competency requirements (e.g. the Institute of Management Accountants emphasizes different digital technology competency requirements to the Association of Chartered Certified Accountants; and the competency requirements for Certified Public Accountants, CPA Canada, and CPA Australia are yet again different). We suggest that the required broadness and depth of working knowledge of different digital technologies is shaped by the particular organizations or industries an accountant works or is expected to work in (e.g. different organizations and industries may leverage different digital technologies to different degrees), shaped by the specific roles occupied or desired to be occupied by an accountant in future (e.g. occupying the digital and technology enabler role may require broader and deeper working knowledge of different digital technologies relative to, say, the sustainability trailblazer), by the professional accreditation sought by an accountant (e.g. AMA, CPA, CFA, CIA, CISA), and by an accountant's career stage (e.g. particular digital technology knowledge may be more relevant to the careers of early stage accountants or prospective accountants).

In relation to the specific emerging technology tools accountants need to be proficient in, a range of these have been identified. They include proficiency with common big data analytics tools[106] (e.g. Tableau, Rapid Miner, Hadoop, SAS, IBM Big Data, Microsoft Power BI, QlikView), proficiency with data science tools[107] (e.g. BigML, Apache Spark, D3.js, MATLAB, NLTK, TensorFlow), proficiency with data visualization tools[108] (e.g. Tableau, Sisense, SAP Analytics Cloud, IBM Watson Analytics), proficiency with artificial intelligence tools[109,110] (e.g. RPA/IPA, chatbots and intelligent assistants, Azure machine learning studio, Deeplearning4j), proficiency with XBRL tools[111,112] (e.g. XINBA, MapForce, Calcbench, CrossView, Altova XBRL tools), proficiency with enterprise level as well as small / medium-sized business level ERP systems[113,114] (e.g. SAP S/4HANA, SAP Business One, Oracle Cloud ERP, Oracle NetSuite, Sage Intacct), proficiency with SME and small business cloud accounting platforms (e.g. Xero, Quickbooks), proficiency with artificial intelligence / RPA / process mining tools relevant to auditing[115,116] (e.g. OCR, Python's Natural Language Toolkit, Blue Prism's RPA software, ProM process mining software), proficiency with key analytics / programming languages[117] (e.g. R programming, Python, Javascript), proficiency with cryptographic asset tools[118,119] (e.g. cryptocurrencies, cryptocurrency exchanges, cryptocurrency wallets), and proficiency with systems design and development tools[120] (e.g. Visio, Agile Scrum Software, Proto.io).

Analytics methods / techniques and systems design / development / implementation methods / techniques

The new technologies and tools discussed thus far result in the need for accountants to be able to use new or enhanced data analytics and data science methodologies and techniques, as well as new or enhanced systems design / development / implementation methodologies and techniques. Accounting researchers and professional / accreditation bodies have discussed some of these different methodologies and techniques. Some of the commonly discussed data analytics and data science methodologies / techniques to date include decision models (e.g. AI-based decision models), regression (e.g. for application to big data analytics), Monte Carlo simulations (e.g. application to budgeting and scenario planning), content analysis (e.g. application to sentiment analysis), narrative analysis, unsupervised learning, neural networks, and predictive modeling[121,122]. Some of the commonly discussed systems design / development / implementation methods include agile scrum, agile project management, lean project management, extreme programming, and design thinking[123,124]. Figure 6.3 outlines stages of the design thinking process and some of the objectives, artefacts, and outputs of each stage[125].

Accelerated change and transformation methods

Digital business transformation and digital business change initiatives often draw on accelerated change and transformation methods most extensively used in high technology industries, albeit not always necessarily originating from those industries. These industries have long been known to be characterized by extraordinary complexity, rapid or high velocity change, and fleeting

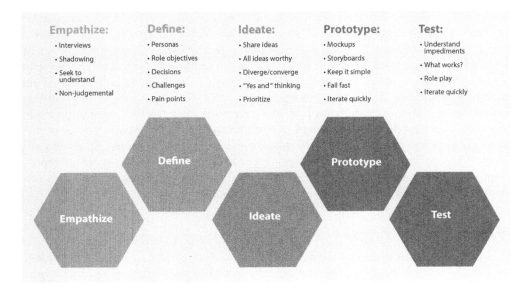

Figure 6.3 The design thinking process and some of each stage's objectives, artefacts, and outputs[126]

opportunity windows[127,128]. As a result, they often rely on change and transformation methods that enable them to make decisions fast, to act or execute on those decisions quickly, to dynamically adapt to rapidly changing circumstances, and, at the same time, keep these decisions and actions aligned to a big picture strategy[129]. We refer to these change and transformation methods as *accelerated change and transformation methods*. Some of the accelerated change and transformation methods that are linked to accounting practice and discussed in the context of accounting competencies include agile principles / methods / practices, design thinking principles / methods / practices[130], and lean thinking principles / methods / practices.[131]. We propose that digital leadership, the ability to effectively lead the implementation of digital transformation / digital business initiatives, or to lead in a highly digital environment, is part of these accelerated change and transformation methods. We have included accelerated change and transformation methods as technology competencies due to their close association (i.e. as they are typically facilitating digital transformation and digital business change initiatives that will be supported by accountants).

Accelerated innovation methods

The speed, dynamism, and disruptive pressures associated with digital technologies, and that are characteristic of the digital technology sector[132], have ushered in new or enhanced ways of innovating. We refer to these as *accelerated innovation methods*, given their focus on, and effectiveness with, accelerated product / service development and commercialization. Some of the commonly discussed accelerated innovation methods include accelerators, hackathons, agile innovation, design thinking, and lean startup methods. Accelerator[133] (startup accelerators, corporate accelerators, impact accelerators), design thinking, hackathon[134,135], and lean startup methods are used by an increasing number of organizations to rapidly speed up the creation and introduction of new products and services, while minimizing the waste commonly associated with these pursuits. Table 6.1 provides examples of different corporate accelerator models and their structure, objectives, and characteristics. Accelerators and hackathons are common to digital technology-related products / services and process innovations; although not limited to them. Accountants are increasingly likely to be involved in assessing the viability and risks of accelerator / lean startup / hackathon methods for an organization, in assessing their effectiveness in organization's innovation efforts, in being a business partner within an accelerator / lean startup / hackathon program, or being a business partner in a change initiative applying hackathon and design thinking methods and practices. In either case, having working knowledge of these methodologies puts accountants in a better value creation position. Similarly, accountants may find themselves working with lean startup concepts (e.g. minimum viable product, pivoting, business model canvas, customer development, innovation accounting) and agile innovation concepts (e.g. sprints, sprint planning, sprint retrospectives, user stories, iterations). Working knowledge of these methods and concepts can greatly enhance their business partnering and value creation capacity.

Digital transformation and digital business competencies

In the various discussions and studies we reviewed during the research for this book, we did not see discussions of specific digital transformation and digital business competencies. However, we did see aspects of these competencies in the AICPA (American Institute of Certified Public Accountants), CGMA (Chartered Global Management

Table 6.1 Examples of different corporate accelerator models and their structures, objectives, and characteristics[136]

	In-house accelerator	Hybrid accelerator	Powered by accelerator	Consortium accelerator
Model				
Participating firms	Single corporate	Single corporate	Single corporate	Multiple corporates
Management structure	Corporate internal	Corporate internal	Corporate independent	Corporate independent
Examples	Wayra (Telefonica)	E.ON a:gile	Metro Accelerator powered by Techstars	TechFounders Startup Autobahn
General overview	• Open innovation collaboration • Brand enhancement and marketing effects • Little experience with innovation and exchange with startups • Large companies listed on the stock market • Providing financial and human resources • Corporate employees, mostly from the corporate development department, acting as accelerator and liaison manages	• Advancement of internal projects • Fostering intrapreneurship and cultural exchange • Brand enhancement and marketing effects • Little experience with open innovation and exchange with startups • Large companies listed on the stock market • Providing human rather than financial resources • Corporate employees acting as accelerator and liaison managers	• Financial gain as a result of startup growth • Evaluating the startups' developments for further investment • Brand enhancement and marketing effects • Little company building experience and expertise with distant knowledge fields • Large companies listed on the stock market • Primarily providing financial resources • Corporate employees support accelerator managers and act as liaison managers	• Pilot project with startups • Little open innovation experience and little exchange with startups • Medium-sized to large companies • Providing few to moderate financial resources • Corporate employees can visit and exchange with startups, but do not have accelerator-managing responsibilities
Program characteristics	• External startups • Exploitative search • Early stage startups • €25,000 – €50,000 • Usually no equity stakes in exchange • 3 months duration • Located close to headquarters • Highly adjustable to the company's needs and startups' feedback	• Internal projects and external startups • Exploitative or explorative search • Early stage startups • €0 – €30,000 • Usually no equity stakes in exchange • 3–6 months duration • Located close to or remotely from the headquarters • Highly adjustable to the company's needs and startups' feedback	• External startups • Exploitative search • Early stage startups • ~€100,000 • Typically 5–6% equity in exchange • 3 months duration • Located remotely from the headquarters • Predefined program structures	• External startups • Exploitative or explorative search • Early stage startups • With investment (~ €25,000) or without investment • Equity stakes or no equity stakes in exchange • 3 months duration • Located remotely from the headquarters • Highly adjustable to the companies' needs and startups' feedback

Accountant), and CPA Canada accounting competency frameworks. Digital transformation competencies include working knowledge of digital business transformation strategies, practices / approaches, challenges, and risks. Accountants will be much better empowered to support digital transformation efforts if they have such working knowledge. For example, in its competency framework, CGMA has management accounting competency requirements such as "Advise on the digital transformation of the organisation as a way of managing and transforming costs"[137]. In contrast, digital business competencies include working knowledge of key digital business capabilities, strategies, and practices (e.g. digital business strategy, digital stakeholder engagement, digital innovation, digital architecture, etc.). Armed with such working knowledge, accountants are better placed to deliver on co-pilot and navigator roles in particular; and all other roles in general. For example, in the brand protector role, accountants are better placed to understand the risks associated with particular digital business strategies or the absence of such strategies. And in relation to accountants' traditional cost management support roles, they are better placed to understand the costs associated with particular digital business models, strategies, and processes. Within its competency framework, CGMA has competency requirements such as "Implement cost transformation programme that spans the organisation's digital ecosystem" and "Develop cost transformation programme based on the features of the organisation's digital ecosystem". Such competencies require working knowledge of digital business capabilities, strategies, and practices.

Complexity management frameworks and strategy-making processes

Expanding on the need to have working knowledge of accelerated change and transformation methodologies, we propose two additional components to this competency area: working knowledge of complexity management frameworks, and working knowledge of strategy-making processes. Disruptive digital technology changes contribute, and often drive, a much more complex and uncertain business environment[138]. The resultant complexity poses significant strategic risk for business decisions that don't take into account the uncertainty associated with this complexity[139]. However, a range of complexity management frameworks exist to improve organizations' and individuals' decision-making in the context of such complexity. Examples of these frameworks include the Cynefin framework (see Figure 6.4)[140], the VUCA framework[141], the Strategy Palette[142], and other complexity conceptualization / sense-making frameworks. In their evolving roles (e.g. co-pilot, navigator, brand protector, trusted professional, digital and technology enabler, process and control expert, storyteller), accountants have to be able to reflect on the implications of complexity for the optimal leveraging of digital technology advancements.

Growing complexity means the business environment is going to be characterized by more and more disruptive or surprise events and crises that businesses have to prepare for and adjust to (e.g. the GFC, Covid-19, and future ones to come)[143]. But the level of disruption faced commonly differs across organizations, and even across stakeholders within the same organization. To this end, a range of complex environments have been identified, each with unique dynamics and implications for organizational decision-making and action. Examples of these different types of environments include obvious, complicated, complex, chaotic, high velocity, and dissipative environments[144]. The different dynamics and demands of these environments has led to evolutions in strategy-making processes[145]. As a result, a range of different strategy-making processes have been identified (e.g. Execution Premium Process, Simple Rules Process, Change Acceleration Process, 7 Factor

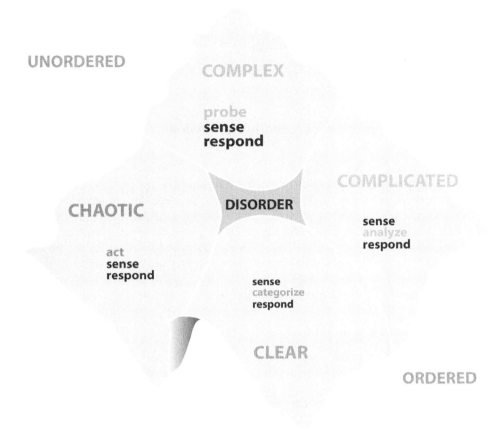

Figure 6.4 The Cynefin framework is one of several frameworks that can be used by individuals and organizations to make sense of information and events in complex settings[146]

Process, Resource Allocation Process)[147]. These different processes have important implications for how digital technology infrastructure ought to be configured (e.g. modular and bimodal or not), how digitalized processes should be configured (e.g. modular or not, digital hybrid or purely digital), what type of information is required by strategy-making and execution leaders (e.g. descriptive, predictive, prescriptive, simulation, real-time, layered), and how that information ought to be provided (real-time monitoring dashboards, big data visualizations, predictive dashboards, customizable / interactive simulations).

Technology learning competency

Given the rapidly expanding digital technology knowledge / skills required of accountants, a natural challenge that arises is keeping up with the growing knowledge / skill requirements. As a result, we propose technology learning (the ability to rapidly and effectively learn digital technology knowledge / skills) as an important digital technology-related competency for accountants. Both this competency and the related challenge are not unique to accountants. For example, within the information systems profession, researchers been explored opportunities and strategies for accelerating the technology learning of information systems professionals[148]. Improving the speed and effectiveness with which accountants learn digital technology knowledge / skills enables them to avoid being overwhelmed, to maintain their confidence when working in digital settings or with different digital technologies, and to keep up with new digital technologies. We expand more on this competency in the chapter on keeping up with digital technologies.

An organizing framework for accounting technology competencies

The abundance and diversity of digital technology-related competencies we have just identified can seem overwhelming. As a result, in Figure 6.5, we present a structured way of viewing them and their interrelationships. As can be seen, this framework is made up of five competency categories, some with subcategories. All the digital technology competencies we have discussed will typically fall into one of these categories, or sometimes have aspects of the competency falling in one category, while other aspects fall into another category (e.g. proficiency with blockchain technology can have a technical aspect that would be in a technical technology proficiency category; but it can also have a strategic aspect that would be in a strategic technology proficiency category).

Technical digital technology competencies

The first category, technical digital technology competencies, refers to competencies that discuss the mechanics of particular digital technologies (e.g. artificial intelligence, computer vision, blockchain) and how to use specific digital technology tools (e.g. specific inventory monitoring / stocktaking drones, specific video analytics software, specific cryptocurrencies and cryptocurrency exchanges). The focus of competencies in this category is on how particular digital technologies work (e.g. blockchain), how to use specific digital technology tools (e.g. how to use the Coinbase or Binance cryptocurrency exchanges), and how to perform accounting-specific roles and activities related to particular digital technologies and tools (e.g. how to audit internal control of blockchain, how to audit AI algorithms). Technical digital technology competencies can be further divided into generic competencies, and accounting function-specific competencies. For example, in relation to blockchain, technical knowledge of how blockchain works and of how to use cryptocurrency exchanges is generic technical knowledge (i.e. not unique to accounting). Whereas, technical knowledge on how to account for cryptographic assets (e.g. cryptocurrencies) is accounting function specific (specifically, the financial accounting and audit functions). Similarly, technical knowledge on how to audit blockchain is accounting function specific (specifically, the auditing function). We propose that generic technical technology competencies make it easier to learn and apply accounting function-specific technical technology competencies. And that accounting function-specific technical technology competencies, in turn, can enhance proficiency with generic technical technology competencies.

Technology learning competencies

The second category, technology learning competencies, refers to competencies related to how accountants can most efficiently and effectively learn required digital technology

Impact on accountants 97

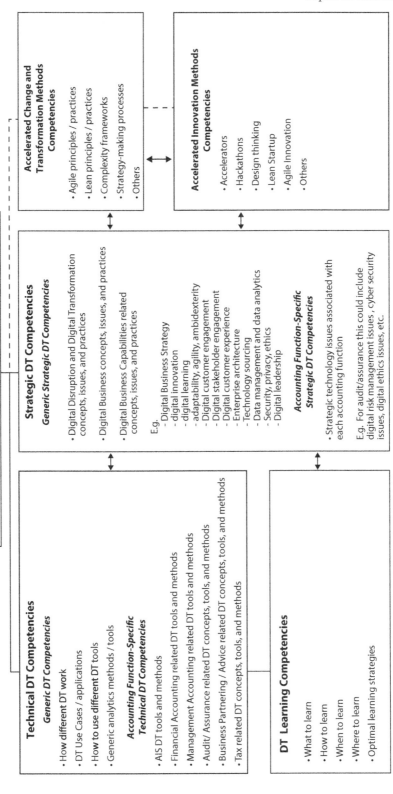

Figure 6.5 Accounting digital technology competencies

knowledge, skills, and abilities. There are specific approaches and strategies for rapidly and effectively acquiring digital technology knowledge, skills, and abilities. These strategies typically address digital technology-related questions such as what to learn (e.g. what is of priority to learn since I can't learn everything?), how to best learn it (e.g. from a book / person / organization / platform, in a face-to-face class / virtual class / self-directed learning, through simulation / practical application / other?), where to best learn (e.g. what physical or virtual settings?), when to learn (e.g. just in time for application or prior?), and the optimal learning strategies to use. Through awareness and practice of these approaches and strategies, accountants are able to overcome technology competency development barriers such as information overload, slippery technical jargon, and feelings of being overwhelmed due to seemingly steep learning curves. We propose that technology learning proficiency accelerates development of all other digital technology competencies.

Strategic digital technology competencies

The third category, strategic digital technology competencies, refers to competencies relating to the strategic uses / applications / implications of digital technologies. Competencies within this category include working knowledge of digital disruption dynamics, digital business transformation concepts / practices / tools, digital business concepts / practices / tools (e.g. nature of digital business, key digital business issues, digital business models, digitalized / hybrid products, digital ecosystems, digital business infrastructure). Competencies also include working knowledge of digital business strategies and key digital business capabilities (e.g. digital innovation, enterprise architecture, digital business strategy, digital risk management). Strategic digital technology competencies can be generic (e.g. the ones discussed thus far within this category). Or they can be accounting function-specific – focusing on strategic digital technologies and issues relevant to a particular accounting function. For example, strategic digital technology issues such as data integrity risks that enhance risks of material misstatement, digital risk management policies / procedures / controls, cybersecurity strategies, and digital ethics issues would fall into the accounting function-specific strategic digital technology competencies category (e.g. for the audit function). These two subcategories can help accountants and educators delineate between learning or CPD activities aimed at building generic strategic digital technology knowledge / skills vs. those aimed at building accounting function specific knowledge / skills.

Accelerated change and transformation methods competencies

The fourth category, accelerated change and transformation competencies, includes all competencies relating to methods and techniques for initiating, facilitating, and bringing about rapid change (e.g. digital transformation). It includes competencies such as working knowledge of agile principles / practices / tools, working knowledge of lean thinking principles / practices / tools, working knowledge of complexity management frameworks, working knowledge of strategy-making processes, and working knowledge of effective digital leadership practices.

Accelerated innovation methods competencies

The final category, accelerated innovation methods competencies, includes competencies relating to methods / practices / tools for accelerating the creation and commercialization of new products and services. These competencies include working knowledge of accelerator methods / practices / tools, working knowledge of hackathon methods / practices / tools, working knowledge of lean startup methods / practices / tools, working knowledge of design thinking methods / practices / tools, working knowledge of agile innovation methods / practices / tools, and more.

Interrelationships between competency categories

The competency categories identified (in Figure 6.5) have important interrelationships. We propose that technology learning competencies accelerate the acquisition / development of technical digital technology competencies (e.g. if accountants can learn digital technologies faster and more effectively, they can acquire more or deeper technical technology competencies). We propose the reverse is also true; that is, acquisition of technical digital technology competencies enhances or accelerates technology learning competencies (e.g. learning a programming language or how artificial intelligence works can enable an accountant to learn other programming languages faster or to learn artificial intelligence-related technologies more rapidly than someone without such a background). We propose that both technology learning and technical digital technology competencies can accelerate acquisition / development of strategic digital technology competencies. For example, it is easier to understand enterprise architecture or digital innovation once an accountant has sufficient background knowledge of how the underpinning digital technologies work (e.g. connectivity technologies, cloud platforms, devices, integration issues). Similarly, we propose that strategic digital technology competencies can enhance technical digital technology competencies and technology learning competencies by enabling accountants to hone in on the most critical knowledge / skills to learn (e.g. working knowledge of IoT-enabled efficiency and effectiveness opportunities may be cultivated in the strategic digital technology competencies category, which may in turn guide an accountant to cultivate deeper technical knowledge / skills in areas such as IoT / drones / robotics-enabled inventory management). This deeper technical knowledge / skill may, in turn, enable an accountant to further enhance their understanding of the IoT efficiency and effectiveness opportunities for organizations (e.g. practical application may provide practice-tested insights that enable them to delineate between real and hypothesized opportunities). Similarly, these three competency categories can enhance the cultivation of accelerated change and transformation methods, and accelerated innovation methods competencies. For example, accountants can better spot risks and issues associated with accelerated change and transformation or accelerated innovation initiatives (e.g. by combining their technical and strategic digital technology competencies with their knowledge of accelerated change and transformation and accelerated innovation processes / practices). In the framework we have provided (see Figure 6.5), the dotted lines to "*accelerated change and transformation*" and "*accelerated innovation*" competency categories highlight that, although these can be argued to belong in the broad management competencies category of the joint AAA and IMA accounting competency framework discussed earlier, they have close relationships with technical and strategic digital technology competencies. That is, they are often associated with or leveraged to facilitate / accelerate digital business transformation and digital business-related initiatives.

Fit with IMA and AAA Joint Task Force's foundational, broad management, and accounting competencies

The accounting digital technology competency framework provided in this chapter expands and complements the IMA and AAA Joint Task Force's broad accounting competency framework. It does this by essentially providing subcategories for the technological and information systems competency categories within the IMA and AAA Joint Taskforce framework digital technology categories. For example, technological competencies can now be divided into generic technical DT competencies, accounting function specific technical DT competencies, generic strategic DT competencies, and accounting function specific strategic DT competencies. Information systems category competencies can also be divided up into those subcategories. The framework we have presented adds technology learning as an important competency area (perhaps as part of the technological category or as a part of both categories) to enable accountants to better keep up with digital technologies. Finally, we identify accelerated innovation and accelerated change and transformation competencies as having such important interrelationships to technical and strategic digital technology competencies that they can almost be thought of as digital technology-related competencies. Either way, accountants require knowledge / skills of those methods / practices to enhance their effectiveness in digital business transformation, digital business, and digital innovation change initiatives.

Fit with IFAC future-fit roles and ACCA career zones

We propose that the type and depth of digital technology competencies required by an accountant is shaped by the particular future-fit roles or career zones an accountant is in or is pursuing. For example, in addition to other relevant competencies, the co-pilot role and the business transformer career zone will require much broader and deeper generic technical digital technology competencies, generic strategic digital technology competencies, accelerated change and transformation method competencies, accelerated innovation method competencies, and technology learning competencies. In contrast, the brand protector role and the assurance advocate career zone are likely to require deeper audit / assurance function related technical digital technology competencies (e.g. big data analytics / artificial intelligence / machine learning technologies, analytics / statistical methods and techniques, risk analysis tools), audit / assurance-specific strategic digital technology competencies (e.g. digital risk management issues, digital risk management frameworks, digital risk management policies / practices, digital ethics issues and risks), and generic technical technology competencies. As demonstrated, the framework can be used by accountants, accounting educators, and accounting accreditation bodies to delineate between generic or accounting function-specific, technical or strategic, broad management or accelerated change and transformation / accelerated innovation, and technology learning competency development efforts. Used this way, the framework complements the IMA and AAA accounting competency framework, the IFAC future-fit accounting roles, and the ACCA career zones.

Google and reflect

data integrity steward, ethics steward, public trust steward, strategy-making, strategy execution, strategic leadership, IFAC future-fit accounting roles, ACCA future career zones, startup accelerator, corporate accelerator, impact accelerator, hackathon, agile innovation, complexity, dynamism, complexity management framework, VUCA framework, Cynefin framework, digital leadership

Discussion questions

1. How do digital technology advancements disrupt the work accountants do?
2. Why isn't a good IT / IS department sufficient, i.e. why do accountants have to develop digital technology, digital transformation, and digital business competencies on top of everything else they have to learn?
3. How do digital technology / digital transformation / digital business competencies enhance the performance of all other accounting roles and activities?
4. Could an accountant work at a more mature digital business like Google or Amazon without digital technology / digital transformation / digital business competencies?
5. Could an accountant lead the finance function at a more mature digital business like Google or Amazon without digital technology / digital transformation / digital business competencies?
6. Which IFAC future-fit accounting roles and ACCA future career zones best fit with your current accounting work aspirations or intentions?
7. Which three IFAC future-fit accounting roles require the greatest breadth and depth of digital technology competencies?
8. Which two IFAC future-fit accounting roles require the strongest strategic digital technology competencies?
9. Which two IFAC future-fit accounting roles require the strongest technical digital technology competencies?
10. Which IFAC future-fit accounting role requires the strongest accelerated change and transformation and accelerated innovation competencies?
11. What is the relationship between new or enhanced accounting roles and new or enhanced competencies required of accountants?
12. Why is the technology learning competency so important to development of technical and strategic digital technology competencies?
13. Could an accountant lead cross-functional teams at a more mature digital business like Google or Amazon without strong digital technology / digital transformation / digital business competencies?
14. Could an accountant review a business case and provide recommendations regarding the introduction of virtual assistants, customer service robots, and cobots without having knowledge / skills / abilities in artificial intelligence?

Notes

1. IFAC. (2018). The changing role of accounting in enterprise performance management. Retrieved August 25, 2020, from: https://www.ifac.org/knowledge-gateway/developing-accountancy-profession/discussion/changing-role-accounting-enterprise-performance-management
2. IFAC. (2017). Professional accountants as business partners and value enablers. Retrieved August 25, 2020, from: https://www.ifac.org/knowledge-gateway/preparing-future-ready-professionals/publications/professional-accountants-business-partners-and-value-enablers
3. IFAC. (2017). Professional accountants as business partners and value enablers. Retrieved August 25, 2020, from: https://www.ifac.org/knowledge-gateway/preparing-future-ready-professionals/publications/professional-accountants-business-partners-and-value-enablers
4. ACCA. (2020). Future ready: Accountancy careers in the 2020s. Retrieved August 28, 2020, from: https://www.accaglobal.com/us/en/professional-insights/pro-accountants-the-future/future_ready_2020s.html

5 ACCA. (2020). Future ready: Accountancy careers in the 2020s. Retrieved August 28, 2020, from: https://www.accaglobal.com/us/en/professional-insights/pro-accountants-the-future/future_ready_2020s.html
6 CPA Canada. (2018). Foresight: Reimagining the profession makes urgent case for change. Retrieved August 25, 2020, from: https://www.cpacanada.ca/en/foresight-initiative
7 IFAC. (2017). Professional accountants as business partners and value enablers. Retrieved August 25, 2020, from: https://www.ifac.org/knowledge-gateway/preparing-future-ready-professionals/publications/professional-accountants-business-partners-and-value-enablers
8 CPA Canada. (2018). Foresight: Reimagining the profession makes urgent case for change. Retrieved August 25, 2020, from: https://www.cpacanada.ca/en/foresight-initiative
9 Coyne, J.G., Coyne, E.M., & Walker, K.B. (2016). A model to update accounting curricula for emerging technologies. Journal of Emerging Technologies in Accounting, 13(1), 161–-69.
10 Sledgianowski, D., Gomaa, M., & Tan, C. (2017). Toward integration of big data, technology and information systems competencies into the accounting curriculum. Journal of Accounting Education, 38, 81–93.
11 Coyne, J.G., Coyne, E.M., & Walker, K.B. (2016). A model to update accounting curricula for emerging technologies. Journal of Emerging Technologies in Accounting, 13(1), 161–169.
12 Coyne, J.G., Coyne, E.M., & Walker, K.B. (2016). A model to update accounting curricula for emerging technologies. Journal of Emerging Technologies in Accounting, 13(1), 161–169.
13 Coyne, J.G., Coyne, E.M., & Walker, K.B. (2016). A model to update accounting curricula for emerging technologies. Journal of Emerging Technologies in Accounting, 13(1), 161–169.
14 Coyne, J.G., Coyne, E.M., & Walker, K.B. (2016). A model to update accounting curricula for emerging technologies. Journal of Emerging Technologies in Accounting, 13(1), 161–169.
15 Janvrin, D.J., & Watson, M.W. (2017). "Big data": A new twist to accounting. Journal of Accounting Education, 38, 3–8.
16 Sledgianowski, D., Gomaa, M., & Tan, C. (2017). Toward integration of big data, technology and information systems competencies into the accounting curriculum. Journal of Accounting Education, 38, 81–93.
17 Coyne, J.G., Coyne, E.M., & Walker, K.B. (2016). A model to update accounting curricula for emerging technologies. Journal of Emerging Technologies in Accounting, 13(1), 161–169.
18 Coyne, J.G., Coyne, E.M., & Walker, K.B. (2016). A model to update accounting curricula for emerging technologies. Journal of Emerging Technologies in Accounting, 13(1), 161–169.
19 Coyne, J.G., Coyne, E.M., & Walker, K.B. (2016). A model to update accounting curricula for emerging technologies. Journal of Emerging Technologies in Accounting, 13(1), 161–169.
20 Coyne, J.G., Coyne, E.M., & Walker, K.B. (2016). A model to update accounting curricula for emerging technologies. Journal of Emerging Technologies in Accounting, 13(1), 161–169.
21 IFAC. (2017). Professional accountants as business partners and value enablers. Retrieved August 25, 2020, from: https://www.ifac.org/knowledge-gateway/preparing-future-ready-professionals/publications/professional-accountants-business-partners-and-value-enablers
22 CPA Canada. (2019). Foresight: The way forward. Retrieved August 25, 2020, from: https://www.cpacanada.ca/foresight-report/en/index.html#page=1
23 CPA Canada. (2018). Foresight: Reimagining the profession makes urgent case for change. Retrieved August 25, 2020, from: https://www.cpacanada.ca/en/foresight-initiative
24 ACCA. (2020). Future ready: Accountancy careers in the 2020s. Retrieved August 28, 2020, from: https://www.accaglobal.com/us/en/professional-insights/pro-accountants-the-future/future_ready_2020s.html
25 IFAC. (2019). Future-fit Accountants: CFO and finance function roles for the next decade. Retrieved from: https://www.ifac.org/system/files/publications/files/IFAC-Future-Fit-Accountant-ROLES-V5-Singles.pdf
26 Lawson, R.A., Blocher, E.J., Brewer, P.C., Cokins, G., Sorensen, J.E., Stout, D.E., ... & Wouters, M.J. (2014). Focusing accounting curricula on students' long-run careers: Recommendations for an integrated competency-based framework for accounting education. Issues in Accounting Education, 29(2), 295–317.
27 Lawson, R.A., Blocher, E.J., Brewer, P.C., Morris, J.T., Stocks, K.D., Sorensen, J.E., ... & Wouters, M.J. (2015). Thoughts on competency integration in accounting education. Issues in Accounting Education, 30(3), 149–171.
28 IFAC. (2019). Future-fit Accountants: CFO and finance function roles for the next decade. Retrieved from: https://www.ifac.org/system/files/publications/files/IFAC-Future-Fit-Accountant-ROLES-V5-Singles.pdf

29 CPA Canada. (2019). Foresight: The way forward. Retrieved August 25, 2020, from: https://www.cpacanada.ca/foresight-report/en/index.html#page=1
30 Busulwa, R., Tice, M., & Gurd, B. (2018). Strategy execution and complexity: Thriving in the era of disruption. Routledge.
31 IFAC. (2019). Future-fit accountants: CFO and finance function roles for the next decade. Retrieved from: https://www.ifac.org/system/files/publications/files/IFAC-Future-Fit-Accountant-ROLES-V5-Singles.pdf
32 Coyne, J.G., Coyne, E.M., & Walker, K.B. (2016). A model to update accounting curricula for emerging technologies. Journal of Emerging Technologies in Accounting, 13(1), 161–169.
33 IFAC. (2019). Future-fit accountants: CFO and finance function roles for the next decade. Retrieved from: https://www.ifac.org/system/files/publications/files/IFAC-Future-Fit-Accountant-ROLES-V5-Singles.pdf
34 ACCA. (2020). Future ready: Accountancy careers in the 2020s. Retrieved from: https://www.accaglobal.com/in/en/professional-insights/pro-accountants-the-future/future_ready_2020s.html
35 IFAC. (2019). Future-fit Accountants: CFO and finance function roles for the next decade. Retrieved from: https://www.ifac.org/system/files/publications/files/IFAC-Future-Fit-Accountant-ROLES-V5-Singles.pdf
36 IFAC. (2019). Future-fit accountants: CFO and finance function roles for the next decade. Retrieved from: https://www.ifac.org/system/files/publications/files/IFAC-Future-Fit-Accountant-ROLES-V5-Singles.pdf
37 IFAC. (2019). Future-fit accountants: CFO and finance function roles for the next decade. Retrieved from: https://www.ifac.org/system/files/publications/files/IFAC-Future-Fit-Accountant-ROLES-V5-Singles.pdf
38 IFAC. (2019). Future-fit accountants: CFO and finance function roles for the next decade. Retrieved from: https://www.ifac.org/system/files/publications/files/IFAC-Future-Fit-Accountant-ROLES-V5-Singles.pdf
39 Busulwa, R., Tice, M., & Gurd, B. (2018). Strategy execution and complexity: Thriving in the era of disruption. Routledge.
40 Busulwa, R., Tice, M., & Gurd, B. (2018). Strategy execution and complexity: Thriving in the era of disruption. Routledge.
41 IFAC. (2019). Future-fit accountants: CFO and finance function roles for the next decade. Retrieved from: https://www.ifac.org/system/files/publications/files/IFAC-Future-Fit-Accountant-ROLES-V5-Singles.pdf
42 Galford, R., & Drapeau, A. S. (2003). The enemies of trust. Harvard Business Review, 81(2), 88–95.
43 Galford, R., & Drapeau, A. S. (2003). The enemies of trust. Harvard Business Review, 81(2), 88–95.
44 ACCA. (2020). Future ready: Accountancy careers in the 2020s. Retrieved from: https://www.accaglobal.com/in/en/professional-insights/pro-accountants-the-future/future_ready_2020s.html
45 ACCA. (2020). Future ready: Accountancy careers in the 2020s. Retrieved from: https://www.accaglobal.com/in/en/professional-insights/pro-accountants-the-future/future_ready_2020s.html
46 ACCA. (2020). Future ready: Accountancy careers in the 2020s. Retrieved from: https://www.accaglobal.com/in/en/professional-insights/pro-accountants-the-future/future_ready_2020s.html
47 ACCA. (2020). Future ready: Accountancy careers in the 2020s. Retrieved from: https://www.accaglobal.com/in/en/professional-insights/pro-accountants-the-future/future_ready_2020s.html
48 ACCA. (2020). Future ready: Accountancy careers in the 2020s. Retrieved from: https://www.accaglobal.com/in/en/professional-insights/pro-accountants-the-future/future_ready_2020s.html
49 ACCA. (2020). Future ready: Accountancy careers in the 2020s. Retrieved from: https://www.accaglobal.com/in/en/professional-insights/pro-accountants-the-future/future_ready_2020s.html
50 ACCA. (2020). Future ready: Accountancy careers in the 2020s. Retrieved from: https://www.accaglobal.com/in/en/professional-insights/pro-accountants-the-future/future_ready_2020s.html
51 ACCA. (2020). Future ready: Accountancy careers in the 2020s. Retrieved from: https://www.accaglobal.com/in/en/professional-insights/pro-accountants-the-future/future_ready_2020s.html
52 ACCA. (2020). Future ready: Accountancy careers in the 2020s. Retrieved from: https://www.accaglobal.com/in/en/professional-insights/pro-accountants-the-future/future_ready_2020s.html
53 ACCA. (2020). Future ready: Accountancy careers in the 2020s. Retrieved from: https://www.accaglobal.com/in/en/professional-insights/pro-accountants-the-future/future_ready_2020s.html
54 ACCA. (2020). Future ready: Accountancy careers in the 2020s. Retrieved from: https://www.accaglobal.com/in/en/professional-insights/pro-accountants-the-future/future_ready_2020s.html

55 ACCA. (2020). Future ready: Accountancy careers in the 2020s. Retrieved from: https://www.accaglobal.com/in/en/professional-insights/pro-accountants-the-future/future_ready_2020s.html
56 ACCA. (2020). Future ready: Accountancy careers in the 2020s. Retrieved from: https://www.accaglobal.com/in/en/professional-insights/pro-accountants-the-future/future_ready_2020s.html
57 ACCA. (2020). Future ready: Accountancy careers in the 2020s. Retrieved from: https://www.accaglobal.com/in/en/professional-insights/pro-accountants-the-future/future_ready_2020s.html
58 Seele, P. (2016). Digitally unified reporting: How XBRL-based real-time transparency helps in combining integrated sustainability reporting and performance control. Journal of Cleaner Production, 136, 65–77.
59 Lawson, R.A., Blocher, E.J., Brewer, P.C., Cokins, G., Sorensen, J.E., Stout, D.E., ... & Wouters, M.J. (2014). Focusing accounting curricula on students' long-run careers: Recommendations for an integrated competency-based framework for accounting education. Issues in Accounting Education, 29(2), 295–317.
60 Lawson, R.A., Blocher, E.J., Brewer, P.C., Cokins, G., Sorensen, J.E., Stout, D.E., ... & Wouters, M.J. (2014). Focusing accounting curricula on students' long-run careers: Recommendations for an integrated competency-based framework for accounting education. Issues in Accounting Education, 29(2), 295–317.
61 Lawson, R.A., Blocher, E.J., Brewer, P.C., Cokins, G., Sorensen, J.E., Stout, D.E., ... & Wouters, M.J. (2014). Focusing accounting curricula on students' long-run careers: Recommendations for an integrated competency-based framework for accounting education. Issues in Accounting Education, 29(2), 295–317.
62 Janvrin, D.J., & Watson, M.W. (2017). "Big data": A new twist to accounting. Journal of Accounting Education, 38, 3–8.
63 Pathways Commission. (2012). The Pathways Commission on higher education: Charting a national strategy for the next generation of accountants. The American Accounting Association and the American Institute of Certified Public Accountants. Retrieved from: http://commons.aaahq.org/files/0b14318188/Pathways_Commission_Final_Report_Complete.pdf
64 Adapted from Lawson, R.A., Blocher, E.J., Brewer, P.C., Cokins, G., Sorensen, J.E., Stout, D.E., ... & Wouters, M.J. (2014). Focusing accounting curricula on students' long-run careers: Recommendations for an integrated competency-based framework for accounting education. Issues in Accounting Education, 29(2), 295–317.
65 Coyne, J.G., Coyne, E.M., & Walker, K.B. (2016). A model to update accounting curricula for emerging technologies. Journal of Emerging Technologies in Accounting, 13(1), 161–169.
66 Coyne, J.G., Coyne, E.M., & Walker, K.B. (2016). A model to update accounting curricula for emerging technologies. Journal of Emerging Technologies in Accounting, 13(1), 161–169.
67 Sledgianowski, D., Gomaa, M., & Tan, C. (2017). Toward integration of big data, technology and information systems competencies into the accounting curriculum. Journal of Accounting Education, 38, 81–93.
68 Coyne, J.G., Coyne, E.M., & Walker, K.B. (2016). A model to update accounting curricula for emerging technologies. Journal of Emerging Technologies in Accounting, 13(1), 161–169.
69 Sledgianowski, D., Gomaa, M., & Tan, C. (2017). Toward integration of big data, technology and information systems competencies into the accounting curriculum. Journal of Accounting Education, 38, 81–93.
70 Coyne, J.G., Coyne, E.M., & Walker, K.B. (2016). A model to update accounting curricula for emerging technologies. Journal of Emerging Technologies in Accounting, 13(1), 161–169.
71 CPA Canada. (2020). Why should CPAs Code? Retrieved from: https://www.cpacanada.ca/-/media/site/operational/rg-research-guidance-and-support/docs/02355-rg-why-should-cpas-code-jan-2020.pdf?la=en&hash=94C6E3DD1C5A5CECDBC0CDAE41A7A92361864180
72 Coyne, J.G., Coyne, E.M., & Walker, K.B. (2016). A model to update accounting curricula for emerging technologies. Journal of Emerging Technologies in Accounting, 13(1), 161–169.
73 Coyne, J.G., Coyne, E.M., & Walker, K.B. (2016). A model to update accounting curricula for emerging technologies. Journal of Emerging Technologies in Accounting, 13(1), 161–169.
74 CPA Canada. (2020). Why should CPAs Code? Retrieved from: https://www.cpacanada.ca/-/media/site/operational/rg-research-guidance-and-support/docs/02355-rg-why-should-cpas-code-jan-2020.pdf?la=en&hash=94C6E3DD1C5A5CECDBC0CDAE41A7A92361864180
75 CPA Canada. (2020). Why should CPAs Code? Retrieved from: https://www.cpacanada.ca/-/media/site/operational/rg-research-guidance-and-support/docs/02355-rg-why-should-cpas-code-jan-2020.pdf?la=en&hash=94C6E3DD1C5A5CECDBC0CDAE41A7A92361864180

76 Sledgianowski, D., Gomaa, M., & Tan, C. (2017). Toward integration of big data, technology and information systems competencies into the accounting curriculum. Journal of Accounting Education, 38, 81–93.
77 Coyne, J.G., Coyne, E.M., & Walker, K.B. (2016). A model to update accounting curricula for emerging technologies. Journal of Emerging Technologies in Accounting, 13(1), 161–169.
78 Coyne, J.G., Coyne, E.M., & Walker, K.B. (2016). A model to update accounting curricula for emerging technologies. Journal of Emerging Technologies in Accounting, 13(1), 161–169.
79 Coyne, J.G., Coyne, E.M., & Walker, K.B. (2016). A model to update accounting curricula for emerging technologies. Journal of Emerging Technologies in Accounting, 13(1), 161–169.
80 Coyne, J.G., Coyne, E.M., & Walker, K.B. (2016). A model to update accounting curricula for emerging technologies. Journal of Emerging Technologies in Accounting, 13(1), 161–169.
81 Coyne, J.G., Coyne, E.M., & Walker, K.B. (2016). A model to update accounting curricula for emerging technologies. Journal of Emerging Technologies in Accounting, 13(1), 161–169.
82 IFAC. (2017a). Developing a future ready profession. Retrieved from: https://www.ifac.org/system/files/publications/files/Developing-a-Future-Ready-Profession.pdf
83 IFAC. (2019). Future-fit accountants: CFO and finance function roles for the next decade. Retrieved from: https://www.ifac.org/system/files/publications/files/IFAC-Future-Fit-Accountant-ROLES-V5-Singles.pdf
84 IFAC. (2017a). Developing a future ready profession. Retrieved from: https://www.ifac.org/system/files/publications/files/Developing-a-Future-Ready-Profession.pdf
85 IFAC. (2019). Future-fit Accountants: CFO and finance function roles for the next decade. Retrieved from: https://www.ifac.org/system/files/publications/files/IFAC-Future-Fit-Accountant-ROLES-V5-Singles.pdf
86 IFAC. (2017a). Developing a future ready profession. Retrieved from: https://www.ifac.org/system/files/publications/files/Developing-a-Future-Ready-Profession.pdf
87 IFAC. (2019). Future-fit accountants: CFO and finance function roles for the next decade. Retrieved from: https://www.ifac.org/system/files/publications/files/IFAC-Future-Fit-Accountant-ROLES-V5-Singles.pdf
88 IFAC. (2017a). Developing a future ready profession. Retrieved from: https://www.ifac.org/system/files/publications/files/Developing-a-Future-Ready-Profession.pdf
89 IFAC. (2017a). Developing a future ready profession. Retrieved from: https://www.ifac.org/system/files/publications/files/Developing-a-Future-Ready-Profession.pdf
90 Sledgianowski, D., Gomaa, M., & Tan, C. (2017). Toward integration of big data, technology and information systems competencies into the accounting curriculum. Journal of Accounting Education, 38, 81_93.
91 IFAC. (2017a). Developing a future ready profession. Retrieved from: https://www.ifac.org/system/files/publications/files/Developing-a-Future-Ready-Profession.pdf
92 AFP. (2017). Emerging technologies and the finance function. Retrieved from: https://www.afponline.org/docs/default-source/default-document-library/pub/afp-mindshift_emergingtech.pdf?sfvrsn=2
93 IFAC. (2017a). Developing a future ready profession. Retrieved from: https://www.ifac.org/system/files/publications/files/Developing-a-Future-Ready-Profession.pdf
94 AFP. (2017). Emerging technologies and the finance function. Retrieved from: https://www.afponline.org/docs/default-source/default-document-library/pub/afp-mindshift_emergingtech.pdf?sfvrsn=2
95 AFA. (2019). Impact of technology to the accounting profession. AFA Connect. Retrieved from: http://www.afa-accountants.org/files/AFA_Connect_03_-_June_2019_(A5)_-_16_Juli_2019.pdf
96 Lynch, E.J., & Andiola, L.M. (2019). If eyes are the window to our soul, what role does eye-tracking play in accounting research?. Behavioral Research in Accounting, 31(2), 107–133.
97 AFP. (2017). Emerging technologies and the finance function. Retrieved from: https://www.afponline.org/docs/default-source/default-document-library/pub/afp-mindshift_emergingtech.pdf?sfvrsn=2
98 AFP. (2017). Emerging technologies and the finance function. Retrieved from: https://www.afponline.org/docs/default-source/default-document-library/pub/afp-mindshift_emergingtech.pdf?sfvrsn=2
99 AFP. (2017). Emerging technologies and the finance function. Retrieved from: https://www.afponline.org/docs/default-source/default-document-library/pub/afp-mindshift_emergingtech.pdf?sfvrsn=2

100 AFP. (2017). Emerging technologies and the finance function. Retrieved from: https://www.afponline.org/docs/default-source/default-document-library/pub/afp-mindshift_emergingtech.pdf?sfvrsn=2
101 AFP. (2017). Emerging technologies and the finance function. Retrieved from: https://www.afponline.org/docs/default-source/default-document-library/pub/afp-mindshift_emergingtech.pdf?sfvrsn=2
102 AFP. (2017). Emerging technologies and the finance function. Retrieved from: https://www.afponline.org/docs/default-source/default-document-library/pub/afp-mindshift_emergingtech.pdf?sfvrsn=2
103 AFP. (2017). Emerging technologies and the finance function. Retrieved from: https://www.afponline.org/docs/default-source/default-document-library/pub/afp-mindshift_emergingtech.pdf?sfvrsn=2
104 AFP. (2017). Emerging technologies and the finance function. Retrieved from: https://www.afponline.org/docs/default-source/default-document-library/pub/afp-mindshift_emergingtech.pdf?sfvrsn=2
105 AFP. (2017). Emerging technologies and the finance function. Retrieved from: https://www.afponline.org/docs/default-source/default-document-library/pub/afp-mindshift_emergingtech.pdf?sfvrsn=2
106 Janvrin, D.J., & Watson, M.W. (2017). "Big data": A new twist to accounting. Journal of Accounting Education, 38, 3–8.
107 Gould, S. (2019). Building data science and analytics capabilities in finance and accounting. IFAC. Retrieved September 2, 2020, from: https://www.ifac.org/knowledge-gateway/preparing-future-ready-professionals/discussion/building-data-science-and-analytics-capabilities-finance-and-accounting
108 Janvrin, D.J., & Watson, M.W. (2017). "Big data": A new twist to accounting. Journal of Accounting Education, 38, 3–8.
109 Pincus, K.V., Stout, D.E., Sorensen, J.E., Stocks, K.D., & Lawson, R.A. (2017). Forces for change in higher education and implications for the accounting academy. Journal of Accounting Education, 40, 1–18.
110 Moffitt, K.C., Rozario, A.M., & Vasarhelyi, M.A. (2018). Robotic process automation for auditing. Journal of Emerging Technologies in Accounting, 15(1), 1–10.
111 Pan, G., & Seow, P.S. (2016). Preparing accounting graduates for digital revolution: A critical review of information technology competencies and skills development. Journal of Education for business, 91(3), 166–175.
112 Sledgianowski, D., Gomaa, M., & Tan, C. (2017). Toward integration of big data, technology and information systems competencies into the accounting curriculum. Journal of Accounting Education, 38, 81–93.
113 Pan, G., & Seow, P. S. (2016). Preparing accounting graduates for digital revolution: A critical review of information technology competencies and skills development. Journal of Education for business, 91(3), 166–175.
114 Lawson, R.A., Blocher, E.J., Brewer, P.C., Cokins, G., Sorensen, J.E., Stout, D.E., ... & Wouters, M.J. (2014). Focusing accounting curricula on students' long-run careers: Recommendations for an integrated competency-based framework for accounting education. Issues in Accounting Education, 29(2), 295–317.
115 Janvrin, D.J., & Watson, M.W. (2017). "Big data": A new twist to accounting. Journal of Accounting Education, 38, 3–8.
116 Moffitt, K.C., Rozario, A.M., & Vasarhelyi, M.A. (2018). Robotic process automation for auditing. Journal of Emerging Technologies in Accounting, 15(1), 1–10.
117 CPA Canada. (2020). Why should CPAs code? Retrieved from: https://www.cpacanada.ca/-/media/site/operational/rg-research-guidance-and-support/docs/02355-rg-why-should-cpas-code-jan-2020.pdf?la=en&hash=94C6E3DD1C5A5CECDBC0CDAE41A7A92361864180
118 CPA Canada. (2020). Audit considerations related to cryptocurrency assets and transactions. Retrieved from: https://www.iasplus.com/en-ca/publications/cpa-canada/audit-considerations-related-to-cryptocurrency-assets-and-transactions
119 Liu, M., Wu, K., & Xu, J.J. (2019). How will blockchain technology impact auditing and accounting: Permissionless versus permissioned blockchain. Current Issues in Auditing, 13(2), A19–A29.
120 Sledgianowski, D., Gomaa, M., & Tan, C. (2017). Toward integration of big data, technology and information systems competencies into the accounting curriculum. Journal of Accounting Education, 38, 81–93.

121 Sledgianowski, D., Gomaa, M., & Tan, C. (2017). Toward integration of big data, technology and information systems competencies into the accounting curriculum. Journal of Accounting Education, 38, 81–93.
122 Gould, S. (2019). Building data science and analytics capabilities in finance and accounting. Retrieved September 2, 2020, from: https://www.ifac.org/knowledge-gateway/preparing-future-ready-professionals/discussion/building-data-science-and-analytics-capabilities-finance-and-accounting
123 Rigby, D. K., Elk, S., & Berez, S. (2020). The agile c-suite. Harvard Business Review, (May–June).
124 Pereira, J.C., & de FSM Russo, R. (2018). Design thinking integrated in agile software development: A systematic literature review. Procedia computer science, 138, 775–782.
125 Fan, D. (2019). Embrace design thinking to advance diversity, equity and inclusion. Retrieved September 21, 2020, from: https://www.chieflearningofficer.com/2019/12/30/embrace-design-thinking-to-advance-diversity-equity-and-inclusion/
126 Fan, D. (2019). Embrace design thinking to advance diversity, equity and inclusion. Retrieved September 21, 2020, from: https://www.chieflearningofficer.com/2019/12/30/embrace-design-thinking-to-advance-diversity-equity-and-inclusion/
127 Davis, J.P., Eisenhardt, K.M., & Bingham, C.B. (2009). Optimal structure, market dynamism, and the strategy of simple rules. Administrative Science Quarterly, 54(3), 413–452.
128 Busulwa, R., Tice, M., & Gurd, B. (2018). Strategy execution and complexity: Thriving in the era of disruption. Routledge.
129 Busulwa, R., Tice, M., & Gurd, B. (2018). Strategy execution and complexity: Thriving in the era of disruption. Routledge.
130 ACCA. (2020). How companies are profiting from design thinking. Retrieved from: https://www.accaglobal.com/gb/en/member/member/accounting-business/2020/04/corporate/design-thinking.html
131 Fullerton, R.R., Kennedy, F.A., & Widener, S.K. (2014). Lean manufacturing and firm performance: The incremental contribution of lean management accounting practices. Journal of Operations Management, 32(7-8), 414–428.
132 Busulwa, R., Tice, M., & Gurd, B. (2018). Strategy execution and complexity: Thriving in the era of disruption. Routledge.
133 Busulwa, R., Birdthistle, N., & Dunn, S. (2020). Startup accelerators: A field guide. John Wiley & Sons.
134 Spaulding, E., & Caimi, G. (2016). Hackathons aren't just for coders. Harvard Business Review, (April 1).
135 Rosell, B., Kumar, S., & Shepherd, J. (2014). Unleashing innovation through internal hackathons. 2014 IEEE Innovations in Technology Conference. https://doi.org/10.1109/innotek.2014.6877369
136 Moschner, S.L., Fink, A.A., Kurpjuweit, S., Wagner, S.M., & Herstatt, C. (2019). Toward a better understanding of corporate accelerator models. Business Horizons, 62(5), 637–647.
137 CGMA. (2020). The CGMA Competency framework guide and tool. (2020, February 3). Retrieved from https://www.cgma.org/resources/tools/cgma-competency-framework/cgma-competency-framework-guide.html
138 Busulwa, R., Tice, M., & Gurd, B. (2018). Strategy execution and complexity: Thriving in the era of disruption. Routledge.
139 Busulwa, R., Tice, M., & Gurd, B. (2018). Strategy execution and complexity: Thriving in the era of disruption. Routledge.
140 Snowden, D.J., & Boone, M.E. (2007). A leader's framework for decision making. Harvard Business Review, 85(11), 68.
141 Bennett, N., & Lemoine, G.J. (2014). What a difference a word makes: Understanding threats to performance in a VUCA world. Business Horizons, 57(3), 311–317.
142 Reeves, M., Love, C., & Tillmanns, P. (2012). Your strategy needs a strategy. Harvard Business Review, 90(9), 76–83.
143 Busulwa, R., Tice, M., & Gurd, B. (2018). Strategy execution and complexity: Thriving in the era of disruption. Routledge.
144 Busulwa, R., Tice, M., & Gurd, B. (2018). Strategy execution and complexity: Thriving in the era of disruption. Routledge.
145 Snowden, D.J., & Boone, M.E. (2007). A leader's framework for decision making. Harvard Business Review, 85(11), 68.

146 Busulwa, R., Tice, M., & Gurd, B. (2018). Strategy execution and complexity: Thriving in the era of disruption. Routledge.
147 Busulwa, R., Tice, M., & Gurd, B. (2018). Strategy execution and complexity: Thriving in the era of disruption. Routledge.
148 Rong, G., & Grover, V. (2009). Keeping up-to-date with information technology: Testing a model of technological knowledge renewal effectiveness for IT professionals. Information & Management, 46(7), 376–387.

Part III

Leveraging digital technologies to thrive in the digital era

Roles of accountants in organization digital business capabilities

7 The role of accountants in digital transformation strategy, digital business strategy, digital innovation, digital learning, adaptability, and agility

Introduction

Becoming a digital business, and effectively competing as a digital business, requires organizations to have unique digital capabilities that are referred to as digital business capabilities. In this part of the book, we look at the digital business capabilities critical to becoming a digital business, to effectively competing as a digital business, to maintaining adaptiveness to ongoing digital disruption, and to making the most of the game-changing opportunities continuing digital technology advancements have to offer. This specific chapter looks at digital transformation strategy (a capability critical to becoming digital business), digital business strategy and digital innovation (capabilities critical to effectively competing as a digital business), adaptability (a capability critical to adapting to ongoing digital disruption), and digital learning and agility (capabilities critical to keeping up with digital technology advancements and seizing the new opportunities they offer). Building, sustaining, and optimizing digital business capabilities is the responsibility of strategic leaders and managers. But accountants can play critical business partnering, trusted advisor, and information provision / assurance roles that enhance and catalyze managers' ability to fulfil their digital business capability responsibilities and aims. To effectively play these roles, accountants have to first understand each digital business capability, and then understand the different roles managers need to play in the building / sustaining / optimization of the capability. Armed with such understanding, they will be well positioned to spot opportunities to better support and catalyze managers' digital business capability-related efforts. The aim of this chapter is to provide a foundation for such an understanding that accountants can build on in their ongoing learning in relation to each digital business capability. Figure 7.1 shows how traditional business capabilities and digital business capabilities have similar aims (improved business performance and longevity). However, they differ in their ability to deliver on those common aims. Digital transformation is required to effect digital business capabilities. And effecting digital transformation also requires particular capabilities (e.g. digital transformation strategy, digital leadership).

The role of accountants in digital business strategy and digital transformation strategy

Unpacking digital business strategy

Digital business strategy is strategy formed and realized by leveraging digital resources to achieve breakthroughs in efficiency, differentiation, adaptability, and agility[1]. It fuses

112 *Leveraging digital technologies*

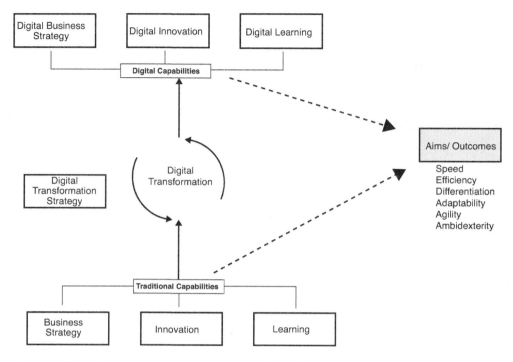

Figure 7.1 Digital business requires new organizational capabilities or digital enhancements of traditional capabilities to achieve the same or enhanced aims to traditional business

together the domains of information systems and business strategy so that, rather than being positioned below business strategy, or being a component of business strategy (like traditional IT strategy), digital business strategy becomes business strategy itself[2]. This is because digital technology advancements continue to rapidly fuse together people, processes, technologies, networks, and things within and outside organizations (or blur the boundaries between them) to such a degree that conceiving strategy separately is increasingly becoming counterproductive. When digital business strategy becomes the business strategy itself, it is able to be a strategic dynamic capability that enables organizations to dynamically configure and orchestrate diverse digital assets to respond to, and shape, changes in marketplaces[3].

Jeanne Ross and Ina Sebastian, researchers at the MIT Centre for Information Systems Research, and Cynthia Beath, emerita professor of information systems at the University of Texas, propose that a great digital business strategy sets a clear direction[4]. In doing so, it enables managers to form and lead digital initiatives, to assess their progress against the set direction, and to adapt their efforts as required[5]. Sunil Gupta, professor of business administration at Harvard Business School, and chair of the executive program on driving digital strategy, warns that digital business strategy shouldn't just be thought of as having an independent digital unit or running digital experiments. That the former is like launching a speedboat to turn around a large ship (lots of activity and speed but it does not move the ship); and the latter, without a clear roadmap, may result in proliferation of disjointed ideas that don't address fundamental strategic issues[6]. He also cautions that, while organizations should always pursue cost reduction and operational efficiency, viewing digital business strategy solely as leveraging technology to reduce costs and improve operational efficiency ignores the potential (and high likelihood) of technology fundamentally disrupting the business and its industry[7]. This is consistent with the thinking of Jeanne Ross, Ina Sebastian, and Cynthia Beath, who clarify that operational excellence (efficiency and effectiveness) is a digital business commodity, not a basis for competitive advantage. These three researchers also argue that organizations should choose between a customer engagement strategy (one that "targets superior, personalized experiences that engender customer loyalty"), or a digitized solutions strategy (one that "targets information-enriched products and services that deliver new value for customers") and not attempt both, as they risk doing both badly[8].

Digital business strategy is about managers determining what combination of digital assets to leverage, and how to leverage them to effectively compete as a digital business. Effectively competing as a digital business requires competing on new and evolving bases of competition such as being able to rapidly flex operations up or down in response to disruptions or changes in demand (e.g. elastic cloud infrastructure)[9], benefiting from network effects and multi-sided business models[10], being able to scale rapidly (e.g. between 1996 and 1999 Amazon grew from 151 employees generating US$5.1 million revenue to 7,600 employees generating $1.64 billion revenue)[11,12], being part of shared digital asset alliances and partnerships (e.g. hospitality and leisure organizations that share reservation systems, loyalty programs, and online cross selling – such as Star Alliance and OneWorld), executing with speed (e.g. speed to market of new products, matching speed of complementary product partners and of competitors, speed of decision-making, real-time customer sensing and responsiveness, speed of supply chain orchestration, speed of network formation and adaptation, etc.)[13], and expanding value creation / capture opportunities (e.g. leveraging growing data availability for product innovation, creating and capturing value from coordinating different business models in networks, building and controlling industry platforms and ecosystems)[14].

The difference between digital transformation strategy and digital business strategy

Whereas digital business strategy focuses on "future states" and how to realize them, *digital transformation strategy* focuses on having, and effecting, the blueprint for navigating the structural and cultural changes required to integrate, and be able to leverage digital technologies to effectively compete as a digital business[15]. Thus, digital business strategy and digital transformation strategy differ, but go hand in hand. For organizations that aren't fully digital, doing both digital business strategy and digital transformation strategy right offers levels of breakthroughs in efficiency, product / service value differentiation, adaptability, and agility that aren't possible without both capabilities. Doing both right can shift organizations into the category of disruptors – organizations that are often rewarded with a lion's share of value capture across markets, industries, and geographies. In contrast, turning a blind eye to digital transformation strategy or digital business strategy capabilities, or doing them in a tokenistic / half-measured manner, is usually the path to loss of competitiveness, disruption, and potentially irreversible survival risks (e.g. at a certain point, organizations like Blockbuster and Kodak could not turn back time and reorient themselves to successfully undertake digital transformation and to effectively compete as digital businesses).

New or enhanced accounting roles and competencies required for digital business strategy and digital transformation strategy

Managers and leaders at all levels and in all parts of an organization need to play critical roles in digital business strategy and digital transformation strategy. These roles include leading the formation and realization of a digital business strategy (e.g. establishing a clear mission / vision / direction for digital business, identifying and leading digital business initiatives, motivating people at different levels and in different parts of the organization to participate in the building and leveraging of digital business capabilities, aligning digital business efforts, etc.), participating in digital business strategy formation (e.g. contributing ideas for business model innovations, digital assets to implement and leverage, networks / ecosystems / communities to participate in, product / service innovations, customer experience innovations, etc.), and championing and supporting digital business strategy initiatives and cultural changes (e.g. leveraging their formal and informal networks to encourage employees to understand and embrace digital business strategy initiatives, ensuring their direct reports have relevant knowledge and skills, modelling appropriate attitudes and behaviors). Accountants can play critical business partnering and information provision / assurance roles that catalyze managers and other leaders' effectiveness in fulfilling the roles we have just described. Through accounting roles such as the business transformer, the digital playmaker, the co-pilot, the navigator, the process and control expert, and the digital and technology enabler, accountants can supercharge managers' and leaders' digital transformation and digital business capability building and maintenance activities.

To effectively support and catalyze managers' and leaders' digital business strategy and digital transformation strategy efforts, accountants need corresponding digital competencies. We propose that these digital competencies include having an understanding of different digital technology advancements and their strategic implications (e.g. what product / service opportunities and what business model opportunities do advancements in internet of things or IoT, artificial intelligence or AI, blockchain, robotics, and drones present?), having working knowledge of the technical aspects of these digital technologies (e.g. how do they work, what are their limitations and issues, what is really involved in implementing and using them, what is hype and what is reality in their value propositions), and having a working understanding of different digital business strategy approaches and benefits (e.g. different business models, approaches to digital infrastructure configuration, approaches to alliances and partnership, approaches to network and ecosystem participation, approaches to product innovation and enhancement, approaches to adaptability and agility, etc.). Further digital competencies include having a working understanding of digital business bases of competition and the value of key platforms and ecosystems, having a working understanding of digital transformation strategies and practices, and having a working understanding of accelerated change / transformation and accelerated innovation approaches (e.g. speed is critical to digital business strategy so managers leading digital strategy initiatives need to understand effective approaches to rapidly implementing and instituting digital business strategy and digital innovation initiatives – so they aren't undermined, rejected, or killed off by the wider organization. We have discussed examples of these accelerated change and transformation approaches including agile[16,17], lean thinking[18,19,20], lean startup[21], design thinking[22], accelerators[23], and change acceleration methods[24]).

The role of accountants in digital innovation

Unpacking digital innovation

From an organizational perspective, innovation refers to the introduction and application of new products, processes, and ideals that have a significant and positive net impact on organizational performance[25]. This definition of innovation refers to both the process or practice of innovating, as well as the outcomes of the innovation process. Thus, innovation discussions or efforts can be focusing on how innovation occurs (e.g. what processes, activities, stakeholders, tools are used), or on what types of new products / services / other benefits are realized from innovation efforts. Digital technology advancements, digital transformation, and digital business change or expand the nature of innovation, as well as the potential impact of innovation. That is, they change or expand how innovation can be done (i.e. what innovation processes / practices are used), the nature of innovation outcomes (i.e. what new products / processes / value can be created), and the impact of innovation outcomes (e.g. the scalability of innovation efforts or outcomes). The changed or expanded ways innovation can occur, the types of new products /services / value creations that can be created, and the speed / scope of innovation impacts that are possible due to digital technology advancements are referred to as *digital innovation*. Digital innovation has been formally defined by researchers as both the new products / services / business processes / business models and other forms of stakeholder value that are created through the use of digital technologies, and the process of using digital technologies to create (and subsequently change) these new products / services / business processes / business models and other forms of stakeholder value[26]. Other formal definitions of digital innovation include that it is "the carrying out of new combinations of digital and physical components to produce novel products"[27], that it is "the use of digital technologies in the process of innovating"[28], and that it is the infusion of digital technologies into innovation outcomes and processes[29].

Digital innovation differs from traditional innovation in four important ways. First, the nature of innovation outputs differs in that the outputs have digital or digital / physical hybrids that are programmable / reprogrammable[30]. Thus, they are malleable, editable, open, transferable, and continuously shifting. They can, and often need to, continue to be improved even once they are in customers' hands. This continued evolution / improvement can even be done by customers[31] or other stakeholders outside of the organization[32,33,34]. The outputs can be both products / services and platforms. The outputs can have several layers (e.g. device layer, network layer, service layer, content layer), with an organization competing on one layer but collaborating on another[35]. The outputs can be made to think for themselves, to continue to work for their creators (e.g. collecting data), to improve themselves (e.g. using AI), to collaborate with other outputs (e.g. AI / IoT products), to exist as orchestrated collections of other outputs, and more (e.g. Apple's iPhone can tick most of these characteristics). Second, the nature of the innovation process differs in that digital innovation processes are digitized, have blurred boundaries between stages of the innovation process (e.g. continuous iterative cycles of empathizing, defining, testing, releasing new innovations), they are much more fluid and non-linear, and more open[36]. For example, digital innovation processes can be both intra and / or interorganizational, and they can leverage community-based generativity and platform-based network effects (e.g. crowdsourcing, crowdfunding, network centric innovation platforms). Third, digital innovation differs from traditional innovation in that the innovation actors, or the people / entities / things doing the innovation aren't just employees. Instead, they can also include dynamic and often unexpected collections of actors (or innovation collectives) with different interests, motivations, abilities, and tools[37,38,39]. Concepts such as distributed innovation, open innovation, network centric innovation, shared cognition, and joint sense-making reflect different approaches to facilitating innovation among diverse actors[40,41,42]. Fourth, and finally, digital innovation involves use of different tools to facilitate the innovation process and to act as components in innovation outputs. For example, a broad swath of new digital technologies (e.g. 3D / 4D printing, AI, blockchain, big data) and tools (e.g. crowdsourcing / crowdfunding platforms, smart devices and algorithms, data analytics / data science models, etc.) can facilitate innovation processes or be built in as components in innovative new products[43,44,45]. Exponential growth in the number and abilities of these tools is rapidly expanding their role in facilitating innovation processes / practices, and as key components of innovation outputs[46]. Fortunately for innovation leaders and innovators, digital innovation can simplify, democratize, and drastically lower the cost of innovation processes and outputs. Table 7.1 provides examples of the different ways digital technology advancements impact digital innovation and provides examples of these impacts in action.

Table 7.1 Impact of digital technology advancements on digital innovation and examples of opportunities that can be leveraged[47]

Impact type	Impact description	Examples
Industry transformation	industry and market convergence; transformation of whole industries	Apple, Bonnier, Netflix, GM OnStar, 3D printing, digital convergence
Distinctive diffusion dynamics	standards wars; risk of stranding	VHS versus Beta; Apple Mac versus Windows; iPhone versus Android; HD DVD versus Blu-ray
Greater diversity of products and services	greater diversity of products and services developed and offered ("long tail" effect)	Netflix, Amazon, Hulu's customized ads, Zara's quicker and more localized market, social media / user-generated content
Greater personalization of products and services	greater personalization of novel processes, products, and services	personalization, mass customization, gamification
Faster innovation cycles and processes	more rapid development and evolution of innovative processes and products	Capital One, Shinsei Bank, Enterprise IT at SYSCO, Zara's Fast Fashion, CVS
Faster / broader product diffusion	accelerated emergence and faster / broader diffusion of new products and business models	DVD players, iPhones / smartphones, tablet computers, Facebook / social networking
Product pricing and delivery flexibility	increased control over how digital products are used, when, and by whom (e.g., bundling, trials, "freemium" models); greater pricing flexibility (e.g., how much is charged, to whom, when, by what mechanism, and for what level of functionality)	Napster, Rhapsody, Hulu, YouTube
New ways to market new products	new avenues for marketing and supporting new products	Google, Facebook, Twitter

Impact type	Impact description	Examples
Move to smart technologies and servitization	widespread emergence of "smart" technologies; accelerated move to servitization (converting products into services) and other kinds of new business models enabled by smart technologies	Rolls-Royce "power by the hour" Progressive Insurance Snapshot program, Zipcar, RFID, Smart Hospitals
Move to real-time question answering systems	new organizational processes and business models based on generalized real-time question answering systems	Apple Siri, streaming data analytics, IBM Watson
Creation of analytics-driven digital innovation opportunities	increased opportunities for process and product / business model innovation	Amazon, Capital One, Harrah's, business analytics
Democratized innovation	process and product innovation discovery and development becomes more open, democratized, and user-driven	Innocentive, P&G connect&develop, open prize competitions, Dell Ideastorm, Whirlpool's Innovation E-Space, Threadless

New or enhanced accounting roles and competencies required for digital innovation

Managers and leaders at all levels can play important roles in digital innovation. Examples of these roles include setting or clarifying the innovation vision and direction, effectively leading / managing / facilitating innovation processes, identifying / ensuring use of the right tools for optimizing innovation process and outcomes, effectively engaging innovation collectives across relevant networks and ecosystems, instituting the right mindsets and behaviors for digital innovation, building / continuously upgrading organizational innovation capacity, and ensuring the effective capture of organizational value from innovation efforts and outputs. Through their business partnering, trusted advisor, and information provision / assurance roles, accountants can enhance the effectiveness of managers in driving digital innovation. Examples of the specific accounting roles that can support digital innovation capability efforts include the business transformer, the digital playmaker, the co-pilot, the navigator, the process and control expert, and the digital and technology enabler roles. To effectively support managers' and leaders' digital innovation efforts, accountants need to understand digital innovation, have working knowledge of different digital innovation platforms / tools / methodologies, have a working knowledge of digital innovation collectives and how to best leverage them, have working knowledge of digital technologies important for innovation processes and innovation outputs, and have strong digital leadership skills.

The role of accountants in organizational digital learning

Unpacking digital learning

Organizations have long been interested in employee / workforce / workplace-based learning as a driver of competitive advantage and a safeguard to disruption or loss of competitiveness. To this end, they have been interested in how to optimize learning (maximize the knowledge / skills / abilities derived by employees from learning efforts and the value created from that learning), and have typically invested in upgrading their workforce learning capability. But for each gain they have made, digital technology advancements, in combination with unprecedented growth in complexity / uncertainty, regulation, compliance requirements, globalization, and competition, have exponentially expanded the nature and amount of learning required. This has resulted in many employees finding themselves unable to keep up with technological advances that affect their everyday work processes; as their knowledge / skills become obsolete quickly and new knowledge / skill requirements grow quickly[48] (e.g. new skills with big data, data analytics, and artificial intelligence). In response, companies have sought ways to close the learning gap (the gap between actual and required workforce knowledge / skills / abilities)[49]. As a result, workforce learning has evolved from traditional, instructor-centered, class-style delivery to become much more online, interactive, multidiscipline, multiplatform, multi-device, portable, user-centered / personalized, self-directed, gamified, always on anywhere / anytime / real-time, immersive, and social, etc.[50]. These evolutions have largely been made possible by digital technology advancements.

Digital learning, then, is employee learning that leverages digital technologies in the learning process, learning content, and / or learning outcomes. It has been described as both planned and / or unplanned, implicit and / or explicit, multi-technology and / or multi-device, intentional and / or unintentional, spontaneous / unconscious and / or defined, independent / autonomous and / or directed / controlled, and occurring in the workplace or outside it[51,52]. It differs from traditional learning in that the nature / characteristics of the learning process are significantly transformed, the learning context is significantly transformed, the teaching methodologies are significantly transformed, the learning participants are expanded, and the learning systems and tools are significantly transformed. The nature and characteristics of digital learning include it being much more online, interactive, multidiscipline, multiplatform, multi-device, portable, user-centered / personalized, self-directed, gamified, always on anywhere / anytime / real-time, immersive, and social etc. Teaching methods wise, digital learning differs from traditional learning in that new teaching methods / approaches are used that better involve learners in the learning process and optimize learning efficiency and effectiveness[53,54]. Examples of these methodologies / approaches include project-based learning, problem-based learning, online learning environments, digital moments, technology integrated teaching methods, digital storytelling, educational games, and authentic learning[55,56]. Learning contexts wise, digital learning differs from traditional learning in that learning contexts which support new and more effective pedagogical models are used. Examples of these include collaborative communities, cooperative learning, collaborative learning, digital combinational systems, digital media-based flipped classrooms, online spaces, experiential online development, open educational practice, and network participation[57,58]. Learning participants wise, digital learning differs from traditional learning in that the participants are expanded to include collaborative community participants, cooperative / collaborative learning participants, network participants, and software algorithms[59,60]. Finally, digital learning differs from traditional learning in that it leverages a diverse collection of digital technology platforms and tools to provide / maintain the learning context, facilitate the learning process, support learners, and report on the effectiveness of both learning processes and learning outcomes. Examples of such tools include web-based video applications, narrated stop-motion animation applications, augmented reality applications, webinar applications, learning management systems (LMS), YouTube, Facebook, Instagram, Wikipedia, LinkedIn, Google / other search engines, mobile learning apps, learning object repositories, Blackboard, Moodle

Learning Manager, Collaborate Ultra, Zoom, Twitter, massive open online courses (MOOC), etc.[61,62].

New or enhanced accounting roles and competencies required for digital learning

Effective digital learning can engage, empower, motivate, and retain employees. In turn, this can accelerate organizational efficiency, adaptability, and agility; and become a strong base for competitive advantage. Managers and leaders at all levels can play important roles in optimizing digital learning. Examples of these roles include setting or clarifying the digital learning vision and direction, effectively leading / managing / facilitating digital learning processes, identifying / ensuring use of the right tools for optimizing digital learning process and outcomes, ensuring access to the best content, identifying / ensuring use of the most effective teaching methodologies and pedagogical models, inspiring and motivating employees to make the most of available learning opportunities, instituting the right mindsets and behaviors for digital learning, building / continuously upgrading organization digital learning capacity, and ensuring effective capture of organizational value from digital learning efforts and outputs. In their business partnering and information provision / assurance roles, accountants can catalyze and improve the effectiveness of managers' and leaders' efforts to build and continuously improve digital learning organizational digital learning capability. In order to support leaders and managers in this way, accountants need to understand digital learning, have working knowledge of different digital learning platforms / tools / methodologies / pedagogical models, have working knowledge of digital technologies important for the digital learning process and to digital learning outputs, and have sufficient digital leadership skills.

The role of accountants in organizational adaptability, agility, and ambidexterity

Unpacking adaptability, agility, and ambidexterity

We previously defined *adaptability* as the ability to dynamically reconfigure routines, processes, and practices to suit the demands of unexpected internal and external events or disruptions. And we defined *agility* as the capacity for flexibility and speed in sensing and responding to such events and disruptions, especially external ones. For example, an agile organization is able to anticipate / spot / understand disruptions (like Covid-19) early, and is able to efficiently and effectively redeploy / redirect its resources to value creating / value capturing / value protecting activities dynamically as the situation warrants[63]. In contrast, we defined *ambidexterity* as having the ability to ensure efficiency / effectiveness in the organization's existing products / services while at the same time ensuring the organization undertakes the exploratory activities necessary to discover future winning products and services[64].

We noted that adaptability capabilities are critical to enabling organizations to reconfigure their operations and offerings to surprising internal and external events such as the global financial crisis (which resulted in lack of access to new credit, clawing back of approved credit facilities, growth in payment defaults, a sharp decline in consumer demand, and the drying up of working capital) or the Covid-19 pandemic (which resulted in social distancing and travel restrictions, inability of staff to attend workplaces, procurement challenges, sharp declines in product / service demand, restrictions on ways in which organizations could serve customers, etc.)[65]. Organizations with established adaptability capabilities would have had the relevant infrastructure, processes, talent, culture, and financial resources to enable them to reconfigure their operations in response to these surprising events or disruptions. For example, during the Covid-19 pandemic, hospitality and leisure organizations that had made significant progress with their digital transformation efforts were able to have their workforce work from home, undertake meaningful work that contributed to the organization's future adaptive capacity, offer existing or new products virtually, and do all of this without compromising customers' and employees' safety and privacy. Organizations with established agility capabilities are able to sense / anticipate surprising events and disruptions, are able to effect fast responses to seize the corresponding opportunities or react to the threats, and have the flexibility to dynamically vary their responses as the situation requires[66]. Organizations with established ambidexterity capabilities are able to build, maintain, and use their adaptability and agility capabilities without those capabilities materially compromising their established operational processes[67].

Digital technology advancements are key drivers of the need for adaptability, agility, and ambidexterity. But paradoxically, they offer unparalleled opportunities to build, maintain, and use adaptability, agility, and ambidexterity capabilities. For example, big data / data analytics / AI technologies and tools can be used for digital scouting and digital scenario planning. Cloud, mobile, and AI based learning platforms can be used for digital learning and digital mindset shaping. Elastic / anywhere / anytime / any device digital infrastructures can be used to enable dynamic flexing of resources in response to customer / demand-side changes, or supplier / supply-side changes. Combinations of digital technologies can be brought together to assemble highly efficient and scalable business models or to build smart products that can sense and report on consumer behavior changes; or to build smart and autonomous processes that can independently flex with demand and supply-side changes. Combinations of digital technologies can be used to effect bimodality (e.g. digital infrastructure to facilitate / support established processes, as well as digital infrastructure to facilitate / support exploratory or experimental products / services).

Accounting roles and competencies required for organizational adaptability, agility, and ambidexterity

Managers at all levels need to play important roles in leveraging digital technologies for building, maintaining, and optimizing the adaptability, agility, and ambidexterity capabilities of their organizations. Examples of these roles include setting or clarifying a vision for firm adaptability / agility / ambidexterity (e.g. what does the future state of this capability look like in practice), maintaining both efficiency and exploratory digital infrastructures and processes, ensuring the right combination of technologies are used and configured in the right way to maximize adaptability / agility / ambidexterity capabilities, instituting conditions / mindsets / attitudes that provide impetus for both exploration and exploitation activities, and cultivating and using ambidextrous leadership styles. As with other organizational digital capabilities we have previously discussed, accountants can support and catalyze managers' adaptability, agility, and ambidexterity capability building and sustaining efforts through information provision / assurance and business partnering roles. That is, accounting roles such as the co-pilot, the navigator, the digital and technology enabler, the data navigator, the digital playmaker, and the business transformer are well suited to supporting and catalyzing managers' adaptability, agility, and ambidexterity capability building efforts. Within these roles, for example, accountants can leverage data to provide predictive insights that enable managers to ensure the right resources and capabilities are in place to adapt disruptions and seize the opportunities associated with disruptions. Or they can evaluate proposed enterprise architecture designs to identify those that maximize the organization's financial resilience. The latter would help managers intelligently choose among proposed enterprise architecture designs or to request modifications to existing ones.

Google and reflect

Table 7.2 Google and reflect

Digital capability	Common terminology
Digital Business Strategy and Digital Transformation Strategy	digital business strategy, digital transformation strategy, digital asset, network effects, elastic infrastructure, dynamic capability, digital infrastructure
Digital Innovation	crowdsourcing, crowdfunding, network-centric innovation platform, innovation collective, shared cognition, joint sense-making, design thinking, layered modular architecture
Digital Learning	digital learning context, digital learning system / platform, gamification, self-directed learning, immersive learning, autonomous learning, learning efficiency, multidisciplinary knowledge, multidisciplinary teaching, interdisciplinary teaching, pedagogical model, collaborative community, cooperative learning, collaborative learning, digital combinational systems, flipped classroom, experiential online development, open educational practice, narrated stop-motion animation application, augmented reality application, webinar application, learning management system (LMS), learning object repository, massive open online courses (MOOC)
Adaptability, Agility, Ambidexterity	adaptability, agility, ambidexterity

Discussion questions

1. How is digital business strategy different from traditional strategy?
2. What is the relationship between accounting roles and managerial roles?
3. Which accounting role in digital business strategy is the most critical to building and maintaining that capability? Why?
4. Which digital business strategy-related accounting competency is likely to have the greatest positive impact on an accountant's career?
5. How is digital innovation different from traditional innovation?
6. Which accounting role in digital innovation is the most critical to building and maintaining that capability? Why?
7. How is digital learning different from traditional learning?
8. Which accounting role in digital learning is the most critical to building and maintaining that capability? Why?
9. Which digital learning competency of accountants is likely to have the greatest positive impact on an accountant's career?
10. Which of the capabilities discussed in this chapter is the most important to succeeding at digital transformation and digital business?

Notes

1 Bharadwaj, A., El Sawy, O.A., Pavlou, P.A., & Venkatraman, N. (2013). Digital business strategy: Toward a next generation of insights. MIS quarterly, 37(2), 471–482.
2 Bharadwaj, A., El Sawy, O.A., Pavlou, P.A., & Venkatraman, N. (2013). Digital business strategy: Toward a next generation of insights. MIS quarterly, 37(2), 471–482.
3 Bharadwaj, A., El Sawy, O.A., Pavlou, P.A., & Venkatraman, N. (2013). Digital business strategy: Toward a next generation of insights. MIS quarterly, 37(2), 471–482.
4 Ross, J. W. (2016, November 8). How to develop a great digital strategy. MIT Sloan Management Review. Retrieved May 31, 2020, from: https://sloanreview.mit.edu/article/how-to-develop-a-great-digital-strategy/
5 Ross, J. W. (2016, November 8). How to develop a great digital dtrategy. MIT Sloan Management Review. Retrieved May 31, 2020, from : https://sloanreview.mit.edu/article/how-to-develop-a-great-digital-strategy/
6 Gupta, S. (2018). Driving digital strategy: A guide to reimagining your business. Harvard Business Press.
7 Gupta, S. (2018). Driving digital strategy: A guide to reimagining your business. Harvard Business Press.
8 Ross, J. W. (2016, November 8). How to develop a great digital strategy. MIT Sloan Management Review. Retrieved May 31, 2020, from: https://sloanreview.mit.edu/article/how-to-develop-a-great-digital-strategy/
9 Bharadwaj, A., El Sawy, O.A., Pavlou, P.A., & Venkatraman, N. (2013). Digital business strategy: Toward a next generation of insights. MIS quarterly, 37(2), 471–482.
10 Bharadwaj, A., El Sawy, O.A., Pavlou, P.A., & Venkatraman, N. (2013). Digital business strategy: Toward a next generation of insights. MIS quarterly, 37(2), 471–482.
11 Hoffman, R., & Yeh, C. (2018, October). The blitzscaling basics. Retrieved June 1, 2020, from: https://www.strategy-business.com/article/The-Blitzscaling-Basics?gko=3ebb0
12 Hoffman, R., & Yeh, C. (2018). Blitzscaling: The lightning-fast path to building massively valuable businesses. Broadway Business.
13 Hoffman, R., & Yeh, C. (2018). Blitzscaling: The lightning-fast path to building massively valuable businesses. Broadway Business.
14 Hoffman, R., & Yeh, C. (2018). Blitzscaling: The lightning-fast path to building massively valuable businesses. Broadway Business.
15 Vial, G. (2019). Understanding digital transformation: A review and a research agenda. The Journal of Strategic Information Systems, 28(2), 118–144. https://doi.org/10.1016/j.jsis.2019.01.003
16 Rigby, D.K., Sutherland, J., & Takeuchi, H. (2016). Embracing agile. Harvard Business Review, 94(5), 40–50.
17 Busulwa, R., Tice, M., & Gurd, B. (2018). Strategy execution and complexity: Thriving in the era of disruption. Routledge.
18 Haque, B., & James-Moore, M. (2004). Applying lean thinking to new product introduction. Journal of Engineering design, 15(1), 1–31.
19 Womack, J.P., & Jones, D.T. (1997). Lean thinking – banish waste and create wealth in your corporation. Journal of the Operational Research Society, 48(11), 1148.
20 Melton, T. (2005). The benefits of lean manufacturing: What lean thinking has to offer the process industries. Chemical Engineering Research and Design, 83(6), 662–673.
21 Ries, E. (2011). The lean startup: How today's entrepreneurs use continuous innovation to create radically successful businesses. Crown Books.
22 Martin, R., & Martin, R.L. (2009). The design of business: Why design thinking is the next competitive advantage. Harvard Business Press.
23 Busulwa, R., Birdthistle, N., & Dunn, S. (2020). Startup accelerators: A field guide. John Wiley & Sons.
24 Kotter, J.P. (2014). Accelerate: Building strategic agility for a faster-moving world. Harvard Business Review Press.
25 West, M. and Farr, J. (1989) Innovation at work: psychological perspectives. Social Behavior, 4, 15–30.
26 Nambisan, S., Lyytinen, K., Majchrzak, A., & Song, M. (2017). Digital innovation management: Reinventing innovation management research in a digital world. Mis Quarterly, 41(1).
27 Yoo, Y., Henfridsson, O., & Lyytinen, K. (2010). Research commentary – the new organizing logic of digital innovation: An agenda for information systems research. Information systems research, 21(4), 724–735.

28 Nambisan, S., Lyytinen, K., Majchrzak, A., & Song, M. (2017). Digital innovation management: Reinventing innovation management research in a digital world. Mis Quarterly, 41(1).
29 Nambisan, S., Lyytinen, K., Majchrzak, A., & Song, M. (2017). Digital innovation management: Reinventing innovation management research in a digital world. Mis Quarterly, 41(1).
30 Nambisan, S., Lyytinen, K., Majchrzak, A., & Song, M. (2017). Digital innovation management: Reinventing innovation management research in a digital world. Mis Quarterly, 41(1).
31 Bradonjic, P., Franke, N., & Lüthje, C. (2019). Decision-makers' underestimation of user innovation. Research Policy, 48(6), 1354–1361. https://doi.org/10.1016/j.respol.2019.01.020
32 Nambisan, S., Lyytinen, K., Majchrzak, A., & Song, M. (2017). Digital innovation management: Reinventing innovation management research in a digital world. Mis Quarterly, 41(1).
33 Yoo, Y., Henfridsson, O., & Lyytinen, K. (2010). Research commentary – the new organizing logic of digital innovation: An agenda for information systems research. Information systems research, 21(4), 724–735.
34 Lee, J., & Berente, N. (2012). Digital innovation and the division of innovative labor: Digital controls in the automotive industry. Organization Science, 23(5), 1428–-447.
35 Nambisan, S., Lyytinen, K., Majchrzak, A., & Song, M. (2017). Digital innovation management: Reinventing innovation management research in a digital world. Mis Quarterly, 41(1).
36 Nambisan, S., Lyytinen, K., Majchrzak, A., & Song, M. (2017). Digital innovation management: Reinventing innovation management research in a digital world. Mis Quarterly, 41(1).
37 Nambisan, S., Lyytinen, K., Majchrzak, A., & Song, M. (2017). Digital innovation management: Reinventing innovation management research in a digital world. Mis Quarterly, 41(1).
38 Yoo, Y., Henfridsson, O., & Lyytinen, K. (2010). Research commentary – the new organizing logic of digital innovation: An agenda for information systems research. Information systems research, 21(4), 724–735.
39 Lee, J., & Berente, N. (2012). Digital innovation and the division of innovative labor: Digital controls in the automotive industry. Organization Science, 23(5), 1428–1447.
40 Nambisan, S., Lyytinen, K., Majchrzak, A., & Song, M. (2017). Digital innovation management: Reinventing innovation management research in a digital world. Mis Quarterly, 41(1).
41 Yoo, Y., Henfridsson, O., & Lyytinen, K. (2010). Research commentary – the new organizing logic of digital innovation: An agenda for information systems research. Information systems research, 21(4), 724–735.
42 Lee, J., & Berente, N. (2012). Digital innovation and the division of innovative labor: Digital controls in the automotive industry. Organization Science, 23(5), 1428–1447.
43 Nambisan, S., Lyytinen, K., Majchrzak, A., & Song, M. (2017). Digital innovation management: Reinventing innovation management research in a digital world. Mis Quarterly, 41(1).
44 Yoo, Y., Henfridsson, O., & Lyytinen, K. (2010). Research commentary – the new organizing logic of digital innovation: An agenda for information systems research. Information systems research, 21(4), 724–735.
45 Lee, J., & Berente, N. (2012). Digital innovation and the division of innovative labor: Digital controls in the automotive industry. Organization Science, 23(5), 1428–1447.
46 Nambisan, S., Lyytinen, K., Majchrzak, A., & Song, M. (2017). Digital innovation management: Reinventing innovation management research in a digital world. Mis Quarterly, 41(1).
47 Fichman, R. G., Dos Santos, B. L., & Zheng, Z. (2014). Digital innovation as a fundamental and powerful concept in the information systems curriculum. MIS quarterly, 38(2), 329-353.
48 Willyerd,K., Grünwald, A., Brown, K., Welz, B., & Traylor, P. (2016). A new model for corporate learning. Digitalit Magazine. March. Retrieved June 2, 2020, from: https://www.digitalistmag.com/executive-research/a-new-model-for-corporate-learning
49 Willyerd,K., Grünwald, A., Brown, K., Welz, B., & Traylor, P. (2016). A new model for corporate learning. Digitalit Magazine. March. Retrieved June 2, 2020, from: https://www.digitalistmag.com/executive-research/a-new-model-for-corporate-learning
50 Willyerd,K., Grünwald, A., Brown, K., Welz, B., & Traylor, P. (2016). A New Model for Corporate Learning. Digitalit Magazine. March. Accessed 2nd June 2020. URL: https://www.digitalistmag.com/executive-research/a-new-model-for-corporate-learning
51 Sousa, M. J., & Rocha, Á. (2019). Digital learning: Developing skills for digital transformation of organizations. Future Generation Computer Systems, 91, 327–334.
52 Sousa, M. J., & Rocha, Á. (2019). Digital learning: Developing skills for digital transformation of organizations. Future Generation Computer Systems, 91, 327–334.
53 Sousa, M. J., Cruz, R., & Martins, J. M. (2017). Digital learning methodologies and tools – a literature review. Edulearn17 Proceedings, 5185–5192.

54 Sousa, M. J., & Rocha, Á. (2019). Digital learning: Developing skills for digital transformation of organizations. Future Generation Computer Systems, 91, 327–334.
55 Sousa, M. J., Cruz, R., & Martins, J. M. (2017). Digital learning methodologies and tools – a literature review. Edulearn17 Proceedings, 5185–5192.
56 Sousa, M. J., & Rocha, Á. (2019). Digital learning: Developing skills for digital transformation of organizations. Future Generation Computer Systems, 91, 327–334.
57 Sousa, M. J., Cruz, R., & Martins, J. M. (2017). Digital learning methodologies and tools – a literature review. Edulearn17 Proceedings, 5185-5192.
58 Sousa, M. J., & Rocha, Á. (2019). Digital learning: Developing skills for digital transformation of organizations. Future Generation Computer Systems, 91, 327–334.
59 Sousa, M. J., Cruz, R., & Martins, J. M. (2017). Digital learning methodologies and tools – a literature review. Edulearn17 Proceedings, 5185–5192.
60 Sousa, M. J., & Rocha, Á. (2019). Digital learning: Developing skills for digital transformation of organizations. Future Generation Computer Systems, 91, 327–334.
61 Sousa, M. J., Cruz, R., & Martins, J. M. (2017). Digital learning methodologies and tools – a literature review. Edulearn17 Proceedings, 5185–5192.
62 Sousa, M. J., & Rocha, Á. (2019). Digital learning: Developing skills for digital transformation of organizations. Future Generation Computer Systems, 91, 327–334.
63 Warner, K. S., & Wäger, M. (2019). Building dynamic capabilities for digital transformation: An ongoing process of strategic renewal. Long Range Planning, 52(3), 326-349.
64 Busulwa, R., Tice, M., & Gurd, B. (2018). Strategy execution and complexity: Thriving in the era of disruption. Routledge.
65 Busulwa, R., Tice, M., & Gurd, B. (2018). Strategy execution and complexity: Thriving in the era of disruption. Routledge..
66 Busulwa, R., Tice, M., & Gurd, B. (2018). Strategy execution and complexity: Thriving in the era of disruption. Routledge.
67 Busulwa, R., Tice, M., & Gurd, B. (2018). Strategy execution and complexity: Thriving in the era of disruption. Routledge.

8 The role of accountants in digital customer engagement, digital stakeholder engagement, and digital customer experience

Introduction

Digital technology advancements have disrupted customer and other stakeholder expectations and behaviors. Owing to this disruption, customers increasingly expect dramatically higher personalization of experiences and interactions, anytime / anywhere responsiveness, any device / any channel service availability, respect for the value of their time in interactions with organizations, to feel valued at all times, and to feel like they are part of a community when they use a product / service or engage with the organization. Living up to these expectations requires fundamental changes in the nature of customer engagement, stakeholder engagement, and customer experience practices. These transformed practices are, respectively, referred to as digital customer engagement, digital stakeholder engagement, and digital customer experience capabilities. They offer the promise of organizations not only being able to live up to changed and rapidly changing customer / stakeholder expectations but also having important bases for building strategic differentiation, adaptability, and agility from state-of-the-art practice of the capabilities. In this chapter, we unpack each capability and discuss what it means, how it differs from its traditional counterpart, and its value to organizational performance and longevity. We identify the key roles managers can play in building and maintaining these organizational capabilities, and the roles of accountants in supporting the development, sustaining, and optimization of these capabilities. Finally, we discuss the new or enhanced accounting competencies required to effectively support managers' efforts to build, sustain, and optimize these capabilities. As with earlier capabilities, each of these capabilities can be a complex area of practice with significant depth, interdisciplinary knowledge, slippery terms and concepts to make sense of, and practical practice challenges. Our aim is to provide a meaningful introduction to each digital capability, the required managerial roles, and the corresponding accounting roles and competencies. We hope accountants find this introduction to be an understandable starting point and a contextual framework to support further and lifelong learning / competency development in these important capability areas.

Required accounting roles and competencies for digital customer engagement and digital stakeholder engagement

Unpacking digital customer engagement

Customer engagement refers to both the process and effect of creating deep connections with customers that drive purchase decisions, interaction, participation, and advocacy[1].

126 *Leveraging digital technologies*

Its value to profitability and competitiveness is well established and includes benefits such as improved customer experience (e.g. through more empathetic service), improved customer relations / retention (e.g. greater trust / forgiveness of organizations' mistakes), improved brand / product awareness and image (e.g. word of mouth), improved product innovation (e.g. customer ideas for new products or for existing product improvements), improved competitor intelligence (e.g. information on competitor activities from customers), and risk mitigation (e.g. discovering information on fatal product flaws, customer grievances, etc.). Given these benefits, competitive organizations have long been interested in building and continuously upgrading their customer engagement capability (i.e. the efficiency and effectiveness of the capability)[2,3,4,5,6,7].

In previous chapters, we have noted how digital technology advancements disrupt consumer expectations and behaviors, disrupt the competitive field and the bases of competition, and disrupt data availability. From a consumer engagement perspective, these disruptions have manifested themselves as, for example, dramatically higher expectations for personalization, anytime / anywhere responsiveness, any device / any channel availability, and having a sense of community. To deliver on these dramatically higher expectations successfully, organizations have transformed the nature of their customer engagement processes and practices.

The new or transformed processes and practices are collectively referred to as *digital customer engagement* (Figure 8.1 contrasts traditional and digital customer engagement). Digital customer engagement is the use of digital technologies and tools in the processes / practices and effects of creating deep connections with customers that drive purchase decisions, interaction, participation, and advocacy. It deals with all the ways

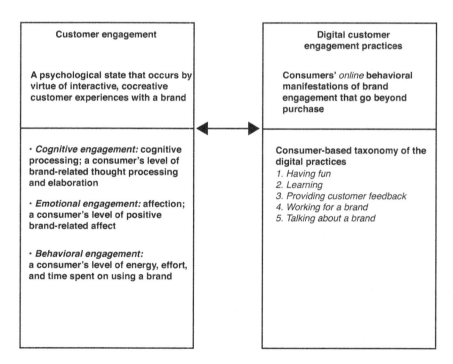

Figure 8.1 Traditional customer engagement vs. digital customer engagement[8]

current and prospective customers can and do interact in relation to an organization, brand, or product across digital channels, platforms, devices, and connected or smart things[9]. Digital customer engagement has rapidly evolved to include a rich repertoire of engagement strategies / approaches and specific engagement practices[10]. Examples of these include digitally managed loyalty programs (e.g. web-based or mobile app frequent flyer programs), online brand communities (e.g. discussion board or chat style interactions with other customers or prospective customers or with the organization, consumers solving other consumers' problems, consumers giving other consumers advice / tips), digital customer engagement platforms (e.g. Zendesk, Freshdesk, HubSpot, Salesforce, Mailchimp), customer co-creation (e.g. product co-creation, product improvement feedback, product testing), brand websites, consumer-generated brand stories, consumer engagement on social media (e.g. liking, commenting, sharing, posting, calling up product photographs, hashtagging), consumer reviews (e.g. search engine reviews, review platform reviews, social media reviews), brand-consumer interactions (e.g. liking a brand on Facebook, following a brand on Twitter), purchase funnel practices, brand fan pages, mobile interactions (e.g. SMS interactions), LiveChat platforms, mobile marketing, consumer-generated advertising (e.g. consumer-generated brand videos), consumer buzz (e.g. consumers generating content by sharing personal experiences, providing online feedback, and expressing sentiments), email marketing, consumers' online brand-related activities or COBRAs, consumption community participation, consumer-initiated mobile marketing, and consumer advocates (e.g. consumers doing remote voluntary work for the organization, acting as multiplier of brand messages, accepting invitations to company-related events, speaking up for the brand at events)[11]. Figure 8.2 provides a taxonomy of business to consumer (B2C), consumer to business (C2B), and consumer to consumer (C2C) engagement types, aims, and example activities.

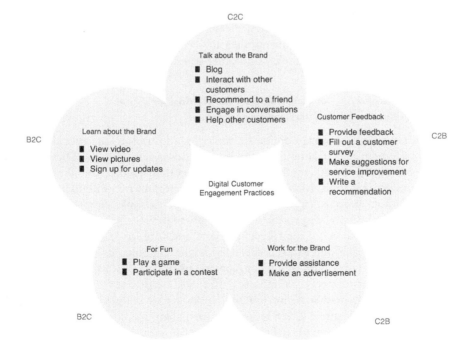

Figure 8.2 A research-derived taxonomy of digital customer engagement practices[12]

Effectively done, digital customer engagement provides organizations with a range of other opportunities including: being able to harness all their customer interactions across channels and platforms to inform decision-making, developing breakthrough and market-validated products (e.g. from spotting new problems to solve for customers, liaising with customers about possible solutions, and receiving product test feedback from customers), involving more customers in digital innovation, cultivating a granular understanding of customer behaviors across market segments, and offering significantly improved customer service and customer experience (e.g. service that leverages interaction data to anticipate and solve customer issues in real time).

Unpacking digital stakeholder engagement

In addition to customers, a range of other stakeholders are critical to organizations' performance and wellbeing. These include employees, suppliers and partners, government and regulatory institutions, competitors, and different local and international communities. Organizations must engage effectively with these different stakeholders in order to safeguard their existence, legitimacy, and the opportunities available to them. For example, organizations must assure governments and regulatory institutions that they are complying with relevant laws or have acceptable reasons for not doing so, they must assure competitors that they are competing fairly, and they must assure different communities that they are not violating their social, environmental, and ethical obligations or their license to operate in those communities and environments. To effectively do this, they must communicate and transact with these stakeholders in such a way as to build positive, trusting relationships. This is the focus of stakeholder engagement. And like digital customer engagement, *digital stakeholder engagement* leverages digital technologies and tools to maximize the practice and outputs of stakeholder engagement. Digital technologies and tools can dramatically improve the cost, speed, scale / reach, transparency, measurability, and effectiveness of stakeholder engagement efforts. In turn, this can translate into organizations enjoying greater trust, empathy, inclusion, growth, profitability, and other benefits from stakeholders.

New or enhanced accounting roles and competencies required for digital customer engagement and digital stakeholder engagement

While organizations may leverage digital technologies and tools to dramatically improve customer engagement and stakeholder engagement, this is not enough. They must also do so more effectively and efficiently than competitors that leverage the same or similar digital technologies and tools. Managers can play an important role in building and continuously upgrading digital engagement capabilities. For example, they can set or clarify the organization's digital engagement vision and strategic objectives, they can help select the right combination of digital technologies and tools to maximize engagement of different customers and other stakeholders (e.g. right technologies / platforms / tools, right configuration and integration of technologies / platforms / tools), they can promote and institute the right supporting mindsets / attitudes / behaviors to support effective digital engagement (e.g. that it is not just the marketing or communications function's job), they can encourage their direct reports to participate in different digital channels in order to better empathize with stakeholders, they can ensure analytics dashboards are built that leverage and integrate interaction data from all channels, they can hire / develop in-house experts across channels and forms of engagement, and much more. Accountants can enhance or accelerate the effectiveness of managers' digital customer and digital stakeholder engagement capability building and optimisation efforts by providing relevant business partnering, trusted advice, and information provision / assurance support. For example, they can help managers to develop business cases for the adoption of particular digital technology tools and practices to drive digital customer engagement and digital stakeholder engagement. They can help managers craft the right integrated dashboards to track the effectiveness of digital customer and digital stakeholder engagement practices and outcomes. They can help managers to effectively communicate the benefits of different digital customer and digital stakeholder engagement initiatives. They can also help managers understand the interrelationships between particular digital customer and digital stakeholder engagement practices / activities and financial performance, and to understand how digital customer and digital stakeholder engagement objectives / ideas may better support broader strategic objectives of the organization. To effectively play this support and catalyst role, accountants need sufficient working knowledge of digital customer and digital stakeholder engagement objectives, processes, and practices. They need to have working knowledge of different digital channels, and of how multichannel works. They also need to understand how value is captured from organizational digital customer and digital stakeholder engagement efforts. Finally, they need the digital leadership skills to enable them to be co-pilots in managers' efforts to develop, continuously upgrade, and realize value from digital customer and digital stakeholder engagement efforts.

Required accounting roles and competencies for digital customer experience

Unpacking digital customer experience

Customer experience refers to the quality of all of a customer's encounters with an organization's products, services, and other brand manifestations[13,14]. Improvements in the quality of these encounters is linked to benefits such as improved customer acquisition, improved customer loyalty, improved revenue growth, and improved profitability. Perhaps it is for this reason that optimizing customer experience has been a strategic priority for organizations since as far back as the nineteenth century; and that today, industry leading brands such as Ritz Carlton, Mirazur, and Singapore Airlines revolve their management strategies around customer experience optimization[15]. As with transformations of customer engagement and stakeholder engagement, digital technology advancements are changing the nature of effective customer experience management. The drivers of this change include customer encounters with an organization's products / services / brand increasingly shifting to digital channels, a proliferation in digital channels (e.g. different search engines, different social media platforms, different payment platforms, different website management platforms, different computing and mobile devices, different mobile apps, different virtual / augmented / mixed reality platforms, different IoT platforms, different online video platforms, different television platforms, etc.), and significant differences in customer interaction requirements across channels. Irrespective of the digital channels they choose, or their location and time of access customers want access to organizations' services and products in the most convenient way possible[16]. They are put off by having to repeat themselves when shifting one channel to another or from one customer representative to another. They hate process and visual inconsistency across channels, as well as having to perform actions that waste their time. And they are far less patient on digital channels than they are in traditional channels (e.g. a study found that waiting ten seconds for a page to load can result in half of customers terminating their encounter with a brand)[17].

Digital customer experience is the quality of all of a customer's encounters with an organization's products, services, and brand across all digital channels, touchpoints, and contact moments[18]. It also refers to the process of optimizing these encounters (e.g. having the right technology / platform / application infrastructure, having the right processes and people, and having the right policies). By having the right supporting technologies, the right platforms / applications, the right management processes, and the right people, organizations can ensure they are available to effectively serve customers in their preferred channels, at their preferred times, in their preferred locations, and in ways that respect their time (i.e. by saving them all possible effort, rather than externalizing more effort to them due to the organization's shortcomings). Digital customer experience optimization strategies typically focus on enhancing reachability (e.g. by customers being able to use their preferred channels to interact with or about the organization, and by customers being aware of all of the organization's available channels), enhancing digital channel flexibility (e.g. by enabling customers to switch between channels without losing context, providing them consistent information across channels, and not requiring them to repeat themselves across channels), enhancing service convenience (e.g. by providing access to clear and up-to-date information, providing access to quick or live support, and providing the ability to receive end-to-end support rather than being bounced across channels). They also focus on enhancing purchase convenience (e.g. by providing the ability to conduct end-to-end transactions, and providing broad payment options), enhancing and ease of use (e.g. through intuitive user interface design, simple and guided customer journeys), and enhancing personalization (e.g. by recognizing each customer as a unique individual, having their personal preferences automatically met, and configuring experiences to suit each customer's unique context)[19]. Organizations can leverage a range of digital technology platforms and tools to achieve these digital customer experience optimization objectives. For example, by using omnichannel support platforms (e.g. Pega CRM, Five9) organizations can track, centralize, and tie together or orchestrate all interactions across channels (e.g. face-to-face, email, phone, social media, and LiveChat so that a customer's digital experience is integrated and smooth, rather than fragmented and conflicting.

New or enhanced accounting roles and competencies required for digital customer experience

To effectively lead or participate in digital customer experience optimization efforts, managers can play roles such as setting / clarifying / communicating the organization's digital customer experience vision and strategic objectives, championing availability of the organization's offerings and support services across as many channels as possible, helping select the right combination of digital technologies / platforms / tools to maximize digital customer experience across customer preferred channels (e.g. right technologies / platforms / tools, right configuration and integration of technologies / platforms / tools), promoting and instituting the right supporting mindsets / attitudes / behaviors to maximize digital customer experience, encouraging their direct reports to participate in different digital channels in order to better empathize with customers' experiences and needs in those channels, ensuring analytics dashboards are built that leverage and integrate digital customer experience data from all channels, hiring / developing in-house experts across channels, and more. Accountants can support and catalyze managers' digital customer experience capability related efforts through business partnering, trusted advice, and information provision / assurance roles. Examples of such support that they can provide includes helping managers develop frameworks for evaluating the ability of different digital technology / platform / tool choices to maximize digital customer experience, helping managers track levels of organizational attitudes / mindsets / behaviors in relation to digital customer experience, helping managers develop integrated digital customer experience measures and dashboards, helping managers to measure and track customer value derived from digital customer experience investments, supporting managers' presentations to the wider organization or to executives, and helping managers respond to executive and broader organizational queries regarding implications / impacts / need for digital customer experience investments. To play such supporting and partnering roles, accountants need to have sufficient working knowledge of digital customer experience objectives, strategies, processes, and practices. They need to have strong working knowledge of customer journey mapping, digital customer journeys, and the key moments of truth in customer journeys across platforms. They need to have working knowledge of different digital channels, and of how multichannel and omnichannel work. Finally, they need the digital leadership skills to enable them to be effective digital customer experience business partners and change enablers.

Google and reflect

Table 8.1 Google and reflect

Digital capability	Common terminology
Digital Customer Engagement	customer engagement, digital customer engagement, digital loyalty program, online brand community, digital customer engagement platform, customer co-creation, brand fan page, LiveChat platform, consumer-generated advertising, consumer buzz, customers' online brand-related practices (COBRAs)
Digital Stakeholder Engagement	stakeholder management, stakeholder engagement, digital stakeholder engagement, organizational legitimacy, social license to operate (SLO), corporate social responsibility (CSR)
Digital Customer Experience	customer experience (CX), digital customer experience (DCX or Digital CX), customer experience management (CEM or CXM), customer experience program, customer sentiment, customer satisfaction score (CSAT), customer effort score (CES), customer delight, brand advocacy, customer lifetime value (CLV), voice of the customer (VoC), Net Promoter Score (NPS®), Customer Effort Score (CES), customer experience design (CXD), customer journey mapping, digital touchpoint, digital customer experience moment of truth (MoT), omnichannel strategy, digital customer experience platform

Discussion questions

1 How is digital customer engagement different from traditional customer engagement?
2 Which accounting role in digital customer engagement is the most critical to building and maintaining that capability? Why?
3 Which accounting related digital customer engagement competency is likely to have the greatest positive impact on an accountant's career?
4 How is digital stakeholder engagement different from traditional stakeholder engagement?
5 Which accounting role in digital stakeholder engagement is the most critical to building and maintaining that capability? Why?

6   How is digital customer experience different from traditional customer experience?
7   Which accounting role in digital customer experience is the most critical to building and maintaining that capability? Why?
8   Which accounting related digital customer experience competency is likely to have the greatest positive impact on an accountant's career?
9   Which of the capabilities discussed in this chapter is the most important to succeeding at digital transformation and digital business?

Notes

1 Sashi, C.M. (2012). Customer engagement, buyer-seller relationships, and social media. Management Decision, 50(2), 253–272. https://doi.org/10.1108/00251741211203551
2 Hueffner, E. (2020). How digital customer engagement can boost your business. Retrieved June 3, 2020, from Zendesk website: https://www.zendesk.com/blog/digital-customer-engagement/
3 Sashi, C.M. (2012). Customer engagement, buyer-seller relationships, and social media. Management Decision, 50(2), 253–272. https://doi.org/10.1108/00251741211203551
4 Bernhard J. Klein Wassink, & Santenac, I. (2019, February 11). How a new digital engagement model attracts and educates customers. Retrieved June 3, 2020, from: https://www.ey.com/en_gl/insurance/new-digital-customer-engagement-model
5 Ebrahim, S., Rabbani, U., & Rosenberg, R. (2015). Making digital customer engagement a reality. McKinsey & Company. Retrieved June 3, 2020, from: https://www.mckinsey.com/business-functions/marketing-and-sales/our-insights/making-digital-customer-engagement-a-reality
6 Ebrahim, S., Rabbani, U., & Rosenberg, R. (2015). Making digital customer engagement a reality. McKinsey & Company. Retrieved June 3, 2020, from: https://www.mckinsey.com/business-functions/marketing-and-sales/our-insights/making-digital-customer-engagement-a-reality
7 Hueffner, E. (2020). How digital customer engagement can boost your business. Zendesk. Retrieved June 3, 2020, from: https://www.zendesk.com/blog/digital-customer-engagement/
8 Eigenraam, A.W., Eelen, J., Van Lin, A., & Verlegh, P.W. (2018). A consumer-based taxonomy of digital customer engagement practices. Journal of Interactive Marketing, 44, 102–121.
9 Hueffner, E. (2020). How digital customer engagement can boost your business. Zendesk. Retrieved June 3, 2020, from: https://www.zendesk.com/blog/digital-customer-engagement/
10 Eigenraam, A.W., Eelen, J., Van Lin, A., & Verlegh, P.W. (2018). A consumer-based taxonomy of digital customer engagement practices. Journal of Interactive Marketing, 44, 102–121.
11 Eigenraam, A.W., Eelen, J., Van Lin, A., & Verlegh, P.W. (2018). A consumer-based taxonomy of digital customer engagement practices. Journal of Interactive Marketing, 44, 102–121.
12 Eigenraam, A.W., Eelen, J., Van Lin, A., & Verlegh, P.W. (2018). A consumer-based taxonomy of digital customer engagement practices. Journal of Interactive Marketing, 44, 102–121.
13 Borowski, C. (2015). What a great digital customer experience actually looks like. Harvard Business Review. Retrieved June 4, 2020, from: https://hbr.org/2015/11/what-a-great-digital-customer-experience-actually-looks-like
14 Meyer, C., & Schwager, A. (2007). Understanding customer experience. Harvard business review, 85(2), 116.
15 Klaus, P. (2014). Towards practical relevance – Delivering superior firm performance through digital customer experience strategies. Journal of Direct, Data and Digital Marketing Practice, 15(4), 306–316. https://doi.org/10.1057/dddmp.2014.20
16 Shep Hyken. (2018). Customer experience is the new brand. Forbes. Retrieved from: https://www.forbes.com/sites/shephyken/2018/07/15/customer-experience-is-the-new-brand/#1e586acf7f52
17 Borowski, C. (2015). What a great digital customer experience actually looks like. Harvard Business Review. Retrieved June 4, 2020, from: https://hbr.org/2015/11/what-a-great-digital-customer-experience-actually-looks-like
18 Borowski, C. (2015). What a great digital customer experience actually looks like. Harvard Business Review. Retrieved June 4, 2020, from: https://hbr.org/2015/11/what-a-great-digital-customer-experience-actually-looks-like
19 TTEC. (2020). Digital customer experience strategy: Six key areas to focus your efforts. Retrieved June 5, 2020, from: https://www.ttec.com/articles/digital-customer-experience-strategy-six-key-areas-focus-your-efforts#:~:text=A%20digital%20experience%20strategy%20requires,service%20interactions%20is%20not%20sufficient.

9 The role of accountants in enterprise architecture, technology sourcing, data analytics, data science, and data management

Introduction

This chapter puts a spotlight on three capabilities that we contend are among most important building blocks for operating and competing as a digital business. The first, enterprise architecture management, relates to how the organization's technology infrastructure, information / data, and business processes are and should be configured. The second, technology sourcing, relates to how an organization goes about finding, choosing, and procuring the technologies and related services to be added as components of its enterprise architecture. The third, data management and data analytics, relates to an organization's ability to collect, validate, store, and leverage internal and external data to spur data-driven decision-making. Taken together, the organization's ability to effectively build and optimize these capabilities can drive or constrain its efficiency, differentiation, adaptability, and agility. This effect can be supercharged through the capacity of these particular capabilities to catalyze all other digital transformation and digital business capabilities. Effectively establishing and continuously upgrading the competitiveness of these capabilities requires organization-wide involvement; and is an important part of managers' roles at all levels (i.e. vertically up and down the hierarchy, and horizontally across functions). Accountants can play critical managerial support and organization-wide leadership roles in these particular capabilities. As a result, they need to understand these capabilities; and to develop competencies to enable them to effectively play required managerial support and organization-wide leadership roles.

Required accounting roles and competencies for enterprise architecture management

Unpacking enterprise architecture

Enterprise architecture (EA) refers to the design or configuration of the different elements / assets of an organization (e.g. hardware, software, networks, business processes, information systems, information, data, etc.) and the resultant levels of efficiency, effectiveness, and longevity they enable an organization to have in the pursuit of its mission within its external environment. For example, one particular design or configuration may lead to mediocre levels of efficiency and effectiveness in the pursuit of the organization's mission (e.g. perhaps due to having a random collection of disparate hardware, software, networks, business processes, and information / data that don't work together – thus constraining connectivity, communication, collaboration, and customer experience). For an organization like the Ritz-Carlton, for example, such enterprise architecture would severely limit its mission of providing guests with the finest personalized service and experience[1]; and, in turn, limit its longevity. Another type of design or configuration might be suited to maximizing connectivity, integrability, communication, collaboration, automation, adaptability, and customer experience – resulting in very high levels of efficiency, effectiveness, and agility. We contend that the latter is the type of enterprise architecture that leading digital businesses like Microsoft, Amazon, Google, and Netflix have. Enterprise architecture has had simpler (although perhaps less complete) definitions, including that it is the process of aligning an organization's strategic vision with its information technology[2], that it is how information / business / technology flow together[3], and that it is the organizing logic for how business processes and IT infrastructure should work together to meet operational requirements[4].

Enterprise architecture is described as being layered (i.e. having business architecture, information architecture, information systems architecture, data architecture, and delivery architecture layers), as spanning the entire organization (i.e. vertically across the hierarchy and horizontally across business functions), as both conceptual and physical (i.e. being visual or written logical representations, or the actual elements / assets), as being iterative (i.e. built or evolving over time through iterative additions / improvements), and as being both current and forward-looking (i.e. enterprise architecture designs or configurations deal with both current and future business needs). According to practitioners and researchers, good enterprise architecture should enable both current and future strategy (e.g. enable both operational efficiency / effectiveness today, and business transformation for the future)[5], it should be proactive (i.e. it should anticipate and prepare for the future needs of the business)[6], it should speed up processes (e.g. digitize, integrate, and automate key processes for efficiency gains), it should enable organizational adaptability (e.g. through plug and play digital assets that can be adapted to different internal and external systems / technologies / processes / ecosystems), it should ensure availability and accessibility of high-quality data across the enterprise to drive decision-making (e.g. by optimizing cleaning, standardizing, sharing, presentation of data), and it should instantiate the organization's digital business model[7].

Enterprise architecture management

Enterprise architecture management refers to the processes and practices of planning, implementing, maintaining, and continuously improving an organization's enterprise architecture. At a high level, it involves continuous and iterative activities of identifying EA stakeholders and their concerns, understanding the existing EA and the value it creates, designing the target EA, planning the implementation, transitioning to the target EA, and ensuring effective EA governance[8]. See Table 9.1[9] providing example EA management activities and tasks, as well as the resultant artefacts (accountants may be presented with and have to interpret some of these artefacts). The benefits of effective EA management are broad and include the capacity for improved communication, increased collaboration, improved decision-making, improved functional and external partner alignment, improved customer satisfaction, reduced complexity, and more. EA researchers identify more than 40 benefits of effective enterprise architecture (see Table 9.2). Given the digital business transformation and digital business imperatives, the most important benefit, and one integrating all the 40 listed benefits into a single benefit, is successful digital business transformation, and therefore the capacity to effectively compete as a digital business. Enterprise architecture leaders can ensure the design or configuration of and transition

Table 9.1 Example enterprise architecture management activities, tasks, and artefacts

EA management activities	EA management tasks	Resultant EA management artefacts
Identifying EA stakeholders and their concerns	Identification of stakeholders and their concerns	List of stakeholders
	Identification of project motivation	Project goals and objectives
Understanding the existing EA and the enterprise value it creates	General view of the enterprise	Business model canvas "as is"
	Identification of company goals, objectives, and indicators for their measurement	Strategy map (or goal tree)
		Balanced scorecard
	Identification of value proposition (VP)	Tree of products / services, value curve
	Identification of the value configuration "as is"	Value creation model
	Identification of the operations architecture "as is"	Function decomposition model
		Processes landscape
		Business process models (if necessary)
	Organizational structure and responsibility matrix "as is"	Organization chart
		Responsibility matrix (or RACI-matrix)
	IT architecture "as is" (existing information systems and technological infrastructure)	Model of application / IS usage
		Description of the application / IS landscape
		Infrastructure use model
	General idea of EA "as is"	High-level (overview) EA model
Designing the target EA (several alternative scenarios may be developed at this stage)	Development of target EA vision	Business model canvas "to be"
	Development of target EA with detailing of representations by layers	High-level (overview) model "to be"
		Particular EA models, which will be affected by changes (composition of models as in the description of the current state), "to be"
Planning and effecting the implementation and transitioning to the target EA	Planning of the transition between the EA states (current, target, transitional)	Transition planning model (linking EA changes / gaps with work packages)
	Formation of development projects portfolio	Transformation and development program cards (proposed initiatives)
	Planning for implementation and transition (see project management)	Schedule of transformation projects (for example, in MS Project)
Ensuring effective EA governance	Establishing and maintaining effective EA organization structure with clear roles and responsibilities	EA organization chart, EA function job descriptions, KPIs
	Establishing and maintaining effective EA governance practices	EA governance model
	Establishing and maintaining effective EA Standards and guidelines	EA framework
	Establishing and maintaining effective EA Management Tools	Architecture repository

to architectures that simultaneously deliver efficiency, differentiation, adaptability, and agility capabilities. Although previously seen as being "either or" choices, simultaneously having these capabilities has been shown to be essential in increasingly complex business environments[10,11].

Table 9.2 Benefits of effective enterprise architecture management

Effective EA management benefits	
Document knowledge of the enterprise	Improve resource quality
Identify resource dependencies	Improve return on investments
Identify resource synergies	Improve situational awareness
Identify suboptimal resource use	Improve solution development
Improve alignment with partners	Improve stability
Improve change management	Increase agility
Improve compliance	Increase economies of scale
Improve customer satisfaction	Increase efficiency
Improve decision-making	Increase growth
Improve employee satisfaction	Increase innovation
Improve enterprise-wide goal attainment	Increase market share
Improve information quality	Increase resource flexibility
Improve investment management	Increase resource reuse
Improve measurement	Increase resource standardization
Improve organizational alignment	Increase revenue
Improve organizational collaboration	Provide a high-level overview
Improve organizational communication	Provide directions for improvement
Improve resource alignment	Provide standards
Improve resource consolidation	Reduce costs
Improve resource integration	Reduce complexity

New or enhanced accounting roles and competencies required for effective enterprise architecture management

Managers can play a range of roles in enterprise architecture management. First, the top enterprise architecture management role can be filled by someone from the IT / IS / technology function but with deep operational process and industry knowledge, or by someone from operations with sufficient IT / IS / technology competencies[12]. Both individuals are likely to be challenging to recruit and to retain. Another option is strong collaboration between someone from the IT / IS / technology function and someone from the operations function with deep industry knowledge. So, operating and functional managers can be involved in directly managing the EA function or having shared responsibility for it. Outside of direct or shared management of EA, managers can play other important roles in enterprise architecture management. For example, they may be involved in hiring the person to directly manage the EA function, they may be involved in setting or approving the EA vision and high-level objectives, they may be involved in interpreting and using EA artefacts, they may be involved in identifying and / or selecting different technology / network/ hardware / software/ process options, they may be asked to participate in EA-related discussions, they may be involved in choosing between different EA target state options, they may participate in EA governance or oversight of EA governance processes / activities, or they may have to change business processes to align with chosen EA target state options. See Figure 9.1 for examples of potential managers' involvement in enterprise architecture governance at different hierarchical levels of an

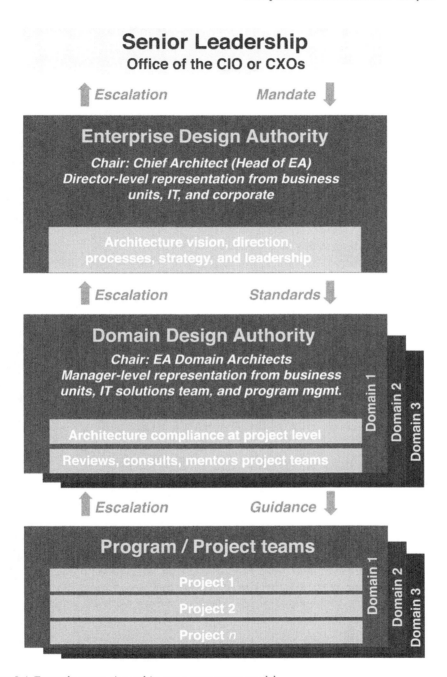

Figure 9.1 Example enterprise architecture governance model

organization. Accountants can support managers' enterprise architecture roles and activities in a range of ways. For example, in their information provision and assurance roles, accountants can provide critical information on the financial and strategic impact of different EA design / configuration options, or they can help identify /

build / review KPI dashboards to support effective EA governance. In their business partnering and trusted advisor roles, accountants can participate in setting EA vision and high-level objectives, they can champion the EA change agenda across functions and up / down the hierarchy, they can support EA leaders to frame the EA change agenda in the context of established business strategy and financial objectives, and they can help EA managers to overcome resistance to change. To effectively support EA management, accountants need a working understanding of enterprise architecture and enterprise architecture management (e.g. what are its aims and value propositions, what are the opportunities and challenges, what are the risks, what constitutes best practice management), they need a working knowledge of EA artifacts (e.g. being able to read EA frameworks, EA plans / designs), and they need a working knowledge of different digital technologies and the implications of these technologies for effective EA designs.

Required accounting roles and competencies for technology sourcing

Unpacking technology sourcing

Technology sourcing capability refers to the effectiveness of an organization's processes / practices for finding, choosing, and procuring the technology resources required for its current and desired enterprise architectures. Digital technology advancements and digital disruption have expanded the focus of technology sourcing from cost minimization and risk mitigation, to driving innovation, revenue growth, customer retention, business process speed, and business adaptability and agility[13]. Through finding, choosing, and partnering with the right vendors, as well as getting contracts right and managing the relationships appropriately, organizations can reap a range of rewards. Examples of such rewards include having superior hardware / software / networks relative to competitors, undertaking product co-creation with vendors, vendor-induced migration to state-of-the-art practices, vendor-induced introduction to new technologies and new customers, etc. Through finding, choosing, and adopting breakthrough technologies and products, an organization can speed up realization of their desired enterprise architectures, or exceed what they thought was possible from enterprise architecture. For example, imagine an organization being one of the first companies to discover, choose, and procure Amazon's Elastic Compute Cloud back in 2006. That organization would have been able to spin up a virtual desktop, fully equipped with all of the organization's systems and data, on any computer, anywhere in the world. Depending on the nature of the business's product offerings, the elastic computing cloud capability could have given the business superior workflow portability, global scalability, and business process speed advantages, relative to competitors.

New or enhanced accounting roles and competencies required for technology sourcing

Managers can play critical roles in technology sourcing. These include scouting for transformative technologies and vendors, building collaborative relationships with vendors, engaging in co-creation efforts with vendors[14], sourcing informal advice from vendors, scouting for innovative business models to apply, scouting for products / services used in the organization that are no longer needed / that need upgrading /

or that have better or cheaper alternatives on the market, engaging their teams to be the organization's eyes and ears with regard to new technology breakthroughs or star vendors, and more. They can also fill formal roles such as procurement director, technology sourcing manager, vendor relationship manager, business engagement manager, contract manager, etc. In their business partnering, trusted advisor, and information provision / assurance roles, accountants can play critical managerial support roles. For example, accountants can enable data-driven decision-making in relation to vendor choices, vendor proposals, and existing vendor terms. Accountants can provide insights with regard to the utilization costs / benefits associated with existing technology products owned or controlled by the organization. Accountants can help technology sourcing leaders to make the business case for choosing different vendors or different products / services. And accountants can help build diagnostic, predictive, and predictive dashboards that drive competitive advantages from technology sourcing. To effectively support technology sourcing leaders, accountants need to build working knowledge of the role, functioning, strategies, and potential value of the technology procurement and sourcing function. They also need a working understanding of different digital technologies, of the products and services related to these technologies, and of the vendor landscape for different products / technologies. They also need to have an understanding of the organization's enterprise architecture, and how to engage constructively with the enterprise architecture management team in technology / vendor sourcing decisions and activities.

Required accounting roles and competencies for data management, data science, and data analytics

Unpacking data management

Digital technology advancements have made and continue to make vast quantities of internal and external data available. For example, more than 500 million tweets, 294 billion emails, five billion search engine searches, and four petabytes of Facebook data are created each day – and it is estimated that there are up to 40 times more bytes of data than there are stars in the known universe[15]. The big challenge for organizations is how to leverage the vast quantities of internal and external data to improve their efficiency, differentiation, adaptability, and agility[16]. Effective data management, which is covered in more detail in the digital technologies deep dive section of the book, plays a critical role in addressing this challenge.

Data management capability refers to an organization's processes and practices for collecting, validating, storing, and using data optimally[17]. This can be a challenge, given the growing avalanche of internal and external data to manage, and the growing sources of such data. For example, data can come from SaaS applications (software as a service applications), ERP systems (enterprise resource planning systems), legacy systems, databases, data warehouses, and data lakes. Or it can come from the web, from social media platforms, and from open data platforms. Alternatively, it may come from any number of devices, including phones, computers, wearable devices, sensors, monitoring devices, etc. All this data has to be collected safely, validated, stored safely, and formatted and presented in such a way that different parts of the organization can access the right information at the right time and in the right format to make the best decisions. This requires that organizations have the right technical leaders, the right technical specialists, the right technology platforms, and the right policies, procedures and practices. The data management function typically plays a leadership role in issues such as data governance (who has what decision rights and what accountability for data management), data architecture (what rules, policies, standards, and models are in place to determine what data is collected, how it is stored, how it is integrated, and how it is used), data modelling and design (how to define and analyze data required to support business processes), database and storage management, and data security and privacy.

Unpacking data analytics and data science

Data analytics (also referred to just as analytics[18]) is an umbrella term referring to any form of analysis of data to uncover trends, patterns, anomalies, or simply to measure performance[19,20,21]. It also includes interpretation, presentation, and communication of discovered patterns to improve decision-making. Analytics approaches or methods can include descriptive analytics (using historic or current data to determine "what" happened and "how" it happened), predictive analytics (understanding the "why" or cause and effect relationships within data in order to be able to make accurate predictions), and prescriptive analytics (using algorithms to suggest optimal decisions based on the results of descriptive and predictive analytics). Often going hand in hand with data analytics, *data science* is a method for drawing insights from large datasets of structured and unstructured data. It draws on approaches, methods, techniques, and theories from disciplines such as mathematics, statistics, computer science, and information science. For example, it may draw on machine learning and deep learning techniques from the computer science field to learn from past decisions in order to improve the quality of automatically prescribed decisions. Or it may draw on statistical methods such as regression analysis and structural equation modelling to improve the reliability of information used as a basis for prescribed decisions. The role of data scientists can include activities such as collecting data, cleaning data, organizing data, making statistical inferences, building / using machine learning or deep learning models, conducting online experiments, building customizable or personalized data products, visualizing data, communicating findings, and much more[22,23]. Collectively, data management, data analytics, and data science capabilities have the same business aims: leveraging internal and external data to drive efficiency, differentiation, adaptability, and agility

New or enhanced accounting roles and competencies required for data management, data analytics, and data science

Managers can play a range of roles in an organization's data management, data analytics, and data science capabilities. These include establishing a data management / data analytics / data science function, establishing data management / data analytics / data science objectives, championing data-driven decision-making, hiring / line managing relevant staff or service providers, sponsoring data management / data analytics / data science leaders, authorizing what systems to map and connect, getting relevant parties on board with change efforts[24], approving funding for data investment projects, approving what data to use from inside or outside the organization, championing or authorizing the release of function-specific data, approving procurement of particular data management technologies, and more.

As well as supporting and catalyzing managers' data management / data analytics / data science roles and activities, accountants need to play an important organizational leadership role in the building, maintaining, and optimization of their organization's data management, data analytics, and data science capabilities. This is a central part of their evolving roles as data stewards, data analysts, systems designers, assurance providers, cyber risk managers, strategic risk navigators, brand protectors, storytellers, trusted professionals, process and control experts, co-pilots, and digital and technology enablers[25,26,27]. In playing this organization-wide leadership role, accountants may need to explain the financial value of different data and data management activities, they may be involved in setting organizational objectives for data management / data analytics / data science, or they may be involved in driving data integration and accessibility across functions and hierarchies. Alternatively, they may be involved in specific data management activities. For example, they may be involved in preparing / reviewing / approving business cases for data projects, they may be involved in advising managers on business intelligence and data analytics requirements, they may be involved in building data products, they may be involved in using data products to improve decision-making, and they may be involved in auditing data products or data management activities.

To play an effective leadership role in data management / data analytics / data science capabilities and activities, accountants require knowledge of and skills in data management / data analytics / data science (e.g. an understanding of the objectives, functioning, methodologies / tools, challenges, state-of-the-art practices, key terminology, and related artefacts). In addition, they need the enterprise architecture management and technology sourcing competencies we described earlier.

Google and reflect

Table 9.3 Google and reflect

Digital capability	Common terminology
Enterprise Architecture Management	enterprise architecture, enterprise architectural planning (EAP), enterprise architecture management (EAM), Enterprise Architecture Body of Knowledge (EABOK), enterprise architect, enterprise architecture modeling (EAM), enterprise architecture framework, business architecture, information architecture, information systems architecture, data architecture, DevOps architecture, architecture repository, service-oriented architecture (SOA), backward compatibility.
Technology Sourcing	procurement market Intelligence, supplier co-creation, internal sourcing, partner-based sourcing, market-based sourcing, value chain sourcing, industry–university collaboration, technology scanning, technology transfer, technology licensing, technological alliance, technology acquisition, joint R&D
Data Management, Data Analytics, and Data Science	database, data mart, data warehouse, data lake, data catalog, enterprise data hub, data fabric, operational data store, data governance, data Architecture, open data, machine learning, deep learning, neural networks, data mining, data set, data democratization, natural language processing, data anonymization, behavioral analytics, citizen data scientist, data classification, decision trees, multidimensional database (MDB), online analytical processing (OLAP), outlier, predictive modelling, Python, R (programming language), random forest, validity, reliability, decision science, association analytics, sentiment analysis, time decomposition, cluster analysis.

Discussion questions

1. What is the difference between enterprise architecture, IT architecture, and technology architecture?
2. What role does enterprise architecture play in digital business capability?
3. Which acccounting role in enterprise architecture management is the most critical to building and maintaining that capability? Why?
4. Which accounting enterprise architecture management competency is likely to have the greatest positive impact on an accountant's career?
5. What is the difference between technology sourcing and technology procurement?
6. Which accounting role in technology sourcing is the most critical to building and maintaining that capability? Why?
7. What is the difference between data management and data analytics?
8. Which is more important, data management or data analytics? Why?
9. Which data management and data analytics related accounting competency is likely to have the greatest positive impact on an accountant's career?
10. Which of the capabilities discussed in this chapter is the most important to succeeding at digital transformation and digital business?

Notes

1. Ritz-Carlton. (2020). Gold standards. Retrieved June 6, 2020, from: https://www.ritzcarlton.com/en/about/gold-standards
2. Daniel, D. (2007, March 31). The rising importance of the enterprise architect. CIO. Retrieved from: https://www.cio.com/article/2439397/the-rising-importance-of-the-enterprise-architect.html
3. White, S.K. (2018, October 16). What is enterprise architecture? A framework for transformation. CIO. Retrieved from: https://www.cio.com/article/3313657/what-is-enterprise-architecture-a-framework-for-transformation.html
4. Ross, J.W., Weill, P., & Robertson, D. (2006). Enterprise architecture as strategy: Creating a foundation for business execution. Harvard Business Press.
5. Daniel, D. (2007, March 31). The rising importance of the enterprise architect. CIO. Retrieved from: https://www.cio.com/article/2439397/the-rising-importance-of-the-enterprise-architect.html
6. Daniel, D. (2007, March 31). The rising importance of the enterprise architect. CIO. Retrieved from: https://www.cio.com/article/2439397/the-rising-importance-of-the-enterprise-architect.html
7. Suer, M. F. (2018, June 26). Enterprise architects as digital transformers. CIO. Retrieved from: https://www.cio.com/article/3284475/enterprise-architects-as-digital-transformers.html
8. Kudryavtsev, D., Zaramenskikh, E., & Arzumanyan, M. (2018). The simplified enterprise architecture management methodology for teaching purposes. Lecture Notes in Business Information Processing, 76–90. https://doi.org/10.1007/978-3-030-00787-4_6
9. Kudryavtsev, D., Zaramenskikh, E., & Arzumanyan, M. (2018). The simplified enterprise architecture management methodology for teaching purposes. Lecture Notes in Business Information Processing, 76–90. https://doi.org/10.1007/978-3-030-00787-4_6
10. Ovans, A. (2015, May 12). What is strategy, again? Harvard Business Review. Retrieved June 7, 2020, from: https://hbr.org/2015/05/what-is-strategy-again
11. Busulwa, R., Tice, M., & Gurd, B. (2018). Strategy execution and complexity: Thriving in the era of disruption. Routledge.
12. Daniel, D. (2007, March 31). The rising importance of the enterprise architect. CIO. Retrieved from: https://www.cio.com/article/2439397/the-rising-importance-of-the-enterprise-architect.html
13. Pettey, C. (2018, July 16). Top trends for the future of IT procurement. Gartner. Retrieved June 7, 2020, from: https://www.gartner.com/smarterwithgartner/top-trends-for-the-future-of-it-procurement/
14. Sinclair, S. (2020). What are the future skills of sourcing? Aalto University. Retrieved June 8, 2020,: https://www.aaltopro.fi/en/aalto-leaders-insight/2020/what-are-the-future-skills-of-sourcing

15 Desjardins, J. (2019, April 17). How much data is generated each day? World Economic Forum. Retrieved June 7, 2020, from: https://www.weforum.org/agenda/2019/04/how-much-data-is-generated-each-day-cf4bddf29f/
16 Brylad, M. (2019). Data literacy: A critical skill for the 21st century. Tableau Software. Retrieved 17 December 2019, from: https://www.tableau.com/about/blog/2018/9/data-literacy-critical-skill-21st-century-94221
17 What Is Data Management? (2019). Oracle.Com. Retrieved December 9, 2019, from: https://www.oracle.com/au/database/what-is-data-management/.
18 Analytics. (2019). Gartner. Retrieved December 16, 2019, from: https://www.gartner.com/en/information-technology/glossary/analytics
19 Comparing business intelligence, business analytics and data analytics. (2019). Tableau Software. Retrieved December 16, 2019, from: https://www.tableau.com/learn/articles/business-intelligence/bi-business-analytics
20 Business analytics: Everything you need to know. (2019). MicroStrategy. Retrieved December 16, 2019, from: https://www.microstrategy.com/us/resources/introductory-guides/business-analytics-everything-you-need-to-know
21 Boulton, C. (2019). Data analytics examples: An inside look at 6 success stories. CIO. Retrieved December 17, 2019, from: https://www.cio.com/article/3221621/6-data-analytics-success-stories-an-inside-look.html
22 Bowne-Anderson, H. (2018). What data scientists really do, according to 35 data scientists. Harvard Business Review. Retrieved December 17, 2019, from: https://hbr.org/2018/08/what-data-scientists-really-do-according-to-35-data-scientists
23 What is data science?. (2019). Oracle.com. Retrieved December 17, 2019, from: https://www.oracle.com/data-science/what-is-data-science.html
24 Daniel, D. (2007, March 31). The rising importance of the enterprise architect. CIO. Retrieved from: https://www.cio.com/article/2439397/the-rising-importance-of-the-enterprise-architect.html
25 Sledgianowski, D., Gomaa, M., & Tan, C. (2017). Toward integration of big data, technology and information systems competencies into the accounting curriculum. Journal of Accounting Education, 38, 81–93.
26 Coyne, J.G., Coyne, E.M., & Walker, K.B. (2016). A model to update accounting curricula for emerging technologies. Journal of Emerging Technologies in Accounting, 13(1), 161–169.
27 IFAC. (2019). Future-fit accountants: Roles for the next decade. Retrieved December 18, 2019, from: https://www.ifac.org/knowledge-gateway/preparing-future-ready-professionals/discussion/future-fit-accountants-roles-next

10 The role of accountants in cybersecurity, information privacy, and digital ethics

Introduction

Depending on how they are used, digital technologies can present significant threats to the rights and wellbeing of individuals and to the effective functioning of political, economic, social, environmental, and legal institutions, processes, and practices. Individuals, societies, and institutions are increasingly conscious of these threats. And they are apprehensive about the trust they place in organizations to safeguard against them. So, in their quest to leverage digital technologies to become and compete as digital businesses, organizations must ensure they are conscious of these threats and have effective practices to safeguard against their enhancement or materialization. Organizations that don't do this can quickly find themselves in a position where they have put customers, societies, and institutions in grave danger; in addition to greatly increasing their chance of going out of business (e.g. consider the case of Cambridge Analytica). In this chapter, we unpack two important capabilities for organizations in the digital era: cybersecurity capability, and information privacy and digital ethics capability. We first outline the meaning of and need for these capabilities. We then discuss the risk of not sufficiently investing in the functions, processes, and practices involved in establishing these capabilities. Finally, we discuss the roles of accountants in establishing and continuously improving these capabilities, as well as the competencies accountants require to play those roles.

Required accounting roles and competencies for cybersecurity

Unpacking cybersecurity

At a very high level, *cybersecurity* refers to the state of or processes for protecting anything in the cyber realm (e.g. devices, software, networks, information, connected "things", etc.) and recovering from cyberattacks[1,2,3]. The terms information security, IT security, ICT security, computer security, and network security are sometimes interchangeably used to refer to cybersecurity – even though there are nuanced differences in meaning[4]. Typically, these terms refer to specific subsets of cybersecurity. For example, information security is mainly focused on protecting physical and digital information from unauthorized access, use, disclosure, disruption, modification, or destruction, in order to provide confidentiality, integrity, and availability[5,6]. And IT security / ICT security / computer security tend to focus more narrowly on protecting computers, networks, and data (but what about the exploding diversity in things and ecosystems?). Given some of the slipperiness, overlaps, and limitations of these terms, the term cybersecurity has emerged as a more flexible and all-encompassing term. But there have still been differences in the way practitioners and researchers have defined cybersecurity. Daniel Schatz, global head of cybersecurity at Qiagen, as well as former director of threat and vulnerability management at Thompson Reuters, and Julie Wall, a senior researcher at the University of East London, reviewed and synthesized the various definitions to arrive at a more specific and all-encompassing definition of cybersecurity. They proposed that cybersecurity is[7]:

> The approach and actions associated with security risk management processes followed by organizations and states to protect confidentiality, integrity and availability of data and assets used in cyberspace. The concept includes guidelines, policies and collections of safeguards, technologies, tools and training to provide the best protection for the state of the cyber environment and its users.

Except for protecting your personal online security and privacy, cybersecurity may not have historically been in your consciousness as a big deal for employees outside the IT or IS function. And you may be wondering what has changed to make it an issue warranting much attention from accountants. If so, consider these questions: How much of your organization's information was indefinitely online in the past vs. now? How many devices within and outside of your organization were "plugged" into that information in the past vs. now? How many people around the world were online and able to hack into your information systems in the past vs. now? How sophisticated was the computation available to hackers in the past vs. now? How fast was internet connectivity speed in the past vs. now? How much integration was there in the past vs. now? As you may be starting to see, digital technology advancements and the associated race to digitally transform and become a digital business have meant that nearly all of most organizations' resources are now online, and potentially accessible by billions of people anywhere in the world (some with sinister motives). On top of this, the exponentially growing proliferation of things, external networks, and ecosystems plugging into an organization's online resources almost creates the effect of having millions, even billions, of potential front doors to your house that you may or may not be aware of. And data flows from and to devices, from and to core systems with sensitive data, from and to external networks and devices, from and to different locations around the world, and from and to different digital ecosystems. At any point during that flow, or while it resides in a particular storage location, digitized data and information can be intercepted by sophisticated cybercriminals anywhere in the world. For example, they may intercept login details, they may steal identification information for selling on to identity thieves, they may steal company trade secrets or key stakeholder intellectual property, they may alter company records for their own gain, they may steal sensitive key person information and hold those people to ransom, they may steal and dump sensitive customer data online in order jeopardize the organization, and much more. Thus, the significantly expanded digitization, connectivity, integration, and ubiquity related to digital transformation and digital business means new and significantly expanded digital vulnerabilities. In fact, massive cybersecurity breaches have become almost commonplace now, with even prestige brands regularly being in attention-grabbing and alarming breach headlines[8]. For example, in early 2020 Marriott International was in one such breach headline[9]. A cybercriminal had hacked the login details of two employees from a franchise property and used those login details to access customer information from the app's backend systems[10]. This impacted 5.2 million customers and included access to personal information such as names, addresses, phone numbers, dates of birth, gender, travel history, travel plans, etc.[11] It followed another incident in 2018 in which 383 million guests' details were stolen (these included names, addresses, passport numbers, credit card numbers, etc.)[12,13]. Imagine how you would feel as a customer, any one of these incidents may have undone any credibility or brand trust. And it could have been much worse, imagine if cybercriminals used guests' travel history and mobile information to track down key persons in remote locations and held them hostage or sold them into human trafficking rings. In addition to ruining customers' lives, almost a century of brand building could have been brought down overnight; and thousands of people could have lost their jobs. Perhaps due to the growing breaches and the significant risks customers are exposed to, a number of governments around the world have started to introduce mandatory data breach reporting laws, requiring organizations to report data breaches where personal information they hold is subject to unauthorized access or disclosure[14,15]. This makes the naming and shaming through attention-grabbing headlines a certainty for organizations that fail to protect the data entrusted into their care. Finally, it goes without saying that the financial costs involved in a breach can be ruinous; these are typically exacerbated by the time it takes to discover the breach, respond to it, and recover from the disruption – to the extent this is actually possible[16]. Table 10.1 shows the top ten messages for leaders synthesized from the World Economic Forum's annual meeting exploring critical and emerging cybersecurity issues.

Table 10.1 Ten messages for global leaders from the 2019 World Economic Forum annual meeting on cybersecurity[17]

No.	Cybersecurity risk / Practice insight
1	Cyberattacks are increasing in frequency and sophistication. It is thus the responsibility of public and corporate leaders to take ownership for ensuring global cybersecurity and digital trust.
2	Board and C-Suite members need to gain a better understanding of the cyber risks to which their organization is exposed and of their cyber readiness.
3	Both public and private organizations need to improve their crisis management, develop holistic responses and recovery plans, including a crisis communication strategy.
4	Leaders need to create a culture of cybersecurity from the entry level to the top leadership of an organization.
5	Leaders may need to rethink organizational structures and governance to enable a more robust cybersecurity posture.
6	Innovation in cybersecurity and rapidly evolving technologies call for greater investment to stay ahead of cybercriminals who are adopting such technologies even faster and to their advantage.
7	Global cooperation across the public and the private sectors is vital. Information-sharing, business cooperation with law enforcement agencies, as well as skills and capacity development need to be prioritized.
8	Maintaining and open and secure internet requires a collaborative effort between the public and private sector.
9	Trusted and verified cybersecurity ratings are required for the improved assessment of an organization's cyber resilience and comparability across peers.
10	The World Economic Forum provides a neutral, trusted, and globally recognized platform to facilitate cooperation and deliver tangible impact on the systemic challenge of global cybersecurity.

Cybersecurity capability and cybersecurity management

Cybersecurity capability refers to how effectively an organization can protect itself against and recover from cyber threats (e.g. how effective its cybersecurity infrastructure consisting of hardware, software, processes, people, etc. is). And *cybersecurity management* refers to the processes and practices of planning, implementing, maintaining, and continuously upgrading an organization's cybersecurity capability. According to the National Institute of Standards and Technology cybersecurity framework[18] (NIST CSF), cybersecurity capability consists of five core functions: identify, protect, detect, respond, and recover (see Figure 10.1). The *identify* function involves developing a clear understanding of the business's processes and environment, its supporting systems / people / assets / data / capabilities, the cyber threats faced by these systems / people / assets / data / capabilities (e.g. ransomware, hacking, data leakage, insider threat), and the potential impact of these threats on the organization. It includes asset management, business environment, governance, risk assessment, and risk management strategy practices. The *protect* function involves establishing and maintaining appropriate safeguards to prevent or limit the impact of a potential cybersecurity event. It includes practices such as identity management and access control, awareness training, data security, information protection processes and procedures, and the use of protective technology. The *detect* function involves establishing and maintaining appropriate activities for the timely identification of cybersecurity events. It includes practice such as anomaly detection, information security continuous monitoring (ISCM), and detection processes. The *respond* function involves establishing and maintaining processes for containing the impact of a detected cybersecurity incident. It includes practices such as response planning, communication, analysis, mitigation and improvements. Finally, the

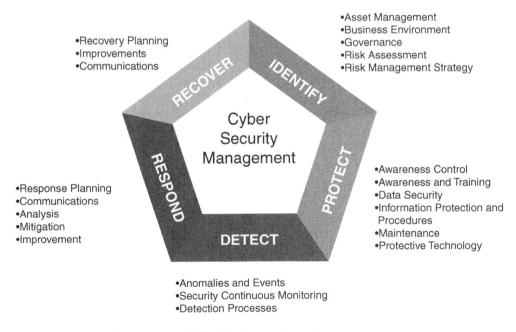

Figure 10.1 NIST cybersecurity capability functions and practices

recover function involves establishing and maintaining resiliency and service / capability restoration plans (i.e. plans that can be effected for timely recovery from a disruptive cybersecurity incident). It includes practices such as recovery planning, communication, and continuous improvement. See the cybersecurity capability maturity model (C2M2) for an example of an alternative cybersecurity capability framework[19].

New or enhanced accounting roles and competencies for cybersecurity management

Effective cybersecurity management and an effective cybersecurity capability require top management team ownership / engagement, a top-down approach to cybersecurity strategy, and integration of cybersecurity policies / activities into operations. This helps to ensure that cyber and privacy risks are managed effectively in every part of the organization[20,21,22]. Effective cybersecurity management and capability also requires leaders to cultivate, and drive the cultivation of, a cyber risk management culture at all levels of the organization. Managers may play the role of a top management team leader with ownership for the organization's overall cybersecurity capability (e.g. hiring the right functional leader, building the credibility and influence of this leader, and establishing cybersecurity objectives and governance mechanisms). Or they may play other roles such as ensuring employee understanding of and compliance with cybersecurity policies, ensuring employees report cybersecurity breach events, and ensuring employees have adequate knowledge of and competency in cybersecurity – so that they are able to avoid cybersecurity compromising behaviors[23]. In their navigator, brand protector, trusted professional, and process and control expert roles, accountants can support and accelerate managers' cybersecurity management efforts; as well as provide organization-wide leadership of cybersecurity attitudes, behaviors, and initiatives. One example of such managerial support and organization-wide leadership of cybersecurity capability by accountants is ensuring the right information is available and accessible at all levels and in all parts of the organization regarding cybersecurity-related risks, threats, events, behaviors, and attitudes. Another is championing a leader's efforts (e.g. an IS security leader) to effectively communicate cyber risk exposures and their implications for the organization's performance and longevity; or supporting IS security leaders to effectively make the case for cybersecurity capability investments. To play effective managerial support and organization-wide cybersecurity leadership roles, accountants need a working understanding of the cybersecurity function's objectives, functioning, and challenges. They also need sufficient understanding of cyber risks and threats, of state-of-the-art cybersecurity practices, and of cybersecurity terminology / language.

Required accounting roles and competencies for information privacy and other digital ethics issues

Unpacking information privacy

Information privacy refers to an individual's interest in and / or ability to control, or at least significantly influence, the handling of data about themselves[24]. Information privacy includes personal communication privacy, personal behavior privacy, and personal data privacy[25]. The handling of data refers to issues like what data is collected and how, the primary use (the purpose for which the data is originally collected), secondary uses (what purposes other than the primary purpose is the data used for), any unauthorized secondary use, what analysis is done on the data, what improper access it is exposed to, what errors are in it, and how long the data will be kept for (e.g. does this impinge on a person's "right to be forgotten"). Although the concept of privacy existed before the advent of digital technologies[26,27,28], the use of digital technologies results in significant privacy threats. For example, consider the expanded access to information (e.g. using big data, data analytics, search engines, social networks, triangulation algorithms), the ubiquity (e.g. digital technologies are with us when we sleep, when we wake up, while we are working, while we are socializing, etc.), the undetectability (e.g. of cookies, location-based services, real-time video analytics, miniaturized devices, etc.) and the invasiveness (e.g. implantable chips) of digital technologies. Also consider the permanency of the data they capture, the near real-time external accessibility to this data, and the ease with which it can be sold on and used anywhere around the world. Unfortunately, although consumers desire privacy, they are often in a situation where they can't receive certain services without sharing personal information. Outside of leveraging privacy-enhancing technologies in the purchasing process and avoiding consumption, consumers typically have to place their trust in particular brands and / or in regulators.

Digital ethics and digital ethics issues

Besides privacy and security, there are a range of other technology-related ethical threats that are generally collated under the umbrella of *digital ethics*[29]. Digital ethics considers the ethicality of the existing and potential impacts of digital technologies on political, social, economic, environmental, and legal dynamics and entities. For example, it considers and builds discussion of issues such as ethics of surveillance, when and what information can be given to the state, digital monopolies (growing concentration of power in large technology companies), uses of and regulation of artificial intelligence, automation and robotics-driven unemployment, disparity between tech-savvy and non-tech-savvy people, transparency in how data is held / where it is held / who has access to it, discrimination embedded in algorithms and big data, environmental impacts of digital technology-related waste, and more. Organizations not conscious of or not reflecting these broader digital ethics issues in their policies and conduct can quickly find themselves on the wrong side of an issue. For example, Cambridge Analytica[30,31], Facebook[32], Google[33], Twitter[34], and Amazon[35] have recently found themselves in the crossfire in relation to one or more of these ethics issues. Thus, when choosing which digital technologies to leverage and how to leverage them, in addition to security and privacy implications, organizations need to consider the broader digital ethics implications relating to use of those digital technologies.

Consumers, governments, and advocacy groups are increasingly conscious of and concerned with the information privacy and other digital ethics practices of organizations. Besides the resultant ethical threats these practices can create, for some consumers the practices are also about respect – and they feel disrespected by organizations that disregard or don't take seriously their privacy and digital ethics concerns. Thus, through their particular actions or non-actions, organizations can alleviate threat or respect concerns and enhance the trust customers have in them; or they can disregard or be oblivious to these concerns and erode consumer trust. Their actions or non-actions, then, can have significant consequences for their brand image, profitability, and longevity.

New or enhanced accounting roles and competencies for information privacy and digital ethics

As with other digital capabilities, managers can play a critical role in their organizations' information privacy and digital ethics capabilities. For example: they can embed a culture of privacy that enables compliance (e.g. ensure staff understand their privacy responsibilities, and assign roles and responsibilities for information privacy and digital ethics management). They can institute reporting processes to keep top management informed of evolving ethics issues and practices. They can put in place effective information privacy and digital ethics practices / procedures / systems (e.g. having an information privacy and digital ethics policy, establishing processes for receiving and responding to information privacy and digital ethics issues or complaints, and integrating information privacy and digital ethics into induction and training processes). And they can evaluate and continuously improve information privacy and digital ethics practices (e.g. regularly review policies / processes / events, monitor performance to plan, establish processes for staff and other stakeholders to provide feedback, establish processes for staying up to date with evolving expectations / best practices in relation to information privacy and digital ethics)[36]. In addition to the aforementioned roles, managers at all levels can set the tone[37] for information privacy and digital ethics through what they say, how they behave, how they handle information privacy and digital ethics situations[38], who they reward, and who they promote. Accountants can play an invaluable role in enabling managers to undertake the aforementioned roles. For example, they can ensure managers have access to the best information to enable them to anticipate or spot early any privacy and digital ethics-related risks / events / behaviors / attitudes. They can ensure managers have the best information to assess the effectiveness of information privacy and digital ethics-related policies and procedures. And they can ensure managers have clear visibility of the contribution of different employees / suppliers / customers / other stakeholders to the organization's information privacy and digital ethics objectives.

To effectively support managers' efforts and provide broader organizational leadership of information privacy and digital ethics, accountants need a working understanding of information privacy and digital ethics issues, risks, and management best practices. They also need to ensure they keep up with evolutions in these issues, risks, and best practices – given they change rapidly with digital technology advancements and growth in number of organizations / other things coming online.

Google and reflect

Table 10.2 Google and reflect

Digital capability	Common terminology
Cybersecurity	cyber risk, cybersecurity, cybersecurity capability, cybersecurity management, cybersecurity framework, NIST CSF, cybersecurity event, cyber resilience, identity management, access control, anomaly detection, security continuous monitoring, cyber response planning, cyber recovery planning, DevSecOps, cyber insurance, ransomware
Information Privacy and Digital Ethics	privacy, information privacy, information privacy threat, right to be left alone, right to be forgotten, digital ethics, privacy-enhancing technologies, breach disclosure, data breach notification, Privacy Act, data breach reporting laws

Discussion questions

1 What is the difference between cybersecurity, IT security, and ICT security?
2 What is the difference between cybersecurity management and cybersecurity?
3 What is the difference between privacy and information privacy?
4 What is the relationship between information privacy and digital ethics?
5 What is the relationship between cybersecurity, information privacy, and digital ethics?
6 What are the top three digital ethics issues at the moment?
7 Which is more important, cybersecurity, information privacy, or digital ethics?
8 Which accounting role in information privacy and digital ethics is most important to an organization's information privacy and digital ethics capability?
9 Which cybersecurity management related accounting competency is likely to have the greatest positive impact on an accountant's career?
10 Which of the capabilities discussed in this chapter is the most important to succeeding at digital transformation and digital business?

Notes

1 Cisco. (2020). What is information security (InfoSec)? Retrieved June 8, 2020, from: https://www.cisco.com/c/en/us/products/security/what-is-information-security-infosec.html
2 Secureworks. (2017). Cybersecurity vs. network security vs. information security. Retrieved June 8, 2020, from: https://www.secureworks.com/blog/cybersecurity-vs-network-security-vs-information-security
3 Norton. (2020). What is cyber security? What you need to know. Retrieved June 8, 2020, from: https://us.norton.com/internetsecurity-malware-what-is-cybersecurity-what-you-need-to-know.html
4 Schatz, D., Bashroush, R., & Wall, J. (2017). Towards a more representative definition of cyber security. Journal of Digital Forensics, Security and Law, 12(2), 53–74.
5 Cisco. (2020). What is information security (InfoSec)? Retrieved June 9, 2020, from: https://www.cisco.com/c/en/us/products/security/what-is-information-security-infosec.html
6 Secureworks. (2017). Cybersecurity vs. network security vs. information security. Retrieved June 8, 2020, from: https://www.secureworks.com/blog/cybersecurity-vs-network-security-vs-information-security
7 Schatz, D., Bashroush, R., & Wall, J. (2017). Towards a more representative definition of cyber security. Journal of Digital Forensics, Security and Law, 12(2), 53–74.
8 Castelli, C., Gabriel, B., Yates, J., & Booth, P. (2017). Strengthening digital society against cyber shocks. PricewaterhouseCoopers. Retrieved June 8, 2020, from: https://www.pwc.com/us/en/services/consulting/cybersecurity/library/information-security-survey/strengthening-digital-society-against-cyber-shocks.html
9 Cimpanu, C. (2020, March 31). Marriott discloses new data breach impacting 5.2 million hotel guests. ZDNet. Retrieved June 8, 2020, from: https://www.zdnet.com/article/marriott-discloses-new-data-breach-impacting-5-2-million-hotel-guests/
10 Cimpanu, C. (2020, March 31). Marriott discloses new data breach impacting 5.2 million hotel guests. ZDNet. Retrieved June 8, 2020, from: https://www.zdnet.com/article/marriott-discloses-new-data-breach-impacting-5-2-million-hotel-guests/
11 Cimpanu, C. (2020, March 31). Marriott discloses new data breach impacting 5.2 million hotel guests. ZDNet. Retrieved June 8, 2020, from: https://www.zdnet.com/article/marriott-discloses-new-data-breach-impacting-5-2-million-hotel-guests/
12 Fruhlinger, J. (2020, February 12). Marriott data breach FAQ: How did it happen and what was the impact? Retrieved June 9, 2020, from: https://www.csoonline.com/article/3441220/marriott-data-breach-faq-how-did-it-happen-and-what-was-the-impact.html
13 Cimpanu, C. (2019, January 4). Marriott says less than 383 million guests impacted by breach, not 500 million. ZDNet. Retrieved June 9, 2020, from: https://www.zdnet.com/article/marriott-says-less-than-383-million-guests-impacted-by-breach-not-500-million/

14 Easton, S. (2019, May 20). Almost 1000 data breaches in a year, and citizens don't know who to trust with privacy. Retrieved June 8, 2020, from: https://www.themandarin.com.au/108762-almost-1000-data-breaches-in-a-year-and-citizens-dont-know-who-to-trust-with-privacy/
15 Innes, K. (2019). One year of mandatory data breach reporting: Insights and lessons. Bradley Allen Love Lawyers. Retrieved June 8, 2020, from: https://ballawyers.com.au/2019/05/28/mandatory-data-breach-reporting/
16 Swinhoe, D. (2020, May 8). What is the cost of a data breach? CSO. Retrieved June 9, 2020, from: https://www.csoonline.com/article/3434601/what-is-the-cost-of-a-data-breach.html#tk.ciofsb
17 Müller, M.S., & Zwinggi, A. (2020, January 19). Global leaders must take responsibility for cybersecurity. Here's why. World Economic Forum. Retrieved June 19, 2020, from: https://www.weforum.org/agenda/2020/01/global-leaders-must-take-responsibility-for-cybersecurity-here-s-why-and-how/
18 Christopher, J. (2018, November 1). Council Post: The cybersecurity maturity model: A means to measure and improve your cybersecurity program. Forbes. Retrieved from: https://www.forbes.com/sites/forbestechcouncil/2018/11/01/the-cybersecurity-maturity-model-a-means-to-measure-and-improve-your-cybersecurity-program/#32e367a680bc
19 Christopher, J. (2018, November 1). Council Post: The cybersecurity maturity model: A means to measure and improve your cybersecurity program. Forbes. Retrieved from: https://www.forbes.com/sites/forbestechcouncil/2018/11/01/the-cybersecurity-maturity-model-a-means-to-measure-and-improve-your-cybersecurity-program/#32e367a680bc
20 Castelli, C., Gabriel, B., Yates, J., & Booth, P. (2017). Strengthening digital society against cyber shocks. PricewaterhouseCoopers. Retrieved June 8, 2020, from: https://www.pwc.com/us/en/services/consulting/cybersecurity/library/information-security-survey/strengthening-digital-society-against-cyber-shocks.html
21 Oltsik, J. (2019, February 19). Enterprises need to embrace top-down cybersecurity management. Retrieved June 9, 2020, from: https://www.csoonline.com/article/3342036/enterprises-need-to-embrace-top-down-cybersecurity-management.html
22 Dutta, A., & McCrohan, K. (2002). Management's role in information security in a cyber economy. California Management Review, 45(1), 67–87. https://doi.org/10.2307/41166154
23 Dutta, A., & McCrohan, K. (2002). Management's role in information security in a cyber economy. California Management Review, 45(1), 67–87. https://doi.org/10.2307/41166154
24 Bélanger, F., & Crossler, R.E. (2011). Privacy in the digital age: A review of information privacy research in information systems. MIS quarterly, 35(4), 1017–1042.
25 Bélanger, F., & Crossler, R.E. (2011). Privacy in the digital age: A review of information privacy research in information systems. MIS quarterly, 35(4), 1017–1042.
26 Bélanger, F., & Crossler, R.E. (2011). Privacy in the digital age: A review of information privacy research in information systems. MIS quarterly, 35(4), 1017–1042.
27 Igo, S.E. (2018). The known citizen: A history of privacy in modern America. Harvard University Press.
28 Holvast, J. (2007). History of privacy. In The history of information security (pp. 737–769). Elsevier Science BV.
29 de Broglie, C. (2016). We need to talk about digital ethics. OECD. Retrieved June 10, 2020, from: https://www.oecd.org/science/we-need-to-talk-about-digital-ethics.htm
30 Facebook and Cambridge Analytica: What you need to know as fallout widens. (2018, March 19). The New York Times. Retrieved from: https://www.nytimes.com/2018/03/19/technology/facebook-cambridge-analytica-explained.html
31 Wong, J.C. (2019). The Cambridge Analytica scandal changed the world – but it didn't change Facebook. The Guardian. Retrieved June 10, 2020, from: https://www.theguardian.com/technology/2019/mar/17/the-cambridge-analytica-scandal-changed-the-world-but-it-didnt-change-facebook
32 Foroohar, R. (2020). EU and US regulators scrutinise big tech and digital "monopoly". Financial Times. Retrieved June 10, 2020, from: https://www.ft.com/content/f7b13372-3797-11ea-a6d3-9a26f8c3cba4
33 Novet, J. (2019). Google cancels A.I. ethics panel after uproar. CNBC. Retrieved June 10, 2020, from: https://www.cnbc.com/2019/04/04/google-cancels-controversial-ai-ethics-panel.html
34 Scott, M. (2020). Twitter labels Trump tweet as "glorifying violence". Politico. Retrieved June 10, 2020, from: https://www.politico.com/news/2020/05/29/twitter-labels-trump-tweet-as-glorifying-violence-288356
35 Biswas, S. (2020). Why India is greeting Amazon's Jeff Bezos with protests. BBC News. Retrieved from: https://www.bbc.com/news/world-asia-india-51117315

36 Office of the Australian Information Commissioner. (2016). Privacy management plan template (for organizations). Retrieved June 10, 2020, from: https://www.oaic.gov.au/privacy/guidance-and-advice/privacy-management-plan-template-for-organizations/
37 Southeastern Oklahoma State University. (2016). Why ethics are still essential in management. Retrieved June 9, 2020, from: https://online.se.edu/articles/mba/why-ethics-are-still-essential-in-management.aspx
38 Southeastern Oklahoma State University. (2016). Why ethics are still essential in management. Retrieved June 9, 2020, from: https://online.se.edu/articles/mba/why-ethics-are-still-essential-in-management.aspx

11 The role of accountants in digital leadership, accelerated change and transformation, digital risk management, and digital governance

Introduction

Digital disruption, digital transformation, and digital business demand rapid shifts in an organization's culture and its execution speed (i.e. speed at which it implements strategies, changes, and plans). Effectively bringing about the required cultural shifts and execution speed requires new or adapted leadership roles and competencies that are conceptualized as digital leadership, and juxtaposed against traditional leadership. As well as being steep achievement challenges, the rapid shifts in culture and execution capability come with significant change risks that leaders have to manage. But, although serious, these change risks are dwarfed by the new risk exposures created by the use of new digital technologies, digital business models, and digital processes. These new and significantly expanded risk exposures demand sophisticated and fast risk management and governance practices. Fortunately, as well as the new risks they create, digital technologies offer a swathe of sophisticated tools that can be leveraged to supercharge the effectiveness of risk management and governance practices. Leveraging of these tools to optimize risk management and governance or managing the unique risks associated with digital technologies what is commonly referred to as digital risk management and digital governance. In this chapter, we introduce accountants to these concepts of digital leadership, accelerated change and transformation, digital risk management, and digital governance (i.e. what are they, how do they differ from their traditional counterpart terms, what is their value proposition, what constitutes best practice for each capability). We then discuss the roles and competencies these organizational capabilities require of accountants.

Required accounting roles and competencies for digital leadership

Digital leadership vs. traditional leadership

Digital disruption, digital transformation, and digital business present unique leadership challenges (e.g. the need for fast decision-making and execution, the need to make rapid shifts in organization culture, the need to transform the workforce into a flexible and distributed workplace, the need for significant efficiency breakthroughs, the need to manage virtual workforces, etc.). These unique challenges require new leadership roles or adaptations of traditional leadership roles and activities. The augmentation of traditional leadership roles and activities with new or adapted roles and activities suited to digital contexts is what is referred to as *digital leadership* (also referred to as e-leadership in academic research). Thus, digital

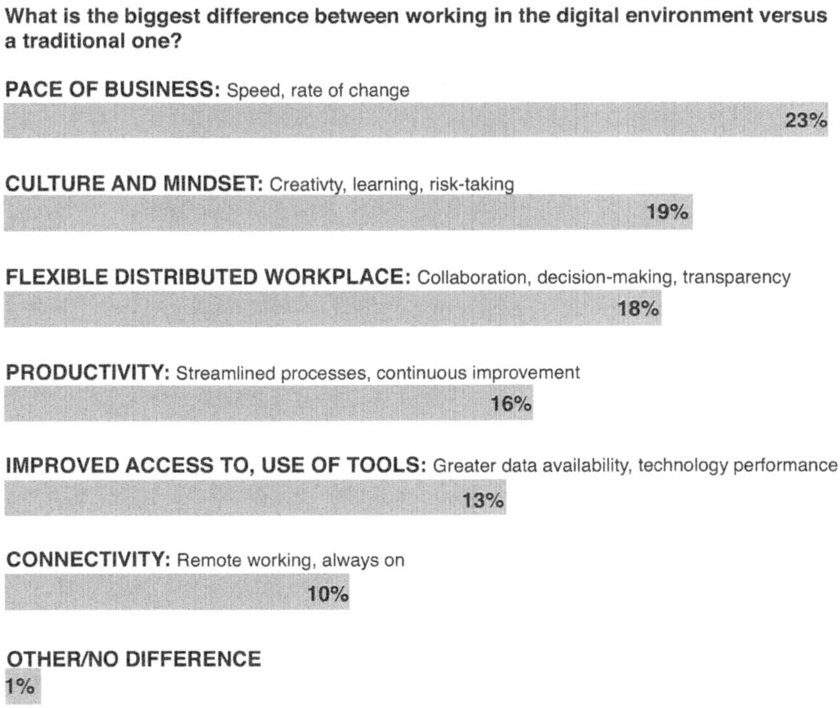

What is the biggest difference between working in the digital environment versus a traditional one?

PACE OF BUSINESS: Speed, rate of change
23%

CULTURE AND MINDSET: Creativty, learning, risk-taking
19%

FLEXIBLE DISTRIBUTED WORKPLACE: Collaboration, decision-making, transparency
18%

PRODUCTIVITY: Streamlined processes, continuous improvement
16%

IMPROVED ACCESS TO, USE OF TOOLS: Greater data availability, technology performance
13%

CONNECTIVITY: Remote working, always on
10%

OTHER/NO DIFFERENCE
1%

Figure 11.1 Results of a survey of 3,300 *MIT Sloan Management Review* readers, Deloitte Dbriefs webcast subscribers, and other interested parties, regarding what is different about working in a digital business environment

leadership refers to the new or adapted roles / activities required of leaders to effectively lead digital transformation and digital business. And it refers to the augmentation of traditional leadership roles / activities with these new or adapted roles and activities. It also refers to the effect of carrying out these roles and activities to lead in a digital environment (e.g. Figure 11.1 identifies how a highly digitalized environment differs from a traditional one). Digital leadership can be considered from an individual leader level (e.g. the capacity of a leader to lead digital transformation and digital business initiatives) or from an organizational capability level (the collective ability of an organization's leaders, at all levels, to lead digital transformation and digital business initiatives). Organization digital leadership capability, then, refers to the presence and collective effectiveness of digital leaders in every part of the organization. Or, put another way, it is the effectiveness of the collection and configuration of an organization's digital leaders at all levels of the organization and across all parts of the value chain.

The new or adapted leadership roles of digital leadership

Several researchers and practitioners have discussed what new or adapted leadership roles / activities are required for digital leadership. Typically, these discussions focus on nine roles / activity groups. The first is that digital leaders have to set a digital transformation / digital

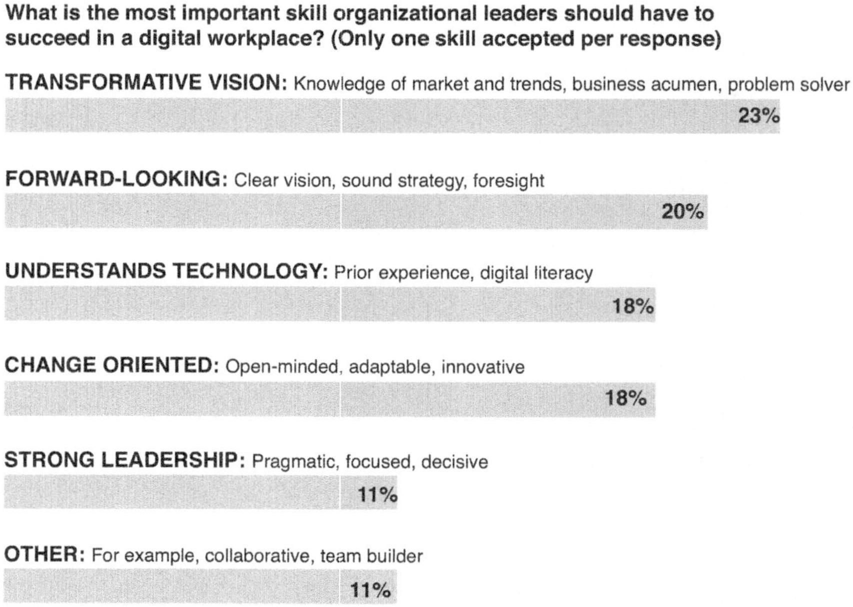

What is the most important skill organizational leaders should have to succeed in a digital workplace? (Only one skill accepted per response)

TRANSFORMATIVE VISION: Knowledge of market and trends, business acumen, problem solver
23%

FORWARD-LOOKING: Clear vision, sound strategy, foresight
20%

UNDERSTANDS TECHNOLOGY: Prior experience, digital literacy
18%

CHANGE ORIENTED: Open-minded, adaptable, innovative
18%

STRONG LEADERSHIP: Pragmatic, focused, decisive
11%

OTHER: For example, collaborative, team builder
11%

Figure 11.2 Results of a survey of 3,300 *MIT Sloan Management Review* readers, Deloitte Dbriefs webcast subscribers, and other interested parties, regarding the most important skill leaders need to succeed in a digital workplace

business vision and direction. This is a critical and unique role in that it requires leaders to understand how digital technology advancements, digital disruption, and digital transformation may play out at consumer, organization, industry, geographic, and societal level[1] – before they can set the digital transformation / digital business vision and direction. It can be considered as an augmentation of the traditional leadership role of vision / direction setting[2] with deep digital technology, digital disruption, digital transformation, and digital business strategy knowledge / skills. And it can be symbolically represented by the visionary digital leadership capabilities of leaders like Bill Gates (Microsoft), Steve Jobs (Apple), Reed Hastings (Netflix), and Andy Grove (Intel). Digital transformation / digital business vision or direction setting, and digital technology competency, are viewed as being among the top two or three leadership skills critical to success in digital workplaces (see Figure 11.2). The second role is that digital leaders have to be strong change agents and digital enablers who are able to push their organizations to seize the opportunities offered by digital technologies and digital disruption. These are typically fleeting opportunities with tight and closing time windows. Thus, they require organizations to change their capabilities quickly, followed by rapid execution, in order to seize the opportunities. For example, Netflix was able to change its capabilities quickly to seize the opportunities offered by the internet and then by cloud computing; whereas the opportunity window closed on Blockbuster. Effective digital leadership plays a critical role in driving the necessary rapid change in capabilities, and subsequent execution speed. The third is that digital transformation and digital business require leaders to use a more inclusive leadership style that involves employees in day-to-day decision processes (often in real time), and takes into account their ideas and concerns in strategic decisions[3,4]. The fourth is that digital leaders need to effectively lead virtual teams and facilitate virtual teamwork. For example, this can involve leveraging the right digital technology tools to facilitate communication, workflows, and resource sharing. It can also involve effectively supporting employees with virtual work issues. Owing to virtual, remote, and autonomous work, employees can be prone to peer alienation, weak social bonds, and challenges dealing with typically greater autonomy and increased job demands. So, digital leaders need to unearth and support employees with these issues.

The fifth discussed role is that digital leaders need to proactively build an enabling digital culture (e.g. digital cultures have been described as being agile and responsive, flexible and adaptive, curious / exploratory / experimental, continuously learning, connected / networked, open, and highly collaborative)[5]. Sixth, digital leaders need to build relationships with stakeholders across partner and competitor networks and ecosystems[6]. Both the way they do this and the extent to which they do it differs from networking and relationship roles / activities associated with traditional leadership. Seventh, digital leadership plays important roles in enabling and maximizing digital innovation effectiveness. In one of the prior chapters, we discussed the importance of digital innovation for effectively competing as a digital business. To drive digital innovation, digital leadership plays important roles such as creating or shaping virtual networks among internal and external communities of practice, breaking down silos, democratizing access to information, enabling the free flow of ideas, and, thus, enabling these communities to rapidly respond to change, solve business problems, and introduce new products / solutions[7]. Eighth, digital leaders determine how sourcing, assessment, and / or approval of the digital technologies, platforms, and tools used in the organization occurs. The choice of technologies, platforms, and tools can significantly impact the efficiency and effectiveness of internal processes (e.g. planning and monitoring, decision-making, customer engagement, collaboration), and of organizational adaptability and agility. For example, use of sophisticated data tools has enabled hospitals to have real-time visibility of hospital capacity, patient flow, and patient conditions – thus dramatically improving the ability of healthcare managers to drive the efficiency and effectiveness of internal processes[8]. Ninth, and finally, digital leaders need to play an important role in building and continuously upgrading the effectiveness of their organizations' digital ethics practices. This requires a clear understanding of cybersecurity, information privacy, and other digital ethics issues to be able to identify and mitigate digital ethics risks. Accountants need to leverage the new or adapted leadership roles of digital leadership to enhance their accounting team leadership, cross-functional leadership, and broader leadership roles or activities. For example, digital leadership's new or enhanced leadership roles can enhance the effectiveness of accountants in their accounting team leadership, as well as their co-pilot, navigator, process and control expert, digital and technology enabler, assurance advocate, business transformer, digital playmaker, and sustainability trailblazer roles.

New or enhanced competencies required for digital leadership

Researchers and practitioners have identified a range of digital leadership competencies including adaptability / flexibility (e.g. being able to effectively respond to new / surprising work demands and events), mastery of a variety of virtual communication platforms (e.g. optimally using those which offer the best richness, synchronicity, speed of feedback, and ease of understanding by non-experts – so as to maximize

158 *Leveraging digital technologies*

communication effectiveness), mastery of virtual communication practices (e.g. how to set the right tone, communicate in a clear, organized, and error / miscommunication-free manner) and management of disruptive change (e.g. being able to guide teams to effectively respond to new / surprise consumer expectations and to technological obsolescence). Other digital leadership competencies identified include management of connectivity (e.g. intraorganizational, interorganizational, extraorganizational connectivity), leadership / facilitation of virtual teams (e.g. managing forming, storming, norming, performing stages), and having sufficiently deep technical knowledge of relevant digital technologies (e.g. IoT, blockchain, edge computing, robotics, cloud) and tools (e.g. teleconferencing, workflow management, and collaboration platforms). In addition to understanding the new or enhanced roles of digital leadership, accountants can enhance their digital leadership effectiveness by understanding and cultivating the digital leadership competencies we have just discussed.

Required accounting roles and competencies for accelerated change and transformation

One of the biggest challenges organizations face in their digital transformation and digital business efforts is the scale and speed with which external change and transformation are occurring. This scale and speed is incompatible with change and transformation approaches which weren't designed for environments characterized by high dynamism, uncertainty,

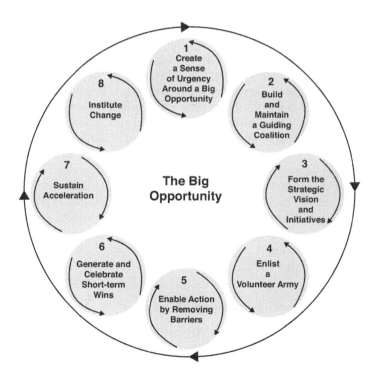

Figure 11.3 Having working knowledge of accelerated change and transformation methodologies like the Change Acceleration Process can be an invaluable tool in digital leaders' rapid change and transformation tool arsenal

technological obsolescence, and disruption. Fortunately, organizations that have long existed in such environments, typically high technology firms, use a range of methodologies to effect rapid transformation and execution, enabling them to adapt and thrive in such environments. We collectively refer to these methodologies as *accelerated change and transformation* methodologies. Examples of these accelerated change and transformation methodologies include agile principles, agile innovation[9,10,11,12], lean thinking[13,14,] lean startup[15,16], strategy-making processes[17], seed accelerator / corporate accelerator practices[18,19,20], blitzscaling practices[21,22,23], and hackathon practices[24,25]. To effectively leverage one or more of these methodologies (e.g. use it to facilitate transformation initiatives or to drive digital innovation, encourage particular teams to use it, or play an effective role in catalyzing its effectiveness), accountants need to have a working understanding of how the different methodologies work, the key roles and responsibilities in each methodology, and the strengths and limitations of each methodology. Armed with such understanding (i.e. both knowledge and experience), they can leverage the right weapon for the right job in digital transformation and digital business enhancement efforts.

Required accounting roles and competencies for digital risk management and governance

Digital risk management and governance vs. traditional risk management and governance

Risk management is concerned with how effectively an organization detects, guards against, responds to, and recovers from risk exposures or events[26]. And governance is concerned with how effectively an organization is led and controlled, as well as how effectively the people operating it are held to account for the efficient, effective, and responsible pursuit of the organization's mission[27,28,29]. Effective risk management is a critical element of effective governance[30]. *Digital risk management* and *digital governance* refer to the management of the unique risk and governance issues associated with digital technologies / digital transformation / digital business, as well as to the leveraging of digital technologies to maximize the efficiency and effectiveness of risk management and governance functions.

The nature of digital risk and the new risk landscape

Digital technology advancements, digital transformation, and digital business bring about new risks that haven't been encountered before and also add complexity to existing risks – thus significantly changing the risk landscape[31]. Examples of the new risks and complexity introduced include: inappropriate employee behaviors on social media; employees inadvertently clicking on suspect links in emails / online or divulging sensitive corporate information; and artificial intelligence product / tool algorithm-related risks (e.g. biased data, unsuitable modeling techniques, algorithmic bias). They also include an expanded number of cyberattack points due to expansion of IoT devices / platforms / networks integrating with an organization's infrastructure; an expanded number of cybercriminals online who also have more sophisticated attack tools; growing misinformation risks (e.g. cybercriminals / nation states / competitors or other troublemakers using sophisticated digital editing and imitation technologies like machine learning, bots, and natural language generation to spread false information, incite adverse reactions, delegitimize leaders and influencers, and damage brands); and data misuse (e.g. lack of transparency, control, accuracy, ethics, security, reliability, and privacy). They further include ubiquitous connectivity (e.g. attack is able to happen any time, most likely when key security staff are offline); digital technology advancements outpacing laws and regulations (e.g. risk of new and less legally bound competitors entering market; or risk that new business models adopted may be rendered obsolete as laws and regulations catch up); culture risk (e.g. pace of change exceeding cultural readiness resulting in destructive resistance to change, disengagement / disenfranchisement, vindictive employees / partners / contractors); and they include digital ethics transgressions (e.g. risk that digital technologies are used for and / or in a manner that current and future societies consider unethical)[32].

The role of digital technologies in digital risk management and governance

As just illustrated, the breadth in risk exposure and the mortal nature of the risks faced makes effective risk management and governance critical in the digital era. Fortunately, accountants can leverage the same sophisticated digital technologies that drive these risk exposures to effectively support managers at all levels to detect, guard against, respond to, and recover from the diverse risk exposures or events[33]. Examples of leveraging such tools to improve risk management and governance include leveraging robotic process automation for accelerated identity and access management, leveraging natural language generation to automate regulatory reporting, leveraging chatbots to improve understanding of policies and compliance requirements, and leveraging computer vision to spot anomalies in an environment. Other examples include leveraging virtual / augmented / mixed reality to simulate crisis management situations, leveraging machine learning to spot policy and ethics violations, and leveraging algorithms for continuous monitoring of credit reports / court filings / sanctions lists / search engines so as to limit third-party risk exposures. Further examples include leveraging blockchain-enabled proof-of-provenance to verify the origin / safety / authenticity of products, leveraging predictive analytics to anticipate and intervene in risky behaviors before the fact, and leveraging digital twins (virtual replicas of physical objects) to anticipate and mitigate risk impacts[34].

New or enhanced accounting roles and competencies required for digital risk management and digital governance

Accountants have shared responsibility with strategic leaders for leading effective risk management and governance. Accounting roles such as the co-pilot, the navigator, the brand protector, the assurance advocate, the process and control expert, and the trusted professional have a central focus on effective risk management and governance. Within these roles, accountants can be establishers / maintainers / continuous improvers of risk management and governance practices, evaluators / procurers / vendor managers of digital risk management and governance technologies, monitors of state-of-the-art risk management and governance practices, monitors and testers of risk management technologies, risk management practice auditors, crisis managers, and more. Effectively carrying out each of these roles requires an understanding of the evolving digital risk landscape, of digital risk management and governance practices, of digital risk management and governance technology tools, and of the broad opportunities and threats presented by digital technology advancements.

Google and reflect

Table 11.1 Google and reflect

Digital capability	Common terminology
Digital Leadership	leadership, digital leadership, e-leadership, digital leadership capability, digital leader, digital transformation vision, digital business vision, change agent, digital change agent, digital enabler, inclusive leadership, virtual team, virtual communication style, digital innovation
Accelerated Change and Transformation	uncertainty, complexity, complicatedness, high velocity environment, fleeting opportunity, change management, organization transformation, agile innovation, lean thinking, lean startup, change acceleration, design thinking, seed accelerator, corporate accelerator, blitzscaling, hackathon
Digital Risk Management and Digital Governance	risk management, digital risk management, governance, digital governance, governance operating model, governance structure, governance infrastructure, governance roles and responsibilities, risk exposure, risk event, biased data, algorithmic bias, attack surface, misinformation, imitation technologies, natural language generation, culture risk, digital ethics risk

Discussion questions

1. What is the difference between traditional leadership, e-leadership, and digital leadership?
2. What is the difference between risk management and digital risk management?
3. What is the relationship between risk management and governance?
4. What is the relationship between information privacy and digital ethics?
5. What is the difference between change and transformation? How do accelerated change and accelerated transformation differ?
6. What are the three most dangerous risk exposures for organizations at the moment?
7. If you were a hacker or cybercriminal, which risk surface or attack point would you consider best to attack and why?
8. What are three ways digital technologies are being leveraged to enhance digital risk management?
9. Which accounting role in digital risk management and governance is most important to an organization's risk management and governance effectiveness?
10. Which risk management and governance-related competency is likely to have the greatest positive impact on an accountant's career?
11. Which of the capabilities discussed in this chapter is the most important to succeeding at digital transformation and digital business?

Notes

1. Kane, G.C. (2019, March 12). How digital leadership is(n't) different. MIT Sloan Management Review. Retrieved from: https://sloanreview.mit.edu/article/how-digital-leadership-isnt-different/
2. Cortellazzo, L., Bruni, E., & Zampieri, R. (2019). The role of leadership in a digitalized world: A review. Frontiers in Psychology, 10, 1938.
3. Cortellazzo, L., Bruni, E., & Zampieri, R. (2019). The role of leadership in a digitalized world: A review. Frontiers in Psychology, 10, 1938.
4. Schwarzmüller, T., Brosi, P., Duman, D., & Welpe, I. M. (2018). How does the digital transformation affect organizations? Key themes of change in work design and leadership. management revue (MREV), 29(2), 114–138.

5 Cortellazzo, L., Bruni, E., & Zampieri, R. (2019). The role of leadership in a digitalized world: A review. Frontiers in Psychology, 10, 1938.
6 Cortellazzo, L., Bruni, E., & Zampieri, R. (2019). The role of leadership in a digitalized world: A review. Frontiers in Psychology, 10, 1938.
7 Cortellazzo, L., Bruni, E., & Zampieri, R. (2019). The role of leadership in a digitalized world: A review. Frontiers in Psychology, 10, 1938.
8 Cortellazzo, L., Bruni, E., & Zampieri, R. (2019). The role of leadership in a digitalized world: a review. Frontiers in Psychology, 10, 1938.
9 Gothelf, J. (2014). Bring agile to the whole organization. Harvard Business Review, 92(11).
10 Busulwa, R., Tice, M., & Gurd, B. (2018). Strategy execution and complexity: Thriving in the era of disruption. Routledge.
11 Rigby, D.K., Sutherland, J., & Takeuchi, H. (2016, April 20). The secret history of agile innovation. Harvard Business Review, 4.
12 Morris, L., Ma, M., & Wu, P.C. (2014). Agile innovation: The revolutionary approach to accelerate success, inspire engagement, and ignite creativity. John Wiley & Sons.
13 Collins, D. (2016). Lean strategy. Harvard Business Review, 94(3), 63–68.
14 Busulwa, R., Tice, M., & Gurd, B. (2018). Strategy execution and complexity: Thriving in the era of disruption. Routledge.
15 Ries, E. (2011). The lean startup: How today's entrepreneurs use continuous innovation to create radically successful businesses. Crown Books.
16 Busulwa, R., Tice, M., & Gurd, B. (2018). Strategy execution and complexity: Thriving in the era of disruption. Routledge.
17 Busulwa, R., Tice, M., & Gurd, B. (2018). Strategy execution and complexity: Thriving in the era of disruption. Routledge.
18 Busulwa, R., Birdthistle, N., & Dunn, S. (2020). Startup accelerators: A field guide. John Wiley & Sons.
19 Say, M. (2016, February 23). Corporate accelerators: What's in it for the big companies? Forbes. https://www.forbes.com/sites/groupthink/2016/02/23/corporate-accelerators-whats-in-it-for-the-big-companies/#7445a2d45f62
20 Hathaway, I. (2016, March 1). What startup accelerators really do. Harvard Business Review, 7.
21 Sullivan, T. (2016). Blitzscaling. Harvard Business Review, 94(4), 15.
22 Kuratko, D.F., Holt, H. L., & Neubert, E. (2020). Blitzscaling: The good, the bad, and the ugly. Business Horizons, 63(1), 109–119.
23 Hoffman, R., & Yeh, C. (2018). Blitzscaling: The lightning-fast path to building massively valuable businesses. Broadway Business.
24 Spaulding, E., & Caimi, G. (2016, April 1). Hackathons aren't just for coders. Harvard Business Review.
25 Rosell, B., Kumar, S., & Shepherd, J. (2014). Unleashing innovation through internal hackathons. 2014 IEEE Innovations in Technology Conference. https://doi.org/10.1109/innotek.2014.6877369
26 Iso.org. (2018). ISO 31000:2018 Risk management – guidelines. Retrieved June 12, 2020, from: https://www.iso.org/obp/ui/#iso:std:iso:31000:ed-2:v1:en
27 Siems, M., & Alvarez-Macotela, O.S. (2017). The G20/OECD principles of corporate governance 2015: A critical assessment of their operation and impact. Retrieved from: https://www.law.ox.ac.uk/business-law-blog/blog/2017/09/g20oecd-principles-corporate-governance-2015-critical-assessment
28 Japan Exchange Group. (2009). Principles of corporate governance for listed companies. Retrieved from: https://www.jpx.co.jp/english/equities/listing/cg/tvdivq0000008j6d-att/principles_200912.pdf
29 Governance Institute of Australia. (2020). What is governance? Retrieved from: https://www.governanceinstitute.com.au/resources/what-is-governance/
30 ISO. (2018). ISO 31000:2018 Risk management – guidelines. Retrieved June 12, 2020, from: https://www.iso.org/obp/ui/#iso:std:iso:31000:ed-2:v1:en
31 Marsh, J., Bhachawat, K., Maheshwari, S., Nagpal, A. (2019). Future of risk in the digital era. Deloitte. Retrieved June 12, 2020, from: https://www2.deloitte.com/content/dam/Deloitte/fi/Documents/risk/future-of-risk-in-the-digital-era.pdf
32 Marsh, J., Bhachawat, K., Maheshwari, S., Nagpal, A. (2019). Future of risk in the digital era. Deloitte. Retrieved June 12, 2020, from: https://www2.deloitte.com/content/dam/Deloitte/fi/Documents/risk/future-of-risk-in-the-digital-era.pdf

33 Marsh, J., Bhachawat, K., Maheshwari, S., Nagpal, A. (2019). Future of risk in the digital era. Deloitte. Retrieved June 12, 2020, from: https://www2.deloitte.com/content/dam/Deloitte/fi/Documents/risk/future-of-risk-in-the-digital-era.pdf
34 Marsh, J., Bhachawat, K., Maheshwari, S., Nagpal, A. (2019). Future of risk in the digital era. Deloitte. Retrieved June 12, 2020, from: https://www2.deloitte.com/content/dam/Deloitte/fi/Documents/risk/future-of-risk-in-the-digital-era.pdf

Part IV

Keeping up with digital technology advancements

12 Keeping up with digital technologies

Introduction

Organizational digital transformation and digital business capabilities depend on employee digital business competencies (e.g. to lead digital transformation and digital innovation efforts, and to effectively leverage digital technology tools). These competencies, in turn, depend on employees' ability to keep up with and, therefore, be able to leverage digital technology advancements. Keeping up with digital technologies is increasingly becoming a critical component of the *expert leadership* required for digitally transforming and effectively competing as a digital business. As a result, it is increasingly critical to the effectiveness of accountants in leadership roles. In this chapter, we conceptualize keeping up with digital technologies as an accelerated learning practice. That is, accountants can keep up with digital technologies to the extent that they can accelerate or align their learning rate to the rate of change in digital technologies. Accelerated learning, or learning efficiency, has individual beliefs / attitudes / traits levers which can be influenced, and it has learning strategy / practice / habit levers which can be adopted / learned. In this chapter, we unpack each of these lever types, and explain how they interact together to drive the accelerated learning / learning efficiency necessary for accountants to keep up with digital technology advancements.

Importance and challenge of keeping up with digital technologies

In the preceding chapters, we outlined the threat of digital disruption, the pressing need for digital transformation, and the digital capabilities required by organizations to effectively compete as a digital business. For each of these organizational digital capabilities, we highlighted required managerial and accounting competencies (knowledge, skills, abilities). A recurring theme in all organizational digital capabilities is the need for managers and their business partners or co-pilots to have sufficient technical and strategic knowledge of and proficiency with a range of different digital technologies. Without this knowledge / skills / abilities across different digital technologies, accountants can become key impediments to their organizations' digital transformation and digital business competitiveness efforts – in addition to limiting their own careers. However, accountants face challenges effectively acquiring the required working knowledge of different digital technologies and keeping it relevant. For example, the range of digital technologies to have working knowledge and skills in is broad, it's ever-changing, and it seems to expand in breadth and depth at an exponential rate. As a result, keeping up with it can easily overwhelm even the most enthusiastic of accountants. Accountants who succeed at it recognize that technology learning is a never-ending process that combines effective technology learning habits / practices with effective strategies to maximize both what is learned and the efficiency with which it is learned.

Common strategies and practices for keeping up with digital technologies

The challenge of keeping up with digital technologies is not unique to accountants. And, across different industries, job functions, and professions, a range of strategies and practices are employed to keep up with digital technologies. In the remainder of this chapter, we've curated a list of commonly used strategies and practices from both the academic research and from practitioners. This list is just a starting point, and what works for one accountant may not work for another. Our aim in putting together this list is to start accountants on the never-ending journey of seeking out effective strategies and practices to add to their repertoire, and leveraging the right strategy or practice for them, at the right time, and for the right technology to maximize their learning and learning efficiency.

Strategies and practices from the research on technological knowledge renewal effectiveness

Framing it as *technological knowledge renewal effectiveness*, researchers exploring challenges and drivers of effectiveness at keeping up with digital technologies have identified three individual beliefs / attitudes / traits drivers and two technology learning strategy drivers. The identified individual beliefs / attitudes / traits are: perceived need for digital technology competencies, sufficient appreciation of the technology learning challenge, and tolerance for ambiguity[1]. The identified driving technology learning strategies are: learning from external experts, and learning from internal experts[2]. We explain each of these below. Each of these individual beliefs / attitudes / traits and learning strategies can be thought of as a lever that can be turned and held in one position to accelerate technology learning, or turned another way to decelerate it.

Perceived need for digital technology competencies, appreciation of the technology learning challenge, and tolerance for ambiguity.

An accountant's perceived need for *digital technology competencies* refers to the accountant's belief or lack of belief that digital technology competencies materially impact their job performance and career prospects[3]. According to the research, accountants who don't believe that digital technology competencies materially impact their job performance and career prospects will lack sufficient motivation to make or sustain the necessary investments in time and effort required to learn and keep up with digital technologies. On the contrary, accountants who see digital technology competencies as being a significant driver of job performance and career success will have far greater motivation and persistence in pursuing these competencies.

Accountants' *appreciation* of the true challenge of keeping up with digital technologies refers to how accurately they understand and take seriously the rate of change in digital technologies and the resultant disruption threats[4]. The more fully accountants appreciate and take seriously the rate of change, the more likely they are to put in and sustain efforts to keep up with digital technologies. Accountants underestimating the nature of the challenge in front of them have been found to make insufficient efforts to keep up with digital technologies[5]. *Tolerance for ambiguity* refers to accountants' tendency to perceive ambiguous situations as tolerable or even desirable[6]. For example, accountants with higher tolerance for ambiguity are more willing to cope with change, modify their opinions in the face of new information, embrace new experiences, and renew their knowledge [7]. Tolerance for ambiguity has been shown to have a positive impact on the ability to learn new technology[8] and, thus, to keep up with digital technologies.

Accountants can leverage these three research findings to enhance their own and their teams' motivation to keep up with digital technologies, as well as resilience in the face of setbacks or overwhelm. For example, they can ensure that they and colleagues fully understand and are continuously reminded of the value of digital technology competencies to their organizations and careers, they can ensure that they and their colleagues understand the true challenge of keeping up with digital technologies and how this challenge is evolving, and they can ensure that they continuously work on improving theirs and colleagues' tolerance for ambiguity (e.g. through work assignments and other learning activities that expand tolerance to ambiguity). For example, accountants can influence their colleagues to see technological change and dynamism as an opportunity rather than a burden. And, where they lead teams, accountant managers can cultivate a culture that encourages and incentivizes employees to take on and overcome challenges, embrace change, and deal with uncertainty. Through recruiting processes, accountant managers can ensure that they hire for ambiguity tolerance, and motivation to learn / keep up with digital technologies.

Leaning from external experts and learning from internal experts

Learning from external experts refers to acquiring new knowledge and skills from professional entities outside the organization. The learning activities can be in the form of reading professional literature (e.g. consulting firm research reports on a topic, professional / academic journals on a topic), attending conferences (e.g. a vendor IoT conference), attending networking events (e.g. an information ethics professionals dinner), participating in online forums and discussion boards, signing up for electronic newsletters, and more. The amount of time spent on such learning activities, and the choice of learning activities, are strongly associated with effectiveness in learning new digital technologies[9], and, thus, with keeping up with digital technologies. In the research, learning from external experts is also referred to as *professional delegation* as the learner "delegates" the identification / curation of what to learn, and how to learn it, to an expert (typically a professional entity). For example, a learner wanting to learn more about artificial intelligence may seek out leading associations, vendors, and research organizations in that area and make a point of reading as much of their content (e.g. blogs, videos, reports) and attending as many of their conferences and networking events as possible. Learning from internal experts refers to acquiring new knowledge and skills from units or departments or individuals with that expertise within the organization[10]. Typically, this might be the IT / IS / technology function. So, for example, an accountant may learn through informal conversations with employees from the IT / IS / technology function. Or they may learn through seeking out the support of or collaborating on projects with employees in the IT / IS / technology function. Accountants can leverage both external and internal experts in both professional and social contexts to improve what they learn and how efficiently and effectively they learn it.

Strategies and practices from practitioners

Have an evolving plan for managing information overload

The relentless torrent of information on just about any technology topic, the proliferation of information sources, the blurring boundaries between uncredible and credible information, and the growth in misinformation can leave accountants feeling overwhelmed. Navigating this situation requires accountants to make decisions about when to pay attention, what information to pay attention to, what information sources to trust, and when to trust both the information and the information sources. Fortunately, there is no shortage of strategies, habits, and tools that practitioners prescribe for dealing with information overload. These include filtering or explicitly deciding which information sources to pay attention to and which to ignore[11,12,13], having a process for prioritizing and sequencing information consumption[14] (e.g. scanning selected information sources in the morning for the day's content and then curating and scheduling when important items[15] will be read and in what order), implementing automated information filtering tools[16] (e.g. recommendation engines, search tools, email inbox rules), and learning to skim-read fast and effectively[17]. Other strategies include curating or eliminating push notifications on smart devices, limiting the amount of incoming information[18] (e.g. via email, social media, adverts, search engine recommendations, smart devices, computers, etc.), and enhancing the ability to effectively process incoming information[19]. We recommend that accountants devise their own information overload management plan (a combination of strategies, practices, and tools that are effective for them), and that they continuously adapt / evolve this plan to maximize its effectiveness at both enabling optimal learning and offsetting information overload-related anxiety / stress.

Continuously upgrade your learning efficiency

Learning efficiency refers to a learner's rate of learning and retention[20]. It can also be thought of as a combination of degree of difficulty in what is being learned, the accuracy of learning, and the quantity of learning that takes place per unit of time[21]. Or, put another way, it is the amount and quality of learning that occurs per unit of time, assuming what is being learned is the same. Researchers have linked learning efficiency to attention control[22], working memory capacity[23], learning strategy use (e.g. which strategy and how well it is applied)[24], curiosity[25], and constructive self-talk[26]. In addition, *learning to learn* and *accelerated learning* are burgeoning fields with contributions from practitioners, education psychologists, and educators across a range of industries. Accountants can leverage this burgeoning research and knowledge to dramatically improve focus, memory, curiosity, constructive self-talk, and learning strategy literacy. In doing so, they can dramatically expand the effectiveness and speed with which they learn new digital technology concepts, tools, and related issues.

Choose the right learning platforms

Learning platforms continue to grow in popularity based on their ability to drive learning efficiency (e.g. through benefits such as curation and serving up of content, personalized learning recommendations, behavioral nudges, learning analytics, device flexibility)[27]. Platforms can differ in the type of content offered, the way in which the content is delivered, cost, learner experience, certification, device flexibility, and more. For example, there are course-style platforms (e.g. CodeSchool, Udemy, Coursera, Job

Ready Programmer, Pluralsight, Cloud Academy, Katacoda, DataCamp, Cybrary, Udacity, Linux Academy, Lynda, Skillshare, Code Academy, GoSkills, Edx, Future Learn), there are coaching / mentoring-oriented platforms (e.g. Masterclass, CrossKnowledge), there are technology-oriented content platforms (e.g. MIT Technology Review, ZNet, Engadget, Thenextweb, Wired, Arstechnica, Techcrunch, Tomshardware, Gizmodo, Forbes), there are specialist industry technology content platforms, and more. By finding and leveraging the right platforms, accountants can significantly improve their ability to discover which technologies to learn, what issues to focus on in relation to use of that technology within and outside of the industry, what technical and strategic skills to develop, and how to develop those skills. In addition, the platforms can make the learning process much more enjoyable (see tables 12.1 to 12.3 for examples of common learning platforms and tools).

Embrace omnichannel learning

Learning can take place in a variety of environments, on a variety of platforms and devices, and at a variety of times – known as *omnichannel learning*. For example, while waiting for a client to arrive, a learner may have 20 minutes to spend on learning activities. Having

Table 12.1 Top learning tools sorted alphabetically by learning tool type and their change in ranking from year to year – part 1[28]

Ranking 2019	Change from 2018	Tool	Learning tool type
181	NEW	Filtered	AI-powered learning platform
182	NEW	Docebo	AI-powered LMS
67	down 22	Powtoon	animated explainer tool
61	up 33	Audible	audio books platform
191	NEW	Fleeq	bite-size training video tool
116	up 74	getAbstract	book abstracts
138	down 17	Blinkist	book abstracts
165	down 15	Omnigraffle	diagramming tool
25	up 13	Evernote	digital notebook
71	down 7	Kindle App	e-books reader
6	same	Google Docs & Drive	file sharing and collaboration
17	down 4	Dropbox	file sharing platform
55	down 5	OneDrive	file sharing platform
91	down 30	Quizlet	flashcard app
164	down 3	PebblePad	learning journey platform
179	NEW	EdCast	learning platform
65	down 18	Degreed	lifelong learning platform
134	NEW	Meetup	local community events app
174	up 9	Office Lens	makes photos of whiteboards readable
158	up 4	Highbrow	micro-course platforms
39	up 12	Google Scholar	web search engine
64	down 15	Webex	webinar platform
113	NEW	Jamboard	whiteboard collaboration
197	NEW	Drafts	writing automation tool

Table 12.2 Top learning tools sorted alphabetically by learning tool type and their change in ranking from year to year – part 2[29]

Ranking 2019	Change from 2018	Tool	Learning tool type
128	down 10	Axonify	micro-learning platform
170	same	Freemind	mind mapping app
133	BACK	XMind	mind mapping tool
63	up 39	Mindmeister	mind mapping app
139	down 17	Google Alerts	monitor the Web
15	down 1	Feedly	news aggregator
76	up 48	Inoreader	news aggregator
183	BACK	Notability	note-taking app
151	NEW	Mind Tools	online business resources
121	down 14	CodeCademy	online coding courses
13	up 21	LinkedIn Learning [Lynda]	online courses
29	up 7	Udemy	online courses
53	down 22	Coursera	online courses
101	down 20	edX	online courses
103	down 17	FutureLearn	online courses
115	up 43	Udacity	online courses
173	up 2	Khan Academy	online courses
176	up 23	Alison	online courses
156	down 43	Pluralsight	online IT courses
24	up 6	TED Talks	online talks
54	NEW	Apple Podcasts	podcast platform
105	BACK	Pocket Casts	podcast player
146	down 16	Overcast	podcast player

Table 12.3 Top learning tools sorted alphabetically by learning tool type and their change in ranking from year to year – part 3[30]

Ranking 2019	Change from 2018	Tool	Learning tool type
155	down 22	Castro	podcast player
157	NEW	Podcast Addict	podcast player
107	BACK	Quora	Q&A website
177	BACK	Quizizz	quizzing app
178	BACK	Zotero	research management app
56	down 21	Pocket	save for later app
27	down 2	Snagit	screen capture tool
110	NEW	Loom	screen recorder
148	NEW	Screencastify	screen recorder
92	down 15	Screencast-O-matic	screencasting app
23	up 1	Camtasia	screencasting tool
77	down 11	Google Maps	searchable / zoomable maps
32	up 17	Diigo	social bookmarking
1	same	YouTube	video platform
66	down 13	Vimeo	video platform

Ranking 2019	Change from 2018	Tool	Learning tool type
159	up 34	Kaltura	video platform
129	NEW	Microsoft Stream	video streaming service
99	down 16	Adobe After Effects	visual effects app
35	up 19	Google Chrome	web browser
125	up 13	Firefox	web browser
167	down 14	Microsoft Edge	web browser
81	down 21	Adobe Connect	web conferencing platform
142	BACK	Big Blue Button	web conferencing platform
94	down 24	Sway	web content app
2	up 1	Google Search	web search engine

mobile access to the relevant learning content (e.g. Kindle book, Audible book, YouTube video, LinkedIn article) can result in seized learning opportunities. And these seized opportunities can accumulate over years to represent significant differences in time spent learning. This a key benefit of embracing learning across a range of channels (e.g. across mobile, desktop, other smart devices; across social; across web; across email marketing; across digital and physical books; etc.). Omnichannel learning can maximize learning flexibility (e.g. there is always a right channel for the learning situation), learning availability (e.g. the right content is always accessible), and learning efficiency (e.g. the most efficient channel in a situation can be used and there are less wasted learning opportunities). We recommend that accountants make deliberate efforts to effect and maximize omnichannel learning (e.g. signing up to platforms across a range of channels, downloading relevant apps, ensuring online / offline availability, ensuring sufficient data, ensuring access to optimal smart devices, etc.). And we recommend they invest time in constantly improving their omnichannel learning approach (e.g. adding new tools, reconfiguring content access processes, integrating content across channels, etc.).

Build and leverage thought leaders on social networks

Social media provides one of the greatest vehicles to access the insights and latest thinking from digital technology, digital transformation, and digital business thought leaders. Through following topic thought leaders (e.g. topics such as digital strategy, AI, data science, blockchain) on social media platforms (e.g. Twitter, LinkedIn, Facebook, and others), accountants can access cutting-edge information directly from people shaping the evolution of these digital technologies. In contrast, this information may take decades to filter down through other information channels like published books and training courses. A range of strategic leaders of world leading technology companies, technical specialists and futurists, and industry technology specialists post regularly on Twitter, LinkedIn, Facebook, and other social media sites (e.g. Bill Gates, Cathy Hackl, Michael Krigsman, QuHarrison Terry, Paul Graham, Lisa Seacat Deluca, Tom Davenport, Michael Fauscette, Bill Marriott, Daniel E. Craig, Jason Q. Feed, Craig Rispin). Through regularly following the posts of these thought leaders on social networks, accountants can learn technology concepts first, spot technology opportunities first, and ensure their organizations profit first from these thought leaders' insights. For example, one early stage company participating in a seed accelerator to raise required funding struggled to raise a million dollars through conventional venture capitalists. In contrast, a cohort company participating in the same seed accelerator acted on a tweet suggesting that there was not an easier startup fundraising opportunity at the time than ICOs (initial coin offerings). The startup spotting and acting on this thought leader insight spent its time setting up an ICO instead of pursuing venture capitalists; it raised millions of dollars in the course of a month, without having to give up any ownership of the company[31]. In contrast, other seed accelerator participants did not understand ICOs and the ICO opportunity until it had passed; and, therefore, never raised anywhere near that level of funding.

Configure your search engines, social media, and email subscriptions

Suggested news articles, social media feeds, and subscription emails can be distractions, drawing time away from priority learning activities. Google's search engine app, for example, automatically suggests news articles a searcher might be interested in. And social media platforms like LinkedIn and Twitter have automatic news / post feeds that platform users see as soon as they log in. Similarly, the majority of people are likely to scroll through a bunch of subscription emails before getting to a personal or work email. But rather than being distractions, suggested news articles, social media feeds, and emails can be configured to be content discovery and learning prompts. For example, Google-suggested news articles can be configured to suggest news articles related to desired technology learning topics (e.g. "digital business model", "digital Innovation"); so that each time a user opens the search app it can automatically deliver the latest news about new digital business models or digital innovation practices. Search results can also be configured to automatically be emailed monthly / weekly / daily. For example, a user may configure weekly alerts for "new digital business model" and receive an email with links to the latest information containing those keywords as soon as such information goes online anywhere in the world. Similarly, social media feeds can be configured so that they automatically serve up information on particular learning topics of interest. For example, on LinkedIn and on Twitter accountants can subscribe to or follow certain hashtags (e.g. #cloudaccounting, #artificialintelligence, #digitalleadership #digitalinnovation) to automatically receive the latest news and posts about these topics. And they can also use those hashtags to filter for and follow particular thought leaders for each hashtag. By configuring the platforms they access most regularly, accountants can ensure they have access to cutting edge news and insights on technology topics as well as near daily curiosity, reflection, and learning prompts for their targeted learning topics.

Have an effective and sustainable personal information management strategy

After configuring channels, platforms, and devices to deliver the best information, there then comes the challenge of capturing each information item, storing each information item, organizing it so it can be found, and leveraging tools that can enable near instant retrieval of the desired information as and when needed, wherever it is needed. Doing so can significantly enhance learning efficiency by minimizing retrieval time. It can also minimize the chance of the desired information not being found (which would result in lost or suboptimal learning opportunities). But having an effective system for storing and retrieving information can be challenging. One issue is the number of channels in which information can be sourced (e.g. social media, YouTube, search engines, email, conversations with people, conferences, books, websites, NFC codes, etc.). For example, it can be challenging to remember in which channel the information resides. Or it can be time consuming to transfer information across channels in order to have all information on a single platform or device. Another issue is that some content requires platform specific storage (e.g. YouTube videos may be better stored on YouTube). Yet another issue is that some platforms and devices significantly simplify the information retrieval and learning experience, but are limited in their ability to integrate information from other platforms / devices. Further, settling on a particular platform or device, and building learning routines around it, needs careful consideration, since the device or platform could be discontinued. Or it may not be updated regularly enough to keep up with changes across other platforms, hence limiting integrability. Fortunately, a range of personal information management platforms and tools exist – and these are continuously improving. Accountants can curate or architect a combination of platforms, devices, and apps that fit perfectly into their routines to maximize learning effectiveness. For example, an accountant may decide on the following configuration / architecture:

- *Email:* use Gmail for personal emails. Set up email folders by technology topic, and then drag and drop information into relevant folders for ease of retrieval (new digital innovation practice-related emails can be moved to a "digital innovation practices" folder, digital business model-related emails can go in the "digital strategies" folder, etc.).
- *Articles:* use Instapaper to save articles for later reading and set up folders in Instapaper (e.g. "digital innovation practices," "new digital tech to explore"). Instapaper is available on almost all devices, can be integrated into most browsers to enable single-button saving of articles, and has built-in search functionality and folder structuring to enable even faster retrieval of articles.
- *YouTube channels:* establish a YouTube account; follow key thought leaders' channels and set up folders for saved videos ("digital innovation practices," "digital strategies").
- *Audio:* set up Audible and Blinkist to be able to listen to books and book summaries; make these apps available on mobile, desktop, and CarPlay.
- *Books:* set up Kindle and Apple Books apps to be able to purchase any book and have lifetime access to it; these apps enable in-book search and have built-in note-taking functions.
- *TV:* set up technology-related channels and apps on your smart TV to enable watching interesting tech documentaries.
- *Notes:* set up Apple Notes or Evernote to enable digital note-taking; these have highly effective built-in search functions to enable fast access to notes.
- *Transcription:* set up audio recording and transcription apps on mobile and desktop (e.g. Otter Voice Meeting); integrate these with virtual meeting apps such as Microsoft Teams and Google Meet.
- *Desktop / laptop:* ensure all selected platforms / apps are cloud based, and can be replicated in the desktop / laptop / web environment.
- *Smart device:* ensure learning apps are also installed on every possible smart device so that if one device is down, learning can occur on another device.

What we have outlined is one example of a personal information management approach, it can be extended and configured differently to suit each individual (e.g. more or better channels, platforms, apps, devices added; and perhaps a better plan for integrating information across channels, devices, platforms, and apps). Most strategies / approaches are being continuously improved as users gauge their effectiveness, discover better tools, and evolve their learning behaviors. Deliberately designing / architecting / configuring a system and continuously improving it can supercharge learning efficiency and effectiveness.

Participate in hackathons and accelerators

Hackathons originated as computer-programming events in which a small group of people work intensely together – sometimes around the clock to solve a difficult programming problem in a fixed (and often very short) amount of time[32]. For example, they could work on "hacking" or solving a complex security problem over the course of a weekend, whereas this problem might otherwise have taken months or years via traditional approaches. Due to their success, hackathons have been applied to solve a range of problems across sectors, industries, and disciplines[33]. Many hackathons focus on leveraging digital technologies and digital business models to solve organization, government, community, and state problems. Many are run in a competitive-style format (different teams competing to solve a problem first or come up with the best solution in the timeframes allowed) for a prize and are open to teams, or individual volunteers, who are then allocated into teams by the hackathon organizers. For example, some nation states have "govhack"-style hackathons in which volunteer teams are formed to leverage publicly available government data to build innovative new products over the course of a weekend (e.g. these products could be mobile apps, smart devices, cloud platforms, etc.). These particular types of hackathons typically have a big data focus, but there are others that focus on leveraging different digital technologies. Accountants can build practical working knowledge of digital technologies, digital business capabilities, and digital innovation by participating as members of hackathon teams, by volunteering as hackathon organizers / facilitators, or by volunteering as judges of hackathon innovations / solutions. In either participation form, accountants can gain a lot of practical know-how about the digital technologies leveraged in that hackathon, about digital innovation and digital business capability issues, and about digital leadership.

In contrast to a hackathon, an *accelerator* (e.g. seed accelerator, startup accelerator, corporate accelerator), is a fixed-term, cohort-based, accelerated learning program that typically focuses on accelerating product development and commercialization processes[34]. An accelerator program is typically run over a 3–6 month period that culminates in a "Shark Tank"-style public pitch event known as demo day[35]. In this time, accelerated or compressed learning occurs through a combination of iterative experimentation, intensive mentoring and coaching, customer and investor feedback, and product / business model pitching. Accelerators usually bring together a network of investors, entrepreneurs, potential strategic partners, and potential customers that cohort companies can draw on to accelerate their learning, product development, and commercialization outcomes. Accountants can participate in accelerators as volunteer organizers, industry or function-specific coaches / mentors, demo day judges, or just as demo day observers. There are even accounting tech-focused accelerators which would expose accountants to emerging accounting technologies and business models, potential areas of profession disruption, and innovation challenges.

Volunteer for a startup

Similar to the learning benefits of hackathons and accelerators, accountants can volunteer to be on the boards of technology startups. For example, an accountant could join an early stage custom software development firm to provide accounting advice. In return, that accountant would have the opportunity to accelerate their learning of different digital technologies, digital business models, and strategic technology issues. They would also have an informal sounding board to run ideas or questions by in relation to digital technology issues or tools use.

Implications for accountants

This chapter had three aims, first we sought to highlight the importance of accelerated learning or learning efficiency as an important accounting competence for keeping up with digital technologies. Second, we sought to highlight the importance of taking a strategic approach to managing accelerated learning, and to provide an example framework of such an approach. Finally, we wanted to provide some example strategies, practices, and habits that accountants can leverage to accelerate their learning. But all this is just a starting point; and our hope is that accountants use this starting point to begin the career-long process of seeking out accelerated learning practices and tools; and leveraging these to adapt and optimize their accelerated learning strategy. Doing so is crucial to keeping up with rapid advancements in digital technologies; and to growing accounting role demands.

Google and reflect

accelerated learning, learning efficiency, learning science, content curation, expert leadership, tolerance for ambiguity, learner self-talk, constructive self-talk, experiential learning, learning platform, learning experience platform (LXP), attention control, memory capacity, learning strategy, curiosity, learning to learn, omnichannel learning, thought leader, futurist, personal information management strategy (PIM), hackathon, accelerator, project-based learning, inquiry-based learning

Discussion questions

1. What is accelerated learning?
2. What is learning efficiency?
3. What is the difference between accelerated learning and learning efficiency?
4. What are three individual beliefs / attitudes / traits that drive learning efficiency?
5. What are the top four drivers of learning efficiency?
6. What is the role of digital technologies in learning efficiency?
7. How do digital technologies enhance learning efficiency?
8. What is the relationship between digital technologies, learning efficiency, and an accountant's ability to keep up with digital technologies?

Notes

1. Rong, G., & Grover, V. (2009). Keeping up-to-date with information technology: Testing a model of technological knowledge renewal effectiveness for it professionals. Information & Management, 46(7), 376–387.
2. Rong, G., & Grover, V. (2009). Keeping up-to-date with information technology: Testing a model of technological knowledge renewal effectiveness for it professionals. Information & Management, 46(7), 376–387.
3. Rong, G., & Grover, V. (2009). Keeping up-to-date with information technology: Testing a model of technological knowledge renewal effectiveness for it professionals. Information & Management, 46(7), 376–387.
4. Rong, G., & Grover, V. (2009). Keeping up-to-date with information technology: Testing a model of technological knowledge renewal effectiveness for it professionals. Information & Management, 46(7), 376–387.
5. Rong, G., & Grover, V. (2009). Keeping up-to-date with information technology: Testing a model of technological knowledge renewal effectiveness for it professionals. Information & Management, 46(7), 376–387.
6. Rong, G., & Grover, V. (2009). Keeping up-to-date with information technology: Testing a model of technological knowledge renewal effectiveness for it professionals. Information & Management, 46(7), 376–387.
7. Rong, G., & Grover, V. (2009). Keeping up-to-date with information technology: Testing a model of technological knowledge renewal effectiveness for it professionals. Information & Management, 46(7), 376–387.
8. Rong, G., & Grover, V. (2009). Keeping up-to-date with information technology: Testing a model of technological knowledge renewal effectiveness for it professionals. Information & Management, 46(7), 376–387.
9. Rong, G., & Grover, V. (2009). Keeping up-to-date with information technology: Testing a model of technological knowledge renewal effectiveness for it professionals. Information & Management, 46(7), 376–387.
10. Rong, G., & Grover, V. (2009). Keeping up-to-date with information technology: Testing a model of technological knowledge renewal effectiveness for it professionals. Information & Management, 46(7), 376–387.
11. Lavenda, D. (2012). 7 time-proven strategies for dealing with information overload. Fast Company. Retrieved June 15, 2020, from: https://www.fastcompany.com/3002467/7-time-proven-strategies-dealing-information-overload
12. Asay, M. (2009). Shirky: Problem is filter failure, not info overload. CNet. Retrieved June 15, 2020, from: https://www.cnet.com/news/shirky-problem-is-filter-failure-not-info-overload/
13. Beaton, C. (2017). The single most effective way to deal with information overload. Inc.com. Retrieved June 15, 2020, from: https://www.inc.com/caroline-beaton/the-single-most-effective-way-to-deal-with-information-overload.html
14. Lavenda, D. (2012). 7 time-proven strategies for dealing with information overload. Retrieved June 15, 2020, from: https://www.fastcompany.com/3002467/7-time-proven-strategies-dealing-information-overload
15. Lavenda, D. (2012). 7 time-proven strategies for dealing with information overload. Retrieved June 15, 2020, from: https://www.fastcompany.com/3002467/7-time-proven-strategies-dealing-information-overload
16. Lavenda, D. (2012). 7 time-proven strategies for dealing with information overload. Retrieved June 15, 2020, from: https://www.fastcompany.com/3002467/7-time-proven-strategies-dealing-information-overload
17. Lavenda, D. (2012). 7 time-proven strategies for dealing with information overload. Retrieved June 15, 2020, from: https://www.fastcompany.com/3002467/7-time-proven-strategies-dealing-information-overload
18. Soucek, R., & Moser, K. (2010). Coping with information overload in email communication: Evaluation of a training intervention. Computers in Human Behavior, 26(6), 1458–1466.
19. Soucek, R., & Moser, K. (2010). Coping with information overload in email communication: Evaluation of a training intervention. Computers in Human Behavior, 26(6), 1458–1466.
20. Zerr, C.L., Berg, J.J., Nelson, S.M., Fishell, A.K., Savalia, N.K., & McDermott, K.B. (2018). Learning efficiency: Identifying individual differences in learning rate and retention in healthy adults. Psychological Science, 29(9), 1436–1450. https://doi.org/10.1177/0956797618772540

21 Bruce, G.S. (2004). Learning efficiency goes to college. In Evidence-based educational methods (pp. 267–275). Academic Press. https://doi.org/10.1016/b978-012506041-7/50016-4
22 Zerr, C.L., Berg, J.J., Nelson, S.M., Fishell, A.K., Savalia, N.K., & McDermott, K.B. (2018). Learning efficiency: Identifying individual differences in learning rate and retention in healthy adults. Psychological Science, 29(9), 1436–1450. https://doi.org/10.1177/0956797618772540
23 Zerr, C.L., Berg, J.J., Nelson, S.M., Fishell, A.K., Savalia, N.K., & McDermott, K.B. (2018). Learning efficiency: Identifying individual differences in learning rate and retention in healthy adults. Psychological Science, 29(9), 1436–1450. https://doi.org/10.1177/0956797618772540
24 Zerr, C.L., Berg, J.J., Nelson, S.M., Fishell, A.K., Savalia, N.K., & McDermott, K.B. (2018). Learning efficiency: Identifying individual differences in learning rate and retention in healthy adults. Psychological Science, 29(9), 1436–1450. https://doi.org/10.1177/0956797618772540
25 Andersen, E. (2016). Learning to learn. Harvard Business Review. Retrieved June 15, 2020, from: https://hbr.org/2016/03/learning-to-learn
26 Andersen, E. (2016). Learning to learn. Harvard Business Review. Retrieved June 15, 2020, from: https://hbr.org/2016/03/learning-to-learn
27 Gullotti, D. (2019, November 26). Leveraging technology platforms for the best learning experiences. Harvard Business Publishing. Retrieved June 15, 2020, from: https://www.harvardbusiness.org/leveraging-technology-platforms-for-the-best-learning-experiences/
28 Hart. J. (2019). Top 200 learning tools for 2019: Results of the 13th Annual Learning Tools Survey published 18 September 2019. Retrieved June 20, 2020, from Toptools4learning.com website: https://www.toptools4learning.com/
29 Hart. J. (2019). Top 200 learning tools for 2019: Results of the 13th Annual Learning Tools Survey published 18 September 2019. Retrieved June 20, 2020, from Toptools4learning.com website: https://www.toptools4learning.com/
30 Hart. J. (2019). Top 200 learning tools for 2019: Results of the 13th Annual Learning Tools Survey published 18 September 2019. Retrieved June 20, 2020, from Toptools4learning.com website: https://www.toptools4learning.com/
31 Busulwa, R., Birdthistle, N., & Dunn, S. (2020). Startup accelerators: A field guide. John Wiley & Sons.
32 Lara, M., & Lockwood, K. (2016). Hackathons as community-based learning: A case study. TechTrends, 60(5), 486–495. https://doi.org/10.1007/s11528-016-0101-0
33 Lara, M., & Lockwood, K. (2016). Hackathons as community-based learning: A case study. TechTrends, 60(5), 486–495. https://doi.org/10.1007/s11528-016-0101-0
34 Busulwa, R., Birdthistle, N., & Dunn, S. (2020). Startup accelerators: A field guide. John Wiley & Sons.
35 Busulwa, R., Birdthistle, N., & Dunn, S. (2020). Startup accelerators: A field guide. John Wiley & Sons.

Part V
Digital technologies deep dive

13 Data, data management, data analytics, and data science technologies

Introduction

Data literacy and proficiency is the unifying theme of the concepts discussed in this chapter. It refers to the ability to leverage the vast quantities of internal and external data to improve the organization's efficiency, effectiveness, and agility[1]. Gartner expects that 80% of organizations have either rolled out internal data literacy initiatives to upskill their workforce, or are intending to do so in the coming year. Reaping major rewards from data has become a critical organizational issue, with data now being argued to be an even more important resource than oil[2,3]. Used effectively, the large volumes of internal and external data being created every minute provide organizations with great opportunities for breakthroughs in how they organize, operate, manage talent, create value, and scale their reach[4]. But effectively capturing, storing, organizing, integrating, protecting, analyzing, and making the most of this data requires an organization-wide team effort[5]. There are limited benefits to doing it in silos or restricting it to a few go-to experts in a technical function within the organization[6]. Given this, non-technical stakeholders in every part of the organization also need to be literate and proficient with data.

Accountants in particular need to be literate and proficient with data, given their evolving roles as data stewards, data analysts, systems designers, assurance providers, cyber risk managers, strategic risk navigators, brand protectors, storytellers, trusted professionals, process and control experts, co-pilots, and digital and technology enablers[7,8,9]. Accountants may need to explain the financial value of different data and data management activities, to be involved in data management activities, to prepare / review / approve business cases for data projects, to advise managers on business intelligence and data analytics requirements, to build data products, to use data products, and to audit data management activities. Their data literacy and proficiency can make them a valuable business partner or an obstacle to reaping major rewards from data. In this chapter, we provide an introduction to data, data management, and data issues from an accounting perspective. Our intention is to provide a starting point to enable accountants to understand the value of data, the key data / data management concepts, key data / data management terminologies, accountants' role in data management, and examples of common data management platforms and vendors.

Data

Data as the new oil

As it relates to digital technologies, the term *data* refers to a collection of the smallest units of information that can be stored, processed, or transmitted by a computer (datum refers to the singular form of data). What constitutes data can range from numbers and letters to pictures, sounds, and videos. Although we only see the video, for example, within digital technologies, data is represented as a series of binary digits or bits. Each binary digit is either a one or zero, so that at the most basic level, all data is a bunch of ones and zeros referred to as binary data. This enables it to be stored, processed, and transmitted by computers. Data can be stored on a physical or virtual computer (e.g. virtual machine) and can be transmitted between computers via a network connection. It can also be stored on a physical storage device (e.g. USB, hard drive) and manually transferred onto another storage device or computer.

In the early days of computing, usable data was limited to the few internal information systems or software applications within an organization (e.g. accounting systems, HR systems, procurement systems) alongside limited external statistical data. But over time, there has been a proliferation in the number of devices and software applications collecting data. These include millions of devices with sensors, cameras, and audio recorders as well as the digitization and facilitation of more and more business processes and workflows through software applications. In addition to this, many of these devices, processes, and workflows are connected to the internet and therefore able to interact with each other, with physical or virtual computers, and with people. This results in vast amounts of data being created, stored, and available to use every second. The opportunities for organizations able to effectively make the most of this data are almost unlimited. For example, organizations can format, integrate, organize, analyze, and leverage insights from this data as a source of vast revenues (e.g. Google and Facebook). They can use it as a source of operational and strategic intelligence, use it to drive product innovation, to enhance customer experience, use it to form and better manage strategic partnerships, use it to disrupt industry offerings, and much more. Given this proliferation in available data and the vast power possible from effectively leveraging it, some experts have contended that data is the new oil. That is, that data may be an even greater source of global power and prosperity than oil[10,11]. Unverified data is data that data managers are not sure is true or untrue. Trusting such data and making decisions based on it can be highly dangerous. For example, imagine having unverified data about customer preferences and investing in capabilities to satisfy those preferences, only to discover after the investment that the preferences were completely wrong.

Types of data

Not all data is the same. Some data is readily usable and of great value. Other data is of little value or can't be used without undergoing extensive formatting, organizing, integration, analysis, and presentation. Accountants may come across a range of terminologies relating to data types including structured data, unstructured data, machine data, open data, dark data, real-time data, spatiotemporal data, unverified data, and outdated data. Structured data is usually pre-formatted and highly organized, making analysis easy (e.g. it could be credit card numbers, first names, or annual revenue figures). In contrast, unstructured data is not pre-formatted or organized, making collection, processing, and analysis challenging (e.g. audio files or Twitter conversations about a brand). Machine data is data created by machines such as planes, elevators, and traffic lights, as well as by devices such as mobile phones and fitness-monitoring devices. It can provide a real-time record of the behavior and activities of customers or other stakeholders (e.g. delays, difficulties, frustrations, hesitations, delights while using a service, etc.) as well as the performance or effectiveness of machines and devices such as servers, networks, heating systems, and mobile devices. Open data refers to data that is free for anyone to use, without the usual copyright, privacy, or other legal restrictions. For example, government and international agencies may make available some of the data they collect as open data. Organizations may then be able to combine this open data with other external and internal data to optimize operational and strategic decisions. Dark data is data that is collected, processed, and stored through the normal course of business but not actually used[12]; making use of such data may open up great new opportunities for an organization. Real-time data is data that is able to be used as it is created. For example, real-time customer experience data may reveal customer frustrations as they happen, enabling a manager to intervene and override routine procedures that may be frustrating the customer, creating risk of loss of repeat business from that customer. We mentioned earlier that unverified data is data that may or may not be correct, making information based on that data potentially dangerous. Information based on outdated data can equally be bad, if not worse. For example, imagine tourism service operators basing destination package information on customer experience satisfaction data from the 1970s. People will most likely want different things out of their package today than they did in the 1970s. This is not an exhaustive list of data types. Rather, we have touched on some of them to illustrate that, when searching for insights, providing advice, or making decisions based on data, understanding the type of data that has been used is important. Similarly, understanding the nature of data and data issues is invaluable when making decisions about who to hire, what data tools and methodologies to use, and what level of investment to make in data formatting, organizing, integration, analysis, and presentation projects. Figure 13.1 provides a visualization of some of the different types of data accountants may be faced with.

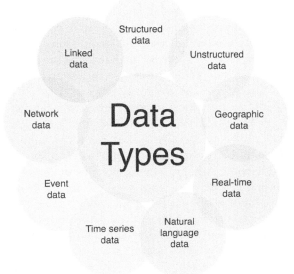

Figure 13.1 An example of different types of data

186 *Digital technologies deep dive*

Data risks and other issues

The growing value and power in data also brings with it great and ever-growing risks. Dark organizations, groups, and individuals getting authorized and unauthorized access to organizations' data can use it for illegal purposes ranging from using customers' data to steal their identity and their property[13,14], selling on customer data to criminal organizations, using customer data to interfere in elections[15,16,17] and stir up social unrest[18,19], using customer data to take customers hostage, and much more. Early on, data-related risks were largely limited to storage, risk of loss, and data recovery challenges. But now, with almost all data being transmitted or stored online, priority data-related risks include data security, user privacy, ethical collection, and ethical use risks. These issues have grown in prominence as the only barrier between organizations' data and reckless, dark, or criminal entities are the measures organizations' employees at all levels take to safeguard their organization's data. In their assurance, data stewardship, and risk management roles, accountants play a crucial role in shaping the responsible use of data. Other data-related issues typically focus on how to make the most of the mounting data organizations are collecting and have access to in order to enhance strategy and operations. These issues involve addressing questions such as how to format, organize, integrate, analyze and, present data to maximize the value derived from it.

Big data

Big data is a term that refers to datasets that are so voluminous, are being created so fast, and are so complex that traditional data processing software and approaches can't handle them. This data can include text, video, images, sounds, sensor data, and more (Figure 13.2 provides example big data source types and specific sources). Six characteristics or dimensions of big data are often discussed: volume, velocity, variety, variability, veracity, and value. Volume simply refers to there being massive amounts of data to capture, organize, store, manage, and / or use. For example, there are more than 500 million tweets per day[20] – which might make it a challenge for some organizations to analyze a year's worth of Twitter data (e.g. in order to understand what is being said about their brand in tweets). Velocity refers to the fast rate at which data is received, processed, and needs to be acted on. For example, every minute on Facebook more than half a million comments and nearly 300,000 status updates are received, analyzed, and stored into Facebook's databases. Acting on the analyzed data, Facebook is able to respond to inappropriate comments in near real time. Variety refers to the many types of data that a dataset may come in. For example, it could be traditional structured data such as numbers and characters in a database. Or it could be unstructured text documents, images, videos, sounds, emails and more. Variability refers to data whose meaning is constantly changing and changing rapidly. For example, in our earlier example of a brand analyzing tweets, the exact same tweets can have different meanings, depending on the context (e.g. one tweet saying "great, I love this brand!" may mean that person loves the brand, while another tweet saying "great, I love this brand!" may be from someone being sarcastic who actually hates the brand). Veracity refers to the quality of the data. Not all the voluminous datasets an organization has access to will be accurate. And those that are accurate are not all likely to be in a format that can be used without significant effort to validate them, separate out what is useful and what isn't, reformat them, integrate them with other data, and make them available in systems where they can be used for decision-making. Some datasets are more reliable and easier to work with than others, making them of better quality. Finally, value is concerned with the potential value that can be derived from datasets.

Data management and data analytics 187

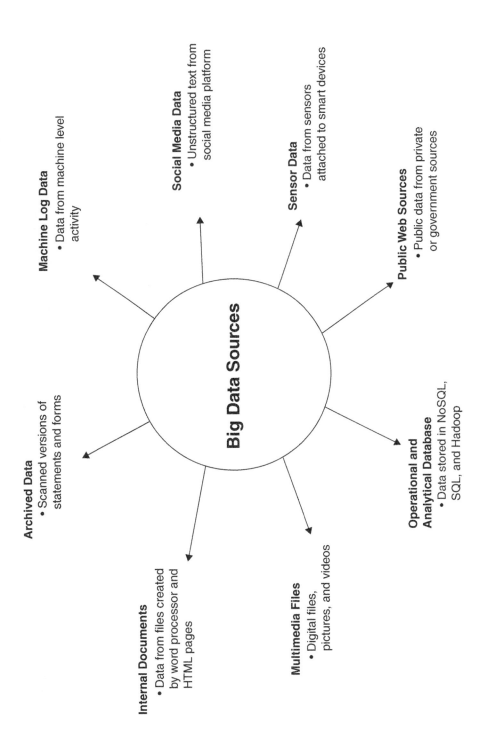

Figure 13.2 Example of sources of big data

188 *Digital technologies deep dive*

In summary, the term big data relates to massive and rapidly expanding datasets from lots of different sources and in lots of different formats. This data is typically noisy, messy, and ever-changing. The conversation about big data can be thought of as being made up of two parts. One part is a conversation about the different voluminous datasets organizations can access, the quality of these datasets, and the potential value or riches that can be discovered in them. The other part is about the approaches, practices, and methodologies to unlocking and leveraging that value (e.g. methodologies and practices for capturing, storing, analyzing, transferring, presenting, and updating big data).

Data management

Given the value, power, and risks associated with data, it may not be surprising that a formal practice has evolved to ensure value derived from data is maximized, while risks and costs are minimized. This practice is known as *data management*, and is concerned with how to collect, validate, store, and use data most effectively[21]. Effective data management is a significant challenge for organizations given the avalanche of internal and external data to manage, and the growing sources of such data. For example, data can come from SaaS applications (software as a service applications), ERP systems (enterprise resource planning systems), legacy systems, databases, data warehouses, and data lakes. Or it may come from the web, social media platforms, open data, and commercial data platforms. Alternatively, it may come from any number of devices including phones, computers, wearable devices, sensors, monitoring devices, etc. All this data has to be collected safely, validated, stored safely, and formatted and presented so that different parts of the organization can access the right information at the right time and in the right format to make the best decisions. This requires that organizations have the right technical leaders, the right technical specialists, the right technology platforms, and the right policies, procedures, and practices. The data management function typically plays a leadership role in issues such as data governance (e.g. determining who has what decision rights and accountability for data activities), data architecture (e.g. considering what rules, policies, standards, and models are put in place to determine what data is collected, how it is stored, how it is integrated, and how it is used), data modeling and design (e.g. defining and analyzing data required to support business processes), database and storage management, and data security and privacy. By having a working understanding of data management practices, accountants will be better positioned to advise on data investment projects, to collaborate with the data management function, to advise on the right data management technologies, to ensure the best data is available for decision-making, and to not inadvertently undermine change efforts intended to deliver effective data management.

Business intelligence and business analytics

The vast amounts of data emanating from business operations are of little value if they are not used to improve operational and strategic decisions. *Business intelligence* (BI) is a term that refers to the collection, storing, and analyzing of this operational data in order to use it to improve operational and strategic decisions[22,23]. It can also refer to the methods and tools used to do so. BI focuses on descriptive analytics, showing "what" has happened in the past or what is currently happening and "how" it happened or is happening[24,25]. So, for example, a BI dashboard may show us that sales have spiked to four times normal levels during the April to June quarter last year. As a result, we need to decide whether to ramp up inventory and staffing by three to four times normal levels for this period. Thus, BI answers what and how questions to help us decide whether we should continue doing what we are doing, do more / less of what we are doing, or completely change what we are doing[26].

Business analytics (BA) is a subset of business intelligence that focuses on predictive analytics[27,28]. That is, it focuses on discovering, interpreting, and communicating meaningful patterns in datasets. It answers why questions or cause and effect determination questions[29]. Armed with answers about cause and effect, we can predict the outcomes of certain actions or non-actions. Whereas BI dashboards showed us that sales previously spiked in the April to June quarter, through BA we may discover that the spike happened because a big festival was relocated to our town for the next three years, bringing an influx of young and hip customers (e.g. we may get this from mining website traffic data and discovering that the increased traffic was the result of a favorable influential blog post relating to the festival). Armed with this "why" information, we may decide not only to ramp up our stock and staffing levels during that period, but to also send a thank you gift to the influential blogger. We might also decide to offer an invitation to other influential bloggers to try / review our products / services at no cost.

Data analytics and data science

The term *data analytics* (also referred to just as *analytics*[30]) is an umbrella term referring to any form of analysis of data to uncover trends, patterns, and anomalies, or simply to measure performance[31,32,33]. It also includes interpretation, presentation, and communication of discovered patterns to improve decision-making. Usage of the terms data analytics or analytics can also be referring to one or more approaches, methodologies, and tools used to achieve the objectives of data analytics. Analytics approaches or methods include:

- *Descriptive analytics:* using historic or current data to determine "what" happened and "how" it happened
- *Predictive analytics:* understanding the "why" or cause and effect relationships within data in order to be able to make accurate predictions
- *Prescriptive analytics:* using algorithms to suggest optimal decisions based on the results of descriptive and predictive analytics

Specialty applications of data analytics include value chain activities (e.g. marketing analytics, HR analytics, supply chain analytics), sectors (e.g. retail analytics, healthcare analytics), workflows (e.g. call analytics), data source (e.g. video analytics, web analytics, speech analytics), and more.

Data science is a method for drawing insights from large datasets of structured and unstructured data[34]. It is a multidisciplinary field, meaning it draws on approaches, methods, techniques, and theories from disciplines such as mathematics, statistics, computer science, and information science. For example, it may draw on machine learning and deep learning techniques from the computer science field to learn from past decisions in order to improve the quality of automatically prescribed decisions. Or it can draw on statistical methods such as regression analysis and structural equation modeling to improve the reliability of information used as a basis for prescribed decisions. The role of data scientists can include activities such as collecting data, cleaning data, organizing data, making statistical inferences, building / using machine learning or deep learning models, conducting online experiments, building customizable or personalized data products, visualizing data, communicating findings, and much more[35,36]. The

190 *Digital technologies deep dive*

value of data science to accountants' key stakeholders includes revenue growth (e.g. from leveraging patterns in data to maximize sales opportunities), cost reduction (e.g. leveraging data insights to eliminate waste), improved customer experience (e.g. from using customer analytics and big data insights), product innovation / new product development (e.g. discovering product shortcomings or unmet customer needs in big data), and improved agility and adaptability (e.g. sensing and preparing for effective adaptation to or benefiting from pending industry disruptions). Figure 13.3 shows that data science brings together operations and business function knowledge, math or statistics knowledge, and data management knowledge. And Table 13.1 provides examples of data analytics and

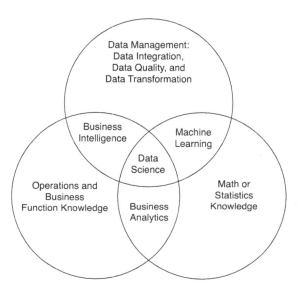

Figure 13.3 Data management, business intelligence, business analytics, and data science overlaps[37]

Table 13.1 Data-related roles and type of expertise[38]

	DSA framework category	Functional role	Sample occupations
Level of Analytical Rigour	Data Driven Decision Makers	Leverage data to inform strategic and operational decisions	IT Project Manager Marketing Manager
	Functional Analysts	Utilize data and analytical models to inform specific functions and business decisions	Business Analyst Financial Analyst
	Analytics Managers	Oversee analytical operations and communicate insights to executives	Chief Analytics Officer Marketing Analytics Manager
	Data Systems Developers	Design, build, and maintain organizations' data and analytical infrastructure	Systems Analyst Database Administrator
	Data Analysts	Leverage data analysis and modelling techniques to solve problems and glean insights across functional domains	Data Analyst Business Intelligence Analyst
	Data Scientists and Advanced Analytics	Create sophisticated analytical models used to build new datasets and derive new insights from data	Data Scientist Economist

data science-related roles and the common job or position titles of employees performing those roles.

Data visualization

Data visualization refers to the communication of insights from data through visual representation[39,40]. The format of visual representation can vary from dashboards, infographics, and interactive charts to heat maps, network diagrams, cartograms, wordclouds, videos, and more[41,42]. The insights discovered in data need to be communicated effectively and efficiently in order for potential users to make the most of them. This can be a challenging task when the interrelationships in data and the related insights are extensive, complex, or scenario dependent. Data visualization expands the repertoire of approaches and tools for communicating insights in the most efficient and impactful way. So, rather than a boring 30-minute PowerPoint, a well-designed and interactive infographic may get the same information across much faster and with much greater impact. Accountants can benefit from the use of data visualization methods, techniques, and tools, given how much of their role involves combining and using different datasets, searching for insights from data, communicating data insights to different stakeholders, and providing advice based on data insights. Data visualization proficiency can improve the insights they discover, the advice they provide, as well as the efficiency and impact of their communications.

Google and reflect

Table 13.2 Google and reflect

Digital capability	*Common terminology*
Data	raw data, clean data, metadata, structured data, unstructured data, semi-structured data, data quality
Big Data	database, data mart, data warehouse, data lake, data catalog, enterprise data hub, data fabric, operational data store, SaaS application, ERP system, legacy system, deployment platform, edge computing, data governance, data architecture, open data
Data Management	online analytical processing (OLAP), data mining, process mining, complex event processing, business performance management, benchmarking, text mining, descriptive analytics, prescriptive analytics, business analytics, business analyst, data analyst
Business Intelligence	backend, front end, BI application designer, BI project sponsor, business driver, business lead, business owner, business user, Cube, dashboard, DBMS, data feed, executive BI
Data Analytics and Data Science	machine learning, deep learning, neural networks, data mining, dataset, data democratization, algorithm, natural language processing, machine vision, data anonymization, artificial intelligence, behavioral analytics, citizen data scientist, data classification, decision trees, multidimensional database (MDB), data wrangling, Outlier, predictive modeling, Python, R (programming language), random forest, validity, reliability, decision science[43], association analytics, sentiment analysis, time decomposition, cluster analysis.
Data Visualization	charts, geospatial visualization, interactive visualization, climate change art, data art, data profiling, infographic, information visualization, interaction design, interaction techniques, scientific visualization, software visualization, statistical graphics, visual analytics, visual journalism, warming stripes, table or crosstab, distribution, flow, spatial, change over time, Part to Whole[44], Brainstorm, Bubble Chart, bubble map, circle packing, connection map, density plot, flow chart, flow map, heat map, network diagram, population pyramid, radar chart, scatterplot, span chart, spiral plot, stacked area graph, stacked bar graph, stem and leaf plot, stream graph, sunburst diagram, tally chart, timeline, timetable, tree diagram, tree map, Venn diagram, violin plot, word cloud

Example tools and vendors

Table 13.3 Example tools and vendors

Digital capability	Common terminology
Data	GoSpotCheck, IBM Datacap, Mozenda, Octoparse, OnBase by Hyland, OpenRefine, Data Ladder, Cloudingo, IBM Infosphere Quality Stage
Big Data	Amazon Redshift, Ataccama ONE, Cloudera, EnterWorks, Google BigQuery, Hortonworks Data Platform, IBM Db2 Hybrid Data Management Hadoop, Quoble, HPCC, Cassandra, MongoDB, Apache Storm, Rapidminer, Talend, Teradata, Apache Spark, Apache SAMOA, DataCleaner, Oracle Big Data Cloud, Oracle Big Data Cloud Service, Oracle Big Data SQL Cloud Service, and Oracle NoSQL Database, SAP master data management software, SAS Data Management.
Data Management	Oracle Data Management Suite, SAP Data Management, IBM Infosphere Master Data Management Server, Microsoft Master Data Services, Microsoft Azure Data Factory, Microsoft SQL Server SSIS, Dell Boomi, Talend, Amazon Web Services – Data Lakes and Analytics, Alooma, Panoply, Informatica MDM Reference 360, Collibra, Profisee
Business Intelligence and Business Analytics	Microsoft (Power BI), Google (e.g. Google Data Studio), Tableau, Qlik, ThoughtSpot, Sisense, Salesforce (e.g. Einstein Analytics), Tibco Software, TIBCO Software, SAS BI, SAP (e.g SAP business intelligence, SAP NetWeaver BW, SAP Business Objects), Oracle (e.g. Oracle BI, Oracle Enterprise BI Server, Oracle Hyperion System), IBM (e.g. IBM Cognos Intelligence), Birst, Yellowfin BI, Domo, Locker, MicroStrategy, GoodData, BOARD International, LogiAnalytics, Information Builders, Pyramid Analytics
Data Analytics and Data Science	R, Python, C/C++, SQL, GoSpotCheck, IBM Data Cap, Mozenda, Paxata, Trifacta, DataRobot, Feature Labs, Anaconda, Tableau, SAS, Alteryx, KNIME, RapidMiner, IBM Cognos, Hadoop, Hive, Pig, Spark[45], GoSpotCheck, IBM Datacap, Mozenda, Octoparse, OnBase by Hyland, Domino Data Lab, Informatica, KNIME Analytics Platform, Alteryx, Domino Data Lab, Informatica, KNIME Analytics Platform, RapidMiner, Anaconda Enterprise, Databricks, DataRobot, Feature Labs, H20.ai
Data Visualization	Tableau, Google Fusion Tables, JReport by Jinfonet, Google Charts, Microsoft Power BI, Infogram, Qlik, SAS, Cluvio, Visme

Discussion questions

Data

1. Do you agree that data is the new oil? What are three arguments for and against the view that data is the new oil?
2. What is the biggest organization to have compromised the security and privacy of customer or employee data? What role could accountants have played in preventing this breach?
3. What personal data are you emitting each day (e.g. via social media, search engines, mobile devices etc.)?
4. What are some practical strategies for protecting your privacy?
5. What can accountants do to minimize the risks to their employers' data?

Big data and data management

1. What is the difference between raw data, unstructured data, and structured data?
2. What is clean data and what does the data cleansing process involve?
3. What is the difference between a database, a data warehouse, and a data lake?
4. If an organization has a data lake, can it do without a data warehouse?
5. What are five free open data sources that could be useful to accountants and how could they be useful?
6. What are three open data use cases in the accounting function?
7. What are three ways you can use big data to improve your performance as an accountant?
8. Imagine you are a finance manager and you have the choice between two candidates to fill a vacant financial accounting position. One candidate has five years more experience including a stint at a well-respected accounting firm. But they have zero data and data management literacy. Another candidate has five years less experience and has not worked at an accounting firm. But this candidate has very strong data literacy (e.g. did a Masters of Data Science with their accounting degree and spent three years working in the data management team at a leading bank). Which candidate would you hire and why?

Business intelligence and business analytics

1. What is the difference between business intelligence and business analytics?
2. Which of the "example tools and vendors" are open source products or product providers?
3. Which of the BA and BI tools identified in "example tools and vendors" are suited to enterprise level customers, and which are suited to small / medium-sized business customers?

Data analytics and data science

1. What is the difference between data science and data analytics?
2. What is the difference between these roles: data analyst, business analyst, data scientist?
3. As a finance manager with a vacancy on the accounting team, who would be more valuable to you: a data analyst, a business analyst, a data scientist, an accountant with deep accounting experience, or a recent graduate with a double major in accounting and data science?
4. What are the top five benefits to an accountant of understanding data analytics and data science terminology, tools, methods, and approaches?

Data visualization

1. As an accountant, how could you benefit from being proficient in one or more data visualization tools?
2. As an accountant, what can you do to benefit from data visualization tools if you are not proficient in them yourself?
3. Which of the data visualization tools in "Example Tools and Vendors" are open source tools?

4 Which of the data visualization tools in "Example Tools and Vendors" would be suited for use in an enterprise level organization and which would be suited for use in a small to medium-sized business?

Notes

1. Brylad, M (2019). Data literacy: A critical skill for the 21st century. Tableau Software. Retrieved 17 December 2019, from: https://www.tableau.com/about/blog/2018/9/data-literacy-critical-skill-21st-century-94221
2. Vanian, J. (2016). Why data is the new oil. Fortune. Retrieved December 9, 2019 from: https://fortune.com/2016/07/11/data-oil-brainstorm-tech/
3. Parkins, D. (2017). The world's most valuable resource is no longer oil, but data. Economist. Retrieved December 9, 2019 from: https://www.economist.com/leaders/2017/05/06/the-worlds-most-valuable-resource-is-no-longer-oil-but-data
4. Mayhew, H., Saleh, T., & Williams, S. (2019). Making data analytics work for you – instead of the other way around. McKinsey & Company. Retrieved 17 December 2019, from: https://www.mckinsey.com/business-functions/mckinsey-digital/our-insights/making-data-analytics-work-for-you-instead-of-the-other-way-around
5. Mayhew, H., Saleh, T., and Williams, S. (2019). Making data analytics work for you – instead of the other way around. McKinsey & Company. Retrieved 17 December 2019, from: https://www.mckinsey.com/business-functions/mckinsey-digital/our-insights/making-data-analytics-work-for-you-instead-of-the-other-way-around
6. Mayhew, H., Saleh, T., and Williams, S. (2019). Making data analytics work for you – instead of the other way around. McKinsey & Company. Retrieved 17 December 2019, from: https://www.mckinsey.com/business-functions/mckinsey-digital/our-insights/making-data-analytics-work-for-you-instead-of-the-other-way-around
7. Sledgianowski, D., Gomaa, M., & Tan, C. (2017). Toward integration of big data, technology and information systems competencies into the accounting curriculum. Journal of Accounting Education, 38, 81–93.
8. Coyne, J.G., Coyne, E.M., & Walker, K.B. (2016). A model to update accounting curricula for emerging technologies. Journal of Emerging Technologies in Accounting, 13(1), 161–169.
9. IFAC. (2019). Future-fit accountants: Roles for the next decade. Retrieved December 18, 2019, from: https://www.ifac.org/knowledge-gateway/preparing-future-ready-professionals/discussion/future-fit-accountants-roles-next
10. Parkins, D. (2017). The world's most valuable resource is no longer oil, but data. Economist. Retrieved December 9, 2019 from: https://www.economist.com/leaders/2017/05/06/the-worlds-most-valuable-resource-is-no-longer-oil-but-data
11. Vanian, J. (2016). Why data is the new oil. Fortune. Retrieved December 9, 2019 from: https://fortune.com/2016/07/11/data-oil-brainstorm-tech/
12. Dark data. (2019). Gartner. Retrieved December 6, 2019, from: https://www.gartner.com/en/information-technology/glossary/dark-data
13. Winder, D. (2018). Hack of Marriott Starwood hotels hits 500 million guests. ABC News. Retrieved December 7, 2019, from: https://www.abc.net.au/news/2018-12-01/massive-data-breach-at-marriott-starwood-hotels/10573562
14. Winder, D. (2018). Hack of Marriott Starwood hotels hits 500 million guests. ABC News. Retrieved December 7, 2019, from: https://www.abc.net.au/news/2018-12-01/massive-data-breach-at-marriott-starwood-hotels/10573562
15. Cadwalladr, C., & Graham-Harrison, E. (2018, March 17). Revealed: 50 million Facebook profiles harvested for Cambridge Analytica in major data breach. The Guardian.
16. Rafter, D. (2018). Cyberthreat trends: 15 cybersecurity threats for 2020. Norton.com. Retrieved December 7, 2019, from: https://us.norton.com/internetsecurity-emerging-threats-cyberthreat-trends-cybersecurity-threat-review.html
17. Cambridge Analytica shuts all operations after Facebook scandal. (2018). Fortune. Retrieved December 7, 2019, from: https://fortune.com/2018/05/02/cambridge-analytica-shutting-down/
18. Anderson, J. (2018). "Fake news" and unrest in Nicaragua. The New Yorker. Retrieved December 7, 2019, from: https://www.newyorker.com/magazine/2018/09/03/fake-news-and-unrest-in-nicaragua

19 Nast, C. (2018). The Co-opting of French unrest to spread disinformation. Wired. Retrieved December 7, 2019, from: https://www.wired.com/story/co-opting-french-unrest-spread-disinformation/
20 58 incredible and interesting Twitter stats and statistics. (2019). Brandwatch. Retrieved December 10, 2019, from https://www.brandwatch.com/blog/twitter-stats-and-statistics/
21 What is data management?. 2019. Oracle.Com. Retrieved December 9, 2019, from: https://www.oracle.com/au/database/what-is-data-management/.
22 Pratt, M., & Fruhlinger, J. (2019). What is business intelligence? Turning data into business insights. CIO. Retrieved December 17, 2019, from: https://www.cio.com/article/2439504/business-intelligence-definition-and-solutions.html
23 Comparing business intelligence, business analytics and data analytics. (2019). Tableau Software. Retrieved December 17, 2019, from: https://www.tableau.com/learn/articles/business-intelligence/bi-business-analytics
24 Pratt, M., & Fruhlinger, J. (2019). What is business intelligence? Turning data into business insights. CIO. Retrieved December 17, 2019, from: https://www.cio.com/article/2439504/business-intelligence-definition-and-solutions.html
25 Tableau Software. (2019). Comparing business intelligence, business analytics and data analytics. Retrieved December 17, 2019, from: https://www.tableau.com/learn/articles/business-intelligence/bi-business-analytics
26 Tableau Software. (2019). Comparing business intelligence, business analytics and data analytics. Retrieved December 17, 2019, from: https://www.tableau.com/learn/articles/business-intelligence/bi-business-analytics
27 Business intelligence vs. business analytics. (2018). Retrieved December 16, 2019, from: https://analytics.hbs.edu/blog/business-intelligence-vs-business-analytics/
28 Ofori-Boateng, C. (2019) Data analytics versus business intelligence – and the race to replace decision making with software. Forbes. Retrieved December 17, 2019, from: https://www.forbes.com/sites/forbestechcouncil/2019/06/21/data-analytics-versus-business-intelligence-and-the-race-to-replace-decision-making-with-software/#29cab372612b
29 Tableau Software. (2019). Comparing business intelligence, business analytics and data analytics. Retrieved December 17, 2019, from: https://www.tableau.com/learn/articles/business-intelligence/bi-business-analytics
30 Analytics. (2019). Gartner. Retrieved December 16, 2019, from https://www.gartner.com/en/information-technology/glossary/analytics
31 Tableau Software. (2019). Comparing business intelligence, business analytics and data analytics. Retrieved December 17, 2019, from: https://www.tableau.com/learn/articles/business-intelligence/bi-business-analytics
32 Business analytics: Everything you need to know . (2019). MicroStrategy. Retrieved December 16, 2019, from: https://www.microstrategy.com/us/resources/introductory-guides/business-analytics-everything-you-need-to-know
33 Boulton, C. (2019). Data analytics examples: An inside look at 6 success stories. CIO. Retrieved December 17, 2019, from: https://www.cio.com/article/3221621/6-data-analytics-success-stories-an-inside-look.html
34 Olavsrud, T. (2019). What is data science? Transforming data into value. CIO. Retrieved December 16, 2019, from: https://www.cio.com/article/3285108/what-is-data-science-a-method-for-turning-data-into-value.html
35 Bowne-Anderson, H. (2018). What data scientists really do, according to 35 data scientists. Harvard Business Review. Retrieved December 17, 2019, from: https://hbr.org/2018/08/what-data-scientists-really-do-according-to-35-data-scientists
36 What is data science? (2019). Oracle. Retrieved December 17, 2019, from: https://www.oracle.com/data-science/what-is-data-science.html
37 Gao Institute of Management. (2020). Retrieved June 17, 2020, from: https://www.gim.ac.in/content.php?name=ABOUT-PGDM-(BDA)&id=134
38 Gao Institute of Management. (2020). Retrieved June 17, 2020, from: https://www.gim.ac.in/content.php?name=ABOUT-PGDM-(BDA)&id=134
39 Data visualization: What it is and why we use it. . (2019). MicroStrategy. Retrieved December 17, 2019, from: https://www.microstrategy.com/us/resources/introductory-guides/data-visualization-what-it-is-and-why-we-use-it
40 Data visualization: What it is and why it matters. (n.d.). SAS. Retrieved December 17, 2019, from: https://www.sas.com/en_au/insights/big-data/data-visualization.html

41 Data visualization beginner's guide: A definition, examples, and learning resources. (2019). Tableau Software. Retrieved December 17, 2019, from: https://www.tableau.com/learn/articles/data-visualization
42 Data visualization: What it is and why we use it. . (2019). MicroStrategy. Retrieved December 17, 2019, from: https://www.microstrategy.com/us/resources/introductory-guides/data-visualization-what-it-is-and-why-we-use-it
43 Data science terminology: 26 key definitions everyone should understand . (2019). Bernard Marr. Retrieved December 17, 2019, from: https://www.bernardmarr.com/default.asp?contentID=1446
44 Glossary of data visualizations. (2019). Tableau Software. Retrieved December 17, 2019, from: https://www.tableau.com/learn/articles/data-visualization/glossary
45 Top data science tools. (2019). James Cook University. Retrieved December 17, 2019, from: https://online.jcu.edu.au/canada/blog/top-data-science-tools.

14 Internet of things (IoT) technologies

Introduction

At the heart of the internet of things (IoT) and related technologies or concepts is the use of connected sensors and algorithms to make things "smart". These "things" can range from devices, equipment, and buildings to factories, biological processes, systems, and business processes. Long established, sensor technology has advanced to the point where there are sensors able to detect almost anything – from motion, voice, proximity, and touch to temperature, light, smoke, and much more. Although sensors have been capable of many of these things for some time, what has changed is the ability to connect them to each other and to the internet. This enables them to share collected information with each other and with any other devices or things or people connected to the internet. Through the use of connected sensors, all manner of things can be connected to the internet. This connection enables these things to communicate the data they collect through inbuilt / embedded sensors with each other. And through the use of software algorithms the things can analyze collected information, use it to make decisions, and issue or follow instructions to and from each other or to and from people. The ability of things to do all this makes them smart.

The sensing, connectivity, and "smartness" of things is set to profoundly alter how organizations create and deliver value. The potential of all things involved in organization workflows becoming smart offers significant opportunities for novel new products / services and enhanced product / service offerings, it also offers vastly improved opportunities for efficiency (e.g. the vast data collected from all the different devices can be integrated and used to pinpoint wasted effort, bottlenecks, activities that could be automated, or costs that could be minimized), for effectiveness (e.g concepts like smart workplaces and smart buildings can be leveraged to improve staff effectiveness), and for agility (e.g. through leveraging data on the things of strategic partners, government, and the community, organizations may be able to better anticipate and adapt to crisis events, disruptions and other changes). Accountants play a critical role in helping leaders and managers understand the financial meaning and strategic implications of the opportunities offered by the internet of things and related technologies and concepts. To deliver on their evolving roles as data stewards, systems designers, assurance providers, cyber risk managers, strategic risk navigators, brand protectors, storytellers, trusted professionals, process and control experts, co-pilots, and digital and technology enablers, accountants must understand the foundations, functioning, opportunities and threats, and use cases of the internet of things and related technologies and concepts. Without such an understanding, their advice would be limited at best and outright dangerous at worst.

The internet of things and the internet of everything

The internet of things

The *internet of things* is a collection of connected or linked things (e.g. computers, devices, cars, industrial equipment, buildings, etc.) that are able to transfer data or communicate with each other, usually without requiring the input or intervention of a human being[1]. The things are usually connected, transfer information, and communicate with each other via a network (e.g. a small private network or a much bigger national or global network). At a global network level, you can think of it as the internet but with many more devices or things being connected in addition to computers (e.g. cars, phones, printers, traffic lights, bridges, planes, pillows, dust, etc.). And these devices or things are able to communicate and transfer data and instructions to each other. For example, this could be as simple as your fridge sending instructions to your phone for it to create a reminder that you need to pick up some milk on the way home. Or, on a more involved level, your fridge could go online to find a same day milk delivery supermarket, order the milk, and notify your door lock to expect the delivery at a certain time and be ready to open the door once the milk arrives. If you have a robot in the home, the fridge or the lock could instruct the robot to pick up the milk from the front door and put it on a particular shelf in the fridge, so it is ready for you when you arrive home. The network connection between devices or things enables them to communicate and send data and instructions to each other (e.g. order information, payment information, instructions for actions to take or places to go). These things also need to be able to read or sense themselves and / or their environment (e.g. the fridge has to be able to sense that the milk is running out, and when the milk has been replaced). Because of this, the devices or things are usually fitted with or have inbuilt / embedded sensors (e.g. these can include touch sensors, proximity sensors, motion sensors, voice sensors, temperature sensors, liquid sensors, light sensors, heartbeat sensors, infrared sensors, gas sensors, smoke sensors, chemical sensors, etc.[2]). The job of the sensors is to collect information that things can communicate or use. In addition, the things are usually also equipped with software systems or algorithms that can then analyze the sensed information and use it to issue corresponding instructions. For example, a sensor in a car may sense that a truck is coming at a particular speed towards the car; the inbuilt software system may analyze this data and determine that the truck is about to collide with the car. The software system may issue instructions for the steering wheel and the brakes to perform actions that will prevent the accident. This is not so different to our eyes seeing that that the truck is speeding towards the car, our brain working out that an accident is going to eventuate, and our brain issuing our body parts instructions for actions to take (e.g. signal with our hands for the truck to stop or for the driver to get out of the way). Taken together, the combination of sensors and software algorithms equip the things with significant ability to emulate or even transcend human ability in some activities. For example, it is more likely that your fridge can reliably ensure that you never run out of milk than you may be able to (you may get distracted, forget, or be too tired whereas this will not happen to the fridge). With the right combination of sensors and software algorithms, almost all things can now be connected to the internet and become smart things with expanding potential for action. That is, things able to act on instructions from anywhere around the world or act independently to serve us, protect us, enhance our performance, and much more.

The internet of everything

The *internet of everything* (IoE) extends the internet of things by connecting people, processes, data, and things (see visualization in Figure 14.1)[3]. These are often referred to as the four pillars of the internet of everything. The IoE's expanded power is derived from the vastly expanded possibilities of everything coming online to share data, communicate, and interact in almost unlimited ways[4]. This differs from the internet of things, which is limited to the connection of physical things[5]. The people pillar refers to people's identity, interests and preferences, interaction, healthcare, work, address, payment, and other information being digitized and being online and being able to be interacted with. Once online, our virtual selves can interact with other people or their virtual selves, with businesses, business processes that are online, and with the things that are online (e.g. machines, devices, etc.). Our virtual selves and our things customize products to suit us and they can intervene in activities we are undertaking if we are at risk (e.g. your car could sense, unbeknownst to you, that you are about to be hit by another car and either warn you to avoid it or take over the steering to avoid it – if legally authorized to do so). The process pillar refers to processes or aspects of processes being able to be done online, inputting into other online processes, or requiring outputs from other online processes. For instance, a connected car may send data to the car manufacturer about the condition of each part in your car, notifying the manufacturer when critical parts will be in poor condition, and enabling them to book you in for a change of brake pads at a service center that is walking distance from your workplace. In this case, information from you and your car has fed into and triggered the manufacturer's vehicle monitoring and servicing processes. The data pillar relates to the collection, analysis, and use of data to facilitate and optimize processes. For example, in the case of our booking for a change of brake pads, it is the collection, analysis, and use of data from people (you) and things (the car) that has enabled that process to occur and to occur at the optimal time. Finally, the things pillar is about the different physical things that are connected to each other and to everything else online (e.g. machines, devices, buildings, traffic lights, car parks, etc.). Bringing these pillars together, the IoE offers greater integration, automation, and "smarts" than has ever been possible. It is set to revolutionize value creation and delivery[6].

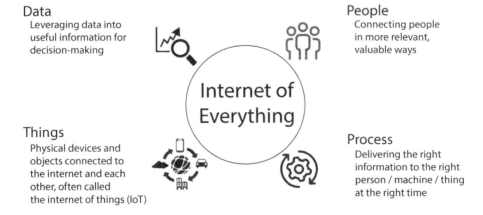

Figure 14.1 The internet of everything extends the internet of things by connecting people, processes, data, and things

Connected vs. smart vs. autonomous

The terms *connected*, *smart*, and *autonomous* often come up in IoT-related topics. In addition to capturing and storing data (e.g. through the use of sensors), IoT devices are "connected" if they can send and receive information. This enables them to, for example, send sensor data they've collected and receive back instructions. For example, your monitoring system may sense that someone is at the door and send you live video of the person. You may decide to send it instructions to not activate the alarm and, instead, to unlock the door because it is one of your relatives at the door dropping off something you forgot at their place. Without the connectivity (which may be via a mobile network such as 5G, a Wi-Fi network, Bluetooth, etc.) the transfer of sensor data and corresponding instructions may be difficult. IoT devices are smart if, in addition to being connected, they can gather information about their environment, process it (e.g. perform computation), and respond to that information. So, for instance, an air conditioner is smart if it can sense the room temperature and adjust its output to ensure the room can remain at a comfortable temperature. An IoT device is "autonomous" to the extent that it can sense, understand, and appropriately respond or adapt to its environment – minimizing the need for human intervention. So, for instance, a smart fridge would be highly autonomous if it can sense (hear) that you are planning to have a large number of guests over, work out that you won't have enough milk to offer them all tea, and order the right amount of extra milk to be delivered in time so you don't run out of milk. Even the smart air conditioner we described earlier is autonomous if it works out on its own how to keep the temperature at a comfortable level for you. Sometimes these terms are used interchangeably through misunderstanding or due to the boundaries between connection, intelligence, and autonomy having some overlaps. There can be degrees to a device's connectivity, smartness, and autonomy such that one device may be smarter and more autonomous than another.

IoT edge

While cloud architecture or "the cloud" offers almost unlimited storage and computation, a major shortcoming for some IoT-related uses is the time delay involved in sending sensor data to the cloud and awaiting computation results or other data to be sent back prior to other actions being able to occur. Sean Bryson, Vice President of Microsoft Technology at Hitachi Consulting, gives the example of an autonomous vehicle traveling down a busy road. He points out that if that car has to stop immediately to prevent an accident, sending sensor data to the cloud and awaiting computation and sending back of the results is not viable – it will just take too long[7]. *Edge computing* provides a solution to this issue for IoT devices. It is a form of distributed computing that brings cloud computing capabilities to local devices (i.e. brings computation and storage capabilities to local devices)[8]. These devices can then collect data via sensors, process it, and use the results for subsequent decisions and actions, instead of having to send sensor data to the cloud and awaiting the results of cloud computation. In the case of the autonomous vehicle needing to stop immediately to prevent an accident, Sean notes that the thousands of sensors within the vehicle can collect necessary data, onboard computation can assess the status of every piece of equipment, and the car can respond in fractions of a second[9]. Subsequent or non-urgent data can still be sent to the cloud for storage and computation (see visualization in Figure 14.2). Thus, *IoT edge* refers to technologies or platforms that bring cloud capabilities locally to IoT devices, enabling

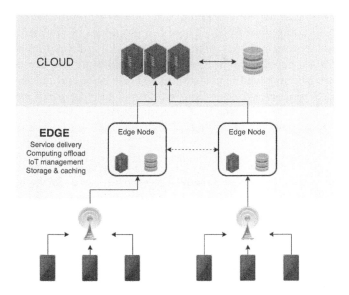

Figure 14.2 Edge computing brings computation and data storage to the locations where they are needed, instead of requiring sensor data to be sent to the cloud and waiting for the cloud to send the results of computation back to the location

them to sense, analyze, and respond in near real time. IoT edge technologies can minimize delays in processing, prevent delay related product quality issues, and minimize financial risks or even fatality risks.

The industrial internet of things

The *industrial internet of things* (IIoT), also known as the industrial internet, is essentially the extension and use of the internet of things in industrial sectors and applications (e.g. in equipment / machine / device-intensive industries such as oil and gas, power generation, manufacturing, aviation, logistics, food and beverage, and healthcare)[10]. The ability of machines and devices to communicate with each other (also known as machine-to-machine or M2M), with people, and with processes, combined with big data and sophisticated analytics algorithms, offers the opportunity for industrial sector organizations to make unprecedented breakthroughs in reliability, efficiency, effectiveness, and agility[11,12]. Industrial machinery and operational processes can be monitored and optimized in ways that have not been possible before. For example, systems can monitor, collect, exchange, analyze, and deliver information on the condition of machines and equipment (e.g. detecting or predicting corrosion inside a refinery pipe), on the interaction of machines with each other and with people (e.g. detecting when one machine is limiting the productivity of others), and on the status, efficiency, and effectiveness of processes (e.g. detecting errors and inefficiencies in the supply chain). Sophisticated algorithms can use the information being collected and analyzed to optimize processes and workflows (e.g. automatically scheduling on-call staff, automatically laying off those who aren't improving, recommending who should receive bonuses, automatically booking machine maintenance calls, or recommending which vendors to continue buying equipment from). These things and more are made possible by real-time data from sensors and the ability for data to be collected, analyzed, and routed between machines, people, and processes anywhere around the world in near real time. Accountants may be involved in evaluating IIoT use cases and innovations or they may be involved in evaluating processes and workflows fully or partly performed by IIoT things. If not, they may evaluate IIoT vendors, strategic partners, or competitors. In either case, a good understanding of IIoT dynamics, use cases, and innovations can be invaluable.

Cyber-physical systems, the Fourth Industrial Revolution, and Industrie 4.0

Cyber-physical systems (CPS) are systems in which integrations of digital and physical things and processes enable the digital management of physical processes and environments (e.g. digital includes software and network connectivity, while physical includes hardware / species / biological / chemical elements). CPS are able to dynamically sense, adapt to, and manage changes in a physical process and in process settings in real time[13,14]. CPS are able to do this by collecting data from different sensors, combining it with data from a range of different systems, analyzing / interpreting this data, using the analysis / interpretations to make decisions (e.g. about how physical processes or environments need to change), and creating and relaying instructions for things and people to perform (e.g. turn up the temperature switch, activate the nurse call alarm, prepare a patient management plan, etc.)[15]. Examples of CPS are abundant in a range of industries. In healthcare, CPS can be used to remotely monitor and manage a patient's health in real time[16]. For example, patient condition data can be collected via sensors in wearable healthcare technologies, this data can be analyzed / interpreted and combined with healthcare information system data to enable the right paramedics team to be called, for the patient to be taken to an emergency department with available capacity, and for the patient's general practitioner to preserve a booking spot to see that patient as soon as possible after they are discharged. This whole process is capable of occurring automatically, with only critical activities being performed by doctors, nurses, and paramedics. In manufacturing, CPS can be used to digitally manage particular manufacturing workflows at a plant, to manage entire plants or groups of plants, or to manage the entire manufacturing process across plants[17]. For manufacturing, Roberto Sabella, head of the Ericsson Research branch in Italy, invites people wanting to understand the power of CPS to imagine a situation in which robots, automated guided vehicles (AGVs), sensors, controllers, raw materials, products, and databases can communicate with one another and where they can all be automatically orchestrated through a central intelligent system[18]. And for an industry such as shipping / logistics, he invites people to imagine a port where cranes, vessels, AGVs, trucks, and containers can communicate with each other, while being orchestrated by a central system aiming to optimize waiting time, damage rates, maintenance costs, environmental impact, safety, etc.[19]. CPS and their elements can leverage technologies such as artificial intelligence, machine learning, and data analytics to be intelligent (or smart) and autonomous. For example, an "intelligent" cyber-physical system (or iCPS) may orchestrate all the activities of a "smart factory", automating and distributing different activity groups among different intelligent agents (e.g. intelligent sub-systems, intelligent things, intelligent processes, human beings, etc.)[20]. CPS leverage the vastly expanded sensing, communication, analytics, automation, intelligence, autonomy, and other possibilities of digital–physical integration for breakthroughs in organizational value creation, efficiency, agility, and adaptability.

The term *Fourth Industrial Revolution* refers to the ushering in of cyber-physical systems and related technologies that are set to drastically change how organizations create and deliver value and, in turn, how societies function and how individuals live their lives[21,22]. This change is anticipated to be similar to, but of an even greater scale, than earlier industrial revolutions that drastically changed the functioning of businesses and societies[23]. For example[24], the First Industrial Revolution ushered in the use of water and steam power to enable the creation of mechanical production facilities. The Second Industrial Revolution ushered in the use of electricity and enabled the division of labor, use of assembly lines, and the mass production of products. The Third Industrial Revolution ushered in IT systems to automate and better control production lines. In each revolution, the change in how organizations created value transformed the nature of work significantly. In turn, each revolution significantly transformed the functioning of cities and nation states and how individuals lived their lives. For example, in the main, we are no longer subsistence farmers, factory laborers, or machine operators. We do more knowledge-oriented and creative work, earn much more, have much more free time, and live in cities and nation states that are very different to those of preceding industrial revolutions. In each revolution, the power and fortunes of individuals, organizations, and nation states leading or keeping up with the revolutions were drastically transformed[25]. For example, the first and second industrial revolutions elevated the wealth and power of nation states like the USA and Japan[26]. It also elevated the fortunes of industrialists like Andrew Carnegie[27] and John Rockefeller[28]. And the third industrial revolution has elevated nations like India and China, as well as modern-day industrialists like Masayoshi Son, Jack Ma, N.R. Narayana Murthy, Bill Gates, and Sergey Brin. For individuals, organizations, and nation states that have not made sufficient effort to keep up with the demands of industrial revolutions, the revolutions have often diminished their wealth and power – if not marginalized them altogether.

Although the term *Industry 4.0* (or *Industrie 4.0*) is sometimes interchangeably used to refer to the Fourth Industrial Revolution, it was originally more specifically used to refer to the digital transformation of the manufacturing industry. Viewed this way, it is a subset of the Fourth Industrial Revolution. Whereas the Fourth Industrial Revolution is an all-encompassing term (i.e. referring to changes in how businesses produce products, in how cities / societies function, and in how individuals live), Industrie 4.0 is limited to digital transformation of the manufacturing industry, manufacturing organizations, and manufacturing processes (e.g. exploring how manufacturing industries, organizations, and processes can be transformed to make the most of the Fourth Industrial Revolution). Industrie 4.0 considers issues such as what "smart manufacturing" and "smart factories" are, how they ought to work, and how to transform manufacturing and factories to be smart.

Smart buildings, smart workspaces, and smart homes

In a nutshell, *smart buildings* are buildings that leverage the internet of things, cyber-physical systems, artificial intelligence, and other technologies to optimize the functioning, usability, and externalities of buildings. The functioning of buildings can be optimized through reduced energy costs, improved temperature and ventilation control, reduced maintenance costs, improved access control, improved useful life, improved safety, improved building condition / value, and more. Externalities, or impacts on communities and the environment, can be optimized through minimization of negative externalities (e.g. carbon emissions, energy consumption, hazardous waste) and maximization of positive externalities (e.g. negative emissions, positive impacts on community wellbeing, etc.). And usability can be optimized through improvements in the efficiency and effectiveness of the activities the building is being used for. Optimizations such as these are logical if we imagine, as an example, every component of a building being fitted with sensors, being online, being able to communicate with all other physical and digital components (e.g. devices, systems, processes, etc.), and being able to leverage artificial intelligence and data science to make smart and autonomous decisions. As a result, a building would be able to know on its own who is in a building, where they are in the building, what their comfort requirements are, who is meeting with them, what devices to activate and when to monitor them, what video footage to analyze, who to notify if security anomalies are detected, what the conditions of a building's external environmental are, when there are likely to be issues with electrical grids and how to avoid the impact of those grids, and much more. Through integrations with workflow management systems, smart buildings may be able to drastically improve process efficiency and effectiveness. For example, a smart building may be able to check which people entering the building have an appointment, automatically register them in the visitor management system, send them an email or SMS confirmation signoff upon arrival, direct them to skip the security cue and scan their QR code, and notify the person they are meeting to go down in the lift at the right time to greet them.

Smart workplaces combine concepts like smart buildings, the internet of things, cyber-physical Systems, artificial intelligence, and other technologies with design and workflow management concepts to optimize the efficiency, effectiveness, and attractiveness of work settings. For example, smart buildings can be leveraged to ensure lighting, airflow, sunlight, heating, and air conditioning that anticipates and caters to workers' needs so as to enable them to do their best work efficiently and effectively (e.g. in regard to lighting, using circadian rhythm lighting can optimize alertness, energy, and focus). IoT, data science, and artificial intelligence can be leveraged to ensure that workplace conditions, equipment, tools, and resources automatically turn on and shut down in time to optimize accessibility and energy efficiency. The right data can be made to be available to the right devices and people, in the right format, in the right places and at the right time – first time, every time. Smart buildings can communicate with other smart buildings, draw data from the external environment, pull in live traffic and public transportation data to ensure employees arrive and leave at the best times, maximize their breaks (e.g. best times to get lunch at their favorite cafes), avoid getting caught in the rain, and avoid areas most often associated with getting sick. Many more smart workplace use cases and best practices are emerging. Smart workplaces can be a potent attraction tool in the war for talent – for instance, consider the word of mouth and pulling power of Apple's and Google's work settings.

Smart homes are essentially like smart workplaces except the focus is on maximizing efficiency, effectiveness, safety, security, livability, and comfort of a home's occupants. For example, smart solar systems, smart meters, and smart devices may ensure that power costs are kept at a minimum or that a household actually generates more electricity than it uses. Or smart fridges, smart washing machines, smart air conditioners, and smart locks may autonomously take care of household tasks like food shopping, washing, climate control, and home access. Through Google's and Apple's connected or smart home platforms, home occupants can interact with devices at their home in real time from anywhere around the world. And these devices can, in turn, interact with each other and with external systems and platforms. For example, a home monitoring system may automatically call police or an ambulance if it senses a security or safety threat within or outside the home.

Smart infrastructure, smart cities, and smart government

Smart infrastructure

Infrastructure refers to the physical structures and facilities needed for the effective functioning of society (e.g. roads, bridges, power lines, public buildings, etc.) and, sometimes, enterprise. Like other IoT things, infrastructure can also be connected, smart, and autonomous through leveraging smart buildings, the internet of things, cyber-physical systems, artificial intelligence, and other technologies[29]. Through leveraging these concepts and technologies, *smart infrastructure* can sense what is happening within itself and in the external environment. It can share the sensed information with other infrastructure (e.g. roads, traffic systems, street lights), with machines and devices (e.g. cars, smartphones, parking meters), with institutions (e.g. the fire service, the local emergency department, policing and intelligence agencies), and with information systems and workflows (e.g. government procurement systems, government healthcare systems, government emergency management systems, tender documents, ambulance diversion workflows). Smart infrastructure can also receive information from external systems and leverage artificial intelligence and data science, for example, to be self-aware and self-managing (e.g. it can sense the need for and coordinate its own maintenance depending on external weather conditions and government budget performance, it can anticipate and prevent public safety issues, it can coordinate with other infrastructure to limit traffic congestion, it can suggest / request changes to other infrastructure that may be creating bottlenecks, it can prevent infrastructure abuse and limit the impact of public disorder events, etc.). The use cases for smart infrastructure are only limited by imagination and political / legal / social constraints. Diverse use cases can include letting swimmers know where it is safe to swim in real time in order to avoid shark attacks and drowning, anticipating wastewater overflow due to rain and coordinating preemptive action (e.g. by removing existing and emerging blockages), eliminating congestion from road networks by analyzing real-time data on the whereabouts of cars and redirecting them to alternate routes, recognizing criminals and stolen cars and directing police to their anticipated getaway routes, automatically analyzing video footage and alerting policing and public safety institutions to current and anticipated risks, optimizing infrastructure performance by pinpointing performance issues and limitations, and enabling real-time changing of public signage (e.g. street signs could automatically change speed limits and street accessibility). Governments that make smart infrastructure data publicly available enable businesses and consumers to leverage that data to improve available products / services and to improve the functioning of cities and regions. For example, when Transport for London shared public transportation data (e.g. pickup spots, pickup times) businesses and individuals used this data to create mobile apps or integrate the data into existing apps to improve public transport accessibility[30,31]. Optimizing the performance and capacity of assets can help meet challenges related to population growth, raise consumer / society expectations and raise national productivity.

Smart cities

Smart cities are cities that enable and leverage smart infrastructure, as well as the integration of smart infrastructure data with data collected from other things, collected from individuals, and collected from institutions, to better govern and serve communities. For example, they can automatically source and integrate data from roads, bridges, buildings, transportation systems, water supply networks, drainage networks, police departments, citizens, schools, libraries, hospitals, social media platforms, and other public services, assets, information systems, and platforms. They can then leverage data analytics, data science, and artificial intelligence to better manage public service quality (e.g. availability of services, accessibility of services, timeliness, efficiency, safety, security, etc.), to reduce service costs (e.g. city capital and operating costs), to reduce resource consumption (e.g. water, energy, labor, etc.), to improve community engagement, and to improve the quality of life satisfaction of citizens. As with smart infrastructure use cases and examples, smart city technology use cases and examples are abundant. For example, on its continuing journey to becoming a smart city, the city of Barcelona implemented a network of optics throughout the city – enabling it to support the IoT and to provide free hi-speed Wi-Fi. This then enabled smart water, smart lighting, and smart parking management – saving the city over US$98 million and creating 47,000 new jobs. In its continuing journey, the city of Boston implemented smart trash cans that automatically determine when trash cans need collection and the most efficient routes for sanitation workers. And the city of Amsterdam has migrated to real-time monitoring of traffic flow, energy usage, and public safety data to enable real-time adjustments to be made about their management[32]. Table 14.1 shows where a range of cities around the world are on the smart city maturity journey.

Table 14.1 Cities around the world and their smart city maturity (e.g. if they have a smart city roadmap or smart city department, and the presence of key smart city domains or application areas)[33]

City name	Roadmap designed	Smart city department	Smart city application domains			
			Business	Citizen	Environment	Government
Bilbao	No	No	Yes	Yes	Yes	Yes
Birmingham	Yes	Yes	No	Yes	No	Yes
Bristol	Yes	Yes	Yes	Yes	Yes	Yes
Cape Town	No	No	No	Yes	Yes	Yes
Cleveland	Yes	No	No	Yes	Yes	Yes
Copenhagen	Yes	Yes	Yes	Yes	Yes	Yes
Fujisawa	Yes	Yes	Yes	Yes	Yes	Yes
Melbourne	No	No	No	Yes	No	Yes
Ottawa	Yes	Yes	Yes	Yes	Yes	Yes
Santander	No	No	No	Yes	No	Yes
Seattle	Yes	Yes	Yes	Yes	Yes	Yes
Seoul	Yes	Yes	No	Yes	No	Yes
Singapore	Yes	No	Yes	Yes	No	Yes
Stockholm	Yes	Yes	Yes	Yes	Yes	Yes
Toronto	Yes	No	No	Yes	Yes	Yes

Smart government

Smart government basically extends the concepts of smart infrastructure and smart cities to optimize governance of democratic processes, to optimize the management of public service institutions, and to optimize the delivery of public services. Given their experiences with the business world, citizens expect responsive, efficient, and accountable government services and institutions. As their expectations grow, they are becoming more intolerant of bureaucratic delays, lack of service availability, lack of service access, siloed government departments that don't talk to each other, and infrastructure that is not digitally enabled or able to interface with consumer devices. Examples of smart government initiatives include mobile apps that enable citizens to be community guardians (e.g. to capture and report incidents, to suggest improvements etc.), they include point sign on to access all government services, they include leveraging business and consumer data to warn consumers about organizations misleading them[34], and they include leveraging big data to anticipate security threats (e.g. leveraging travel / aviation data, traffic data, social media data, search engine to anticipate terrorist threats). They further include optimizing security and privacy of government information, enabling the use of digital IDs and digital government workflows, and enabling the secure integration of business and consumer systems and devices with government systems and devices.

Risks and other issues

As with many other digital technologies, key risks and issues of IoT-related technologies include privacy, security, ethics, and constantly changing technology standards. Examples of privacy-related issues include increased risks of unauthorized exposure of customer, citizen, or organization data. Examples of security risks include increased points of access to sensitive information for almost anyone around the world (e.g. whereas a hacker once upon a time was limited by availability of an internet connection, internet speed, lower availability of hacking targets, only computers as an access / breach point, and minimal online information to use – today, all these things are almost unlimited). This creates a very big security challenge for organizations that may impact how they manage all their people, things, systems, and processes[35,36]. Organizations and governments are expected to be ethically responsible in how they use the vast treasure troves of data available to them. This becomes a much bigger challenge with so many connected, smart ,and autonomous devices. For example, it can be easy for artificial intelligence algorithms to create new information (by integrating and analyzing integrated data) but for it not to be acceptable for an organization to use or even access that information (e.g. it wouldn't be difficult for Google to create digital profiles of citizens and use artificial intelligence algorithms to comb the internet and internet-connected devices for extensive personal data about citizens, but this would likely be met with community outrage that could even lead to communities taking away Google's license to operate in those communities). Finally, constantly changing technology standards mean that IoT-related technology users must always keep in mind that technology standards could change rapidly (e.g. from NFC to Bluetooth to 5G) and they ought to have platforms and devices that can accommodate new standards (e.g. ones that are able to adapt to new standards or are cheap to replace).

Google and reflect

licensing and entitlement management, IoT-enabled product as a service, things as customers, IoT-enabled applications, edge AI, infonomics, managed IoT services, IoT edge

208   *Digital technologies deep dive*

analytics, IoT cloud platform, mobile IoT (MIoT), IoT protocol, narrowband IoT (NB-IoT), quality of service (QoS), mesh network, telematics, IoT business solutions, digital business technology platform, digital twin, IoT security, digital ethics, IoT services, IoT Platform, event stream processing, automotive, real-time data analytics, IoT edge architecture, LPWA, autonomous vehicles, low-cost development boards, commercial UAVs (drones), intelligent building automation systems, IT / OT alignment, asset performance management, managed machine-to-machine services, IoT integration, smart lighting, cloud MOM services (momPaaS), MDM of product data, MDM of "thing" data, internet of meat

Example tools and vendors

Google Home voice-controlled speaker, Amazon Echo Plus, August Doorbell Cam, Nest Smoke Alarm, NETGEAR Orbi Ultra-Performance Whole Home Mesh Wi-Fi System, Kuri Mobile Robot, August Smart Lock, Arm Pelion, Bosch IoT Suite, Bosch Sensors, Cambium Networks cnReach Narrowband Wireless Solution, Cisco Intent-Based Networking (IBN) Solutions, Dell IoT Connected Bundles, Eaton PredictPulse, HP Enterprise Edgeline OT Link Platform, Intel OpenVINO, Intel IoT Market Ready Solutions, Lenovo ThinkSystem SE350, Particle IoT Rules Engine, Qualcomm Vision Intelligence Platform, Qualcomm 9205 LTE modem, Rigado Cascade Edge-as-a-Service, Roambee sensors and beacons, Roambee Honeycomb IoT API platform, Siemens / Alibaba MindSphere, Software AG Cumulocity IoT platform, Hitachi Lumada, PTC Thingworx, Nexiot Globehopper smart sensors, Huawei NB-IoT platform, SAP Leonardo, GE Predix, Ingenu RPMA device management platform, AWS IoT Core, Google Cloud IoT Core, Microsoft Azure IoT, Arundo Analytics, Bright Machines, Dragos, FogHorn, Iguazio, Preferred Networks, READY Robotics, SparkCognition, Element Analytics [37,38]

Discussion questions

1 What is the best metaphor you can think of to explain how the internet of things works?
2 Is it possible for every single thing (living or nonliving) to be connected to the internet (e.g. could dust, water, bacteria, diseases, plates, trees, volcanoes, etc. be connected to the internet)?
3 What do we mean when we say things can communicate with each other? What types of communication can they undertake?
4. What is a sensor? How is a connected sensor different?
5 What are ten different types of sensors?
6 What sensors could you attach to a chair to give it human like senses?
7 What is the difference between the internet of things (IoT), the internet of everything (IoE), and the industrial internet of things (IIoT)?
8 What is the difference between a connected IoT device, a smart IoT device, and an autonomous IoT device?
9 What is edge computing? What is the IoT edge?
10 What is a cyber-physical System (CPS)? Are there different types of cyber-physical systems?
11 What is the difference between Industry 4.0, Industrie 4.0, and the Fourth Industrial Revolution?

12 Are Industry 4.0 and the Fourth Industrial Revolution possible without cyber-physical systems?
13 What is the difference between a smart building, a smart workplace, and a smart home?
14 Can you have smart workplaces and smart homes without smart buildings?
15 Which comes first, smart infrastructure, smart cities, or smart government?
16 What are five ways IoT and IoT-related technologies can compromise a person's privacy, security, and health?

Notes

1 Frangoul, A. (2017). The internet of things: Why it matters. CNBC. Retrieved December 23, 2019, from: https://www.cnbc.com/2017/10/23/the-internet-of-things-why-it-matters.html
2 What is a sensor? Different types of sensors, applications. (2017). Electronics Hub. Retrieved December 23, 2019, from: https://www.electronicshub.org/different-types-sensors/
3 The internet of everything. (2019). Cisco. Retrieved December 20, 2019, from https://www.cisco.com/c/dam/en_us/about/business-insights/docs/ioe-value-at-stake-public-sector-analysis-faq.pdf
4 The internet of everything. (2019). Cisco. Retrieved December 20, 2019, from https://www.cisco.com/c/dam/en_us/about/business-insights/docs/ioe-value-at-stake-public-sector-analysis-faq.pdf
5 The internet of everything. (2019). Cisco. Retrieved December 20, 2019, from https://www.cisco.com/c/dam/en_us/about/business-insights/docs/ioe-value-at-stake-public-sector-analysis-faq.pdf
6 Seven things you need to know about IIoT in manufacturing. (2019). Forbes. Retrieved December 23, 2019, from: https://www.forbes.com/sites/louiscolumbus/2019/06/02/seven-things-you-need-to-know-about-iiot-in-manufacturing_updated/#7de9c6095f56
7 Bryson, S. (2019). Internet of things (IoT) – five components of IoT edge devices. Cisco. Retrieved December 30, 2019, from: www.cisco.com/c/en/us/solutions/internet-of-things/iot-edge-devices.html
8 Bryson, S. (2019). Internet of things (IoT) – five components of IoT edge devices. Cisco. Retrieved December 30, 2019, from: www.cisco.com/c/en/us/solutions/internet-of-things/iot-edge-devices.html
9 Bryson, S. (2019). Internet of things (IoT) – five components of IoT edge devices. Cisco. Retrieved December 30, 2019, from: www.cisco.com/c/en/us/solutions/internet-of-things/iot-edge-devices.html
10 Everything you need to know about IIoT. (2019). GE Digital. Retrieved December 23, 2019, from: https://www.ge.com/digital/blog/everything-you-need-know-about-industrial-internet-things
11 Industrial internet of things (IIoT) - definition. (2019). Trend Micro USA. Retrieved December 23, 2019, from: https://www.trendmicro.com/vinfo/us/security/definition/industrial-internet-of-things-iiot
12 Everything you need to know about IIoT. (2019). GE Digital. Retrieved December 23, 2019, from: https://www.ge.com/digital/blog/everything-you-need-know-about-industrial-internet-things
13 Sabella, R. (2018) Cyber physical systems for Industry 4.0. Retrieved December 30, 2019, from: https://www.ericsson.com/en/blog/2018/10/cyber-physical-systems-for-industry-4.0
14 Sabella, R. (2018) Cyber physical systems for Industry 4.0. Retrieved December 30, 2019, from: https://www.ericsson.com/en/blog/2018/10/cyber-physical-systems-for-industry-4.0
15 Sabella, R. (2018) Cyber physical systems for Industry 4.0. Retrieved December 30, 2019, from: https://www.ericsson.com/en/blog/2018/10/cyber-physical-systems-for-industry-4.0
16 Sabella, R. (2018) Cyber physical systems for Industry 4.0. Retrieved December 30, 2019, from: https://www.ericsson.com/en/blog/2018/10/cyber-physical-systems-for-industry-4.0
17 King, A. (2019) What are cyber-physical systems? (2019). RMIT University. Retrieved December 30, 2019, from: https://www.rmit.edu.au/industry/develop-your-workforce/tailored-workforce-solutions/c4de/articles/what-are-cyber-physical-systems
18 Sabella, R. (2018) Cyber physical systems for Industry 4.0. Retrieved December 30, 2019, from: https://www.ericsson.com/en/blog/2018/10/cyber-physical-systems-for-industry-4.0
19 Sabella, R. (2018) Cyber physical systems for Industry 4.0. Retrieved December 30, 2019, from: https://www.ericsson.com/en/blog/2018/10/cyber-physical-systems-for-industry-4.0

20 Sabella, R. (2018) Cyber physical systems for Industry 4.0. Retrieved December 30, 2019, from: https://www.ericsson.com/en/blog/2018/10/cyber-physical-systems-for-industry-4.0
21 Wilson, B. (2016). What is the Fourth Industrial Revolution & how will it affect you? Oracle Blogs. Retrieved December 30, 2019, from: https://blogs.oracle.com/oracleuniversity/what-is-the-fourth-industrial-revolution-how-will-it-affect-you
22 Schulze, E. (2019). Everything you need to know about the Fourth Industrial Revolution. CNBC. Retrieved December 30, 2019, from: https://www.cnbc.com/2019/01/16/fourth-industrial-revolution-explained-davos-2019.html
23 Sabella, R. (2018) Cyber physical systems for Industry 4.0. Retrieved December 30, 2019, from: https://www.ericsson.com/en/blog/2018/10/cyber-physical-systems-for-industry-4.0
24 Wilson, B. (2016). What is the Fourth Industrial Revolution & how will it affect you? Oracle Blogs. Retrieved December 30, 2019, from: https://blogs.oracle.com/oracleuniversity/what-is-the-fourth-industrial-revolution-how-will-it-affect-you
25 Diamond, J.M. (1998). Guns, germs and steel: A short history of everybody for the last 13,000 years. Random House.
26 Porter, M.E. (2011). Competitive advantage of nations: Creating and sustaining superior performance. Simon and Schuster.
27 Nasaw, D. (2007). Andrew Carnegie. Penguin.
28 Rockefeller, J.D., & Chernow, R. (1998). Titan: The life of John D. Rockefeller, Sr. Ballantine Books.
29 Siemens (2020). Intelligent infrastructure: How to make a smart building more profitable. Retrieved January 3, 2020, from https://assets.new.siemens.com/siemens/assets/api/uuid:396710f1-ea9e-4089-ae2f-8408528094c7/version:1560771253/cc-us-bt-cpp-intel-infrstrctr-wp.pdf
30 Macaulay, T. (2019). How startups aim to transform cycling with enormous new TfL dataset. Techworld. Retrieved January 3, 2020, from: https://www.techworld.com/data/startups-aim-transform-urban-cycling-with-enormous-new-tfl-dataset-3701170/
31 Uber integrates Transport for London info into app. (2020). Financial Times. Retrieved January 3, 2020, from: https://www.ft.com/content/d557d9ec-6a8e-11e9-80c7-60ee53e6681d
32 Ellsmoor, J. (2019). Smart cities: The future of urban development. Forbes. Retrieved January 3, 2020, from: https://www.forbes.com/sites/jamesellsmoor/2019/05/19/smart-cities-the-future-of-urban-development/#8ee0ae72f900
33 Sánchez-Corcuera, R., Nuñez-Marcos, A., Sesma-Solance, J., Bilbao-Jayo, A., Mulero, R., Zulaika, U., ... & Almeida, A. (2019). Smart cities survey: Technologies, application domains and challenges for the cities of the future. International Journal of Distributed Sensor Networks, 15(6), 1550147719853984.
34 Grieve, C. (2019). Worst performing superannuation funds exposed by APRA "heatmap". The Sydney Morning Herald. Retrieved January 3, 2020, from: https://www.smh.com.au/business/banking-and-finance/worst-performing-superannuation-funds-exposed-by-apra-heatmap-20191210-p53ihq.html
35 Trendmicro. (2019). IIoT security risk mitigation in the Industry 4.0 era. Retrieved January 3, 2020, from: https://documents.trendmicro.com/assets/rpt/IIoTsecurity-risk-mitigation-in-the-industry-4-era.pdf
36 Wood, E. (2019) It's Time to secure the internet of everything: Regulations rise as the IoT continues to expand. Forbes. Retrieved January 3, 2020, from: https://www.forbes.com/sites/forbestechcouncil/2019/09/30/its-time-to-secure-the-internet-of-everything-regulations-rise-as-the-iot-continues-to-expand/#711b22f7fa44
37 Martin, D. (2019). 2019 internet of things 50: 15 coolest IoT hardware companies. CRN. Retrieved January 5, 2020, from: https://www.crn.com/slide-shows/internet-of-things/2019-internet-of-things-50-15-coolest-iot-hardware-companies/1
38 Staff, C. (2020). The most powerful IoT companies in the world. Computerworld. Retrieved January 5, 2020, from: https://www.computerworld.com/article/3412287/the-most-powerful-internet-of-things-iot-companies-to-watch.html#slide16

15 Artificial intelligence technologies

Introduction

The overarching theme of the digital technologies and concepts covered in this chapter is the design, use, and optimization of information systems and applications that can sense, comprehend, and recommend or take action. The design and use of such digital technologies and concepts is collectively referred to as artificial intelligence (or AI for short). Artificial intelligence includes but extends far beyond familiar AI technologies like robots, smart devices, chatbots, and virtual assistants. AI is set to fundamentally transform how products and services are delivered and how the organizations delivering these products and services operate. Andrew Ng (co-founder of Coursera, AI Fund, Landing.AI, and Google Brain) uses the metaphor of the disruptive and transformative power of the internet to explain the disruptive and transformative power of AI[1]. The advent of the internet saw some companies aspire to become internet-enabled companies and others aspire to become true internet companies. While those aspiring to be internet-enabled companies focused on building and operating a website, those aspiring to be true internet companies focused on re-architecting the whole company to fully leverage the new capabilities of the internet[2]. Many companies focusing on being internet-enabled companies missed the point (the disruptive and transformative power of the internet) and were leapfrogged by true internet companies (e.g. Blockbuster vs. Netflix, Borders vs. Amazon). In the same way, today many companies may be aspiring to become AI-enabled companies when they really ought to be aspiring to become true AI companies (re-architecting the whole organization to fully leverage the new capabilities of AI).

AI technologies and related practices offer organizations significant efficiency opportunities (e.g. using AI to perform routine tasks that can be automated through "if this, then that" rules), significant effectiveness opportunities (e.g. using AI to augment human decision-making in order to enhance decisions), significant product and business model innovation opportunities (e.g. using AI to create new AI-based products and services such as automated analysts, digital assistants, robots, AI-augmented services, data management services, etc.), and significant scalability opportunities (e.g. being able to offer automated AI-based services, 24/7, worldwide), and significant adaptability and agility opportunities (e.g. leveraging AI's sensing and intelligence capabilities to anticipate disruptions and opportunities, to better adapt to disruptions, or to seize opportunities first).

Early adopters of AI in accounting have used AI to improve audit quality and efficiency, to better manage risk (e.g. KPMG is leveraging IBM's Watson cognitive platform and other AI technologies to automate document reviews and therefore free auditors up to focus on areas requiring their judgement and expertise), to automate transaction reconciliations (e.g. German accounting software firm SMACC leverages AI to enable its software to convert receipts and invoices into machine-readable format, encrypt them, and allocate them to an account), to improve regulatory compliance and reporting (e.g. AI algorithms are being used to parse through large quantities of structured and unstructured data for evidence of fraud, misconduct, and other regulatory violations), and to offer management teams better predictive and prescriptive analytics (e.g. accountants are getting involved in AI model requirements definition and AI model testing and validation). But this is just the beginning, in their evolving roles as data stewards, systems designers, assurance providers, cyber risk managers, strategic risk navigators, brand protectors, storytellers, trusted professionals, process and control experts, co-pilots, and digital and technology enablers, accountants can play a critical role in supporting organizations to transform into true AI companies that leverage the full benefits of AI in a safe, efficient, and effective manner. To effectively play this role, accountants have to at the very least understand and keep up with AI terminologies and concepts. Although this is an iterative process of learning to keep up with rapidly evolving digital technologies, in this chapter we provide a basic starting point. The chapter begins by introducing high-level AI and machine learning concepts. It then goes on to introduce interpretation, modeling, learning and prediction tools and concepts which underpin the "intelligence" in artificial intelligence (e.g. natural language processing, speech recognition, computer vision, knowledge graphs, artificial neural networks, deep learning, expert systems). Finally, the chapter identifies some of the key AI-related issues and risks. Taken together, we hope readers will get a high-level understanding of AI and machine learning as well as a high-level understanding of the interpretation, modeling, learning and prediction tools and concepts underpinning AI. If so, this will enable them to pursue self-directed follow on learning with confidence, so they can keep up with evolving AI developments and applications.

Artificial intelligence and machine learning

Artificial intelligence

Artificial intelligence (also referred to as machine intelligence, computational intelligence, or cognitive computing) is intelligence demonstrated by machines (e.g. computers and computer-based or computer-like machines). As a branch of computer science, it is the study of how intelligent agents (e.g. computer programs or computer-based machines) can best sense and adapt to changes in their environment to achieve their goals (e.g. winning a chess game, driving a car on a busy road, completing an obstacle course, dealing with a customer inquiry, or even taking out a military threat during a war). Artificial intelligence is often a foundational building block, enabler, catalyst, and / or extender of many other digital technologies and related applications such as predictive and prescriptive data analytics, IoT smart devices, robotics, drones, and cyber-physical systems. The term "artificial" is used in contrast to natural human intelligence to signify that artificial intelligence attempts to mimic human intelligence or cognitive functions and behaviors (such as attention, memory, learning, thinking, problem-solving, decision-making, natural language literacy, motor coordination, planning, manipulation, social intelligence, and creativity). When used, the term artificial intelligence (or its abbreviation AI) can be referring to the definition of AI (discussed earlier), or it can be referring to one or more AI-based technologies and applications.

General AI vs. narrow AI

There are two broad types of AI: *general AI* and *narrow AI*. General AI, also referred to as artificial general intelligence (AGI), strong AI, full AI, or general intelligent action, is the type of adaptable and adaptive intelligence that humans are capable of; and that enables them to autonomously perform a diverse range of actions by leveraging all human cognitive functions. This is the type of AI in Hollywood depictions of AI, like in the movie *The Terminator*. Such depictions usually refer to general AI or to super-intelligence – artificial intelligence that exceeds human cognitive capabilities. New York University professor Meredith Broussard, who researches the role of artificial intelligence in journalism, proposes that general AI can be thought of as achieving the equivalent of putting a human brain inside machines; thus enabling them to learn or be taught the full range of human capabilities (e.g. from empathizing and falling in love, to building a spreadsheet or a computer program, to raising children or leading a nation state)[3]. Meredith contends that this type of AI is mostly fantasy, and that we are very far from achieving it. Although some artificial intelligence researchers contend it may be possible to achieve general AI at some point, others contend it is not possible for us to ever achieve it. Table 15.1 shows the different types of AI, what they are capable of, and the performance implications resulting from their capability.

Narrow AI (also known as weak AI or applied AI) is actually a commercial reality today. Narrow AI refers to programs or machines that can be taught or can learn to perform specific and well-defined tasks without explicitly being programmed to do so (e.g. analyze a dataset of past winning and losing moves in chess, learn from them, and determine the optimal move to make in order to beat a chess grandmaster). Narrow AI can be thought of as AI that can perform a single activity or a narrow set of related activities that would typically require a human brain to be done. This is the type of AI in virtual assistants like Siri and Google Assistant (which can learn to decipher and respond to human speech in limited ways). It's also the type of AI used in purchase recommendation engines that suggest what other products you might like to buy based on yours or others' past behavior. Professor Meredith Broussard contends that narrow AI is really just beautiful math, or computational statistics on steroids. That is, it is largely about machines being taught or learning to find patterns in datasets and then using these patterns as the basis for optimal recommendations, decisions, instructions, or actions. This type of AI is very different from the Hollywood stereotypes of machines like the Terminator, with broad

Table 15.1 Types of AI, their capabilities, and implications for human beings

Types of AI	Artificial Narrow Intelligence (ANI)	Artificial General Intelligence (AGI)	Artificial Super Intelligence (ASI)
What is it capable of?	Execute specific tasks without ability to self-expand functionality.	Perform broad tasks, reason, and improve capabilities in a way that is comparable to humans.	Demonstrate intelligence beyond human capabilities.
What are the implications?	Outperform humans in specific repetitive functions like driving, medical diagnosis, games, etc.	Compete with humans on all fronts, such as earning university degrees, and convincing humans that it is human (Turing Test).	Outperform humans, helping to achieve societal objectives or threatening the human race.

human-like intelligence and capabilities. While narrow AI is limited to specific tasks, the number and range of specific tasks it can perform are almost limitless. And different types of tasks can be combined and can build on each other to expand what is possible so that narrow AI is not so narrow. For example, a range of specific tasks can be integrated and sequenced in such a way as to manage a smart home, a smart workplace, a smart factory, or even a smart city.

Bots

Bots are an application of narrow AI. A bot is a software application or program that runs / performs an automated task (or a script). Bots usually operate over the internet and are hence sometimes referred to as internet robots or web robots. Bots can be taught or can learn to perform a vast array of processes, activities, and routines using business datasets as well as publicly available online datasets or search engines. For example, chatbots are programs that interact with people in written or voice format to answer their questions, provide them services, or entertain them. Applications like Siri and Google Assistant are examples of voice-based chatbots. The range of bots available on the market is extensive and includes friend bots, digital assistants (like Siri), meeting planners, bot writers, language tutoring bots, legal bots (e.g. querying and refuting parking tickets), Q & A bots (e.g. customer support), therapy bots, survey bots, sales bots, insurance claim bots, and many more. Although they can't solve all customer service / support issues, bots can enable 24/7 availability of a limited level of service / support.

Machine learning

Machine learning (ML) is a subset of artificial intelligence. As a subset, it is artificial intelligence that focuses on algorithms for equipping machines with the ability to analyze and automatically learn from datasets and then using this learning as the basis for recommendations, decisions, instructions, or actions. This is not so different to the way a human being analyzes or reflects on their past experiences, learns from them, and uses this learning to guide future actions. Typically, machine learning involves machines being fed large amounts of historical data, and the ML algorithms using this data as "training data" (e.g. data from which to identify cause and effect patterns and make inferences based on statistical methods and mathematical optimization). Bots and recommendation engines are examples of machine learning applications. It is machine learning algorithms in GPS maps that anticipate upcoming traffic and offer optimal routes to take. And it is machine learning that enables clinicians to be alerted by a wearable healthcare device that a patient is about to have a heart attack if there isn't an intervention immediately. In commercial uses, machine learning can also be referred to as predictive analytics.

Knowledge graphs, neural networks, and deep learning

Knowledge graphs

A *knowledge graph* is a graphical representation of the links between data and its meaning[4]. The links can be between different types of data in a dataset (e.g. text, images, video), they can be between data subgroups (e.g. homes in a particular country as a subgroup of homes in a dataset), and the links can be between different datasets (databases, data stores, data lakes, external knowledge graphs, and other information). The links and meaning are represented in a natural language like format. The "graph" is usually in a network-like format, making it one of the most flexible formal data structures. It makes it easy to add on other data links or to modify a data link. Figure 15.1 shows part of a knowledge graph representing information about an aspect of the US election at a point in time. Knowledge graphs are data and thus require graph databases as well as related components (e.g. taxonomy and ontology editors, entity extractors, graph mappers, validation, visualization and search tools, etc.[5]). While technical specialists maintain knowledge graphs, non-technical specialists can contribute their domain expertise to improve the quality and meaningfulness of the connections. There is huge power in having meaningful links between information that is constantly evolving as new datasets are added or as patterns are found in existing datasets. Both human beings and artificial intelligence algorithms can query this data using natural language or using graph computing techniques and algorithms (like shortest path computations, or network analysis). Knowledge graphs bring together disparate data silos to provide an integrated view of the available information for problem-solving, they link structured and unstructured data to illuminate relationships between them, and they provide a structured way to capture and store the insights of non-technical domain experts (e.g. with regard to the links and the meaning of links between a company's different data and information). In doing so, they enable better and faster decisions to be made and at scale (i.e. decisions able to be made quickly, 24/7, by both people and machines anywhere in the world).

Neural networks

Neural networks are a branch of machine learning. Neural networks (also referred to as *neural nets* or *artificial neural network* or NN or ANN) are algorithms that mathematically model the relationship between inputs and their outputs to enable accurate prediction to occur. The "neural" part of the term is derived from the neural networks approach having been inspired by and attempting to mimic the biological functioning of brains (e.g. brain neural pathways are comprised of connected neurons that communicate with each other and with other cells via a process called "neuronal firing"). And the "network" part of the term is derived from the connections. Although mimicking biological brain

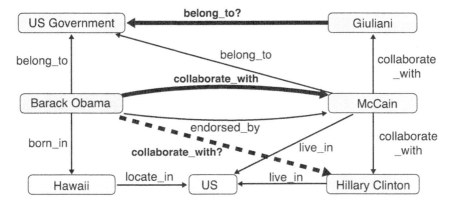

Figure 15.1 Part of a knowledge graph showing information about key figures in US politics at a point in time[6,7]

216 *Digital technologies deep dive*

functioning in problem-solving was the original inspiration, neural networks have somewhat deviated away from this and moved more towards mathematical modeling. Still, artificial neural networks are made up of neurons as the basic computational unit that receives data, processes it, and sends signals to other neurons connected to it within the neural network-like structure. In this way, it emulates a simplified form of brain functioning. Nevertheless, neural networks are still able to automatically learn from data and adapt signals and predictions to changing inputs. Business applications of neural networks are extensive and include evaluating loan applications (in banking), customer behavior modeling, facial recognition (in security and law enforcement), and medical image / scan analysis (in healthcare). Extending neural networks, *deep learning* (also referred to as *deep structured learning* or *hierarchical learning* or *deep neural learning* or *deep neural networks*) is a machine learning method that uses multi-layer neural networks to solve complex problems. Figure 15.2 contrasts a simple neural network with a deep learning neural network.

Natural language processing, speech recognition, and computer vision

Natural language processing and speech recognition

Natural language processing (NLP), *speech recognition*, and *computer vision* are important subfields of artificial intelligence. Natural language processing is concerned with how to get machines to understand and process natural human language (e.g. English or Chinese or Spanish). Advances in natural language processing are enabling machines to understand instructions from us, and to converse with us, in our natural language. Natural language processing applications usually focus on enabling machines to understand and process speech and text (i.e. understand spoken language and written language). Applications of NLP include assistants such as Google Assistant and Siri. Speech recognition is concerned with finding the best way to get machines to understand speech and translate it into machine-readable format. Applications of speech recognition include call routing (e.g. when you call a bank or a phone company and are directed to a sales service based on you saying you want a new product), voice dialing (e.g. "call Jonathan"), and voice search (e.g. "OK Siri, what is the weather tomorrow?"). Speech recognition and NLP are often used together in applications like Google Assistant and Siri. For example,

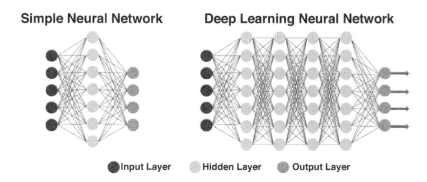

Figure 15.2 A simple neural network vs. a deep learning neural network

speech recognition may hear what is being said and convert it to text but then NLP is needed for machines to understand what the text actually means or what commands the person is actually issuing.

Computer vision

Computer vision and its subset *machine vision* are concerned with enabling machines to "see" (e.g. through capturing, analyzing, and understanding captured images and video). Through image and video analysis, computer vision algorithms can detect faces of specific people or groups of people, shapes of objects, writing, movement, poses, motion, emotion, and changes in objects and environments. Combined with additional information that a whole range of different sensors can pick up, it is not hard to imagine how computer vision and machine vision can be very powerful. For example, they can provide machines such as robots and drones with vastly expanded possibilities (e.g. to fly through a dense and obstacle-filled rainforest at high speed or to recognize a suspect walking in a crowd and immediately call the police or to give robots the type of movement and body control that a human being has). Figure 15.3 shows how computer vision can enable self-driving cars to "see" better than humans (e.g. having simultaneous 360-degree sight, being non-distractible, being better at multi-tasking, and having much faster processing / computation).

Figure 15.3 Computer vision can enable self-driving cars to "see" better than humans[8,9]

https://creativecommons.org/licenses/by/2.0/

Expert systems

Expert systems were one of the early successful applications of AI. As they sound, they are basically systems that emulate the decision-making ability of human experts to solve complex problems. Expert systems have inbuilt "if this, then that" type rules that enable them to make decisions based on a large number of inputs[10]. Expert systems are usually made up of an inference engine and a knowledge base. The inference engine applies the rules to the knowledge base (the knowledge base represents both the facts and the rules). Expert systems are used in healthcare for medical diagnosis (e.g. early diagnosis of cancer[11]), in banking to assess mortgage applications, and to diagnose the condition of infrastructure (e.g. the condition of dams).

Common AI issues and risks

Although AI has been around for a long time, it has gone through phases where it has been overhyped and subsequently under-delivered. In addition, it has often received negative media attention and warnings regarding its associated risks to society (e.g. potential loss of jobs, potential unintended consequences such as machines taking unethical actions or their intelligence outpacing the ability of humans to control them[12,13]). Because of background issues such as this, proposed AI ideas, projects, or strategies in organizations may have been or may still be met with disregard, skepticism, trivialization, passive aggressiveness, or even hostility. Other AI-related issues or risks include data management issues (e.g. organisations may face challenges ingesting, sorting, linking, and properly using the vast amounts of data from sensors, devices, machines, people, media, and digital platforms – not managing this data properly limits the reliability of AI algorithms), they include technology and process issues (e.g. technical issues or process breakdowns resulting in AI malfunction such as oversights or incorrect decisions), they include privacy and security issues (e.g. hackers and fraudsters breaching stored data or AI instructions in transit, resulting in violations in customer privacy as well as related legal issues), they include misguided AI models (e.g. incomplete or biased AI models making blatantly sexist or racist decisions), and they include AI interaction limitations (e.g. empathy and social skill limitations of AI can ruin customer experience and brand credibility)[14].

Google and reflect

algorithm, heuristic programming, inductive reasoning, reinforcement learning, backpropagation, convolutional neural network (CNN), forward chaining, generative adversarial networks (GAN), unsupervised machine learning, Turing Test[15], chatbots (or bots), cluster, cognitive science, image recognition, semantic analysis, supervised learning[16], autonomous artificial intelligence, black box, transfer learning[17], bias, semi-supervised learning, autonomic computing, classification algorithm, cognitive computing, game AI, genetic algorithm, logic programming, machine intelligence, recurrent neural network (RNN), swarm behavior[18], AlphaGo, neuromorphic computing, spiking neural networks (SNN).

Example tools and vendors

Apple HomePod, Apple FaceID, Apple Siri, IBM Project Debater, Microsoft Cortana, Google Assistant, Amazon Alexa, Baidu Deep Voice, Facebook DeepFace, Alibaba City Brain, Google Deep Mind, Waymo self-driving technology, Google Duplex, Amazon

Go, Microsoft AIaaS, MATLAB, IBM Watson Machine Learning, IBM Watson Studio, Google Cloud AI Platform, Microsoft Azure Machine Learning Studio, Salesforce Einstein, Pega Platform, Amazon SageMaker, Microsoft Azure Machine Learning, TensorFlow, Box Skills, DataRobot, Deep Cognition, Anaconda Enterprise, Oracle Data Science Cloud Service, Azure Batch AI, IBM Watson Machine Learning Accelerator, Infosys Nia, H2O Driverless AI, Infor Coleman, Microsoft Cognitive Toolkit (CNTK), NVIDIA AI Platform for Developers, Apple Core ML 3, Apple Create ML, Apple A-series chips, Apple Neural Engine, Intel's OpenVINO Toolkit, CyberInt, HEALTH[at] SCALE Technologies, Algolux, Brodmann17, Dynamic Yield, SoundHound, AntWorks, Zimperium, Sensory TrulySecure, Awake Security Knowledge Graph, Stardog enterprise knowledge graph platform, Franz Semantic Graph Database technology, Pilot.ai, Shazura, Nyris, 20 Billion Neurons, EVK, SpiNNaker, Intel Loihi.

Discussion questions

1 What is the difference between artificial intelligence, machine learning, and deep learning?
2 What is the difference between general AI and narrow AI?
3 Are there more applications of general AI or of narrow AI in accounting practice?
4 What is the difference between an artificial neural network and a deep neural network?
5 What is the difference between an AI-enabled company and a true AI company?
6 What are the top seven AI use cases in the accounting profession?
7 What is the difference between a bot, a chatbot, and a robot?
8 What types of things can you do with a neural network that you can't do with a knowledge graph?
9 What is the difference between computer vision and machine vision?
10 What is an example of an expert system use case in the accounting profession?
11 Rank the top six biggest risks and issues in relation to using artificial intelligence.
12 What organizational capabilities do organizations need in order to become true AI companies?

Notes

1 Ng, A., &Chui, M. (2018). How artificial intelligence and data add value to businesses. McKinsey & Company. Retrieved January 13, 2020, from: https://www.mckinsey.com/featured-insights/artificial-intelligence/how-artificial-intelligence-and-data-add-value-to-businesses
2 Ng, A., & Chui, M. (2018). How artificial intelligence and data add value to businesses. McKinsey & Company. Retrieved January 13, 2020, from: https://www.mckinsey.com/featured-insights/artificial-intelligence/how-artificial-intelligence-and-data-add-value-to-businesses
3 Broussard, M., & Lowe, L. (2019) Author discussion on technology series: Artificial unintelligence. C-SPAN. Retrieved September 20, 2020, from: https://www.c-span.org/video/?457638-2/artificial-unintelligence
4 Stichbury, J. (2017). WTF is a knowledge graph? Hackernoon. Retrieved January 9, 2020, from: https://hackernoon.com/wtf-is-a-knowledge-graph-a16603a1a25f
5 Semantic Web Company (2020).What is a knowledge graph – transforming data into knowledge. PoolParty Semantic Suite. Retrieved January 9, 2020, from: https://www.poolparty.biz/what-is-a-knowledge-graph
6 Anadiotis, G. (2019, March 18). Salesforce research: Knowledge graphs and machine learning to power Einstein. ZDNet. Retrieved June 21, 2020, from: https://www.zdnet.com/article/salesforce-research-knowledge-graphs-and-machine-learning-to-power-einstein/

7 Lin, Y., Liu Z., Luan H., Sun M., Rao S, & Liu S. (2015). Modeling relation paths for representation learning of knowledge bases. arXiv preprint arXiv, 1506:00379. Retrieved from: https://arxiv.org/abs/1506.00379
8 Tara, R. (2018) Technology vs humans. Engineers seek answers in Uber's fatal self driving car accident. Retrieved June 21, 2020, from: https://www.engineering.com/Hardware/ArticleID/16756/Technology-vs-Humans-Engineers-Seek-Answers-in-Ubers-Fatal-Self-Driving-Car-Accident.aspx
9 Burke, K. (2019). How does a self-driving car see? Nvidia. Retrieved June 22, 2020, from: https://blogs.nvidia.com/blog/2019/04/15/how-does-a-self-driving-car-see
10 Leonard-Barton, D and Sviokla, J. (1988). Putting Expert Systems to Work. Harvard Business Review. Retrieved 12 January 2020, from https://hbr.org/1988/03/putting-expert-systems-to-work
11 Başçiftçi, F., & Avuçlu, E. (2018). An expert system design to diagnose cancer by using a new method reduced rule base. Computer Methods and Programs in Biomedicine, 157, 113–120.
12 Clifford, C. (2018). Elon Musk: "Mark my words – A.I. is far more dangerous than nukes". CNBC. Retrieved January 8, 2020, from: https://www.cnbc.com/2018/03/13/elon-musk-at-sxsw-a-i-is-more-dangerous-than-nuclear-weapons.html
13 Marr, B. (2018). Is artificial intelligence dangerous? 6 AI risks everyone should know about. Forbes. Retrieved January 8, 2020, from: https://www.forbes.com/sites/bernardmarr/2018/11/19/is-artificial-intelligence-dangerous-6-ai-risks-everyone-should-know-about/#3c5d4a942404
14 Cheatham, B., Javanmardian, K., & Samandari, H. (2020). Confronting the risks of artificial intelligence. McKinsey & Company. Retrieved January 13, 2020, from: https://www.mckinsey.com/business-functions/mckinsey-analytics/our-insights/confronting-the-risks-of-artificial-intelligence
15 Rosso, C (2018). Defining artificial intelligence: A glossary of key AI terms. Psychology Today. Retrieved January 13, 2020, from: https://www.psychologytoday.com/au/blog/the-future-brain/201810/defining-artificial-intelligence-glossary-key-ai-terms
16 Kniahynyckyj, R. (n.d.). Artificial intelligence: Terms marketers need to know. Business Twitter. Retrieved January 13, 2020, from: https://business.twitter.com/en/blog/artificial-intelligence-terms-marketers-need-to-know.html
17 Greene, T. (2017). A glossary of basic artificial intelligence terms and concepts. The Next Web. Retrieved January 13, 2020, from: https://thenextweb.com/artificial-intelligence/2017/09/10/glossary-basic-artificial-intelligence-terms-concepts/
18 Davis, S. (2017). 27 artificial intelligence terms you need to know. DZone AI. Retrieved January 13, 2020, from: https://dzone.com/articles/ai-glossary

16 Video analytics, computer vision, and virtual reality technologies

Introduction

The digital technologies discussed in this chapter enable organizations to leverage the growing troves of video data captured from a range of devices and stakeholders (e.g. CCTV, smartphones, online uploads), to offer new virtual products and services (e.g. virtual world products and experiences or enhanced real-world products and experiences), to make new operational efficiency breakthroughs (e.g. drastically improving staff training and enhancing technology based support for staff through the use of augmented and mixed reality), to craft novel marketing campaigns (e.g. novel virtual, augmented, or mixed reality marketing campaigns), to approach after sales support differently (e.g. virtual, augmented, or mixed reality-guided repairs performed by customers), and much more. Given their potential impact on customer experience, operational efficiency, product innovation, and marketing, these digital technologies are important to all organizations and industries. As a result, a number of organizations are taking the lead in applying or experimenting with their applications for a range of different purposes. These range from augmented products, to augmented or mixed reality-driven training and coaching, to processes that allow customers to virtually experience what they are buying before making the purchase. Realizing the business value of these digital technologies requires accountants to have a working understanding of how the technologies work, to understand the current and potential use cases for these technologies, and to understand how their stakeholders can leverage these technologies to enhance efficiency, differentiation, and agility. In this chapter, we provide an introductory overview of the technologies, how they work, their business value, example use cases, common terminologies, and example vendors and platforms. The aim of the chapter is to provide a base-level overview of the technologies (i.e. video analytics and computer vision, virtual reality, augmented reality, and mixed reality) in order to enable accountants to undertake their own self-directed and more in-depth learning. This is an essential requirement in order to keep up with rapid developments in these technologies and their applications.

Video analytics and computer vision

Video analytics (also referred to as *video content analysis, intelligent video analytics, video content analytics,* or *VCA*) involves the use of software algorithms to analyze or check video data for particular objects, events, patterns, people, or issues. Once one or more particular issues, events, patterns, objects, or people are identified, the software can report that or it can generate automatic alerts, prescribe action, or take follow-on actions in response to

222 *Digital technologies deep dive*

Figure 16.1 An example of VCA / computer vision software developed by Voxel51[1]

what has been identified. For example, if the software recognizes a known criminal walking down the street it can immediately alert police or request a police squad and direct it to the specific spot that the criminal is about to walk to. Or the software may identify that vandalism has occurred or that it routinely occurs at particular times of the day. Based on analysis of historical video footage, VCA software may even identify that theft is about to occur in a particular location and alert security or request police attendance (e.g. raising an urgent call request via the company's workflow management systems). Or VCA software may notice a confused or lost guest and request someone from guest services to check in on them. Alternatively, it might notice people entering a restricted area or that a guest room has not been made up in time for a guest's arrival. In either case, it can alert or request the right people to take action and even prescribe the optimal actions to take. Although lacking the benefit of different colors, Figure 16.1 shows VCA / computer vision software identifying different people, different cars, different cross walks, road conditions, traffic conditions, and more.

Video analytics is a subset of computer vision, which in turn is a subset of artificial intelligence. Thus, VCA works by leveraging image processing / image enhancement technologies and techniques like image sensors, image pixelation, image compression, image stabilization (reducing blurring associated with an imaging device), unsharp masking (sharpening an image), super-resolution (improving the resolution of an image), plus other AI learning and prediction algorithms. Basically, a video is just a series of image frames[2]. So analyzing video requires extracting and interpreting what is in its image frames. An algorithm (e.g. a recurrent neural network algorithm) can be trained to do this. This involves providing it with lots of data to compare what it is seeing in video image frames to. In this case, the data would consist of a sequence of image frame descriptions (e.g. we can provide it with a sequence of image frames for taking cleaning equipment to a room door and label this sequence "room cleaning preparation". We can then provide it with a sequence of image frames for opening the room door for cleaning and label it "room cleaning start". We can also provide it with a series of images for packing up cleaning equipment and label it "room cleaning completion". We can then collectively label the three groups of images as "room cleaning".). The algorithm is able to learn from these images and labels so that when new video data is fed to it, the algorithm can go through the video's image frames and identify any image, sequences of image frames, groups of sequences of image frames that it already knows (e.g. it might notice a sequence of image frames corresponding to the existing sequence of image frames for "room cleaning completion" and, triangulating this with other data available to it, work out that a room has been cleaned or that it will be cleaned in time for a guest's arrival). The algorithm can learn from its calculations, conclusions, decisions, and mistakes to get more accurate over time. Video analytics can thus be used to detect faces of particular people or groups of people in videos, to detect shapes of objects in videos, to detect writing in videos, to detect movement, to detect poses, to detect motion, to detect emotion, to detect particular events, to detect changes in objects and environments, and much more. Figure 16.2 shows VCA / computer vision software recognizing people, their actions, and occurring events. The exponentially growing number of devices capturing or able to capture video, the exponentially growing availability of images and video footage available online, and the growing sophistication of VCA algorithms make video footage a potently powerful source of value right now. Organizations are capturing some video data but they can capture much more, they can access vast troves of video data on the internet to train their VCA algorithms (e.g. YouTube videos and associated chat history, Facebook videos and associated chat history, LinkedIn videos and associated chat history), and they can access sophisticated VCA platforms to make the most of all the internal and publicly available video data.

Figure 16.2 An example of VCA / computer vision software recognizing both people and actions/events[3]

The business value of VCA includes product innovation opportunities (e.g. offering new VCA-related products and services like an industry-specific VCA platform), product / service enhancement opportunities (e.g. using VCA to anticipate and respond to guest issues before they occur, thus optimizing customer experience), business model innovation opportunities (e.g. video-based service delivery models), operational efficiency opportunities (e.g. using VCA to anticipate, prevent, or minimize disruptive events such as vandalism or theft that may slow down operational processes or result in higher costs), and risk mitigation opportunities (e.g. learning from VCA when or how particular security and other threats occur and taking action to prevent or minimize them). This business value can be expanded and significantly enhanced with real-time VCA that is combined with smart things[4] (e.g. devices, robots, bionics) to provide real-time, human-like sensing and responding.

VCA use cases to date have included enhanced customer and staff security through incident detection (e.g. identifying unattended objects in main lobbies or in car parks, identifying disruptive individuals, identifying camera tampering, identifying suspicious activity), they have included intrusion management (detecting unauthorized people in secure zones), they have included people / crowd counting (e.g. counting foot traffic and attendance for analyzing patronage and conversion), they have included automatic number plate recognition (e.g. detecting unauthorized tailgating in secure car entrances), and they have included facial recognition (e.g. monitoring faces as they enter premises and high-risk areas, searching through faces for an investigation, searching for the location of particular individuals across a large facility). They have further included management (e.g. using heat maps to understand customer traffic density and traffic choke points by time of day, understand customer traffic movement and areas of interest), and also included demographic analytics (e.g. identifying the demographic profile of people entering as well as where they stay, how long they stay, where they go, and what their mood is)[5,6,7,8]. Some organizations are integrating VCA with customer service and customer loyalty data to provide even better value for their most valuable customers. An example of VCA in action is the Hawaii Tourism Authority's "Discover Your Aloha" campaign, which analyzed the expressions on travelers' faces in video captured via webcams to determine what custom offers to push to them (i.e. it used facial recognition in videos as well as predictive analytics to identify the best offer for a particular traveler and push it to them along with a booking link)[9]. Similarly, Cherokee Nation Entertainment (CNE) used VCA across its ten casinos in Oklahoma to relieve its security team of the need to review video footage manually. As a result, they could focus on more proactive and preventative tasks. VCA analyzed camera footage from entrances and exits, from gaming machines, and from other areas – enabling Cherokee Nation Entertainment to have real time visibility and alerts of traffic patterns, people counts, and any risky events or situations unfolding[10]. Although early VCA use cases have focused on security / access control and sales / marketing, VCA offers many possibilities for understanding customers, for optimizing customer experiences, for enhanced operational insights, and for optimizing operations management.

Virtual reality, augmented reality, and mixed reality

Virtual reality (VR), *augmented reality* (AR), and *mixed reality* (MR) represent continuing breakdowns of the boundaries between the real world and the virtual world that enable enhanced or new experiences as well as enhanced or new business opportunities[11].

Virtual reality

Virtual reality has been around since the 1930s as a technology for enabling users to experience a fully computer-generated or digital environment[12]. Once in the digital environment, users can see, hear, and interact with the digital environment. Although other senses can be incorporated to make the digital world experience more immersive, VR is not yet at the fully immersive, nerve-connected experiences depicted in movies like *The Matrix*. Still, VR can provide highly immersive experiences through great graphics, 360-degree visuals, binaural sound (3D stereo sound sensation that emulates actually being there to hear the full, rich sound), and tapping into other human senses[13,14]. Virtual worlds or environments can be unique digital creations that don't exist in the real world, recreations or emulations of the real world, or somewhere in between. For example, virtual reality games can be played in fantasy digital worlds completely devoid from reality or they can be played in emulations of real world conditions and rules such as a World War II setting. In contrast to games, tourism operators may replicate the experience of navigating protected environments to enable tourists to "see" them without putting those environments and species at risk. Virtual reality experiences typically require specialized hardware such as VR headsets. Depending on how immersive the VR experience needs to be, other sensory optimization hardware like noise-cancelling headphones, cameras to track room space and boundaries, and motion capture technology may also be required.[15]

Augmented reality

The term "augment" means to make something greater by adding to it. Thus, as it sounds, augmented reality refers to adding or superimposing digital data and / or images and animations on real-world elements to enhance them[16]. That is, it involves enhancing the real world with digital details that can, for example, improve understandability of the digital world or engagement with the real world[17]. Augmented reality devices and applications can place digital objects in the real world (e.g. Pokemon Go game creators enabled overlaying of the game's buildings and characters over real-world areas like streets and buildings in a town so players could play the game by navigating real-world streets and buildings) – they can overlay animations, they can overlay information, or they can overlay a combination of objects, animations, and information[18]. Examples of AR-capable hardware includes mobile phones (e.g. AR apps available on most app stores) and smart tablet devices (e.g. the iPad), wearable AR devices (e.g. AR glasses like Epson MOVERIO or AR headsets like Oculus Go), and custom enterprise AR equipment. AR offers organizations the opportunity to significantly expand customer engagement and customer experience through AR-enriched experiences, products, and services.

Mixed reality

Drawing on next generation sensing and imaging technologies, mixed reality "mixes" real with virtual worlds and allows users to see, immerse, and interact with both virtual and real worlds[19,20]. Users can manipulate the virtual world using their own hands, or they can make changes to the real world guided by virtual objects, or make changes to the real world by making changes to virtual objects[21]. For example, surgeons at Imperial College London use Microsoft's HoloLens mixed reality devices to enable them to see "inside" a patient's body during an operation[22] (e.g. bones, blood vessels, and other body parts

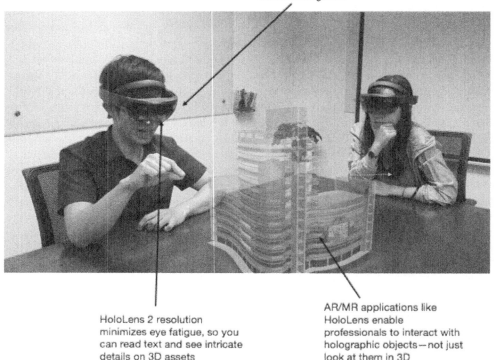

Figure 16.3 Using a HoloLens 2 headset
https://creativecommons.org/licenses/by-sa/4.0/

revealed in scans can be reconceptualized, animated, and superimposed onto the patient's body so that surgeons can move them around as in a real surgery, and see exactly where to cut, or where to implant a device without obstructing the functioning of other body parts). Perhaps less complex, a patient's blood vessels can be superimposed onto their arm so that nursing staff can see exactly where the best spot to inject a needle is and trial the injection virtually in that spot before actually doing it. Figure 16.3 shows architecture students interacting with their building design using a Microsoft HoloLens 2 headset.

Business value of VR, AR, and MR

Although VR, AR, and MR technologies are of value to all areas of business, they hold standout value in areas like product innovation, operational efficiency and effectiveness, marketing, HR, and after sales support. In the product innovation area, they offer the opportunity to provide customers new or improved products (e.g. to create and offer virtual versions of any real-world environment or experience, to augment existing products and services with digital data and virtual objects, to create new products and services leveraging mixed reality, etc.). In the operational efficiency area, these technologies offer businesses the opportunity to provide their staff with an almost x-ray vision-like ability to see through opaque things and interact with them (e.g. see through and interact with underground infrastructure, cabling in walls, vessels in the brain, arteries in the body, etc.). This can result in faster repair times, minimization of costly errors, avoidance of equipment damaging actions, and more. And what is seen through this x-ray-like vision and interacted with is increasingly able to be an exact representation of the real thing thanks to connected IoT sensors and AI algorithms. For example, the superimposed blood vessel can expand or contract or burst in sync and to the same degree as the real thing – enabling whoever is interacting with it to see, for example, the implications of shifting it one way or applying a little bit more pressure to it. AR and MR can also enable remote or automatic interaction with things, thanks to IoT and AI. For example, virtual versions of things can be linked to real versions so that a change in the virtual-world version automatically results in a change in the real-world one. Taken together, these abilities provide organizations with opportunities to redesign their workflows for greater efficiency and effectiveness (e.g. greater possibilities for automation, greater possibilities for remote supervision and management). From an HR perspective, VR, AR, and MR can enable provision of real-time, on-site, interactive, step-by-step training, guidance, or coaching that is superior to any manual or a video. And it could be used for better assessing aptitude prior to giving someone the responsibility for a task. For example, before undertaking a high-risk task in the real world, an employee may be required to first competently perform that task in the virtual world. Using analytics, employee's performance of such tasks in the virtual world could be contrasted to their performance in the real world to improve VR-based training. From a marketing perspective, VR, AR, and MR can be powerful marketing tools (e.g. enabling virtual experiences of products and services to drive sales, enabling customers to place a product into their home settings to see how it fits in, enabling gamification of marketing campaigns drawing on viral games like Pokemon Go). From an after sales perspective, VR, AR, and MR can be used to enable customers to effectively do their own repairs or to do assembly quicker or to coach customers through the repair process (e.g. imagine VR or AR-guided assembly of IKEA furniture). Together, these different value propositions can transform how employees learn, the quality of the decisions they make, how they interact with customers, how they buy and who they buy from, how customers interact with a business's products, and much more.

Early VR, AR, and MR use cases have included virtual experiences, virtual purchasing processes, interactive facilities, Pokemon Go-style gamified entertainments, and augmented environments[23,24]. An example of virtual experiences in action is the Atlantis Dubai, which provides a very inviting virtual tour of its premises. An example of virtual booking processes in action is Amadeus, which set up a virtual booking process that enables customers to enter a virtual world where they can look for flights, walk on the plane to inspect it and find the perfect seat, then compare hotel prices and look inside the hotel room before finally making a booking. On completion, they exit the virtual world but have made real-world bookings which they don't need to be anxious about since they have experienced most aspects of the bookings[25]. An example of interactive hotel rooms is The Hub Hotel from Premier Inn in the United Kingdom, which used a combination of maps on hotel room walls and AR to enable guests to point their phones at different map locations to see additional information and places of interest in those locations – thus enhancing customer experience[26,27]. An example of gamification is organizations incorporating their physical sites or services in established AR games or creating their own

VR / AR gaming apps for promotional purposes. For example, hospitality and leisure organization Best Western Kelowna set up an Augmented Reality Quest for kids staying at the hotel to play alone or with other kids or with their parents[28]. Most early use cases have focused on VR and AR applications for entertainment and consumer engagement, for providing X-ray like vision, and for delivering training or simulating situations. But there are great possibilities for VR, AR, and MR beyond this.

Google and reflect

Table 16.1 Google and reflect

Digital technology	Common terminology
Video Analytics and Computer Vision	Recurrent neural network (RNN), CCTV, OpenCV, rule-based analytics, area of interest (AOI), region of interest, region of uninterest, smart surveillance engine, video management system, view group, dynamic masking, motion detection, shape recognition, object detection, tamper detection, video tracking, video error level analysis (VELA), object co-segmentation
Virtual, Augmented, and Mixed Reality	Immersive VR, virtual space, AR space, head mounted display (HMD), haptics, VR head tracking, VR eye tracking, VR position tracking, VR field of view, VR blind spot, VR headset latency, VR headset interpupillary distance (or IPD), VR judder, VR headset refresh rate, 360 video, VR video stitching, VR sickness, low persistence, VR 1 to 1 movement, asynchronous timewarp, spatial desync, VR ride, social VR platform, cinematic VR, fish tank VR, virtual theater, directional sound, motion platform / omnidirectional treadmill, discrete graphics processor, computer-aided design (CAD), extended reality (XR), GL Transmission Format (gITF), hologram, Simultaneous Localization and Mapping (SLAM), six degrees of freedom (6DoF) tracking, visual-inertial odometry (VIO), waveguide displays, augmented face mesh, simulation-based learning, blended space, lifelike experience, multimodal interaction, simulated reality, Supranet, Telexistence, multiexperience development platform (MXDP), Google ARCore, PTC Vuforia, Augmentir, Amazon Sumerian, HP Reveal, SmartReality.

Example tools and vendors

Digital technology	Tools and vendors
Video Analytics and Computer Vision	Google Cloud Vision, Cloud Vision Intelligence, Agent Vi savVi, Agent Vi innoVi, NVIDIA DeepStream SDK, NVIDIA Jetson, NVIDIA Tesla, NVIDIA GPU Cloud (NGC)[29], Oculus Rift, HTC Vive, and PlayStation VR, Google Cardboard, Python Imaging Library (PIL), Open Source Computer Vision (OpenCV), Tensorflow
Virtual, Augmented, and Mixed Reality	HTC Vive, iStaging LiveTour, Cupix, Viar360, BRIOVR, Scanta, Fishermen Labs, Groove Jones, Program-Ace, Xtrematic, Niantic Real World Platform, Windows Mixed Reality platform, Zappar ZapWorks platform, Lucyd Lab AR, Qualcomm® Snapdragon™ platforms, Apple ARKit 3, Apple Reality Composer, Apple RealityKit, Magic Leap 1, PlayStation VR, FOVE Eye Tracking Virtual Reality Headset, Samsung Gear VR, Epson Drone Soar augmented reality app, Epson Moverio AR glasses, DAQRI Worksense, Bosch Common Augmented Reality Platform (CAP)

Discussion questions

1 What are the similarities and differences between VCA and other forms of data analytics?
2 What is a recurrent neural network? How is it different to other neural networks?
3 Where can organizations get the vast quantities of data required to train recurrent neural network algorithms to understand what they are seeing in video data?
4 Can VCA be applied to virtual reality, augmented reality, and mixed reality?
5 How can an organization use VCA to improve its operational efficiency?
6 What is an example of an innovative new product leveraging VCA that an organization could offer?
7 What are the top three enterprise grade VCA platforms and which is the best?
8 What are the top three SME grade VCA platforms?
9 How can VCA be used to improve the quality of products and of customer experience?
10 Would adding real-world objects into a virtual reality setting fit the definition of augmented reality?
11 Would adding real-world objects into a virtual reality setting fit the definition of mixed reality?
12 How could organizations use augmented reality to improve real-life products and services?
13 How could organizations use mixed reality to attract more customers?
14 What are the top five challenges to adopting and using VR, AR, and MR?
15 What are the top five risks associated with using VR, AR, and MR in accounting practice?
16 What are the top three risks to organizations not adopting or at least experimenting with VR, AR, and MR?
17 Within the example tools and vendors provided, identify three leading vendors and products in each of these product categories: virtual reality, immersive VR, augmented reality, mixed reality.
18 Within the example tools and vendors provided, identify three leading vendors and products in each of these product categories: consumer, small business, enterprise.
19 Within the example tools and vendors provided, identify three leading vendors and products in each of these product categories: gaming, marketing, healthcare, hospitality / tourism.
20 Group the example tools and vendors provided into the following categories: hardware products, software products, VR / AR / MR development platforms.

Notes

1 NIST. (2019). Enhancing public safety video analytics with computer vision and artificial intelligence. Retrieved June 21, 2020, from: https://www.nist.gov/news-events/news/2019/11/enhancing-public-safety-video-analytics-computer-vision-and-artificial
2 Robinson, S. (2018) How computer vision works. YouTube. Retrieved January 27, 2020, from: https://www.youtube.com/watch?v=OcycT1Jwsns
3 NIST. (2019). Enhancing public safety video analytics with computer vision and artificial intelligence. Retrieved June 21, 2020, from: https://www.nist.gov/news-events/news/2019/11/enhancing-public-safety-video-analytics-computer-vision-and-artificial

4 Ganesan, V., Ji, Y., & Patel, M. (2020). Video meets the internet of things. McKinsey & Company. Retrieved January 24, 2020, from: https://www.mckinsey.com/industries/technology-media-and-telecommunications/our-insights/video-meets-the-internet-of-things
5 Hughes Systique Corp. (2019) The role of video analytics in tourism, travel & hospitality industry. Retrieved January 27, 2020, from: https://hsc.com/Blog/The-Role-of-Video-Analytics-in-Tourism-Travel-Hospitality-Industry
6 Agent Vi. (2020). Entertainment and hospitality solutions. Retrieved January 27, 2020, from: https://www.agentvi.com/portfolio-items/entertainment-hospitality/?portfolioCats=19
7 Security Magazine. (2017). Using video analytics to create efficiencies. Retrieved January 27, 2020, from: https://www.securitymagazine.com/articles/89083-using-video-analytics-to-create-efficiencies
8 UBAC Group. (n.d.). Face recognition & video analytics for campus & retail hospitality. Retrieved January 27, 2020, from: https://ubacgroup.com/face-recognition-data-analytics/intelligent-surveillance-face-detection/
9 Bhattacharjee, D., Seeley, J., & Seitzman, N. (2017). Advanced analytics in hospitality. McKinsey & Company. Retrieved January 27, 2020, from: https://www.mckinsey.com/business-functions/mckinsey-digital/our-insights/advanced-analytics-in-hospitality
10 Agent Vi. (2020). Entertainment and hospitality solutions. Retrieved January 27, 2020, from: https://agentvi.com/wp-content/uploads/2018/10/Agent_Vi_Solutions_Entertainment_Hospitality-1.pdf
11 Intel. (2019). Virtual reality vs. augmented reality vs. mixed reality. Retrieved January 30, 2020, from: https://www.intel.com.au/content/www/au/en/tech-tips-and-tricks/virtual-reality-vs-augmented-reality.html
12 Intel. (2019). Virtual reality vs. augmented reality vs. mixed reality. Retrieved January 30, 2020, from: https://www.intel.com.au/content/www/au/en/tech-tips-and-tricks/virtual-reality-vs-augmented-reality.html
13 Intel. (2019). Virtual reality vs. augmented reality vs. mixed reality. Retrieved January 30, 2020, from: https://www.intel.com.au/content/www/au/en/tech-tips-and-tricks/virtual-reality-vs-augmented-reality.html
14 Ambalina, L. (2019). Augmented reality vs. mixed reality vs. virtual reality. Hackermoon. Retrieved January 28, 2020, from: https://hackernoon.com/augmented-reality-vs-mixed-reality-vs-virtual-reality-ik8730gv
15 Ambalina, L. (2019). Augmented reality vs. mixed reality vs. virtual reality. Retrieved January 28, 2020, from: https://hackernoon.com/augmented-reality-vs-mixed-reality-vs-virtual-reality-ik8730gv
16 Intel. (2019). Virtual reality vs. augmented reality vs. mixed reality. Retrieved January 30, 2020, from: https://www.intel.com.au/content/www/au/en/tech-tips-and-tricks/virtual-reality-vs-augmented-reality.html
17 Ambalina, L. (2019). Augmented reality vs. mixed reality vs. virtual reality. Hackermoon. Retrieved January 28, 2020, from: https://hackernoon.com/augmented-reality-vs-mixed-reality-vs-virtual-reality-ik8730gv
18 Ambalina, L. (2019). Augmented reality vs. mixed reality vs. virtual reality. Hackermoon. Retrieved January 28, 2020, from: https://hackernoon.com/augmented-reality-vs-mixed-reality-vs-virtual-reality-ik8730gv
19 Intel. (2019). Virtual reality vs. augmented reality vs. mixed reality. Retrieved January 30, 2020, from: https://www.intel.com.au/content/www/au/en/tech-tips-and-tricks/virtual-reality-vs-augmented-reality.html
20 Marr, B. (2019). The important difference between augmented reality and mixed reality. Retrieved January 30, 2020, from: https://bernardmarr.com/default.asp?contentID=1912
21 Ambalina, L. (2019). Augmented reality vs. mixed reality vs. virtual reality. Hackermoon. Retrieved January 28, 2020, from: https://hackernoon.com/augmented-reality-vs-mixed-reality-vs-virtual-reality-ik8730gv
22 Microsoft News Centre UK. (2018, February 8). Surgeons are using HoloLens to "see inside" patients before they operate on them. Retrieved from: https://news.microsoft.com/en-gb/2018/02/08/surgeons-use-microsoft-hololens-to-see-inside-patients-before-they-operate-on-them/
23 Revfine.com. (2019). How virtual reality (VR) can enrich the hospitality industry. Retrieved January 30, 2020, from: https://www.revfine.com/virtual-reality-hospitality-industry/
24 Revfine.com. (2019, August 8). How augmented reality is transforming the hospitality industry. Retrieved January 30, 2020, from: https://www.revfine.com/augmented-reality-hospitality-industry/

25 Revfine.com. (2019). How virtual reality (VR) can enrich the hospitality industry. Retrieved January 30, 2020, from: https://www.revfine.com/virtual-reality-hospitality-industry/
26 Revfine.com. (2019). How virtual reality (VR) can enrich the hospitality industry. Retrieved January 30, 2020, from: https://www.revfine.com/virtual-reality-hospitality-industry/
27 Revfine.com. (2019, August 8). How augmented reality is transforming the hospitality industry. Retrieved January 30, 2020, from: https://www.revfine.com/augmented-reality-hospitality-industry/
28 Revfine.com. (2019). How virtual reality (VR) can enrich the hospitality industry. Retrieved January 30, 2020, from: https://www.revfine.com/virtual-reality-hospitality-industry/
29 MSV, J. (2019) Microsoft and NVIDIA deliver intelligent video analytics at the edge. Forbes. Retrieved January 27, 2020, from: https://www.forbes.com/sites/janakirammsv/2019/03/23/microsoft-and-nvidia-deliver-intelligent-video-analytics-at-the-edge/#16eba1927623

17 Robotics, drones, and 3D / 4D printing technologies

Introduction

The overarching theme of the digital technologies discussed in this chapter is the ability to outsource surveillance (e.g. drone-based surveillance), physical actions or activities (e.g. robot-based action), and manufacturing (3D / 4D printed objects) to smart machines (i.e. drones, robots, 3D / 4D printers). These capabilities of drones, robots, and 3D / 4D printers represent significant product innovation, cost-saving, productivity improvement, operational effectiveness, risk mitigation, customer experience enhancement, staff engagement optimization, and organization agility opportunities. While initially seen by many as fads or playthings, commercial applications of these technologies are growing rapidly and they are expected to impact almost every sector at a pace and scale not so different to that of personal computers and mobile phones. Hospitality organizations are using robots like the Hilton's robot concierge Connie, who complements or covers staff absences – taking actions like greeting guests, interacting with them, and answering their questions. In the healthcare industry, systems like the da Vinci Surgical System improve the productivity of surgeons by enabling them to perform surgery using surgical robots and 3D-vision systems. And in logistics, robots are being used to autonomously manage warehouse inventory (e.g. autonomously lift it, store it in the right place, retrieve it, and maintain appropriate inventory levels). In accounting, early accounting workflow-focused robotics use cases have focused on robotic process automation (RPA), using virtual robots to perform routine accounting tasks (e.g. rules-based, routine, or calculation tasks). And accountants have been focused on identifying, or separating from the hype, the real efficiency / cost-saving opportunities offered by robotics, drones, and 3D / 4D printing. But even without this, accountants are deeply involved in almost any use case of these digital technologies (e.g. assessing business value / business benefits, identifying opportunities and risks, tracking implementation effectiveness, and optimization effectiveness, etc.). As a result, it is essential for accountants to keep up with the evolution and use cases of these technologies, to be able to support strategic leaders and operating managers to safely adopt them, and to contribute to maximum business value being leveraged from them. As a starting point, we provide an overview of each of these technologies, how it works, its business value and use cases, as well as some of the key issues associated with the digital technologies.

Robots and robotics

Robotics is the field of study concerned with how to best design, build, operate, and use robots. *Robots* are machines that can be programmed to physically interact with the world around them and can automatically carry out a series of actions / motions or a range of actions with varying levels of autonomy and intelligence[1]. Or, put differently, robots are artificially intelligent agents existing in a physical form that can take actions to affect the physical world[2]. Robots can be designed to carry out an astounding variety of tasks, particularly when they leverage sophisticated artificial intelligence algorithms. For example, robots can manufacture product parts, assemble cars, fill prescriptions, play with kids, provide customer service, fight wars, spy, and much more.

Building blocks of robots

Robots can differ greatly in their design, capabilities, and uses. For example, a robot for customer service is quite different from a robot for fighting wars or a robot for assembling cars. In spite of this, they usually share common building blocks. At a very high level, they all have mechanical, electrical, and computer program elements. The mechanical element is the physical forms, frames, or constructs of the robot. The design of the mechanical element is usually based on the specific tasks or actions the robot will be performing (e.g. this could be a human-like form for a customer service robot or it could just be a mechanical arm for welding car parts together). The electrical element is all the electrical and electronic components that operate in concert to power the robot, collect information via sensors from the robot's environment, enable controlled movement of the robot, and enable it to perform its task. The electrical element incorporates sub-elements like power supplies (e.g. batteries, solar, AC), motors / actuators (to convert electrical energy into movement), driving mechanisms (e.g. gears, chains, pulleys, belts, and gearboxes to enable movement in different directions and at different speeds), electronic controls (to control mechanical systems like brakes and suspension through switches), sensors (to sense things like proximity, sound, light, etc.), and effectors (to affect a change on an object or the environment or to do the task the robot is meant to do − such as pick up a box or push an item in place). The computer program element is the embedded computer hardware and software code that either enables the robot to be instructed on what to do (e.g. through an internet-based software program) or enables the robot to autonomously work out what to do (e.g. via artificial intelligence algorithms). As with other computer programs, there are specific programming languages used to write the software code or programs for robots to understand and act on. Examples of these languages include Variable Assembly Language (VAL), Robotic Markup Language (Robo ML), Extensible Robot Control Language (XRCL).

How robots work

In a nutshell, you can think of the functioning of a robot in terms of an input, processing, and output system. The input involves the robot's sensors gathering information from the robot's environment (e.g. images, object proximity, temperature, smoke, pressure, light, color, light and color intensity, touch etc.). Or the input could be human-originated data entered via a keyboard, microphone, and / or user interface. The collected sensor data is passed onto the embedded computer program which interprets it (e.g. determines what specific objects are in front of the robot, anticipates the actions and risks of those objects, determines how to best respond to them, and creates a set of response action instructions for the robot to take). The instructions are translated into electrical signals that are sent directly to the robot's hardware (e.g. switches might be turned on to activate particular wheels and move the robot into a particular position, then signals might be sent to move arms into a particular position so as to grab and then throw an object). The effect of the robot on the physical world (e.g. spinning wheels to move, picking up an object) is the output. During this whole input / processing / output process, the robot's sensors can still be picking up real-time information and passing it back to the computer program to do near real-time processing – thus enabling response instructions to be adapted, and therefore the actions that the robot takes to be adapted as necessary.

Types of robots

There are many different types of robots. The different types are commonly classified by the environment in which they operate or by their application field. Other typologies focus on their level of autonomy or human resemblance. Classified by environment, there are fixed robots (ones that exist and operate in fixed and therefore well-defined environments e.g. a robotic assembly line arm mounted on the ground) and mobile robots (ones that operate in changing environments and therefore face the additional challenges of accurately interpreting and operating in those different environments, e.g. mobile vacuum cleaners and self-driving cars). Mobile robots may operate in environments as diverse as underwater, in the air, in a dense jungle, or on the surface of the moon. These different environments may require robots to have one or more features such as wheels, legs, propellers, wings, or parachutes to enable them to navigate an environment. Classified by field of application, there are industrial robots (e.g. large mounted robotic arms for assembling cars or mobile robots for moving inventory around in a warehouse) and service robots (robots that assist people to carry out tasks, e.g. dull, repetitive, dangerous aspects of work). Service robots can be further classified into specific service areas or industries. For example, service robots can be further divided into healthcare / medical robots (e.g. surgical robots that perform surgeries requiring a very high degree of precision), home robots (e.g. robot vacuum cleaners, mobile webcam robots, robotic lawn mowers), defense or military robots (e.g. armed robotic vehicles or military drones), and educational robots (e.g. educational robot kits such as mBot-STEM Educational Robot Kit). Other types of robots include agricultural robots (robots that can perform agricultural activities such as fruit picking or farming activities like herding livestock or wildlife)[3,4,5], collaborative robots (robots designed to work safely with humans in a shared space), nanorobots (robots that operating at the atomic or molecular level), swarm robots (the coordination of multiple robots to interact with each other and their external environment so as to collectively achieve a particular task, e.g. similar to swarms of fish or birds), and telepresence robots (robots that double as a person, can be controlled remotely, and provide an alternative to physically being at a particular event or location)[6].

Business value and use cases of robotics

The business value of robotics includes cost savings, enhanced productivity, reduced risk, overcoming skill shortages, improved staff engagement, new or enhanced products, operational effectiveness, and more[7]. Robotics-related cost savings can come from robots performing activities previously performed by humans. Such activities can include repetitive but low-skill activities, high-risk activities, or low error tolerance activities (e.g. fast food outlets like Wendy's and McDonalds have implemented automated order kiosks / robots to reduce staffing levels at particular outlets. And mining companies like Rio Tinto are leveraging robotics to remotely manage mining operations, for autonomous drilling and autonomous haulage[8,9]). A robot replacement can work 24 hours a day, 7 days a week without needing to take a break or experiencing stress and strain – it does not need line management to maximize its productivity once programmed appropriately, does not require privacy from monitoring, does not require leave, and does not get involved in costly political conflicts. In addition to the benefits we've just discussed, robotics-related productivity improvements can come from improved output per employee if organizations augmenting employees' work with the strengths of robots[10] (e.g. the da Vinci Surgical System in healthcare discussed earlier)[11,12]. And, in industries like manufacturing and logistics, companies such Carlsberg, the beer and beverage maker, use collaborative robots, or "cobots", to work in tandem with employees, doing the heavy lifting or the unsafe work, so employees do the tasks that necessitate human intelligence or input[13]).

Robots can be used in many different ways to reduce risks. For example, robots can perform tasks that are unsafe for humans (e.g. lifting back-straining loads, deactivating bombs, entering infectious areas to enforce infection control measures, welding intricate components at very high temperatures, entering terrorist zones). Robots can also mitigate or reduce risk by anticipating or spotting risks and taking mitigating action or alerting people to take mitigating action. For example, in aged care robots are being used to anticipate and or prevent falls[14]. Robots can be used to overcome skill shortages, for example, in aged care, robots are being used to provide nursing and patient support services either in aged care facilities or in patients' own homes[15]. Robots can be used to provide companionship, to ensure patients take their medications, to facilitate patient exercise, to manage patients' daily routines, and more[16,17]. Robots can also be used to improve staff engagement and reduce absenteeism by taking over less desirable parts of a job and freeing employees to focus on the more desirable aspects. For example, robots can take over manual, repetitive, and time-consuming tasks and thus enable employees to do more creative or strategic work. This may even result in employees having more work-life balance flexibility, once they are not bogged down with repetitive tasks that have to routinely occur at a set time in a set location.

Robotics can be leveraged for product innovation and / or business model innovation. On the product innovation front, robotics can be used to create new products / services or to enhance existing products / services. Disruptive new consumer, SME, and enterprise robotics products or services that leverage the capabilities of robotics are possible. Examples of robotics-driven product innovations in action are numerous across industries. In education, institutions are leveraging robots to innovate teaching delivery (e.g. some educators are using Sphero's app-enabled robotic ball in classrooms to teach through play). In healthcare, companies are designing intelligent robots for hospitals and other care facilities (e.g. Diligent Robotics designed "Moxi", an autonomous robot that can independently navigate hospital hallways and tight spaces, find relevant medical equipment, set up patient rooms, and restock supply rooms). In agriculture and farming, specialty robots are being designed to perform or assist in the management of agricultural and farming processes. The increased use of robots in business operations and in homes creates a need for new software platforms, robotics support, and other services. Thus, product innovation is possible from offering new robot forms, leveraging robots to carry out new forms of service delivery, leveraging robots to augment existing product or service offerings, and offering new services for robot users or owners. Robotics can also be leveraged to create entirely new business models or to enhance existing business models[18,19,20]. For example, some companies servicing the agricultural industry are shifting to a robots as a service (RaaS) business model (e.g. to provide robot-based weeding services that limit the need for their agricultural customers to purchase and manage robots for so many different farming activities). Other industries have started to develop similar RaaS offerings such as delivery RaaS, security RaaS, and cleaning RaaS[21]. For example, RaaS startup Robomart, is trialing a driverless grocery-on-wheels service enabling people in the Boston area to grocery shop from their door stop[22]. Finally, robotics can be leveraged to improve operational effectiveness. The combination of enhanced employee capability and the speed, precision, and 24/7 capabilities of robots can be leveraged to deliver better quality products and customer experiences.

Within the accounting function or the finance department, robotic process automation (or virtual robots) has been an important focus. RPA is software that mimics human interaction with different systems in much the same way as Excel Macros do, except that macro-like routines can be set to work across systems (e.g. move data between systems, use it to perform calculation, use the calculation results in other automated workflows, etc.)[23,24]. Thus, instead of only working in Excel, the macro-like algorithms can open different programs, log in, and interact with systems almost like a real person – except much faster, more accurately, and more reliably[25]. RPA is being used to automate routine and rule-based accounting workflows like movement of data across systems, cleansing of data, reconciliations, journal entries, accounts payable and accounts receivable processing, pricing reviews, expenditure authorizations, debt recovery, and management accounting and financial accounting reports[26]. RPA software applications like UiPath, Blue Prism, and Automation Anywhere simplify the creation of the automated processes mimicking human action. RPA could have been covered in the chapter on artificial intelligence but has been covered here to limit potential confusion.

Drones

Drones, also known as unmanned / uncrewed aerial vehicles or systems (UAV or UAS), are aerial vehicles or aircraft that are remotely or autonomously piloted (i.e. not piloted by a human on board)[27,28,29]. Their counterparts are unmanned or uncrewed ground vehicles (UGV), which are also remotely or autonomously driven with no human on board. Drones and UGVs can come in many sizes and have many different designs, depending on the task or activities they are designed to carry out[30,31]. For example, military-style drones and UGVs can be up to the size of commercial airplanes or larger, whereas hobby-style drones are typically much smaller. As well as having flight capability, drones can be fitted with a wide variety of sensors to gather information about their environment and robotic capabilities to take actions in that environment[32]. For example, drones for military purposes may be equipped with computer vision as well as machine guns, whereas drones for agricultural purposes may be equipped with different sensors and with crop spraying or crop harvesting mechanics. In contrast, drones for zoological purposes may have a combination of sensors and robotic features that enable them to enter a species' territory, pretend to be one of the species, and fit into a species' social hierarchy[33] (e.g. for recording video footage of the social dynamics of species[34]).

Building blocks and functioning of drones

Like robots, drones can differ greatly in their design, capabilities, and uses[35], but they all share some common high-level building blocks (see Figure 17.1 for a visualization of the common building blocks of a drone). All drones usually have a body or frame that is suited to the desired flight approach (e.g. fixed-wing or rotary), and the types of tasks or activities the drone is to perform (e.g. surveillance, aerial photography, transporting people, etc.)[36]. Fixed-wing drones fly in a similar way to or emulate the flight of normal planes. Therefore, they have a body very similar to normal planes, with the rigid wings that can generate lift, and engines to generate thrust (e.g. to move the drone along the ground fast enough so air pressure can be generated below the wings for lift off). Rotary drones, on the other hand, have two or more rotor blades that turn on fixed masts and generate lift, as well as shape flight direction and speed as the blades rotate through the air. Drone body size, shape, and internal / external configuration are dependent on the task the drone is to do[37]. For example, a drone to spy on birds or bees may emulate the shape and appearance of the birds or bees being spied on[38,39]. Whereas a drone to transport people may be designed to prioritize the safety and comfort of passengers as well as the aesthetics of the drone[40,41]. Drones usually have some sort of landing gear (e.g. helicopter-style for rotary drones and airplane-style for fixed-wing drones). This landing gear may be an obvious part of the drone's body / frame or it may require activation. The design of the landing gear depends on the nature of the task to be performed by the drone and the constraints of the environment (e.g. landing on a hostile ocean cliff face vs. a flat football field or a still river).

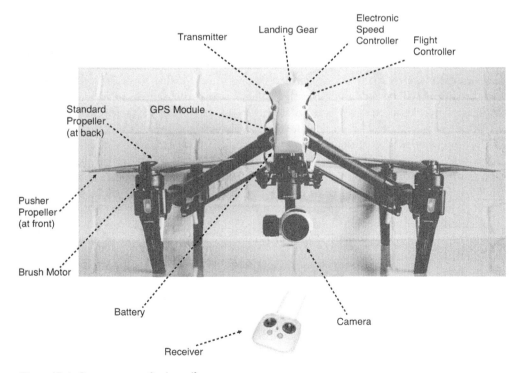

Figure 17.1 Components of a drone[42]

Drones usually have propellers, motors, and some form of power supply[43]. For fixed-wing drones, propellers propel or provide the forward propulsion to enable the rigid wings to generate lift. For rotary drones, the propellers provide lift as well as enabling speed and steering (e.g. a rotary drone with four propellers may have two standard propellers for lift and two pusher propellers for forward and backward thrust)[44]. Motors spin the propellers to enable flight (e.g. typically a brushless motor[45] but could be other types of motors or even a miniature engine[46]). A rotary drone with four propellers typically has a motor for each propeller. And motors draw on the drone's power supply (e.g. batteries, solar cells, hydro fuel cell, combustion engine, AC cable tethering, laser transmitter[47]). The power supply is usually encased in the body of the drone. Without the power supply, it would be difficult to activate all the onboard components (e.g. motors, sensors, cameras, computers, robot-like mechanics, etc.). Drones also have a flight controller and electronic speed controllers (ESC). A flight controller is an onboard computer that receives control information from the pilot on the ground (e.g. instructions such as: more lift, more speed, change direction), receives information from onboard sensors (e.g. objects in the way, wind speed and direction), and receives information from the GPS module (e.g. specifying location in longitude, latitude, and elevation terms)[48]. The flight controller combines this information to send instructions to the propellers (e.g. spin the forward propellers this direction, create this much lift). The electronic speed controllers connect the flight controller to the motors (so a four-propeller drone or quadcopter would need an ESC for each propeller motor)[49]. The ESCs take instructions from the flight controller and power from the drone's power supply to make propeller motor's spin a particular way)[50]. Drones usually have a transmitter and receiver to enable communication with the drone. The transmitter is a remote control-like device that the pilot on the ground or drone operator uses to send instructions (e.g. radio signals) to the receiver on the drone[51]. The job of the receiver is to receive the instructions or signals and pass them onto the flight controller[52]. The receiver may also pass data back to the transmitter for the pilot or operator on the ground to use. Drones usually have one or more onboard sensors, which can vary from drone to drone depending on what the drone will be used for[53]. Examples of onboard drone sensors include gyroscopes, barometers, accelerometers, GPS, magnetometers, range finders, obstacle sensors, distance sensors, thermal sensors, chemical sensors, and orientation sensors.

The components we've discussed thus far are found on most drones. Cameras, onboard computers, smartphone-like capabilities, and robotic capabilities are other less common components. Although less common, these components can significantly enhance the capabilities of drones and their business value. For example, sophisticated cameras and computation can enable sophisticated surveying and computer vision-based remote monitoring. Robotic capabilities and onboard computers can enable remote action (e.g. picking up and moving objects, taking out a terrorist, cleaning skyscraper windows, etc.). Adding sophisticated artificial intelligence algorithms can empower drones to take autonomous action (e.g. search for and chase a person of interest while deploying and directing nearby police squads to capture them, rescue people from burning buildings, map a neighborhood or construction site, herd livestock, identify and remove dangerous obstacles, fight fires, find and destroy other drones, and more)[54]. Smartphone like capabilities can enable remote voice-based instructions, the building of apps to expand the drone's capabilities, and more[55,56]. An important issue for many geographies is ensuring drones operate in an aerial space in which they don't interfere with aircraft space, suburban infrastructure, and dwelling spaces (e.g. see Figure 17.2 for NASA's proposed space for drone operation).

Figure 17.2 NASA's proposed space for drone operation: below aircraft space and above suburban infrastructure and dwellings[57]

Business value and use cases

Drone use cases to date have included 3D mapping, delivery or transportation, inspection or monitoring, infrastructure maintenance, expanded internet connectivity, video data collection, search and rescue, firefighting / disaster response, filmmaking, lighting, inventory tracking, insurance, policing, and more[58,59,60]. For 3D mapping, drones have been used in industries such as agriculture, construction, and mining to survey sites, take photos, and create more accurate contour maps than would otherwise be impossible or that are much more efficient to produce[61,62]. For delivery and transportation, drones have been used to deliver parcels (e.g. Zipline is a US-based company that uses drones for delivering blood and vaccine to regions in developing countries still lacking infrastructure) and even to deliver hot food much more efficiently than a driver[63,64,65]. And in some regions of the world drones-based taxi or Uber services are being offered[66]. For inspection and monitoring, drones have been used to inspect site, building, and other infrastructure conditions[67,68]. For infrastructure maintenance, companies such as Aerones produce industrial drones that can remove ice build-up on wind turbines, drones that can clean skyscraper windows, drones that can stitch or fill cracks, drones that clean drainage areas, and drones that sand and paint[69,70]. For expanded internet connectivity, drones are being used to establish or amplify wireless internet connectivity during large-scale events or in regions where this previously was not possible without expensive infrastructure[71,72,73,74,75]. For video data collection, drones can be used to capture video footage in remote or hard to access locations, as well as sensitive settings (e.g. silently and inconspicuously capturing wildlife interactions up close)[76,77,78].

For search and rescue, drones have been used in a variety of challenges including monitoring beaches and dropping life buoys to swimmers in trouble, spotting shark threats and alerting swimmers, finding lost hikers, locating people in burning buildings, and assessing the status or impact of disaster events[79,80]. For filmmaking, filmmaking drones like the DJI Inspire 2 put cinema-quality filming capabilities in the hands of the average person and provide film professionals with the opportunity to film at angle, stability, and focus types not possible with normal film cameras[81]. For lighting, drones can be used to create completely new spectacles at concerts, fireworks, and sporting events. For inventory tracking, drones with time-of-flight (ToF) sensors are used in industries like mining, agriculture, and forestry to measure piles of stuff (e.g. piles of soil, timber, stones, waste, etc.)[82]. For insurance, drones can fly over natural event or accident sites to assess damage severity and causes, which can help with claim applications[83,84]. And for policing, drones can be applied for a wide variety of uses including as helicopter replacements, as self-directing monitoring devices, and as crowd or population control devices (e.g. a drone could be used to inconspicuously follow a fugitive, leading police right to him without the commotion of a car or helicopter chase)[85]. These example use cases are just the beginning, many more exist and even more will emerge each year as drone technologies impact every industry. Drones are not a fad; in fact, some observers have equated the evolution and impact of drones to that of the personal computers and mobile phones – while the potential value of computers and mobile phones was clear, the eventual pace, scale, and sustained pervasiveness of their impact was hard to imagine.

3D and 4D printing

3D printing (also known as additive manufacturing or desktop fabrication) refers to the use of commercial or consumer equipment (known as printers) that, under computational control, deposits material layer by layer until a three-dimensional object is created in accordance with the specifications of a computer-aided design (CAD) model[86]. Originally, the printed object may have been scanned with 3D object scanners or designed with CAD software. Irrespective, 3D printers can recreate the object with superior precision, accuracy, and efficiency[87]. *4D printing* also builds 3D objects layer by layer but, unlike 3D printing, smart materials are used that enable an object to change its shape over time if exposed to water, heat, light, current, or magnetic fields – this change in shape is the "fourth dimension" that gives 4D printing its name. So 4D printing brings together 3D printing, smart materials (e.g. photo-polymeric liquid that hardens when exposed to light or photoresist material that decomposes solid polymers into liquids), and shape change accommodating design.

3D / 4D printer building blocks and functioning

Although what they do is sophisticated, the common elements of 3D printers are straightforward (see Figure 17.3 for common elements of a basic 3D printer). 3D printers usually have a frame, power supply, and motion components. The frame houses or holds together all the components of the 3D printer. The frame design affects stability and durability of the machine as well as the size of what can be printed on the 3D printer (assuming what is printed does not later expand). Some 3D printers have an open frame and others have a semi-closed or completely enclosed frame. The benefits of an enclosed frame include temperature stability and protection from dust and other things that could get stuck in the 3D printer. The power supply powers everything in the 3D printer. It is commonly encased together with the user interface and mounted onto the frame. The power supply influences

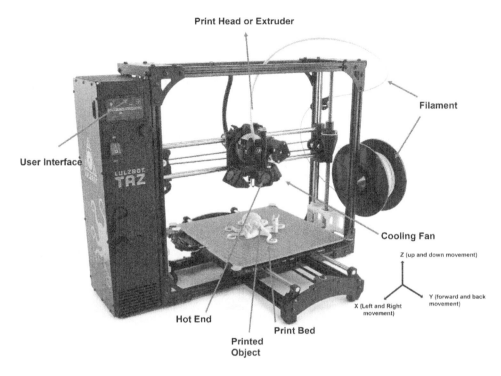

Figure 17.3 Anatomy of a basic 3D printer

the temperature or heat the 3D printer can generate and thus the type of layering material (or filament) that can be used to print with. The motion components are the combination of motors, belts, and other parts that ensure the nozzle depositing the layering material and / or the object being worked on are continuously moved into the right position along the three dimensions (e.g. the right combination of left and right, up and down, and forward and backwards). The motion components basically translate computational instructions into the right physical movement or the positioning of the nozzle and object being worked on.

3D printers have a controller board and some form of user interface. The controller board (sometimes referred to as the motherboard or mainboard, or brain of the 3D printer) sends motion instructions to the motion components based on commands it receives from a computer and on information it gets from sensors (e.g. heat and motion sensors). The user interface is a screen that enables a user to receive status information and make adjustments (e.g. pause layering, reload layering material, etc.). The user interface is usually already built into the frame but can also be a separate unit. Either way, the user interface can be a basic LCD screen controlled with knobs, dials, and buttons or it could be a high-end touchscreen.

For the layering process, 3D printers have filaments, print heads (or extruders), and a print bed. The filament is the material deposited in the layering process, or what the 3D printed objects are made out of. It is similar to ink for a normal 2D printer. There are many different types of filaments (e.g. made of different materials, different colors, different sizes / diameters, etc.). Filaments usually come on a spool (like those used to coil wire around), which is loaded onto the 3D printer's spool holder. One end of the filament is inserted into the print head (or extruder) and gradually feeds into the print head (e.g. at the rate the depositing is occurring). The print head is made up of cold end and hot end sections. The cold end clamps the filament and pushes it into the hot end. The hot end then melts the filament and deposits it or layers it (via the print head nozzle) as per the CAD model specifications of the object being printed. The sections of the print head have various drives, fans, and sensors to ensure that the filament is kept at the right temperature as it is fed from the spool and out the print head nozzle. Nozzles can be interchangeable and come in different sizes depending on what is being printed and the desired print speed. 3D printers can have a print head with more than one nozzle or they can have more than one print head. In turn, the different print heads or nozzles can use different filaments at the same time (e.g. to enable printing of an object with more than one material). The print bed on 3D printers is the surface on which the layered printing of the object occurs. In Figure 17.3 you can see that the print bed moves the object being printed forward and back to have it in the required position for depositing. The print bed surface can be made of various materials which can influence how flat the surface is kept, how easy it is to remove the printed object, how easy it is to clean the surface, and more. 3D printers may be connected to a network to enable remote control or monitoring of the printing process. And they may have one or more file transfer options (e.g. USB or SD card) so users can upload files for printing and initiate the print job using the available user interface.

There are different types of 3D printers, with the types differing in their approach to 3D printing. The most common types include Fused Deposition Modeling (FDM) printers, Stereolithography (SLA) Printers, and Laser Sintering (SLS) Printers. For FDM printers, the approach is as we have just described (i.e. filament is fed into a print head and melted and extruded through the print head nozzle for layering). These types of printers are inexpensive (e.g. starting at a few hundreds of dollars), widely used, and therefore have a wide variety of parts and materials available. In contrast, SLA printers start out with a liquid resin which then gets hardened by a beam of UV light (i.e. instead of starting out with filament that needs to be melted). This type of printer is ideal for printing objects that contain great detail and require a smooth finish. Prices for this type of printer start from two to five times those of FDM printers. Recent adaptations of this approach enable a whole object to be printed in seconds by using algorithms to calculate exactly where in the liquid resin to point the beams, from what angles, and at what dose. Finally, SLS printers work like SLA printers except that they start off with a powder instead of a liquid (e.g. nylon). This type of printer spreads powder layer by layer or segment by segment and then uses laser beams to sinter or raise the temperature of specific parts of the powder so as to trace out and solidify a part of the object being printed. This process is repeated layer by layer until the physical object is fully printed. This type of printing enables printing using aluminum, nylon, sandstone, silver, and steel. It also enables very finely detailed objects to be made. Pricing for these types of printers start at around forty thousand to fifty thousand times the price of SLA printers.

3D printing business value and use cases

Early value from 3D printing includes product innovation, business model innovation, efficiency, effectiveness, product / service differentiation, and improved customer experience. The emphasized value and use cases have varied from industry to industry[88]. For product innovation, a number of organizations in different industries are using 3D printing for cost-effective and faster prototyping of product designs. Yet more organizations are using 3D printers to create add-on components that significantly expand the usability of existing products used in day-to-day operations. For business model innovation, some organizations are offering completely new 3D printing-based business models that include licensing of 3D printing designs and 3D printing as a service (e.g. HP Inc. established HP 3D Printing Solutions as a new business that offers 3D printers, 3D printing care services, 3D printing lifecycle management, 3D printing training, and 3D printing optimization advisory services)[89,90]. For efficiency, organizations in a range of industries are using 3D printing for low-volume manufacturing of custom products and parts, thereby saving on costly engagement of high-volume manufacturers (e.g. creating and using highly customized products that improve the efficiency of value chain processes or recreating a version of existing products / components that are too expensive via existing sourcing channels)[91]. Some organizations are creating novel components to fit onto existing equipment, thus greatly expanding the usability of that equipment and therefore the efficiency of processes using it. For effectiveness, 3D printers are being used to plug component / part accessibility gaps for parts / components that are out of production but still required for a particular business's operations (e.g. it may be that the sole manufacturer has shut down or ceased making the part). In healthcare, this includes custom organs or other body parts for which there may not be enough human donors[92]. For product differentiation, some organizations are using 3D printers to create unique branded accessories and art that enhance brand awareness and value as well as enhancing consumer experiences of particular settings. 3D-printed products and parts eliminate shipping costs, minimize inventory costs (e.g. by enabling 3D designs to be "stored in the cloud" so physical versions can be printed on demand[93]), they eliminate product portability issues (e.g. the design can simply be emailed and printed, rather than needing to package it and send it to different locations), and more. As with other digital technologies we have covered, these use cases are just the beginning[94].

Issues and challenges

While the digital technologies discussed in this chapter are evolving quickly and create significant efficiency, effectiveness, differentiation, and organization adaptability opportunities, they come with inherent risks. These include ambiguous and underdeveloped regulation, security and privacy challenges, uncertain attitudes towards them, dependability and reliability issues, and lack of sufficient assurance and support services. Regulation-wise, it is easy for staff using drones or 3D printers, for example, to be unaware of and breach civil aviation safety laws (e.g. flying drones into prohibited areas) or to copy copyrighted 3D / 4D designs. It is also easy for staff to use these digital technologies for activities which have no restricting regulation as yet but that may be frowned on by society (e.g. robots or drones may capture and use sensitive video footage that causes community outrage). Security and privacy-wise, early versions of digital technologies are typically made by startup companies that may not address possible security breach and privacy risk flaws. As a result, use of these technologies may lead to unethical organizations accessing sensitive customer data. Social attitudes towards digital technologies also have to be considered, for instance, while robots may provide efficiency breakthroughs, organizations have to consider community concern about robots taking their jobs. If organizations don't consider such concerns, they may find communities boycotting their services. Finally, digital technologies go through hype and disillusionment cycles (e.g. as depicted in the Gartner Hype Cycle) and organizations have to ensure they don't get carried away with the hype (thus pushing the implementation of uses for technologies that aren't quite dependable / reliable yet) or carried away with the disillusionment (thus turning a blind eye to technology adoption, only to become another Kodak or Blockbuster).

Google and reflect

Table 17.1 Google and reflect

Digital technology	Common terminology
Robotics	robot axis / degrees of freedom, robot hand guiding, robot reach, robot repeatability, exoskeleton robot, social robots, robot payload, robot grip force, force limited robot, actuator, bionics, robot CPU, cloud robotics, cobots, cyborg, robot end effector, humanoid robot, gynoid robot, android robot, industrial robot, nanobot, RPA, robot uptime, Adaptive Motion Control, robot path simulation, aerobot, combat robot, cruise missile, delta robot, forward chaining, haptic, robot hydraulics, service robot
Drones	ready-to-fly (RTF) drone, almost-ready-to-fly (ARTF) drone, bind-and-fly (BNF) drone, quadcopter, octocopter, multicopter, drone flight time, Gimbal, drone collision / obstacle avoidance, drone pitch, drone roll, drone yaw, UAS (unmanned aircraft system), drone frequency, drone S mode, drone P mode, drone A mode, dronie, field of view (FOV), drone firmware, FPV (first person view) drone, geofencing, GLONASS, gyroscope, inertial measurement unit (IMU), infrared drone / UAV, photogrammetry, PIC (pilot in command), racing drone, drone Return to Home (RTH), target drone, decoy drone, reconnaissance drone, combat drone.
3D / 4D Printing	acrylonitrile butadiene styrene (ABS), 3D printing G-code, polylactic acid (PLA), RepRap, 3D printer slicer, STL file format, 3D model Slicer, heated print bed, Kapton tape, subtractive manufacturing, 3D print shell, 3D print raft, 3D print infill, 3D print curing, 3D sculpting, 3D printing overhang

Example tools and vendors

Table 17.2 Example tools and vendors

Digital technology	Tools and vendors
Robotics	iRobot Roomba 960, iRobot Braava 380T, GreyOrange Butler, GreyOrange Flexo, Arduino, Epson SCARA robots, Boston Dynamics, Boston Dynamics' ATLAS, Boston Dynamics' SPOT, Locus Robotics, SCHUNK, SCHUNK SVH, SCHUNK PGN-plus-E, ASI robots, ASI Chaos High Mobility Robot, ASI Forge Robotic Platform, Honda ASIMO, Softbank Robotics, Softbank's Pepper, Samsung Bot Retail, SamsungBot Care, SamsungBot Air, Sanbot by Qihan technology, Romeo by Softbank Robotics, by Blue Frog Robotics, Aibo by Sony, PIAGGIO 'GITA' Cargo Bot, HRP-5P by AIST, Sphero, Diligent Robotics, Picknik Robotics, Sarcos, Bluefin Robotics, Petronics, AMP Robotics, Left Hand Robotics, Harvest Automation, Intuitive Surgical, Myomo, MakerBot Industries, Autodesk Fusion 360, ABB Robotics, Kuka industrial robots
Drones	DJI drones, GoPro Karma Drone, 3D Robotics IRIS+, Hubsan Zino, Lockheed Martin RQ-170 Sentinel, Parrot AR.Drone 2.0, Yuneec Typhoon Q500 quadcopter, EVO by Autel Robotics, ambulance drone by Delft Technical University, Plan Bee drone, Volocopter, Flirtey Eagle drone, SureFly, GimBall, PD-100 Black Hornet, Aerix Aerius, RoboBee X-Wing, DJI MG-1P Agricultural Spraying Drone, Neurala, Skycatch software, Alive software platform, Skydio drone.
3D / 4D Printing	Lulzbot Mini, Prusa i3 MK2, Formlabs Form 2, Anycubic Photon, Monoprice Maker Select Plus, Stratasys Fortus 250mc, MakerBot Replicator Z18, HP Jet Fusion 3D 4200 Printer, ProJet MJP 3600, Tronxy X5ST-500, BigRep ONE v3, Erectorbot EB 2076 LX, Builder Extreme 2000, BLB Industries THE BOX, Sciaky EBAM 110, AutoDesk Inventor, Autodesk 123D, Google SketchUp Make, Slic3r, Skeinforge, KISSlicer, HP 3D printing, Proto Labs, 3D Systems, Materialise 3D printing, Arcam AB, Autodesk, Stratasys Ltd, The ExOne Company, Hoganas AB, Optomec, Inc., Organovo Holdings, Inc., Ponoko Limited, Voxeljet AG, Formlabs 3D printers, Revolution 3D printers, Airwolf 3D printers

Discussion questions

Table 17.3 Discussion questions

Digital technology	Discussion questions
Robotics	1. What is the difference between robots and robotics? 2. What is the difference between robotics and artificial intelligence? 3. What is the difference between a humanoid, android, and gynoid robot? 4. What is the most important part of a robot? Why? 5. What is the most common robotic programming language? 6. What is the best way to classify robots? Why? 7. What is the most important business value of robots? 8. How can using robots improve work satisfaction and engagement? 9. How can human beings best compete with robots in the workplace? 10. What five types of sensors can have the greatest impact on the capability of a robot and how can a robot use the information from each type sensor? 11. What is the most important ethical issue in relation to using robots? 12. How can robots be used to reduce business risk? 13. What are three examples of product innovation using robots? 14. What are three examples of business model innovation using robots?
Drones	15. What is the difference between a helicopter-sized drone, a helicopter, and a flying robot? 16. What is the most important sensor on a drone? 17. What is the smartest part of a drone? 18. What is the minimum and maximum number of propellers a drone can have? 19. How could artificial intelligence be used in a drone? 20. Could a drone be used to autonomously trim a hedge? How could it work? 21. What is the biggest public concern about drones? 22. What is the biggest legal issue in relation to drones? 23. What is the most important business value of drones?
3D/4D Printing	24. How is a 3D printer different from a 2D printer? 25. Can a 3D printer be used for 4D printing? 26. Which is a more important technology, 3D printing or additive manufacturing? 27. If you had an old machine for which there were no longer any repair parts being made, how would you go about using a 3D printer to solve that problem? 28. What is the cheapest and most expensive type of 3D printing technology? 29. Which 3D printing technology is best for making products out of metal? 30. Which 3D printing technology is best for making decorative glass products? 31. Are 3D-printed products as good as those manufactured traditionally? 32. Will 3D printing be bigger than the internet? Why? 33. What is the best 3D printer for consumer use? Why? 34. What is the best 3D printer for industrial use? Why? 35. What types of services are provided for 3D printing as a service (3DaaS)? 36. What is the most serious strategic risk for businesses in relation to adopting 3D printing?

Notes

1 Nichols, G. (2018). Robotics in business: Everything humans need to know. ZDNet. Retrieved February 3, 2020, from: https://www.zdnet.com/article/robotics-in-business-everything-humans-need-to-know/
2 Simon, M. (2017, August 24). What is a robot? Wired. Retrieved February 3, 2020, from: https://www.wired.com/story/what-is-a-robot/
3 Holley, P. (2019). New Zealand farmers have a new tool for herding sheep: Drones that bark like dogs. The Washington Post. Retrieved from: https://www.washingtonpost.com/technology/2019/03/07/new-zealand-farmers-have-new-tool-herding-sheep-drones-that-bark-like-dogs/

4 Christian, J. (2019). This drone is a sheepdog. World Economic Forum. Retrieved February 11, 2020, from: https://www.weforum.org/agenda/2019/03/new-zealand-farmers-are-using-drones-to-herd-sheep/
5 Paranjape, A.A., Chung, S.J., Kim, K., & Shim, D.H. (2018). Robotic herding of a flock of birds using an unmanned aerial vehicle. IEEE Transactions on Robotics, 34(4), 901–915.
6 Double Robotics. (2020). Telepresence robot for telecommuters. Retrieved from: https://www.doublerobotics.com/
7 Wolfgang, M., Vladimir, L., Sander, A., Martin, J., and Küpper, D. (2017). Gaining robotics advantage. Retrieved from: https://www.bcg.com/en-au/publications/2017/strategy-technology-digital-gaining-robotics-advantage.aspx
8 Crozier, R. (2018). Rio Tinto to build new "intelligent" mines. ITnews. Retrieved from: https://www.itnews.com.au/news/rio-tinto-to-build-new-intelligent-mines-494651
9 Mining Global. (2014). Rio Tinto: Mine of the future. Retrieved from: https://www.miningglobal.com/operations/rio-tinto-mine-future
10 Wilson, H.J & Daugherty, P.R. (2018). How humans and AI are working together in 1,500 companies. Harvard Business Review. Retrieved from: https://hbr.org/2018/07/collaborative-intelligence-humans-and-ai-are-joining-forces
11 Siegel, E.R., McFadden, C., Monahan, K., Lehren, A.W., & Siniauer, P. (2018). The da Vinci surgical robot: A medical breakthrough with risks for patients. NBC News. Retrieved February 4, 2020, from: https://www.nbcnews.com/health/health-news/da-vinci-surgical-robot-medical-breakthrough-risks-patients-n949341
12 Wolfgang, M., Vladimir, L., Sander, A., Martin, J., and Küpper, D. (2017). Gaining robotics advantage. Retrieved from: https://www.bcg.com/en-au/publications/2017/strategy-technology-digital-gaining-robotics-advantage.aspx
13 Francis, S. (2020). Carlsberg reduces risk of accidents with universal robots. Robotics & Automation News. Retrieved February 4, 2020, from: https://roboticsandautomationnews.com/2020/01/06/carlsberg-reduces-risk-of-accidents-with-universal-robots/28215/
14 Maneeprom, N., Taneepanichskul, S., Panza, A., & Suputtitada, A. (2019). Effectiveness of robotics fall prevention program among elderly in senior housings, Bangkok, Thailand: A quasi-experimental study. Clinical Interventions in Aging, 14, 335–346. https://doi.org/10.2147/cia.s182336
15 Fischinger, D., Einramhof, P., Papoutsakis, K., Wohlkinger, W., Mayer, P., Panek, P., . . & Vincze, M. (2016). Hobbit, a care robot supporting independent living at home: First prototype and lessons learned. Robotics and Autonomous Systems, 75, 60–78. https://doi.org/10.1016/j.robot.2014.09.029
16 Bemelmans, R., Gelderblom, G. J., Jonker, P., & de Witte, L. (2012). Socially assistive robots in elderly care: A systematic review into effects and effectiveness. Journal of the American Medical Directors Association, 13(2), 114–120.e1. https://doi.org/10.1016/j.jamda.2010.10.002
17 Aged Care Guide. (2016). The future is here – robots in aged care. Retrieved February 5, 2020, from : https://www.agedcareguide.com.au/talking-aged-care/the-future-is-here-robots-in-aged-care
18 PricewaterhouseCoopers. (2015). CEO pulse: Pulse on robotics: PwC. Retrieved February 14, 2020, from: https://www.pwc.com/gx/en/ceo-agenda/pulse/robotics.html
19 Accenture. (2018). Foster innovation with enterprise robotics. Retrieved from: https://www.accenture.com/_acnmedia/pdf-71/accenture-robotics-pov-web.pdf
20 AMFG. (2019). 5 examples of how 3D printing is creating new business models. Retrieved February 14, 2020, from: https://amfg.ai/2019/11/29/5-examples-of-how-3d-printing-is-creating-new-business-models/
21 PR Newswire (2019). New robotics: Shifting business models. Retrieved February 5, 2020, from: https://www.prnewswire.com/news-releases/new-robotics-shifting-business-models-300818816.html
22 Dumont, J. (2019, January 17). Stop & Shop will pilot driverless delivery in Boston. Grocery Drive. Retrieved February 5, 2020, from: https://www.grocerydive.com/news/stop-shop-will-pilot-driverless-delivery-in-boston/546223/
23 ACCA, CAANZ, & KPMG. (2018). Embracing robotic automation during the evolution of finance. A report by ACCA and CAANZ in collaboration with KPMG. Retrieved from: https://assets.kpmg/content/dam/kpmg/cn/pdf/en/2018/11/embracing-robotic-automation-evolution-of-finance-acca-kpmg-caanz.pdf
24 EY. (2017). The dawn of a new partnership: A robotics-led finance function. Financial Accounting Advisory Services. Retrieved February 14, 2020, from https://www.ey.com/Publication/vwLUAssets/ey-faas-finance-function-automation/$FILE/ey-faas-finance-function-automation.pdf

25 ACCA, CAANZ, & KPMG. (2018). Embracing robotic automation during the evolution of finance A report by ACCA and CAANZ in collaboration with KPMG. Retrieved from: https://assets.kpmg/content/dam/kpmg/cn/pdf/en/2018/11/embracing-robotic-automation-evolution-of-finance-acca-kpmg-caanz.pdf

26 ACCA, CAANZ, & KPMG. (2018). Embracing robotic automation during the evolution of finance A report by ACCA and CAANZ in collaboration with KPMG. Retrieved from: https://assets.kpmg/content/dam/kpmg/cn/pdf/en/2018/11/embracing-robotic-automation-evolution-of-finance-acca-kpmg-caanz.pdf

27 Taking flight. (2016). The Economist. Retrieved from: https://www.economist.com/technology-quarterly/2017-06-08/civilian-drones

28 Corrigan, F. (2019). How do drones work and what is drone technology. DroneZon. Retrieved from: https://www.dronezon.com/learn-about-drones-quadcopters/what-is-drone-technology-or-how-does-drone-technology-work/

29 Pierce, D. (2018). Drones: The complete guide. Wired. Retrieved February 11, 2020, from: https://www.wired.com/story/guide-drones/

30 Taking flight. (2016). The Economist. Retrieved from: https://www.economist.com/technology-quarterly/2017-06-08/civilian-drones

31 Corrigan, F. (2019). How do drones work and what is drone technology. DroneZon. Retrieved from: https://www.dronezon.com/learn-about-drones-quadcopters/what-is-drone-technology-or-how-does-drone-technology-work/

32 Corrigan, F. (2019). How do drones work and what is drone technology. DroneZon. Retrieved from: https://www.dronezon.com/learn-about-drones-quadcopters/what-is-drone-technology-or-how-does-drone-technology-work/

33 Baggaley, K. (2019). Forget props and fixed wings. New bio-inspired drones mimic birds, bats and bugs. NBC News. Retrieved February 6, 2020, from: https://www.nbcnews.com/mach/science/forget-props-fixed-wings-new-bio-inspired-drones-mimic-birds-ncna1033061

34 Mingle, J. (2019). Saving the planet one drone at a time. Department of Zoology. Retrieved February 6, 2020, from: https://www.zoo.ox.ac.uk/article/saving-planet-one-drone-time

35 Corrigan, F. (2019). How do drones work and what is drone technology. DroneZon. Retrieved from: https://www.dronezon.com/learn-about-drones-quadcopters/what-is-drone-technology-or-how-does-drone-technology-work/

36 Corrigan, F. (2019). How do drones work and what is drone technology. DroneZon. Retrieved from: https://www.dronezon.com/learn-about-drones-quadcopters/what-is-drone-technology-or-how-does-drone-technology-work/

37 Corrigan, F. (2019). How do drones work and what is drone technology. DroneZon. Retrieved from: https://www.dronezon.com/learn-about-drones-quadcopters/what-is-drone-technology-or-how-does-drone-technology-work/

38 Baggaley, K. (2019). Forget props and fixed wings. New bio-inspired drones mimic birds, bats and bugs. NBC News. Retrieved February 6, 2020, from: https://www.nbcnews.com/mach/science/forget-props-fixed-wings-new-bio-inspired-drones-mimic-birds-ncna1033061

39 New Scientist. (2005). Airborne robotic spycraft inspired by seagulls. (2020). Retrieved February 11, 2020, from: https://institutions.newscientist.com/article/mg18725155-900-airborne-robotic-spycraft-inspired-by-seagulls/

40 Flanagan, B. (2019, September 9). The maker of Dubai's flying taxi aims to set flight within the next three years. Wired Middle East. Retrieved February 6, 2020, from: https://wired.me/science/transportation/dubai-drone-flying-taxis-volocopter/

41 Blanchard, S., & Randall, I. (2019). Self-driving FLYING TAXI with 18 drone-like propellers is tested in the skies of Singapore. Mail Online. Retrieved February 6, 2020, from: https://www.dailymail.co.uk/sciencetech/article-7599343/Hover-taxi-whizzes-Singapore-firm-eyes-Asian-push.html

42 Grind Drone. (2017). Drone components – quick list of it's parts. Retrieved from: http://grinddrone.com/drone-features/drone-components

43 Corrigan, F. (2019). How do drones work and what is drone technology. DroneZon. Retrieved from: https://www.dronezon.com/learn-about-drones-quadcopters/what-is-drone-technology-or-how-does-drone-technology-work/

44 Corrigan, F. (2019). How do drones work and what is drone technology. DroneZon. Retrieved from: https://www.dronezon.com/learn-about-drones-quadcopters/what-is-drone-technology-or-how-does-drone-technology-work/

45 Renesas Electronics. (n.d.). What are brushless DC motors. Retrieved February 11, 2020, from: https://www.renesas.com/us/en/support/technical-resources/engineer-school/brushless-dc-motor-01-overview.html
46 Nichols, G. (2019). Why don't drones use small versions of commercial aircraft engines? ZDNet. Retrieved from: https://www.zdnet.com/article/why-dont-drones-use-small-versions-of-commercial-aircraft-engines/
47 Arriansyah, A. (2016). The 6 known ways to power a drone. Retrieved from: Techinasia. https://www.techinasia.com/talk/6-known-ways-power-a-drone
48 Corrigan, F. (2019). How do drones work and what is drone technology. DroneZon. Retrieved from: https://www.dronezon.com/learn-about-drones-quadcopters/what-is-drone-technology-or-how-does-drone-technology-work/
49 Corrigan, F. (2019). How do drones work and what is drone technology. DroneZon. Retrieved from: https://www.dronezon.com/learn-about-drones-quadcopters/what-is-drone-technology-or-how-does-drone-technology-work/
50 Corrigan, F. (2019). How do drones work and what is drone technology. DroneZon. Retrieved from: https://www.dronezon.com/learn-about-drones-quadcopters/what-is-drone-technology-or-how-does-drone-technology-work/
51 Corrigan, F. (2019). How do drones work and what is drone technology. DroneZon. Retrieved from: https://www.dronezon.com/learn-about-drones-quadcopters/what-is-drone-technology-or-how-does-drone-technology-work/
52 Corrigan, F. (2019). How do drones work and what is drone technology. DroneZon. Retrieved from: https://www.dronezon.com/learn-about-drones-quadcopters/what-is-drone-technology-or-how-does-drone-technology-work/
53 Corrigan, F. (2019). How do drones work and what is drone technology. DroneZon. Retrieved from: https://www.dronezon.com/learn-about-drones-quadcopters/what-is-drone-technology-or-how-does-drone-technology-work/
54 Wyder, P.M., Chen, Y.S., Lasrado, A.J., Pelles, R.J., Kwiatkowski, R., Comas, E.O., ... & Xiong, Z. (2019). Autonomous drone hunter operating by deep learning and all-onboard computations in GPS-denied environments. PloS One, 14(11): e0225092.
55 Daley, S. (2018). Fighting fires and saving elephants: How 12 companies are using the AI drone to solve big problems. Retrieved February 10, 2020, from: https://builtin.com/artificial-intelligence/drones-ai-companies
56 Leswing, K. (2015). DJI's powerful new computer will lead to better drone apps. Fortune. Retrieved February 11, 2020, from: https://fortune.com/2015/11/02/dji-manifold-computer/
57 McLellan, C. (2018, May 15). The new commute: How driverless cars, hyperloop, and drones will change our travel plans. Retrieved June 21, 2020, from: https://www.techrepublic.com/article/the-new-commute-how-driverless-cars-hyperloop-and-drones-will-change-our-travel-plans/
58 McKinsey & Company. (2017). Commercial drones are here: The future of unmanned aerial systems. Retrieved from: https://www.mckinsey.com/industries/capital-projects-and-infrastructure/our-insights/commercial-drones-are-here-the-future-of-unmanned-aerial-systems
59 Taking flight. (2016). The Economist. Retrieved from: https://www.economist.com/technology-quarterly/2017-06-08/civilian-drones
60 Corrigan, F. (2019). What are drones used for from business to critical missions. DroneZon. Retrieved from: https://www.dronezon.com/drones-for-good/what-are-drones-used-for-and-best-drone-uses/
61 Taking flight. (2016). The Economist. Retrieved from: https://www.economist.com/technology-quarterly/2017-06-08/civilian-drones
62 Corrigan, F. (2019). What are drones used for from business to critical missions. DroneZon. Retrieved from: https://www.dronezon.com/drones-for-good/what-are-drones-used-for-and-best-drone-uses/
63 Taking flight. (2016). The Economist. Retrieved from: https://www.economist.com/technology-quarterly/2017-06-08/civilian-drones
64 Corrigan, F. (2019). What are drones used for from business to critical missions. DroneZon. Retrieved from: https://www.dronezon.com/drones-for-good/what-are-drones-used-for-and-best-drone-uses/
65 Amazon. (2019) Amazon.com: Prime Air. Retrieved from: https://www.amazon.com/Amazon-Prime-Air/b?node=8037720011
66 Flanagan, B. (2019). The maker of Dubai's flying taxi aims to set flight within the next three years. Wired Middle East. Retrieved February 11, 2020, from: https://wired.me/science/transportation/dubai-drone-flying-taxis-volocopter/

67 Taking flight. (2016). The Economist. Retrieved from: https://www.economist.com/technology-quarterly/2017-06-08/civilian-drones
68 Corrigan, F. (2019). What are drones used for from business to critical missions. DroneZon. Retrieved from: https://www.dronezon.com/drones-for-good/what-are-drones-used-for-and-best-drone-uses/
69 Heater, B. (2018). Aerones makes really big drones for cleaning turbines and saving lives. TechCrunch. Retrieved from: https://techcrunch.com/2018/03/17/aerones-makes-really-big-drones-for-cleaning-turbines-and-saving-lives/
70 Aerones. (2018). Aerones. Retrieved from: https://www.aerones.com
71 Etherington, D. (2014). Google acquires Titan Aerospace, the drone company pursued by Facebook. TechCrunch. Retrieved from: https://techcrunch.com/2014/04/14/google-acquires-titan-aerospace-the-drone-company-pursued-by-facebook/
72 Taking flight. (2016). The Economist. Retrieved from: https://www.economist.com/technology-quarterly/2017-06-08/civilian-drones
73 Russell, J. (2019). Facebook is reportedly testing solar-powered internet drones again – this time with Airbus. TechCrunch. Retrieved from: https://techcrunch.com/2019/01/21/facebook-airbus-solar-drones-internet-program/
74 Hickey, M. (2016). Report: Google working on awesome solar-powered broadband drones for 5G wireless internet. Forbes. Retrieved February 10, 2020, from: https://www.forbes.com/sites/matthickey/2016/01/31/report-google-working-on-awesome-solar-powered-broadband-drones-for-5g-wireless-internet/#23e6c2f96a43
75 Hickey, M. (2016). Report: Google working on awesome solar-powered broadband drones for 5G wireless internet. Forbes. Retrieved February 10, 2020, from: https://www.forbes.com/sites/matthickey/2016/01/31/report-google-working-on-awesome-solar-powered-broadband-drones-for-5g-wireless-internet/#23e6c2f96a43
76 Taking flight. (2016). The Economist. Retrieved from: https://www.economist.com/technology-quarterly/2017-06-08/civilian-drones
77 Corrigan, F. (2019). What are drones used for from business to critical missions. DroneZon. Retrieved from: https://www.dronezon.com/drones-for-good/what-are-drones-used-for-and-best-drone-uses/
78 Baggaley, K. (2019). Forget props and fixed wings. New bio-inspired drones mimic birds, bats and bugs. NBC News. Retrieved February 6, 2020, from: https://www.nbcnews.com/mach/science/forget-props-fixed-wings-new-bio-inspired-drones-mimic-birds-ncna1033061
79 Taking flight. (2016). The Economist. Retrieved from: https://www.economist.com/technology-quarterly/2017-06-08/civilian-drones
80 Corrigan, F. (2019). What are drones used for from business to critical missions. DroneZon. Retrieved from: https://www.dronezon.com/drones-for-good/what-are-drones-used-for-and-best-drone-uses/
81 Corrigan, F. (2019). What are drones used for from business to critical missions. DroneZon. Retrieved from: https://www.dronezon.com/drones-for-good/what-are-drones-used-for-and-best-drone-uses/
82 Corrigan, F. (2019). What are drones used for from business to critical missions. DroneZon. Retrieved from: https://www.dronezon.com/drones-for-good/what-are-drones-used-for-and-best-drone-uses/
83 Corrigan, F. (2019). What are drones used for from business to critical missions. DroneZon. Retrieved from: https://www.dronezon.com/drones-for-good/what-are-drones-used-for-and-best-drone-uses/
84 Taking flight. (2016). The Economist. Retrieved from: https://www.economist.com/technology-quarterly/2017-06-08/civilian-drones
85 Corrigan, F. (2019). What are drones used for from business to critical missions. DroneZon. Retrieved from: https://www.dronezon.com/drones-for-good/what-are-drones-used-for-and-best-drone-uses/
86 Gewirtz, D. (2020). Everything you need to know about 3D printing and its impact on your business. ZDNet. Retrieved February 14, 2020, from: https://www.zdnet.com/article/everything-you-need-to-know-about-3d-printing-and-its-impact-on-your-business/
87 Gewirtz, D. (2020). Everything you need to know about 3D printing and its impact on your business. ZDNet. Retrieved February 14, 2020, from: https://www.zdnet.com/article/everything-you-need-to-know-about-3d-printing-and-its-impact-on-your-business/
88 Conlin, B. (2018). More than prototypes: A look at the 3D printing industry. Business News Daily. Retrieved February 14, 2020, from : https://www.businessnewsdaily.com/9297-3d-printing-for-business.html
89 Hewlett Packard Inc. (2017) HP 3DaaS – 3D printer services, supplies and support. HP® Official Site. Retrieved February 12, 2020, from: https://www8.hp.com/us/en/printers/3d-printers/services/3daaS.html

90 Rayna, T., & Striukova, L. (2016). From rapid prototyping to home fabrication: How 3D printing is changing business model innovation. Technological Forecasting and Social Change, 102, 214–224. https://doi.org/10.1016/j.techfore.2015.07.023
91 Graphic Display World. (2019). The new business case for 3D Printing. Retrieved February 14, 2020, from: https://www.graphicdisplayworld.com/features/the-new-business-case-for-3d-printing
92 Starr, M. (2015). Cancer patient receives 3D-printed sternum and ribs. CNET. Retrieved February 14, 2020, from: https://www.cnet.com/news/cancer-patient-receives-3d-printed-sternum-ribs/
93 Gannes, L. (2013). With KeyMe, an iPhone pic now means you can always print more house keys later. AllThingsD. Retrieved from: http://allthingsd.com/20130808/with-keyme-an-iphone-pic-now-means-you-can-always-print-more-housekeys-later/
94 Columbus, L. (2018). The state of 3D printing, 2018. Forbes. Retrieved from: https://www.forbes.com/sites/louiscolumbus/2018/05/30/the-state-of-3d-printing-2018/#423edb287b0a

18 Network and connectivity technologies

Introduction

The overarching theme of the digital technologies discussed in this chapter is connectivity. The digital technologies discussed play a critical role in the ability of people, systems, devices, and other things to pass and receive information from each other. It is this information, combined with computation, that is at the heart of and extends the power of other digital technologies like cloud computing, the internet of things, artificial intelligence, robotics, and drones. There are a range of connectivity technologies and standards, each offering strengths in areas like data transmission speed, transmission range, amount of data that can be sent, connection reliability, connection security, connection availability, connection portability, and more. These technologies and standards also have limitations such as power consumption, infrastructure setup and maintenance costs, durability, hackability, standard adoption levels, connectivity equipment availability / reliability, and much more. In this chapter, we first provide an overview of cellular networks (6G, 5G, 4G, LTE, and others), then we provide an overview of global navigation satellite systems (e.g. those used by GPS devices) and low earth orbit satellite systems, and finally we provide an overview of low-power wide-area networks, NFC, Smart Bluetooth, iBeacon, and other technologies that are at the heart of device-to-device connectivity. The range of available connectivity technologies / standards requires accountants and accounting leaders to understand how different technologies / standards work and what their strengths and shortcomings are. It also requires them to be able to evaluate and advise on the financial and strategic implications of choices about which standards to go with for what purposes, when to experiment with a particular technology / standard, when to cut the cord on an existing connectivity technology / standard, and when to undertake large-scale adoption of a new standard. As we've previously mentioned, without such understanding, accountants may provide advice which costs organizations operational efficiency, product innovation, business model innovation, agility, and adaptability opportunities. In this chapter, we provide a simplified introduction to these technologies. As with other technologies, this is meant to be a starting point to enable current and prospective accountants to catch up, keep up with, and make the most of this group of digital technologies.

6G, 5G, 4G, LTE, and other cellular networks

Cellular networks

If you look in the top corner of your phone, you are likely to see a 5G, 4G, 3G, or, in the worst case, a 2G symbol. These symbols indicate the type of cellular or mobile

252 *Digital technologies deep dive*

network you are using to send and receive data to and from other devices and equipment. *Cellular networks* use land-based towers (also referred to as cell towers, cell sites, cellular base stations, or base transceiver stations) for sending and receiving data. Essentially, a cellular network divides up geographic areas into transmission areas called "cells". The cell towers or transceiver stations have all the necessary components to serve that cell (e.g. antennas, transceivers, control electronics, backup power, sheltering, etc.). The transceiver stations provide the network coverage that devices or equipment then use to send or receive different types of data. The bigger the geographic area requiring network coverage, the more transceiver stations need to be built and operated. There can be set up and maintenance costs, demand issues, environmental degradation issues, and other issues that limit the size and types of areas that can or can't be covered. This is why you might suddenly lose the ability to send or receive data on your device in particular locations – you may be out of range of a transceiver station for your cellular network or the signal may be unable to reach you. Cellular networks can be contrasted to *satellite networks* which transmit data through satellites orbiting the earth. Unlike the relatively short range of transceiver stations and the large number of transceiver stations required to create a big cellular network, satellites can beam coverage to very large and even hard-to-reach areas. But satellites have traditionally been much more costly to build, put in orbit, and maintain. Figure 18.1 provides a visualization of a cellular network and how it works to enable connectivity / data exchange.

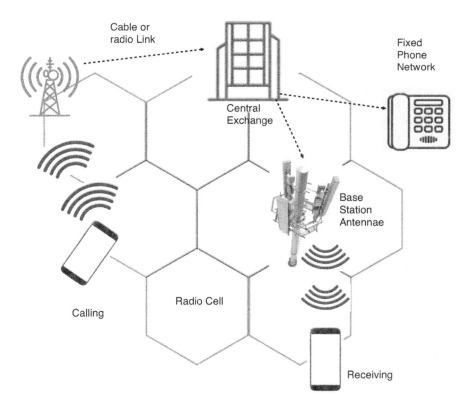

Figure 18.1 How cellular phones work[1]

4G, LTE, and other cellular networks

The "G" in cellular network symbols stands for "generation"; and subsequent generations (or increments) of the "G" symbol (e.g. from 1G and 2G to 3G and 4G to 5G and 6G) represent breakthroughs or expansions in the minimum speed, connectivity, and reliability of cellular networks as set by the International Telecommunication Union Radiocommunication Sector (or ITU-R). For example, while 1G enabled us to be able to talk to each other over a cellular network, 2G expanded this to include the ability to send text messages and limited MMS (i.e. multimedia messages like images). 3G further expanded this to include webpages, music, and videos. But speeds were very slow, relative to, say, a broadband internet connection. 4G and LTE extended cellular network speeds to more closely resemble the speed of a broadband internet connection. This enabled users to enjoy rich experiences on their mobile devices including, for example, streaming video, high-quality music, and multimedia apps – all almost instantaneously (i.e. without the long load or buffering times). The ITU-R set standards for 4G in early 2008, requiring any cellular service referred to as 4G to have peak speeds of at least 100 megabits per second for high-mobility communication (e.g. moving cars and trains) and 1000 megabits per second (or 1 gigabit per second) for stationary or low-motion communication (e.g. walking or not moving). These standards represented a significant leap over existing speeds and, in spite of significant investments, the cellular industry could not reach 4G standards. However, a new technology standard known as LTE (Long Term Evolution), first proposed in Japan in 2004 had evolved from proposal to successful trials to adoption in 2010. By 2011 / 2012 LTE had become an international standard. Although quite short of 4G standards, LTE offered significant improvements on 3G speeds[2]. Due to the significant improvements on 3G and perhaps to the challenges attaining 4G standards, the ITU-R allowed LTE to be called 4G. Cellular networks varied in whether they labelled their LTE offerings 4G LTE or just 4G. But in either case, it wasn't true 4G as it wasn't up to the original ITU-R standards. Over time, improvements in LTE technology resulted in LTE Advanced (LTE-A) and LTE-Advanced Pro, reaching and even surpassing the true 4G standards.

5G and 6G cellular networks

As good as 4G technology has been, advancements in IoT technologies and exponential growth in the number of connected things have pushed it to its capacity limits (e.g. as of 2020 there were an estimated 20 billion connected devices). Fortunately, 5G technology has been in development and, as early as 2018 and 2019, most major economies had trialed or already started to provide a 5G network service. 5G is expected to have significantly greater capacity, with speeds of between 10 and 20 times faster than 4G initially, but potentially up to 100 times faster than 4G[3]. Among other things, it is expected to have greater latency (the time required for data to travel from one point to another) of one to four milliseconds, be more energy efficient, be able to support up to a million connected devices per square foot, and be able to work at greater speeds. It is expected to be a major step towards satisfying the connectivity requirements of advancements in technologies like cloud, IoT, big data, artificial intelligence, augmented / mixed reality, and robotics / drones[4]. As 5G is being rolled out and improved, research on 6G has already begun to explore the types of use cases that won't be possible with 5G and that will require a 6th generation network. Such use cases identified to date include solving remaining accessibility problems (e.g. connecting all people, information, and things in ultra-real time irrespective of location), improving communication between humans and things (e.g. ultra-high definition VR / AR / MR, ultra-real-time communication with things), an expanded communication environment (e.g. high rise buildings, remote geographic areas, the sky, underwater, and space will all become high activity / communication areas), and increasing the sophistication of cyber-physical fusion (e.g. greater integration of cyberspace with human bodily functions, human thought, and human action)[5].

GPS III, GPS Block III, and low earth orbit (LEO) satellites

GPS and GPS III and other global navigation satellite systems (GNSS)

GPS (*Global Positioning System*) is a constellation of space-based satellites that orbit the earth at an altitude of about 20,000 km. At regular intervals, the satellites transmit information about their position and the current time. These signals travel at the speed of light and can be intercepted by GPS receivers. GPS receivers can use the intercepted signals to provide precise location, navigation, and timing information. How do GPS receivers do this? At any point or location on the earth, there is line visibility to at least four GPS satellites[6]. A GPS receiver is able to intercept the signal from each of these four satellites and use it to calculate how far away each satellite is (based on how long it takes for the signal to travel from the satellite to the receiver at the speed of light)[7,8]. Once it knows how far away at least three of the satellites are, the GPS receiver can use a process called trilateration to pinpoint its exact location (or your location)[9]. We use GPS almost daily, sometimes without even realizing it. We use it for directions, to provide pilots with real-time positioning information, to survey, to track the movement of things, for live recording, for military purposes, to avoid collision in shipping, for self-driving cars, and much more[10]. The GPS system was originally developed and is owned by the US Department of Defense, though anyone with a receiver can use it. But it isn't the only system used around the world. Europe has a similar system known as Galileo, China's system is known as BeiDou, and Russia's system is known as GLONASS (*Globalnaya navigatsionnaya sputnikovaya sistema*). Even though the term GPS is often used to refer to all these systems, GPS is technically only the US system, and the better name to refer to all systems is *global navigation satellite systems* (GNSS)[11].

GPS III refers to the next generation of GPS satellites designed and built by Lockheed Martin; with the first of these satellites launched in December 2018[12]. GPS III brings significant improvements in pinpointing location accuracy[13] (e.g. from within 3m to within 1m), significant improvements in signal strength (e.g. signals will be much easier to pick up even in obstructed areas like tree canopies and inside buildings), significantly improved security and reliability (e.g. GPS signals will be much harder to maliciously or accidentally jam / obstruct), and improvements in interoperability with other global navigation satellite systems. Advancements in GPS III hold a range of benefits for organizations including improved user experience, product innovation, and new market potential – so long as device makers have devices available to take full advantage of GPS III[14]. GPS III is anticipated to be fully capable by mid-2023 and to improve when another ten satellites go into orbit between 2026 and 2034[15]. Other global navigation satellite systems have also been working on upgrading their systems. GPS III is anticipated to be fully capable by mid-2023 and to improve when another ten satellites go into orbit between 2026 and 2034. Other global navigation satellite systems have also been working on upgrading their systems.

Low earth orbit satellites (LEO)

Low earth orbit satellites (or LEO) are satellites that orbit the earth at a much lower altitude (e.g. about 400km to 2,000km)[16], unlike conventional satellites that orbit at about 36,000km and GNSS that orbit at about 20,000 to 26,000km. There are several benefits to a low orbit including better signal strength and less power to transmit the signal (as the satellite is near the earth), lower propagation delay (good for applications requiring real-time data), and lower priced satellite equipment. But there are also disadvantages including more satellites being needed to cover the earth (as the lower a satellite is, the less area it can cover), regular maintenance requirements (due to having to continuously travel through the much denser atmosphere), and shorter lifespan of satellites. One aim of LEO satellites is to reach the more than four billion people on earth who are without high-speed internet (e.g. due to cellular infrastructure being too expensive)[17]. Companies such as OneWeb are working on provision of wifi hotspots connected to their LEO satellites[18]. LEO satellites also offer new scientific exploration opportunities at significantly reduced cost (e.g. miniature satellite versions of between 1g and 100kg are now possible)[19]. On the IoT front, LEO satellites offer a way to connect "things" no matter where they are on earth. Their lower orbits (therefore higher detail) also enhance remote sensing capabilities of smart devices. Companies such as Iridium and Globalstar recently launched 64 and 24 LEO satellites respectively, Amazon intends to launch 3,236 LEO satellites to provide internet to areas without it, and SpaceX has sought permission to launch more than 30,000[20,21]. LPWAN technology (see next section) companies like Semtech, the owner of LoRa technology, are experimenting with LEO satellite-connected LoRa connectivity that covers the whole planet. And Iridium has been working with Amazon to develop a satellite cloud-based solution with global coverage for IoT applications[22]. Figure 18.2 and Table 18.1 show the different types of orbits and their different uses.

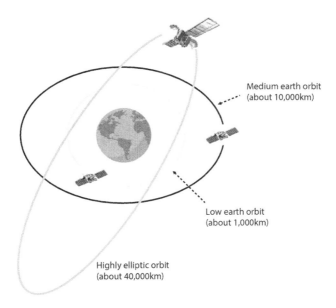

Figure 18.2 Low earth orbit (LEO), medium earth orbit (MEO), and highly elliptical orbit (HEO)[23,24]

Table 18.1 Types of satellite or orbit, and what they are used for[25]

Type of use	Type of orbit / type of satellite
Astronomy	Several orbits
Climate, weather forecast	LEO, GEO
Communications	GEO(low latitude), Molniya(high latitude)
Earth observation	GEO, LEO, global coverage
Global positioning, navigation	LEO, MEO, global coverage
Military	Several LEO orbits
Space environment	Several, including sounding rockets
Space station	LEO
Technology development	Several orbits

Note: Low earth orbit (LEO), medium earth orbit (MEO), geostationary orbit (GEO).

NBIoT, LTE Cat-M1, LoRaWAN and other low-power wide-area network technologies

Devices using cellular networks use a lot of power to send a lot of data over medium distances (which is why they require constant power access or regular recharging). But many IoT devices only need to send a little bit of data over much longer distances, can't be regularly recharged, and, thus, need to make the most of battery life. *Low-power wide-area* (LPWA) and *low-power wide-area network* (LPWAN) technologies provide a solution to this. They are a type of wireless technology that allows for data to be sent at low bit rates (e.g. 0.3kbit/s to 50kbit/s) over long distances (e.g. a few kilometres to tens of kilometres)[26]. The technology for this type of network enables very low power consumption, so that an IoT device can use a standard AA battery for many years (contrast this to a battery-powered device using a cellular network – such a device typically needs to be recharged daily)[27]. LPWA technologies' simpler, lightweight protocols translate into less complex / less costly hardware, less complex / less costly infrastructure requirements, and, thus, significantly reduced IoT connectivity costs (e.g. cents per device per month, as opposed to tens of dollars per month)[28]. Thus, the technologies provide the ability for IoT devices to transfer data to each other over significantly longer distances, at significantly lower power consumption, and significantly lower cost. This makes the idea of an organization connecting hundreds, thousands, or even hundreds of thousands of devices a much more realistic proposition. There are a range of LPWA or LPWAN technologies including LTE-M, NBIoT, LoRaWaN, and others. These typically vary on dimensions such transmission speed, power consumption, latency, availability, mobility, extent of coverage, transmission distance, number of devices that can be connected per unit area, and cost. Thus, the right one for an organization will depend on what the organization's use case is.

NBIoT

As it sounds, NBIoT (or *narrowband internet of things*) is a low bandwidth LPWA cellular technology standard (low bandwidth meaning that very small amounts of data can be sent per second). NBIoT is classified as a 5G technology and has the proven security and privacy features of LTE mobile networks[29,30]. Key strengths of NBIoT over other standards include its super low device power consumption, its capacity to have a massive number of devices connected per unit area, and its potential for ultra-cost efficiency (it eliminates the need to aggregate sensor data before sending it to the primary server, thus reducing hardware costs)[31,32]. Limitations of NBIoT include it being more suited to static devices than mobile ones, its low latency and its low speed (e.g. 26kbit/s to 159kbit/s). In fact, although low device power consumption is a strength of NBIoT, when large amounts of data have to be sent, NBIoT can end up using more power since a device has to be active for a longer period of time[33,34]. Given its current strengths and limitations, NBIoT has been viewed as being suited for use cases involving static devices that send minimal data, and do so infrequently – thus maximizing battery life[35]. Examples of such use cases can include smart power meters and battery-powered smart locks.

LTE-M

LTE-M (also commonly referred to as LTE Machine Type Communication or LTE MTC, enhanced Machine Type Communication or eMTC, and LTE Cat-M1) is another cellular LPWA standard for IoT and machine-to-machine communication[36,37]. Although NBIoT is stronger than LTE-M on the low device power consumption dimension, LTE-M is stronger than NBIoT on mobility, speed (e.g. up to six times that of NBIoT), and latency dimensions[38]. LTE-M is also backward compatible with existing 4G LTE networks, making it more likely to be available / accessible in certain parts of the world than NBIoT[39]. LTE-M is seen as being suited for use cases involving mobility, sending lots of data, and doing so frequently. LTE-M use cases include wearable devices, connectivity with devices in thick walls or deep basements, and asset tracking / monitoring.

LoRa / LoRaWAN

LoRa (long range) is a LPWAN technology and LoRaWAN is a network protocol using LoRa that connects things (e.g. sensors) to the internet to enable bidirectional communication[40,41]. LoRa technology's key strengths are its long-range transmission (2 to 15km) and low device power consumption (e.g. extending battery life by up to ten years)[42]. One of its limitations is the amount of data that can be sent per second (0.3kbps to 5kbps). As with NBIoT, this data transmission rate can result in high device power consumption if large amounts of data need to be sent. LoRa and LoRaWAN use cases include fleet tracking, livestock tracking, and sensors in very hard to reach places (e.g. in concrete or far away)[43,44].

Other LPWAN technologies

Other LPWAN technologies include Signfox and EC-GSM-IoT (Extended Coverage-GSM-internet of things). EC-GSM-IoT works over 4G, 3G, and even 2G mobile networks. This makes EC-GSM-IoT technology valuable in parts of the world that don't have access to the latest cellular networks. Yet others include Weightless, Wize, and Chirp.

NFC, Smart Bluetooth, iBeacon, and other communication protocols

NFC

NFC is short for *near-field communication*. It is a short-range wireless data transmission technology based on older RFID electromagnetic induction ideas. It enables two electronic devices to communicate with each other using electromagnetic waves when brought within 2 to 10cm of each other[45,46,47]. NFC use cases include contactless payments (e.g. pay wave, pay pass, Apple pay, etc.)[48], access control[49] (e.g. digital keys for smart locks), identification of objects via NFC tag scanning, speeding up pairing of Bluetooth objects, improved product authentication via scanning of NFC tags, provision of product on NFC tags, proof of compliance by checking if people with an NFC tag came in proximity with an area they were meant to inspect, and much more[50]. NFC technology enables devices or tags or other things embedded with an NFC chip to receive and / or transmit information which can be used in many different areas including customer engagement, product and supply chain management, marketing, asset management, workflow management, and more. Key benefits of NFC over technologies like Bluetooth or Wi-Fi include its much lower power consumption and its ability to operate without a power source. A device with an NFC chip can create a magnetic field which is able to power or induce current in another NFC device, enabling that device to transmit data even if it has no power source of its own. This is referred to as inductive coupling, and is also how wireless chargers work (e.g. a charging device creates an electromagnetic field which induces charge in a wire connected to a rechargeable battery). An active NFC device (one with power source and capable of both sending and receiving data, e.g. a smartphone) can interact with another active device so both can send and receive data. Or an active device can interact with a passive device (one without a power source and only capable of transmitting data, e.g. an NFC tag or tag embedded with an NFC chip). In this case, the active device powers the passive device (e.g. see Figure 18.3).

NFC chips transmit data at up to 424kbit/s which is significantly less than Bluetooth's 2.1Mbits/s. But this is still adequate for sending text, photos, and even audio. NFC is also considered to be of high security given the need for devices to be right next to each

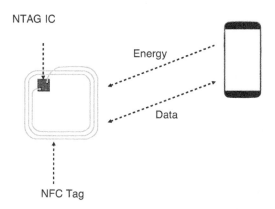

Figure 18.3 An NFC-enabled phone sets up a current, the NFC tag receives the "induced current", and, recognizing it is a valid signal, offers connection to the phone and begins data transfer[51]

other. This limits the opportunity for others to eavesdrop or intercept the data transfer. Other benefits, as far as access control, include limiting the ability for people to lend their access to others or have it stolen (e.g. if NFC access is via a smartphone). And, as far as efficiency, smartphone-enabled NFC access minimizes instances of people forgetting their keys or keycards (assuming they are less likely to forget their phone at home).

Bluetooth 5.0 and Bluetooth Low Energy (BLE)

Traditional or classic Bluetooth (Bluetooth 1.0 to 3.0) was often criticized for the difficulty in pairing devices and maintaining pairing, its slow transmission speeds, and its high device battery power consumption. Bluetooth 4.0 (also referred to as Bluetooth Smart or Smart Bluetooth) evolved as a response to this, offering high-speed and low-energy versions or categories of the technology. The low-energy category (Bluetooth Low Energy or BLE or Bluetooth LE) was designed for lower data rates (e.g. 1Mbps), but with much lower energy consumption. It allows Bluetooth devices to "sleep" while idle and only "wake up" or initiate Bluetooth functionality when data transmission is initiated. By reducing power consumption, BLE technology enables Bluetooth devices to operate for months or even years on a single coin-cell battery. Reducing data transmission rates to elongate battery life means that BLE is not suitable for devices that require a continuous stream of data (e.g. wireless headphones, speakers, radios, etc.). But the reduced transmission rate can work for devices that only need to send small bits of data or send data infrequently (e.g. wearable devices, periodic monitoring devices, etc.). Thus, these devices can benefit from longer battery life without a compromised ability to send data. BLE-enabled devices are capable of multi-point data transmission, as well as co-working with different Bluetooth specifications (e.g. earlier versions of Bluetooth, or Bluetooth high speed)[52]. So, a device with both BLE and high-speed Bluetooth Classic installed (Dual Mode Bluetooth) can switch between high-speed or low-energy uses as the situation demands. For example, if the device is a smartphone, BLE can take over the less intensive data tasks to preserve battery and Bluetooth Classic can take over for tasks that require continuous connectivity or large data transmission[53]. If the device is a sphygmomanometer (blood pressure measuring device), it can use BLE to record blood pressure status, and then use Bluetooth Classic to transmit images or other larger data.[54]

As at the time of writing this book, Bluetooth 5.0 was the latest evolution in the Bluetooth standard. This version doubles the data transmission rate, making audio transmission possible, and edging closer towards video. It quadruples the transmission range from 50m to 200m (enough to cover all the devices in a house or office). It enables the selection of 2Mbps, 1Mbps, 500kbps, and 125kbps transmission rates so device use can be optimized for data rate and / or data range. Finally, Bluetooth 5.0 brings eight times the broadcast capacity[55]. The improvements in data transmission rate, range, and broadcast capability expand the longevity and connection capabilities of IoT devices both indoors and outdoors[56].

Beacon technology

Beacons are small devices that use Bluetooth Low Energy to send you data or content based on where you are (e.g. information about a sale at your favorite store as you walk into a shopping center)[57,58]. Beacons are usually mounted or stuck in the particular location that targeted users are likely to pass and thus where location-based content is best served for the particular purpose it is aimed at. Apps on a user's phone pick up the beacon signals and execute response actions (e.g. as you walk past it, you might receive a push notification from your favorite store's app, if it is installed on your phone, offering 50% off select items if you visit the store today)[59]. Beacon technology has been seen as ideal for indoor settings where GPS can't reach. Beacon use cases include location-based or proximity marketing (e.g. Best Buy serves up different ads to customers depending on which section of the store they are in[60]. But beacons can be put anywhere, even in novel outdoor locations), access control (e.g. smart locks that automatically unlock when an authorized user walks up to the front door), and automated check-in (e.g. once a guest passes the front desk or arrives in their room). They further include location-based content delivery (e.g. delivering information or other resources like emergency warnings, PowerPoint slides, directions, etc.), resource tracking (e.g. tracking people, assets, etc.), ticketing / passes (e.g. tickets or passes purchased on your phone automatically present themselves as you walk in, saving search and presentation time), and much more[61]. iBeacon is the Apple standard-specific version of beacons first introduced in 2013.

Google and reflect

Table 18.2 Google and reflect

Digital technology	Common terminology
Cellular Networks	Hz/MHz/GHz, cellular bandwidth, Cellular Network Latency, 4G LTE, 5G New Radio (5G NR), eMBB, mMTC, URLLC, 10-nanometer chip, 7-nanometer chip, Cloud Radio Access Network (cRAN), mmWave spectrum, 5G Massive Machine-Type Communication (mMTC), cellular network capacity, MIMO, network slicing, small cell densification, licensed spectrum, unlicensed spectrum, 3GGP, carrier aggregation, cell tower, evolved packet system
GPS III and LEO Satellites	GPS accuracy, GPS bearing, GPS coordinate systems, GPS navigation, NAVSTAR, Wide Area Augmentation System (WAAS), medium earth orbit (MEO), geosynchronous equatorial orbit (GEO), picosatellite, microsatellite, minisatellite
LPWAN	Cellular LPWAN, Cellular LPWA, EC-GSM-IoT, IoT stack, IoT gateway,
NFC, Smart Bluetooth, and Beacons	NFC device, RFID, inductive coupling, proximity coupling device (PCD), host controller interface (HCI), inductive coupling, active NFC device, NFC tag, NFC card emulation, NFC encoding, ferrite sheet, passive NFC device, NFC forum, NFC-F, NFC-V, Bluetooth LE, Bluejacking[62], Bluesnarfing, Bluespamming, Bluebugging, Bluecasting, Bluetooth douche, Bluetooth pairing, Bluetooth virus, Bluetooth personal area network, active slave broadcast (ASB), Bluetooth device address, Bluetooth host

Example tools and vendors

Table 18.3 Example tools and vendors

Digital technology	Tools and vendors
Cellular Networks	Verizon 4G LTE, T-Mobile HSPA+, AT&T 5G+, Telstra 5G, Optus 5G, Deutsche Telekom, EE, Vodafone, China Mobile, SK Telecom
GPS III and LEO Satellites	Else Astrocast LEO constellation for IoT communications, OneWeb satellites, Space Exploration Technologies Corp satellites, Iridium satellites, Virgin Orbit satellites, Amazon satellites, Eutelsat Communications SA satellites.

Digital technology	Tools and vendors
LPWA and LPWAN	Ingenu RPMA, Sigfox 0G network, LoRa Alliance, Weightless (SIG), Wize, Chirp, Huawei NBIoT, Ericsson cellular IoT, Vodafone NBIoT, LEAPIN Digital Keys' Smart Locks, iMETOS® NB IoT
NFC, Bluetooth Smart and Beacons	Broadcom Topaz chip, MIFARE DESFire®, NXP MIFARE Classic®, Texas Instruments Bluetooth products, Nordic Semiconductor Bluetooth products, Silicon Labs Bluetooth products, Quuppa Bluetooth products, u-blox Bluetooth products, UnSeen Technologies Bluetooth products, Fanstel Bluetooth products, Laird Connectivity Bluetooth products.

Discussion questions

Table 18.4 Discussion questions

Digital technology	Discussion questions
Cellular Networks	1. Explain in plain language how a cellular network works? 2. What could you do with 2G that was not possible with 1G? 3. What can you do with 5G that you can't do with 4G? 4. What is an example of a product innovation opportunity presented by 5G and 6G? 5. What is an example of a business model innovation opportunity presented by 5G and 6G? 6. What are the potential financial costs and risks of adopting 5G too early? What about the risks of adopting it too late?
GPS III and LEO Satellites	7. What is an example of a product innovation opportunity presented by GPS III or LEO satellites? 8. What is an example of a business model innovation opportunity presented by GPS III or LEO satellites?
LPWA and LPWAN	9. Which LPWA or LPWAN technology would you use if you frequently took travelers on remote tours and relied on IoT devices to improve the traveler experience? 10. Which type of LPWA or LPWAN is likely to be the most widely accepted and why?
NFC, Smart Bluetooth, and Beacons	11. What is an example of a product innovation opportunity presented by NFC, Smart Bluetooth, or Beacons? 12. What is an example of a business model innovation opportunity presented by NFC, Smart Bluetooth, or Beacons?

Notes

1 Telstra. (2014). Mobile base stations and health - Consumer advice. Retrieved June 21, 2020, from: https://www.telstra.com.au/consumer-advice/eme/base-stations
2 Segan, S. (2015, February 10). 3G vs. 4G: What's the difference? PCMag. Retrieved from: https://www.pcmag.com/news/3g-vs-4g-whats-the-difference
3 Whyte, J. (2018, March 14). What is the difference between 4G and... Just Ask Gemalto. Retrieved from: https://www.justaskgemalto.com/en/difference-4g-5g/
4 BBC News. (2020). What is 5G and what will it mean for you? Retrieved from: https://www.bbc.com/news/business-44871448
5 NTT DOCOMO. (2020) 5G Evolution and 6G. Retrieved March 2, 2020, from: https://www.nttdocomo.co.jp/english/binary/pdf/corporate/technology/whitepaper_6g/DOCOMO_6G_White_PaperEN_20200124.pdf
6 Physics.Org. (2020). How does GPS work? Retrieved from: http://www.physics.org/article-questions.asp?id=55

7 Physics.Org. (2020). How does GPS work? Retrieved from: http://www.physics.org/article-questions.asp?id=55
8 Dempster, A. (2013, March 7). Explainer: what is GPS? The Conversation. Retrieved from: https://theconversation.com/explainer-what-is-gps-12248
9 Physics.Org. (2020). How does GPS work? http://www.physics.org/article-questions.asp?id=55
10 Dempster, A. (2013, March 7). Explainer: what is GPS? The Conversation. Retrieved from: https://theconversation.com/explainer-what-is-gps-12248
11 Dempster, A. (2013, March 7). Explainer: what is GPS? The Conversation. Retrieved from: https://theconversation.com/explainer-what-is-gps-12248
12 Pappalardo, J. (2018, December 26). USAF's next-gen GPS satellites will be a huge upgrade… eventually. Popular Mechanics. Retrieved from: https://www.popularmechanics.com/space/satellites/a25683704/gps-iii/
13 Lockheed Martin. (2018). Unbelievable accuracy: GPS III. Retrieved from: https://www.lockheedmartin.com/en-us/news/features/history/gps-iii.html
14 Cozzens, T. (2019, January 9). GPS III finally aloft, benefits on the way. GPS World. Retrieved from: https://www.gpsworld.com/gps-iii-finally-aloft-benefits-on-the-way/
15 Cozzens, T. (2019, January 9). GPS III finally aloft, benefits on the way. GPS World. Retrieved from: https://www.gpsworld.com/gps-iii-finally-aloft-benefits-on-the-way/
16 Allain, R. (2015, September 15). What's so special about low earth orbit? Wired. Retrieved from: https://www.wired.com/2015/09/whats-special-low-earth-orbit/
17 Ritchie, G. (2019, August 9). Why low-earth orbit satellites are the new space race. Bloomberg. Retrieved from: https://www.bloomberg.com/news/articles/2019-08-09/why-low-earth-orbit-satellites-are-the-new-space-race-quicktake
18 Ritchie, G. (2019, August 9). Why low-earth orbit satellites are the new space race. Bloomberg. Retrieved from: https://www.bloomberg.com/news/articles/2019-08-09/why-low-earth-orbit-satellites-are-the-new-space-race-quicktake
19 Avnet Silica, & Avnet Silica. (2019, June 27). Low-Earth-Orbit Satellites and IoT | Avnet Silica. Avnet.Com. https://www.avnet.com/wps/portal/silica/resources/article/low-earth-orbit-satellites-and-iot/
20 Ritchie, G. (2019, August 9). Why low-earth orbit satellites are the new space race. Bloomberg. Retrieved from: https://www.bloomberg.com/news/articles/2019-08-09/why-low-earth-orbit-satellites-are-the-new-space-race-quicktake
21 Blackman, J. (2019, November 4). What is LEO, and how will LEO satellites transform the IoT sector? Enterprise IoT Insights. Retrieved from: https://enterpriseiotinsights.com/20191104/channels/fundamentals/what-is-leo-and-how-will-leo-satellites-transform-iot
22 Blackman, J. (2019, November 4). What is LEO, and how will LEO satellites transform the IoT sector? Enterprise IoT Insights. Retrieved from: https://enterpriseiotinsights.com/20191104/channels/fundamentals/what-is-leo-and-how-will-leo-satellites-transform-iot
23 Borthomieu, Y. (2014). Satellite lithium-ion batteries. Lithium-Ion Batteries, 311–344. https://doi.org/10.1016/b978-0-444-59513-3.00014-5
24 Meseguer, J., Pérez-Grande, I., & Sanz-Andrés, A. (2012). Keplerian orbits. Spacecraft Thermal Control, 39–57
25 Meseguer, J., Pérez-Grande, I., & Sanz-Andrés, A. (2012). Keplerian orbits. Spacecraft Thermal Control, 39–57
26 Wedd, M. (2018, September 26). What is LPWANs and the LoRaWAN Open Standard? IoT for All. Retrieved from: https://www.iotforall.com/what-is-lpwan-lorawan/
27 Upale, A. (2018). LTE Cat M1 vs NB-IoT vs LoRa – Comparing LPWANs. Semiconductorstore. Retrieved from: https://www.semiconductorstore.com/blog/2018/LTE-Cat-M1-vs-NB-IoT-vs-LoRa-Comparing-LPWANs-Symmetry-Blog/3496/
28 Wedd, M. (2018, September 26). What is LPWANs and the LoRaWAN Open Standard? IoT for All. Retrieved from: https://www.iotforall.com/what-is-lpwan-lorawan/
29 Hwang, Y. (2020, January 17). Cellular IoT explained – NB-IoT vs. LTE-M vs. 5G and more. IoT For All. Retrieved from: https://www.iotforall.com/cellular-iot-explained-nb-iot-vs-lte-m/
30 Øyvann, S. (2017, January 26). From parking to farming, applications for NB-IoT are heading out into the real world. ZDNet. Retrieved from: https://www.zdnet.com/article/from-parking-to-farming-applications-for-nb-iot-are-heading-out-into-the-real-world/
31 Hwang, Y. (2020, January 17). Cellular IoT explained – NB-IoT vs. LTE-M vs. 5G and more. IoT For All. Retrieved from: https://www.iotforall.com/cellular-iot-explained-nb-iot-vs-lte-m/

32 Thales. (2020). Narrowband IoT overview (NB-IoT). Retrieved from: https://www.gemalto.com/iot/resources/innovation-technology/nb-iot
33 Hwang, Y. (2020, January 17). Cellular IoT explained – NB-IoT vs. LTE-M vs. 5G and more. IoT For All. Retrieved from: https://www.iotforall.com/cellular-iot-explained-nb-iot-vs-lte-m/
34 Øyvann, S. (2017, January 26). From parking to farming, applications for NB-IoT are heading out into the real world. ZDNet. Retrieved from: https://www.zdnet.com/article/from-parking-to-farming-applications-for-nb-iot-are-heading-out-into-the-real-world/
35 Øyvann, S. (2017, January 26). From parking to farming, applications for NB-IoT are heading out into the real world. ZDNet. Retrieved from: https://www.zdnet.com/article/from-parking-to-farming-applications-for-nb-iot-are-heading-out-into-the-real-world/
36 Hwang, Y. (2020, January 17). Cellular IoT explained – NB-IoT vs. LTE-M vs. 5G and more. IoT For All. Retrieved from: https://www.iotforall.com/cellular-iot-explained-nb-iot-vs-lte-m/
37 SierraWireless. (2018, April 3). LTE-M vs. NB-IoT: Make the best choice for your needs. Retrieved from: https://www.sierrawireless.com/iot-blog/iot-blog/2018/04/lte-m-vs-nb-iot/
38 Hwang, Y. (2020, January 17). Cellular IoT explained – NB-IoT vs. LTE-M vs. 5G and more. IoT For All. Retrieved from: https://www.iotforall.com/cellular-iot-explained-nb-iot-vs-lte-m/
39 SierraWireless. (2018, April 3). LTE-M vs. NB-IoT: Make the best choice for your needs. Retrieved from: https://www.sierrawireless.com/iot-blog/iot-blog/2018/04/lte-m-vs-nb-iot/
40 Wedd, M. (2018, September 26). What is LPWANs and the LoRaWAN Open Standard? IoT for All. Retrieved from: https://www.iotforall.com/what-is-lpwan-lorawan/
41 I-SCOOP. (2015). LoRa and LoRaWAN: The technologies, ecosystems, use cases and market. Retrieved from: https://www.i-scoop.eu/internet-of-things-guide/lpwan/iot-network-lora-lorawan/
42 Maker.io Team. (2016, August 10). Introduction to LoRa technology – The game changer. Retrieved from: https://www.digikey.com/en/maker/blogs/introduction-to-lora-technology
43 Wedd, M. (2018, September 26). What is LPWANs and the LoRaWAN Open Standard? IoT for All. Retrieved from: https://www.iotforall.com/what-is-lpwan-lorawan/
44 Pike, J. (2017, August 21). Understanding LoRa WAN basics: A non-technical explanation. Metova. Retrieved from: https://metova.com/understanding-lora-basics-a-non-technical-explanation/
45 Triggs, R. (2019, June 30). What is NFC and how does it work. Android Authority. Retrieved from: https://www.androidauthority.com/what-is-nfc-270730/
46 Joshi, C. (2019). What is NFC & how does it work? Retrieved from: https://blog.beaconstac.com/2019/05/what-is-nfc-and-how-does-it-work/
47 Triggs, R. (2019, June 30). What is NFC and how does it work. Android Authority. Retrieved from: https://www.androidauthority.com/what-is-nfc-270730/
48 Profis, S. (2014, September 9). Everything you need to know about NFC and mobile payments. CNET. Retrieved from: https://www.cnet.com/how-to/how-nfc-works-and-mobile-payments/
49 Saritag. (2019). NFC tag authentication explained – Seritag Learn NFC. Retrieved from: https://learn.seritag.com/tech/nfc-tag-authentication-explained
50 Ratna, Sneh. (2019). Best use cases of NFC to implement in 2019: Proximity marketing without an app. Beaconstac. Retrieved from: https://blog.beaconstac.com/2019/01/proximity-marketing-without-an-app-best-use-cases-of-nfc-to-implement-in-2019/
51 Camperi, A. (2018). How to use an NFC reader. Retrieved June 21, 2020, from: https://www.getkisi.com/lessons/how-to-use-an-nfc-reader
52 Allion Labs. (2012). The next Bluetooth wave: High speed & low energy technology. Retrieved from: https://www.allion.com/the-next-bluetooth-wave-high-speed-low-energy-technology/
53 Nguyen, A. (2018). When would you have BOTH Bluetooth Classic and Low Energy? Semiconductorstore. Retrieved from: https://www.semiconductorstore.com/blog/2018/When-Would-You-Have-BOTH-Bluetooth-Classic-and-Low-Energy-Symmetry-Blog/3110
54 Technical Direct. (2012). The next Bluetooth wave: High speed & low energy technology. Retrieved from: http://www.technical-direct.com/en/the-next-bluetooth-wave-high-speed-and-low-energy-technology/
55 Heukelman, C. (2017). Bluetooth 5 versus Bluetooth 4.2, what's the difference? (2017). Semiconductorstore. Retrieved from: https://www.semiconductorstore.com/blog/2017/Bluetooth-5-versus-Bluetooth-4-2-whats-the-difference/2080
56 Heukelman, C. (2017). Bluetooth 5 versus Bluetooth 4.2, what's the difference? Semiconductorstore. Retrieved from: https://www.semiconductorstore.com/blog/2017/Bluetooth-5-versus-Bluetooth-4-2-whats-the-difference/2080

57 Ranger, S. (2014, June 10). What is Apple iBeacon? Here's what you need to know. ZDNet. Retrieved from: https://www.zdnet.com/article/what-is-apple-ibeacon-heres-what-you-need-to-know/
58 Maycotte. H.O. (2015, September 1). Beacon technology: The where, what, who, how and why. Forbes. Retrieved from: https://www.forbes.com/sites/homaycotte/2015/09/01/beacon-technology-the-what-who-how-why-and-where/#4fd0c53e1aaf
59 Ranger, S. (2014, June 10). What is Apple iBeacon? Here's what you need to know. ZDNet. Retrieved from: https://www.zdnet.com/article/what-is-apple-ibeacon-heres-what-you-need-to-know/
60 Lighthouse. (2019). The beginners guide to beacons. Retrieved from: https://lighthouse.io/beginners-guide-to-beacons/beacon-use-cases/
61 Lighthouse. (2019). The beginners guide to beacons. Retrieved from: https://lighthouse.io/beginners-guide-to-beacons/beacon-use-cases/
62 PCMAG. (2020). Definition of Bluetooth glossary. Retrieved from: https://www.pcmag.com/encyclopedia/term/bluetooth-glossary

19 Blockchain and other distributed ledger technologies

Introduction

Blockchain and other distributed ledger technologies offer new tamper-proof ways to verify identity and ownership, to make near instant payments without the need for the involvement of third parties, to store value (e.g. through cryptocurrency), to facilitate peer-to-peer fundraising and lending (e.g. through ICOs and STOs), to automate the execution of contractual agreements and related workflows (e.g. via smart contracts), to improve auditability, to distribute data storage, and to do all of this more securely and at lower cost[1,2]. The transformative impact of blockchain technologies has been equated to the advent of the internet[3]. As with early applications of the internet, the applications of blockchain technologies are just in their infancy but hold much more potential for growth in breadth and impact on business and society[4]. The business value of these expanding blockchain applications include: expanded opportunities for product innovation (e.g. companies offering new or enhanced products and services enabled by use of blockchain technologies), business model innovation (i.e. finding more efficient, effective, and profitable ways to serve existing and / or new customers), operational efficiency (e.g. automating workflows, removing third parties and related costs, reducing downtime and errors), customer access (e.g. being able to remotely serve billions of customers in developing economies who previously couldn't be served due to lack of bank accounts and identity verification mechanisms, and high third-party costs), risk mitigation (enhanced security, privacy, and auditability from blockchain's sophisticated cryptography, distributed consensus, immutability and ability to shard data so it does not exist in complete form on any one node), and social change (e.g. enhanced transparency may lead to changes in customer behaviors that businesses can capitalize on or may need to adapt to)[5,6,7,8,9,10].

Accounting strategic leaders have contended that blockchain technology is fundamentally an accounting technology[11], given its role in facilitating accounting-related workflows like measuring and reporting financial information, ascertaining asset ownership and value, accounting for asset ownership transfer, accounting for transaction payments, recording transactions, verifying and authorizing transactions, auditing transactions, and quantifying and mitigating risk. The accounting profession's blend of technical accounting and business knowledge positions accountants well for supporting leaders and managers to understand the business value and financial implications of adopting blockchain technology, to work with blockchain specialists to effectively implement blockchain technologies and platforms, to work with strategic leaders in identifying effective business models, to work with blockchain consortiums and policymakers to set effective standards, and to advise on blockchain-related investment and risk management decisions[12]. Using blockchain for accounting functions can provide greater transparency, improve efficiency, and provide indisputable certainty about the nature and history of transactions and asset ownership. Adoption of blockchain technologies can free accountants up from low value-adding activities (e.g. reconciliation, bookkeeping, finding source documents) to focus on greater value-adding roles like data stewardship, valuation of information assets, systems design, assurance, cyber risk management, strategic risk management, brand protection, engaging communication, building trust, and digital technology enablement.

Blockchain applications, use cases, and impacts on the accounting profession are in the early stages but advancing rapidly with blockchain technology growth. It is the responsibility of accountants to understand and be able to use blockchain technology, to understand the business value and use cases of blockchain technology, to advise on its safe adoption, and to champion and support managers leading the investment and implementation of tested and proven blockchain adoption decisions. Abdicating this responsibility may result in accountants being sidelined in some operational and strategic decisions.

Distributed ledger technology (DLT)

In contrast to an accounting ledger (such as a general ledger, purchase ledger, or sales ledger), a digital ledger is a digital file, or collection of files, or a database (a database is an organized collection of data or files). In contrast to a centralized database (a database that exists in a fixed location like a particular computer or cloud location), a *distributed ledger* (also referred to as a shared ledger or distributed ledger technology or DLT) is a database that exists in several locations and among several participants (e.g. several sites, several institutions, several geographies, several computers, several devices)[13,14]. The term "distributed" (also referred to as decentralized) basically refers to this existence across several locations. Being distributed, any additions or updates to the ledger (the collection of files or the database) are synchronized or copied to all participants' version of the ledger almost instantly (in seconds or minutes). But before any additions or updates can occur, they have to be agreed on and accepted by other participants (i.e. authorized, validated, and accepted). The process of "agreeing" is referred to as distributed ledger consensus or a consensus mechanism. It is facilitated by sophisticated algorithms. Because of this consensus mechanism, no centralized agent (e.g. a bank, a government, a corporation, a person) is needed to authorize, validate, and accept proposed updates[15,16]. A peer-to-peer network is required in order for the distributed ledger to exist in several locations and among several participants (e.g. this peer-to-peer network could be as simple as two computers being connected via a USB or it could be as complex as several computers being connected by a network infrastructure). Distributed ledgers are immutable, meaning that once ledger records are created, they cannot be deleted or altered – instead, other records are added to correct errors or omissions or to make improvements (e.g. if the record was a transaction where a US$100 purchase was made, but which was meant to be US$80, then a US$20 refund transaction is added rather than altering the original transaction). All records or files in a distributed ledger are date / timestamped and have a unique cryptographic signature. This provides a verifiable and auditable history of record creation and any subsequent updates.

Brought together, all these features of distributed ledgers (i.e. existing in several locations via a peer-to-peer network, consensus mechanism algorithms to facilitate updates, record immutability, date / timestamping, and cryptographic signature) offer new levels of efficiency (e.g. minimizing or eliminating the need for centralized monitoring, authorization, and updating activities and related infrastructure) as well as new levels of security (e.g. due to the decentralized nature, immutability, cryptographic signatures, and auditability)[17]. For example, regarding security, distributed ledgers ensure that the record of a financial transaction is near impossible to fake, create without permission, delete, modify, or hide. Not only would this be near impossible to achieve on every computer (or node) within the peer-to peer-network, an incriminating auditable trail would likely catch up with the perpetrator.

Blockchain

What it is and how it works

Blockchain is one type of distributed ledger that (as its sounds) structurally consists of blocks of data linked or "chained" together using high-end cryptography (cryptography is concerned with how to best convert information into unintelligible codes to prevent it being decoded and accessed by unauthorized people or entities)[18,19]. Each block in a blockchain stores information or data (e.g. it could be transaction information like date, purchaser, seller, payment amount). Each block also has a unique code called a "hash" that is unique to the information stored in that block. Figure 19.1 shows the elements of a block.

So, if the information stored in a block is modified in any way, the block's hash also changes to a different code that is unique to the modified or changed information. As well the information or data stored in it, a block also contains a timestamp of when that information was created or edited. In addition, each block stores the hash (or unique code) of its previous block. Before a new block can be added to the blockchain, it must correctly refer to the hash of the previous block – this can't happen if the previous block has been modified (and thus its hash is different to what it should be). Storing the hash of its preceding block is how a block is linked or "chained" to preceding blocks. This link or chain between blocks is what makes blockchain so secure. Besides making tampering or modification of blocks nearly impossible (e.g. through need to refer to correct previous hash which is copied across many nodes in the peer-to-peer network), blockchain provides a perfect audit trail or log of every change that occurs on the blockchain. Figure 19.2 shows a chain of blocks within blockchain, including the genesis block.

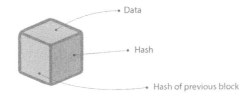

Figure 19.1 Each blockchain block contains some data, the hash of the block, and the hash of the previous block

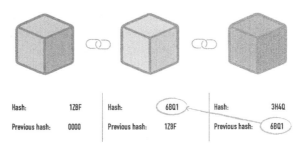

Figure 19.2 A chain of blocks, with each block other than the genesis block having the hash of the previous block

In addition to its linked block structure, blockchain functions with all the features of distributed ledgers (since it is a type of distributed ledger). That is, it operates over a peer-to-peer network, uses consensus mechanism algorithms to facilitate blockchain updates, uses date / timestamping, cryptographic signatures, and has immutable records). Blockchain technology platforms enable people to transact without the need for a central third party to assess and approve the authorization, validity, or security of the transaction (therefore no need to pay the third party, no need to wait for third party, no need to trust the third party, no need to disclose personal information to third party, no need to be exposed to third-party risks). This means cheap, instant, secure, anonymous, and risk-minimized transactions.

Other blockchain terminology

In addition to the distributed ledger and blockchain terminology we've already discussed above, it is often difficult to discuss or read about blockchain without one or more of the below terminologies coming up. Therefore we provide some plain language explanations below:

Append-only data structure

This refers to the fact that you can only add new blocks to the blockchain, which then get chained to previous blocks – you can't alter or delete blocks once they've been added. This is one of the main contributors to blockchain being tamper-proof and having an auditable history of record creation.

Permissionless vs. permissioned blockchain

A *permissionless* blockchain is one where anyone can join the network and perform certain actions on the network without requiring permission from anyone else on the network. In contrast, a *permissioned* network is one in which the network owner decides who can join a network and who can verify blocks. The consensus approach can still be the same or it can be tailored to the owner's preferences (e.g. it could be authority or credibility based).

Mining vs. miners

Mining is the process of verifying transactions to enable new blocks to be added to the blockchain network. *Miners* are blockchain nodes or participants that use their computers / computing power to perform this process. The process usually involves participants using mining programs for performing complex mathematical calculations to verify transactions and enable the creation of new blocks. In return, miners are usually paid a reward (e.g. on the Bitcoin blockchain the reward is an amount of Bitcoin). Miners may compete to be the first to perform the mathematical calculations and verify the transaction, as only the first person to verify is paid the reward. Mining can also cost miners money (e.g. cost of computing power or loss of deposit money they may pay to verify transactions in accordance with the rules). Some miners build massive infrastructure (e.g. buildings or computing hardware and software infrastructure) and hire large numbers of people to mine or verify blockchain transactions as a key source of income.

Proof of work

This is a widely used type of consensus algorithm for verifying transactions and adding new blocks to the blockchain. It involves miners competing with each other to be the first to solve the mathematical calculations required to verify transactions. Once the first miner solves the mathematical puzzle, it is broadcast it to the network so other miners can confirm the solution is correct and that the block can be added to the blockchain. The first miner then receives a reward for being first to solve the mathematical puzzle and thus enable appending of the new block.

Public key vs. private key

To read or add data to the blockchain, you need a *public key* and a *private key*. A public key is like the address or location where the information is stored. And everyone knows that address. But, although they may know where it is stored, it is encrypted (or locked) and can only be unlocked or decrypted with a personal key or private key that authorizes reading or updating of the information stored in that location. A private key is what prevents other people from reading or updating your information and thus keeping it secure.

Genesis block

Also referred to as block zero, a *genesis block* is the first block created on a blockchain.

Smart contract

Smart contracts are legal contracts that self-execute on the blockchain once the terms and conditions of the contract have been satisfied. This is possible because the contract details (e.g. parties, terms, and conditions) have already been agreed to and converted into self-executing code (e.g. the self-executing code might equate to something like: if prospective purchasers meet the seller's criteria for sale of land plus the government's criteria for purchase of land and the seller pays the specified amount, then transfer title ownership over the land to the purchaser). This self-executing code sits on the blockchain, ready to be run or executed on the blockchain once triggered (by the satisfaction of the contract terms and condition). Once on the blockchain, a smart contract cannot be changed, it automatically happens without a third party once triggering criteria are met. Being on the blockchain, the transaction can occur anonymously, it can occur without corruption, and it can occur without one or more of the parties coming back to muddy the meaning or interpretation of the contract terms.

Types of blockchain

There are four common types of blockchains, the types being differentiated by who can join and what

Public blockchains

A *public blockchain* is a permissionless blockchain. The "public" in its name means that anyone can join this blockchain network with read and write permissions. They do not need authorization from anyone else on the network. This is the main type of blockchain we've discussed so far with features and advantages such as openness (anyone can join and view / add to it), distributed consensus, immutability (once a block is added it can't be deleted or altered), scalability (existing on a large and ever-expanding network of nodes), and transparency. Disadvantages of public blockchains include difficulty changing the rules governing them once these are set, and risk that the blockchain can be compromised if the rules are not strictly enforced.

Private blockchains

A *private blockchain* is a permissioned blockchain. It is owned by an entity (e.g. a person, an organization, or other group). That entity or its delegate decides who can access this blockchain, what type of access they can have (e.g. read, write, or audit), and how consensus will be achieved (e.g. who can mine and what rules apply). Private blockchains bring together some of the benefits of central control and some of the benefits of distributed ledgers, usually with aims such as reduced transaction cost, transaction efficiency, improved security, improved auditability, and the flexibility to change blockchain read, write, and audit rules. An example of a private or permissioned blockchain is Hyper Ledger (a blockchain funded to enable industry collaboration for advancing blockchain-based distributed ledgers).

Consortium or federated blockchains

This type of blockchain is like a private blockchain but instead of a single individual or company making all the decisions, a group of companies or their representative individuals make decisions collectively for the benefit of the whole blockchain network (e.g. decisions about who can access the blockchain, who can read / write to the blockchain, and what operating rules apply to the blockchain). Benefits of *consortium* or *federated blockchains* include pooling together of resources to establish and operate the blockchain network, better quality decisions from broader expertise of consortium members and representatives, and better security from curation of blockchain participants and their access rights. Examples of consortium blockchains include the R3 blockchain consortium (established as an invitation-only blockchain consortium for major banks like JP Morgan and Santander) and EWF or Energy Web Foundation (an enterprise grade blockchain for organisations in the energy industry including Mercados Electricos, FlexiDAO, Scytale Horizon, and Wirepas).

Hybrid blockchains

As they sound, *hybrid blockchains* aim to leverage the benefits of both public and private blockchains. Aspects of the network can be made private so transactions with some types of stakeholders or things are permissioned, whereas other aspects of the network are public or open to anyone. For example, Facebook's proposed cryptocurrency Libra may need a hybrid blockchain composed of an open consumer-facing network as well as a private blockchain network for banks backing the currency.

Blockchain applications and use cases

Although many blockchain and other distributed ledger technology applications are still in their early stages, the applications are broadening rapidly and more and more applications are maturing[20]. For example, applications of blockchain technologies to cryptocurrency, smart contracts, bank settlement systems, and data storage are creating real customer and business value today[21,22]. We discuss some of these applications further below:

Cryptocurrency

Cryptocurrency is a type of digital currency or electronic money. Although it only exists in digital form, it can be converted into physical or government-issued currency via cryptocurrency exchanges (e.g. at the time of writing this paragraph, the cryptocurrencies Bitcoin and Etherium were trading at US$8,671 and US$166 respectively. Meaning that if you had 1 Bitcoin, you could exchange it for US$8,671 USD). There are thousands of cryptocurrencies in existence and, with almost any organization or individual able to create their own currency, this number is likely to keep growing. Each cryptocurrency has unique features and benefits which influence its value – not too different to the unique features and benefits of different nations' currencies influencing their value. Examples of these features and benefits include: supply limitations (e.g. there was a limited number of Bitcoins created and this cannot be increased), transaction acceptability (e.g. Bitcoin has been the most widely accepted cryptocurrency for ordinary transactions like buying a home or buying food), public interest (e.g. part of the reason behind Bitcoin's stellar price is it being the most well known and talked about cryptocurrency), stability (e.g. the value of Bitcoin is generally seen as being more stable than lesser known cryptocurrencies), and risk (e.g. during the boom and bust cycles of cryptocurrencies, some rose to price levels thousands of times their initial purchase price only for prices to subsequently fall way below the initial purchase price and remain there – this was especially the case for lesser known cryptocurrencies). Typically, anyone can purchase cryptocurrencies on a cryptocurrency exchange using real money; and they can exchange one cryptocurrency owned for another at the prevailing exchange rate. Although some fees are involved, these are miniscule compared to ordinary currency exchange rates, and transaction fees are usually negligible. The benefits of cryptocurrencies over government-issued currencies include the ability to transact directly without third parties and third-party fees (e.g. banks, brokers, agents, legal representatives), the clear and permanent audit trail of each transaction, confidentiality (nobody needs to know who you are, where you come from, who you bank with, where you live, where you work, what your credit card number is, etc.), reduced privacy risks (e.g. if personal information isn't collected, it can't be accidentally accessed), faster transactions (e.g. a cryptocurrency transaction can happen almost instantly, while a similar bank transaction can take days), stronger security (e.g. the risk of someone discovering and using your private key is very low), and the ability to transact with people who previously couldn't be reached (e.g. people in some developing countries who previously had no access to bank accounts). Disadvantages of cryptocurrency include complexity (although it is improving, a high level of technical expertise is still needed to purchase and use cryptocurrency), risk of loss (cryptocurrency exchanges have been breached, resulting in cryptocurrency losses, and scammers have posed as cryptocurrency platform agents to steal money intended to purchase cryptocurrencies), price volatility (e.g. in one year the Bitcoin price has risen to US$22,000 then crashed back to US$6,000, and it is one of the less volatile cryptocurrencies), and lack of regulation (there is as yet very little regulation of cryptocurrencies relative to government currencies. This often results in unwitting users being scammed, results in criminal enterprises using cryptocurrency as a money-laundering and criminal activity payment vehicle, results in people losing large amounts of money speculating on future cryptocurrency price growth, and results in people buying cryptocurrencies that are worthless).

Some organizations have had great success using cryptocurrency for fundraising purposes. These organizations have used Initial Coin Offerings (ICOs) as a fundraising mechanism in which they create and sell their own coins or tokens in much the same way that another company may sell its shares on a stock exchange to investors. For example, Block.one raised US$4 billion via its 2018 ICO despite its blockchain development product not being fully launched and investors not being clear on exactly how the funds would be spent[23]. Government interventions in ICOs have reduced the number and size of ICOs but they remain viable fundraising vehicles that can result in higher fundraising success (e.g. speed, amount, and cost of fundraising) similar to or better than traditional fundraising channels (e.g. banks, professional investors, stock exchange listings). ICOs are increasingly being replaced by STOs (Security Token Offerings) which are essentially the same thing but, thanks to government intervention, offer better protection against fraud, are based on real registered assets, comply with consumer financial safeguard laws, and are incorporated into the established securities market.

Smart contracts

We defined smart contracts earlier as contracts whose terms and conditions exist on the blockchain as self-executing algorithms[24]. Smart contracts have been applied to numerous types of contracts in different industries[25,26]. In trade finance, smart contracts have been used to automate approval workflows and clearing calculations; in healthcare, smart contracts can be used to authorize access to patient records; in real estate, smart contracts can be used to automate property leasing and purchase agreements as related or integrated workflows (e.g. paying bond, holding bond, releasing bond, cooling off, title search, settlement, rent payment reconciliation)[27,28]; in insurance, smart contracts can be used to automate claims processing; in government, smart contracts can be used to record election votes and announce the winner in a tamper-proof way; and obviously smart contracts can be used in peer-to-peer transactions[29].

Banking

Banks are using or exploring using blockchain for clearing and settlement activities (e.g. the Australian stock exchange is exploring shifting its post-trade clearing and settlement onto a blockchain system to improve the efficiency and effectiveness of these activities), using blockchain for payments (e.g. creating their own cryptocurrencies or utility tokens – such as UBS's utility settlement coin for financial markets which works like other cryptocurrencies but is convertible into cash on deposit at central banks), using blockchain to facilitate trade finance processes and authorization documents (e.g. bill of lading or letter of credit), and using blockchain to facilitate identity verification and to facilitate syndicated loans[30]. Figure 19.3 shows the funds transfer process in a traditional digital ledger vs. in a blockchain network (adapted from Figure 1 by Kean Wu, Manlu Liu, Jennifer Xu in the 2019 issue of *Current Issues in Auditing*).

Data storage

The application of blockchain technology to *data storage* is anticipated to disrupt cloud data storage[31]. Proponents of this application of blockchain technology (e.g. FileStorm,

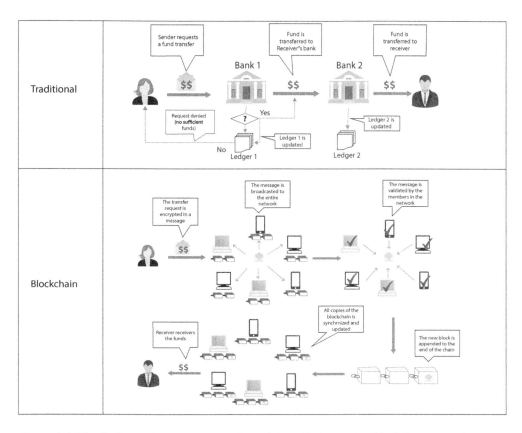

Figure 19.3 The funds transfer process in a traditional digital ledger vs. in a blockchain network

Sia, Storj, and Maidsafe) propose that decentralized data storage (distributing data files across a large peer-to-peer node network) is much more secure, makes it harder to lose data, and will be cheaper than the current centralized cloud infrastructure approach[32]. In addition, blockchain-based data files can be split up and spread piecemeal across nodes all over the world – thus restricting who can see the full integrated file[33].

Other applications

Other blockchain applications include verification of the authenticity of goods through blockchain-enabled supply chains, notarization to ensure proof of existence, validity of intellectual property origins, and more. Blockchain use cases are rapidly expanding in diversity with realization of the business benefits they promise[34,35].

Blockchain use cases in accounting

As noted at the start of this chapter, blockchain and distributed ledger technologies provide opportunities for product innovation, business model innovation, operational efficiency breakthroughs[36], access to new markets, and mitigation of risks[37]. Early adopters of blockchain and distributed ledger technology in accounting have initially been focused on auditing and analyzing blockchain transactions (e.g. in 2018 Ernst and Young launched "EY Blockchain Analyzer" to enable audit teams to review and analyze blockchain transactions[38]), reviewing smart contracts (e.g. in 2019 Ernst and Young launched "EY Smart Contract Analyzer" for monitoring smart contracts for security risks), and auditing the use of blockchain (e.g. PriceWaterhouseCoopers established a service for auditing organizations' blockchain services to ensure they're using the technology correctly and effectively[39]). Accounting applications have also focused on enabling and integrating cryptocurrency payments (e.g. eliminating intercompany reconciliation work by sharing a single ledger system instead of two double ledger systems), simplifying interdepartmental transfers (e.g. IBM's budgeting and forecasting team uses the Stellar cryptocurrency to allowing transfer of value / cash between departments[40]), using smart contracts to improve cash flow (e.g. building automatic payment into smart contracts to improve timeliness of payments), and facilitating shareholder voting (e.g. Santander bank uses blockchain technology to allow its shareholders to vote, reducing vote counting errors and vote tampering, as well as easing counting, accessibility, and accountability[41]). Making voting digital, through using blockchain technology, enables people to vote via mobile devices, reduces errors from manual paper-based systems, and allows real-time analysis and updates of whom and how votes have been cast. Diversity in blockchain applications and use cases in accounting continue to grow at a rapid pace. Table 19.1 shows opportunities and challenges of blockchain applications in auditing (adapted from Table 1 by Kean Wu, Manlu Liu, and Jennifer Xu in the 2019 issue of *Current Issues in Auditing*).

Table 19.1 Blockchain opportunities and challenges for auditing

	Opportunities	Challenges
Permissionless blockchain	• Examine transaction record on blockchain; • Develop novel audit process on blockchain transactions; • Verify the consistency between items on blockchain and in the physical world.	• No reversal of erroneous transactions; • No centralized authority to verify the existence, ownership, and measurement of items recorded on blockchains; • Data retrieval due to clients' loss of private key;
Permissioned blockchain	• Develop guidelines for blockchain implementation; • Leverage industry knowledge and experience to offer advice for best practices for blockchain consensus protocols; • Leverage business networks to form permissioned blockchain based on market demand; • Act as planner and coordinator of potential participants of a blockchain; • Leverage their expertise on IT auditing to audit internal control of blockchain, including data integrity and security; • Offer independent rating services to a specific blockchain; • Act as administrator of blockchain.	• No centralized authority to report cyberattack. • Need to be proficient in various blockchain technologies; • Difficult to reach consensus rules among all participants, when acting as an organizational agent; • Audit transaction linked to a side agreement that is "off-chain"; • Tackle the situation when central authority has power to override information on blockchains; • Cope with change of consensus in a blockchain.

Risks and issues

Early adopters of blockchain technology will have significant advantages for locking in key partnerships (e.g. Hilton and its partnership with IBM or consider the way Microsoft locked in key distributors in the PC business), locking in valuable customer segments (e.g. the way Microsoft locked in enterprise customers or the way Bitcoin is more trusted than other cryptocurrencies), setting industry use case standards, and enjoying superior profits. But such firms have to take care not to overinvest or attempt to scale too early (e.g. before customers are ready or before the technology is ready for certain types of use cases)[42,43,44]. Other blockchain issues include lack of regulation (e.g. unsuspecting customers may fall for scammer platforms pretending to be the real platform, or people pretending to be representatives of organizations involved in a transaction), and significant power consumption requirements and related environmental implications (e.g. the sophisticated blockchain calculations require significant power). Blockchain application issues also include complexity (e.g. the benefits of blockchain products and services can be obscured by complex processes required to identify users and for users to use them), sometimes being slow and cumbersome (e.g. due to their complexity and sophisticated calculations), and resistance or trivialization by entrenched entities (e.g. wide-scale adoption of blockchain will disrupt the existing order in much the same way that the internet disrupted business. As a result, entrenched entities may be incentivized to discredit or fight blockchain adoption). Early adopters must tread with care as the aforementioned issues result in risks that could derail their efforts or bring harm to their organizations.

Google and reflect

Blockchain node, blockchain address, P2P network, blockchain block, block explorer, block height, chain linking, hash, hashing, hash rate, Satoshi, Altcoin, blockchain wallet, hot wallet, cold wallet, blockchain forking, hard fork, soft fork, dApp, nonce, proof-of-stake, proof-of-authority, lightning network, stale block, orphan block, uncle block, multi-signature, blockchain oracle, whitepaper, byzantine fault-tolerance, cryptographic hash function (CHF), Merkle Tree, cryptography, double spending problem, hashcash, computational trust, public key cryptography, Ripple currency (XRP), Etherium currency, Libra currency, Monero currency, cryptocurrency exchange, blockchain sharding

Example tools and vendors

IBM Blockchain, Ripple, Coinbase, Hyperledger Fabric, Microsoft Azure Blockchain, Stellar, Quorum, Blockstream, NEO, Oracle Blockchain Cloud Service, Hyperledger Iroha, MultiChain, Tendermint, ConsenSys[45], PixelPlex, Accubits, SoluLab, PATRON, Celsius Network, Hyperledger Sawtooth, R3 Corda, Menlo One, Gameflip, DACC, Goldilock, FCoin[46], Factom.

Discussion questions

1 What is the difference between blockchain and a distributed ledger?
2 What are three different metaphors you could use to explain to your grandmother how blockchain works?
3 Is blockchain trustworthy? Why?
4 What is the difference between blockchain, Bitcoin, Ethereum, and Ripple (XRP)?

5   What is the difference between a public key and a private key?
6   What are the four main components of a blockchain ecosystem?
7   What are the different types of blockchain and what is the value of each?
8   Identify and explain the six top features or properties of blockchains.
9   What is a blockchain block and how is it created?
10 Can blockchain blocks be modified?
11 What type of data can be stored in a blockchain?
12 What is the double spending problem and how does blockchain overcome it?
13 What is a consensus algorithm?
14 Identify and explain ten different types of consensus algorithm.
15 What are the top five platforms for developing blockchain applications?
16 How is a smart contract different from a normal contract?
17 How is a dApp different from a normal app?
18 Explain how cryptocurrency mining works.
19 What problems does blockchain sharding solve?
20 What are the top five blockchain applications or types of use cases?
21 What are the top five accounting organizations successfully leveraging blockchain technology and how are they using it?
22 What is the business value of blockchain? What six areas of business value have been identified in this chapter?
23 Of all the blockchain use cases, which offers the biggest opportunity for cost reduction?
24 Of all the blockchain use cases, which offers the best opportunity for business model innovation?
25 Of all the blockchain use cases, which offers the best opportunity for product innovation?
26 Of all the blockchain use cases, which offers the best opportunity for safeguarding the security and privacy of stakeholder data?
27 Of all the blockchain use cases, which offers the best opportunity to enhance the adaptability and agility of organizations?

Notes

1 Finley, K. & Barber, G. (2019). Blockchain: The complete guide. Wired. Retrieved January 22, 2020, from: https://www.wired.com/story/guide-blockchain/
2 Mearian, L. (2020). What is blockchain? The complete guide. Computerworld. Retrieved January 22, 2020, from: https://www.computerworld.com/article/3191077/what-is-blockchain-the-complete-guide.html?page=2
3 Tapscott, D & Kirkland, R. (2016). How blockchains could change the world. McKinsey & Company. Retrieved January 22, 2020, from: https://www.mckinsey.com/industries/technology-media-and-telecommunications/our-insights/how-blockchains-could-change-the-world
4 Tapscott, D & Kirkland, R. (2016). How blockchains could change the world. McKinsey & Company. Retrieved January 22, 2020, from: https://www.mckinsey.com/industries/technology-media-and-telecommunications/our-insights/how-blockchains-could-change-the-world
5 Bender, J.P , Burchardi, K. & Shepherd, N. (2019). Capturing the value of blockchain. Retrieved January 22, 2020, from: https://www.bcg.com/en-au/publications/2019/capturing-blockchain-value.aspx
6 Bender, J.P , Burchardi, K. & Shepherd, N. (2019). Capturing the value of blockchain. Retrieved January 22, 2020, from: https://www.bcg.com/en-au/publications/2019/capturing-blockchain-value.aspx
7 Panetta, K. (2019). The CIO's guide to blockchain. Gartner. Retrieved January 22, 2020, from: https://www.gartner.com/smarterwithgartner/the-cios-guide-to-blockchain/

8 Carson, B., Romanelli, G., Walsh, P., & Zhumaev, A. (2018). Blockchain beyond the hype: What is the strategic business value?. McKinsey & Company. Retrieved January 22, 2020, from: https://www.mckinsey.com/business-functions/mckinsey-digital/our-insights/blockchain-beyond-the-hype-what-is-the-strategic-business-value
9 Scribani, J (2018) This is the value of Blockchain to different industries. World Economic Forum. Retrieved January 22, 2020, from: https://www.weforum.org/agenda/2018/12/the-business-value-of-the-blockchain/
10 Plansky, J., O'Donnell,T., & Richardsa, K. (2016). A strategist's guide to blockchain. strategy+business. Retrieved January 22, 2020, from: https://www.strategy-business.com/article/A-Strategists-Guide-to-Blockchain?gko=9d4ef
11 Institute of Chartered Accountants in England and Wales. (2018). Blockchain and the future of accountancy. Retrieved January 22, 2020, from: https://www.icaew.com/-/media/corporate/files/technical/information-technology/thought-leadership/blockchain-and-the-future-of-accountancy.ashx
12 Institute of Chartered Accountants in England and Wales. (2018). Blockchain and the future of accountancy. Retrieved January 22, 2020, from https://www.icaew.com/-/media/corporate/files/technical/information-technology/thought-leadership/blockchain-and-the-future-of-accountancy.ashx
13 Finley, K. & Barber, G. (2019). Blockchain: The complete guide. Wired. Retrieved January 22, 2020, from: https://www.wired.com/story/guide-blockchain/
14 Mearian, L. (2020). What is blockchain? The complete guide. Computerworld. Retrieved January 22, 2020, from: https://www.computerworld.com/article/3191077/what-is-blockchain-the-complete-guide.html?page=2
15 Finley, K. & Barber, G. (2019). Blockchain: The complete guide. Wired. Retrieved January 22, 2020, from: https://www.wired.com/story/guide-blockchain/
16 Mearian, L. (2020). What is blockchain? The complete guide. Computerworld. Retrieved January 22, 2020, from: https://www.computerworld.com/article/3191077/what-is-blockchain-the-complete-guide.html?page=2
17 Mearian, L. (2020). What is blockchain? The complete guide. Computerworld. Retrieved January 22, 2020, from: https://www.computerworld.com/article/3191077/what-is-blockchain-the-complete-guide.html?page=2
18 Mearian, L. (2020). What is blockchain? The complete guide. Computerworld. Retrieved January 22, 2020, from: https://www.computerworld.com/article/3191077/what-is-blockchain-the-complete-guide.html?page=2
19 CompTIA. (2018). Harnessing the blockchain revolution – CompTIAs practical guide for the public sector. Retrieved January 22, 2020, from: https://www.comptia.org/content/research/harnessing-the-blockchain-revolution-comptia-s-practical-guide-for-the-public-sector
20 Blockchain-council.org. (2019). Top 10 promising blockchain use cases. Retrieved January 22, 2020, from: https://www.blockchain-council.org/blockchain/top-10-promising-blockchain-use-cases/
21 Carson, B., Romanelli, G., Walsh, P., & Zhumaev, A. (2018). Open interactive popup Blockchain beyond the hype: What is the strategic business value?. McKinsey & Company. Retrieved January 22, 2020, from: https://www.mckinsey.com/business-functions/mckinsey-digital/our-insights/blockchain-beyond-the-hype-what-is-the-strategic-business-value
22 Bender, J.P , Burchardi, K. & Shepherd, N. (2019). Capturing the value of blockchain. Retrieved January 22, 2020, from: https://www.bcg.com/en-au/publications/2019/capturing-blockchain-value.aspx
23 Silva, M. (2019). Crypto companies are settling with the SEC, but that's not stopping them. Quartz. Retrieved January 20, 2020, from: https://qz.com/1720295/after-4b-ico-block-ones-24m-sec-settlement-lets-it-keep-building/; Rooney, K. (2018). A blockchain start-up just raised $4 billion without a live product. CNBC. Retrieved January 20, 2020, from: https://www.cnbc.com/2018/05/31/a-blockchain-start-up-just-raised-4-billion-without-a-live-product.html
24 Deloitte CFO Insights. (2016). Getting smart about smart contracts. Retrieved January 22, 2020, from: https://www2.deloitte.com/tr/en/pages/finance/articles/cfo-insights-getting-smart-contracts.html
25 Cheng-Shorland, C. (2018). Moving beyond smart contracts: What are the next generations of blockchain use cases? Retrieved January 22, 2020, from: https://www.forbes.com/sites/forbestechcouncil/2018/12/05/moving-beyond-smart-contracts-what-are-the-next-generations-of-blockchain-use-cases/#259adfdb13e5

26 Ream, J., Chu, Y., & Schatsky, D. (2016). Upgrading blockchains. Deloitte Insights. Retrieved January 22, 2020, from: https://www2.deloitte.com/us/en/insights/focus/signals-for-strategists/using-blockchain-for-smart-contracts.html
27 Cheng-Shorland, C. (2018). How technology is changing the real estate market. Forbes. Retrieved January 22, 2020, from: https://www.forbes.com/sites/forbestechcouncil/2018/07/31/how-technology-is-changing-the-real-estate-market/#40ff325b6d06
28 Deloitte. (2018) Blockchain and smart contracts could transform property transactions. Retrieved January 20, 2020, from: https://deloitte.wsj.com/cfo/2018/01/03/blockchain-and-smart-contracts-could-transform-property-transactions/
29 Ream, J., Chu, Y., & Schatsky, D. (2016). Upgrading blockchains. Deloitte Insights. Retrieved January 22, 2020, from: https://www2.deloitte.com/us/en/insights/focus/signals-for-strategists/using-blockchain-for-smart-contracts.html
30 Arnold, M. (2017) Five ways banks are using blockchain. Financial Times. Retrieved January 20, 2020, from: https://www.ft.com/content/615b3bd8-97a9-11e7-a652-cde3f882dd7b
31 Nelson, P. (2019). How data storage will shift to blockchain. Network World. Retrieved January 22, 2020, from: https://www.networkworld.com/article/3390722/how-data-storage-will-shift-to-blockchain.html
32 Nelson, P. (2019). How data storage will shift to blockchain. Network World. Retrieved January 22, 2020, from: https://www.networkworld.com/article/3390722/how-data-storage-will-shift-to-blockchain.html
33 Nelson, P. (2019). How data storage will shift to blockchain. Network World. Retrieved January 22, 2020, from: https://www.networkworld.com/article/3390722/how-data-storage-will-shift-to-blockchain.html
34 CompTIA. (2018). Harnessing the blockchain revolution – CompTIAs practical guide for the public sector. Retrieved January 22, 2020, from: https://www.comptia.org/content/research/harnessing-the-blockchain-revolution-comptia-s-practical-guide-for-the-public-sector
35 Scribani, J. (2018) This is the value of Blockchain to different industries. World Economic Forum. Retrieved January 22, 2020, from: https://www.weforum.org/agenda/2018/12/the-business-value-of-the-blockchain/
36 Accenture. (2020). Unlock trapped value with blockchain. Retrieved January 22, 2020, from: https://www.accenture.com/au-en/insight-blockchain-business-value
37 Carson, B., Romanelli, G., Walsh, P., & Zhumaev, A. (2018). Open interactive popup Blockchain beyond the hype: What is the strategic business value?. McKinsey & Company. Retrieved January 22, 2020, from: https://www.mckinsey.com/business-functions/mckinsey-digital/our-insights/blockchain-beyond-the-hype-what-is-the-strategic-business-value
38 Ernst and Young. (2019). EY announces blockchain audit technology. Retrieved January 22, 2020, from: https://www.ey.com/en_gl/news/2018/04/ey-announces-blockchain-audit-technology
39 Vetter, A. (2018). Blockchain is already changing accounting. Accounting Today. Retrieved January 22, 2020, from: https://www.accountingtoday.com/opinion/blockchain-is-already-changing-accounting
40 Fry, J. (2019). How blockchain technology could change an accountant's role. Medium. Retrieved January 22, 2020, from: https://medium.com/@jonnyfry175/how-blockchain-technology-could-change-an-accountants-role-bb727d26e6b0
41 Mooney, A., & Megaw, N. (2018). Santander shows potential of blockchain in company votes. Financial Times. Retrieved January 22, 2020, from: https://www.ft.com/content/c03b699e-5918-11e8-bdb7-f6677d2e1ce8
42 Gartner. (2019) Gartner 2019 hype cycle for blockchain business shows blockchain will have a transformational impact across industries in five to 10 years. Retrieved January 22, 2020, from: https://www.gartner.com/en/newsroom/press-releases/2019-09-12-gartner-2019-hype-cycle-for-blockchain-business-shows
43 Panetta, K. (2019). The CIO's guide to blockchain. Gartner. Retrieved January 22, 2020, from: https://www.gartner.com/smarterwithgartner/the-cios-guide-to-blockchain/
44 Raconteur. (2016). The future of blockchain in 8 charts. Retrieved January 22, 2020, from: https://www.raconteur.net/business-innovation/the-future-of-blockchain-in-8-charts
45 Gartner Peer Insights. (2020). Blockchain platforms reviews. Retrieved January 22, 2020, from: https://www.gartner.com/reviews/market/blockchain-platforms
46 Rossow, A. (2020). 10 new blockchain companies to watch for in 2018. Forbes. Retrieved January 22, 2020, from: https://www.forbes.com/sites/andrewrossow/2018/07/10/top-10-new-blockchain-companies-to-watch-for-in-2018/#40d089705600

Index

Note: Information in figures and tables is indicated by page numbers in **bold** and *italic*.

3D printing 240–243, *241*
4G networks 252
5G networks 253–254
6G networks 253–254

AAA *see* American Accounting Association (AAA)
ACCA *see* Association of Chartered Certified Accountants (ACCA)
accelerated change and transformation competencies 98, *158*, 158–159
accelerated change and transformation methods *91*, 91–92
accelerated innovation methods 92
accelerated innovation methods competencies 98–99
accelerators 176–177
accountant(s): adaptability and 119–121; agility and 119–121; ambidexterity and 119–121; as assurance advocate 85, *85*, 86; as brand protector 82–83; as business transformer 85, *85*, 86; in change 80–81; competencies 87–96, *88*, *91*, **93**, *95*; as control expert 84; as co-pilot 81–82; data integrity and 80; digital business and 35–36; in digital business strategy 111–114, *112*; digital disruption and 72, 77–100; in digital learning 117–119; as digital playmaker 85, *85*, 87; digital technology advancements and 26; as digital technology enabler 84–85; digital transformation and 77–100; as enablers of data leveraging 78–79; enhanced roles of 78–81; ethics and 80; future career zones for 85, 85–87; as handlers of digital technology demands 79; information systems and 16–17; as navigator 82; new roles of 78–81; as process expert 84; in process redesign 80–81; as public trust stewards 80; as storyteller 83; in strategy making 80–81; as sustainability trailblazer 85, *85*, 87; as trusted professional 83–84

accounting: digital disruption of 43–50, **48**, *49*
accounting functions: disruption of 52–63, *53*, *55*, *59*
accounting information systems (AIS): digital disruption and 62–63
accounting tools: digital disruption of 47–48, **48**
accounting value proposition: capacity and 51; defined 50; digital disruption of 50–52; realization of 51
adaptability 25–26, 119–121
advisory accounting 60–62
agility 25–26, 119–121
AI *see* artificial intelligence (AI)
AIS *see* accounting information systems (AIS)
ambidexterity 25–26, 119–121
ambiguity tolerance 169
American Accounting Association (AAA) 80, 99–100
analytics methods 91; *see also* business analytics (BA); data analytics; video analytics
append-only data structure 268
AR *see* augmented reality (AR)
articles: in personal information management strategy 175
artificial intelligence (AI): bots as 214; computer vision and 217, *217*; defined 212; disruption and 45, 68–69, **69**, **70**; efficiency and 211; expert systems and 218; general **213**, 213–214; issues with 218; knowledge graphs and 214–215, *215*; machine learning and 214; narrow **213**, 213–214; natural language processing and 216–217; neural networks and 215–216, *216*; risks with 218; speech recognition and 216–217; super **213**; tools 218–219; vendors 218–219
Association of Chartered Certified Accountants (ACCA) 78–79, 81; future career zones *85*, 85–87
assurance advocate 85, *85*, 86
audio: in personal information management strategy 175

280 Index

audit: digital disruption and 57–60, *59*
augmented reality (AR) 225, 226–228

BA *see* business analytics (BA)
banking 272
beacon technology 259–260
Beath, Cynthia 112, 113
BI *see* business intelligence (BI)
big data 66–67, 186–188, *187*, **191**
Bitcoin 268, 271–272
BLE *see* Bluetooth Low Energy (BLE)
blockchain 265–266; in accounting 273–274, **274**; applications 270–273, *273*; consortium 270; defined 267; in digital transformation 71–72; federated 270; genesis block 267, 269; hybrid 270; issues with 275; mining in 268; permissioned 268; permissionless 268; private 270; private key in 269; proof of work in 269; public 269–270; public key in 269; risks with 275; terminology 268–269; tools 275; use cases 270–273, *273*; vendors 275; workings of- *267*, 267–268
Bluetooth 259
Bluetooth 4.0 259
Bluetooth 5.0 259
Bluetooth Low Energy (BLE) 259
books: in personal information management strategy 175
bots 214
brand protection 82–83
buildings, smart 203–204
business analytics (BA) 188–189, *190*, **192**
business intelligence (BI) 188–189, *190*, **191, 192**
business partnering 60–62
business transformer 85, *85*, 86

cellular networks 251–254, *252*
CGMA *see* Chartered Global Management Accountants
change acceleration *158*, 158–159
change methods 91–92
change process: digital business as 31
Chartered Global Management Accountants 92, 94, 107
Chartered Institute of Management Accountants 75
CIMA *see* Chartered Institute of Management Accountants
cities, smart 206, **206**
cloud computing 63–64, *64*
cognitive computing 68–69, **69**
communication: in management accounting 55–56
competencies: accelerated change and transformation methods 98, *158*, 158–159; accelerated innovation methods 98–99; adaptability 120–121; agility 120–121; ambidexterity 120–121; complexity management 94–95, *95*; cybersecurity management 148; digital business 92–94, **93**; digital business strategy 114; digital customer engagement 128–129; digital customer experience 130–131; digital ethics 150; digital innovation 117; digital leadership 157–158; digital learning 119; digital risk management 160; digital stakeholder engagement 128–129; digital technology 89–91, 168; digital transformation strategy 114; disruption of *49*, 49–50; enterprise architecture 136–138; foundational IT 88, *88*; IMA and AAA Joint Task Force 99–100; information privacy 150; information systems 89; interrelationships between 99; required 87–96, *88*, *91*, **93,** *95*; strategic digital technology 98; strategy-making 94–95, *95*; technical 96; technology 96–100, *97*; technology learning 95–98, *97*; technology sourcing 138–139
competition: digital disruption and 21–22
complexity management frameworks 94–95, *95*
compliance, tax 56–57
computer vision 217, *217*, 221–223, *222*, *223*
consumer engagement channels 25
contracts, block 272
control expert: accountant as 84
co-pilot: accountant as 81–82
corporate accelerator models **93**
Covid-19 pandemic 46, 63, 82, 94, 119–120
CPA Australia 74, 75, 76, 90
CPA Canada 75, 79, 80, 90, 94, 102, 103, 104, 106
CPS *see* cyber-physical systems (CPS)
cryptocurrency 271–272
culture: digital leadership and 157
customer expectations 21
cyber-physical systems (CPS) 202–203
cybersecurity: capability *147*, 147–148; defined 144, *145*; management *147*, 147–148; risks **146**; unpacking 144–146, **146**
Cynefin framework 94, *95*

DaaS *see* data as a service (DaaS)
data: big data 66–67, 186–188, *187*, **191**; defined 184; event *185*; geographic *185*; in information systems 11, *11*; leveraging of 78–79; linked *185*; machine 184–185; natural language *185*; network *185*; as "new oil" 184; open 185; real-time 185, *185*; risks 186; roles and expertise **190**; structured 184, *185*; time series *185*; tools **192**; types of 184–185, *185*; unstructured 184, *185*; vendors **192**
data analytics 66–67, **191**; audits and *59*; defined 140, 189; descriptive 189; as indirect disruption 45; predictive 189; prescriptive 189; tools **192**; unpacking 140–141; vendors **192**

data as a service (DaaS) 63, *64*
data availability: business partnering and 61; digital disruption and 22–23, 45–47
data ethics 80
data integrity 80
data literacy 183
data management 188, *190*, **191, 192**; defined 139; unpacking 139–140
data navigator 85, *85*, 86–87
data proficiency 183
data science 140–141, 189–191, **190**, *190*, **191, 192**
data science technologies 66–67
data storage 272–273
data visualization 191, **191, 192**
data visualization algorithms 45
data visualization technologies 67
data warehousing systems 13
decision-making: data leverage and 78–79; information systems and 12–13
decision support systems 13, *14*
delegation, professional 169
descriptive analytics 189
design thinking process 91, *91*
digital business: accountants and 35–36; benefits of 31–32, *32*; as change journey or change process 31; defining 29–30; as future state 30–31; imperative 33; maturity models 31–32, *32*; as slippery term 29–30; transformation 33–35, *35*
digital business strategy: accounting roles for 114; competencies 114; defined 111–112; digital transformation strategy *vs.* 113; role of accountants in 111–114, *112*; unpacking 111–113, *112*
digital customer engagement: accounting roles for 128–129; competencies 128–129; defined 125–126; practices 127, *127*; traditional *vs.* *126*; unpacking 125–128, *126*, *127*
digital customer experience: accounting roles for 130–131; competencies 130–131; defined 130; unpacking 129–130
digital disruption 3–4; accountants and 72, 77–100; of accounting 43–50, **48**, *49*; of accounting competencies *49*, 49–50; of accounting functions 52–63, *53*, *55*, *59*; accounting information systems and 62–63; of accounting tools 47–48, **48**; of accounting value proposition 50–52; advisory accounting and 60–62; artificial intelligence and 68–69, **69**; audit and 57–60, *59*; big data and 66–67; blockchain and 71–72; business partnering and 60–62; cloud computing and 63–64, *64*; cognitive computing and 68–69, **69**; of competitive field and bases of competition 21–22; customer engagement and 126; of customer expectations and behaviors 21;

data analytics and 66–67; of data availability 22–23, 45–47; data science technologies and 66–67; data visualization technologies and 67; defined 20; digital technology and 19–21, *20*; direct 45; distributed ledger technologies and 71–72; drivers of 19; of financial accounting 52–54, *53*; impact of 77–78; indirect 44–45; internet of things and 69–71; of management accounting 54–56, *55*; manifestations of 19; network connectivity technologies and 69–71; robotic process automation technologies and 68–69, **69**; tax accounting and 56–57; unpacking 21–23
digital ethics 149
digital innovation: accountant role in 115–117, **116–117**; competencies 117; defined 115; opportunity leveraging **116–117**; unpacking 115–116, **116–117**
digital leadership: competencies 157–158; culture and 157; defined 154; roles 155–157, *156*; skills *156*; traditional *vs.* 154–155, *155*
digital learning: accountant role in 117–119; competencies 119; defined 118; traditional learning *vs.* 118–119; unpacking 117–119; *see also* learning
digital playmaker 85, *85*, 87
digital risk management and governance: accounting roles 160; competencies 160; defined 159; digital technologies in 160; and nature of digital risk 159–160; traditional *vs.* 159
digital stakeholder engagement: accounting roles for 128–129; competencies 128–129; defined 128; unpacking 128
digital technology(ies): accountants and 26; accounting information systems and 62–63; accounting value proposition and 50–51; advancements 19–21, *20*; advisory accounting and 61–62; ambiguity tolerance and 169; auditing and 58–60; business partnering and 61; competencies 89–91, 168; customer engagement and 126; defined 15; digital business transformation and 34; digital disruption and 19–21, *20*; in digital risk management and governance 160; existential threats and 23–24; exploration of 78; external experts and 169; financial accounting and 52–54, *53*; game-changing opportunities and *24*, 24–26; information overload and 170; information systems and 15–16; internal experts and 169; keeping up with 167–177, **171–173**; learning efficiency and 170; learning platforms and 170–171; leveraging of 78; management accounting and 54–56, *55*; omnichannel learning and 171–173, **171–173**; risk landscape and 60; tax accounting and 56–57; technological knowledge renewal

effectiveness and 168; thought leaders and 173–174

digital transformation: accelerated *158*, 158–159; accountants and 77–100; digital business competencies and 92–94, **93**; impact of 77–78; as term 3

digital transformation strategy: accounting roles for 114; competencies 114; digital business strategy *vs.* 113

distributed ledger technologies 71–72, 266–267

Dörner, Karel 30

drones 236–240, *237*, *239*

EA *see* enterprise architecture (EA)

edge computing 200–201, *201*

education: in information systems 13–14

efficiency, learning 170

email: in personal information management strategy 175; subscriptions 174

enterprise architecture (EA) 134–135, **135, 136**; accounting roles for 136–138; competencies 136–138; defined 133; governance model *137*; as layered 134; management 134–135, **135, 136**; unpacking 133–134

enterprise resource planning (ERP) systems 13, 188

ERP *see* enterprise resource planning (ERP) systems

ethics 80, 149

executive information systems 13, *14*

expert systems 218

FaaS *see* function as a service (FaaS)

financial accounting: digital disruption of 52–54, *53*

Fourth Industrial Revolution 203

function as a service (FaaS) 63, *64*

future-fit accounting roles 81–85

genesis block 267, 269

global navigation satellite systems (GNSS) 254

GNSS *see* global navigation satellite systems (GNSS)

government, smart 207

GPS (Global Positioning System) 234, 254

GPS III 254

graphs, knowledge 214–215, *215*

Gupta, Sunil 112

hackathons 176–177

hardware: in information systems 10–11, *11*

homes, smart 204–205

IaaS *see* infrastructure as a service (IaaS)

ICT *see* information communications technology (ICT)

IFAC *see* International Federation of Accountants (IFAC)

IIOT *see* industrial internet of things (IIoT)

IMA *see* Institute of Management Accountants (IMA)

imperative, digital business 33

industrial internet of things (IIoT) 201–202

Industrie 4.0 202–203

information communications technology (ICT) 14

information overload 170

information privacy: accounting roles 150; defined 148; unpacking 148–149

information system(s) (IS): accountants and 16–17; competencies 89; as competency 88, *88*; components of 10–12, *11*; computer-based 13; data in 11, *11*; decision-making and 12–13; defined 10; digital technologies and 15–16; education in 13–14; hardware in 10–11, *11*; management 13; managers in 12; manual-based 13; network in 11, *11*; people in *11*, 12; processes in *11*, 11–12; roles of 12–13; software in 11, *11*; strategic 15; types of 13–14, *14*; *see also* accounting information systems (AIS)

information technology 14

infrastructure, smart 205

infrastructure as a service (IaaS) 63, *64*

innovation methods, accelerated 92; competencies in 98–99; *see also* digital innovation

Institute of Management Accountants (IMA) 80, 99–100

International Federation of Accountants (IFAC) 4, 5, 78, 81

internet of everything (IoE) 69–71, 199, *199*

internet of things (IoT) 14; autonomous 200; connected 200; cyber-physical systems and 202–203; defined 198; digital business transformation and 35; disruption and 20, 47, 69–71; edge computing and 200–201, *201*; industrial 201–202; narrowband 256–257; as network 198; risks with 207; smart buildings and 203–204; smart cities and 206, **206**; smart government and 207; smart homes and 204–205; smart infrastructure and 205; "smartness" and 197, 200; smart workplaces and 204

IoE *see* internet of everything (IoE)

IoT *see* internet of things (IoT)

IS *see* information system(s) (IS)

knowledge graphs 214–215, *215*

learning: competencies 96–98, *97*; efficiency 170; omnichannel 171–173, **171–173**; platforms 170–171; tools **171–173**; *see also* digital learning

Lopez, Jorge 30
LoRa 257
LoRaWAN 257
low earth orbit satellites (LEO) 255, *255*, **256**
low-power wide-area (LPWA) 256
low-power wide-area network (LPWAN) 256, 257
LPWA *see* low-power wide-area (LPWA)
LPWAN *see* low-power wide-area network (LPWAN)
LTE networks 252, 257

machine learning (ML) 214
management accounting: digital disruption of 54–56, *55*
management information systems 13, *14*
managers: in information systems 12
Marchand, Donald 33
maturity models 31–32, *32*
mining, blockchain 268
mixed reality (MR) 225–226, *226*, 226–228
ML *see* machine learning (ML)
MR *see* mixed reality (MR)

natural language processing (NLP) 216–217
navigator: accountant as 82, 85, *85*, 86–87
NBIoT (narrowband internet of things) 256–257
network(s): cellular 251–254, *252*; in information systems 11, *11*; satellite 252, *252*
network connectivity technologies 69–71
neural networks 215–216, *216*
NFC (near-field communication) *258*, 258–259
Ng, Andrew 211
NLP *see* natural language processing (NLP)
notes: in personal information management strategy 175

office automation systems 13
omnichannel learning 171–173, **171–173**
operating systems 11
opportunities, game-changing *24*, 24–26

PaaS *see* platform as a service (PaaS)
people: in information systems *11*, 12
permissioned blockchain 268
permissionless blockchain 268
personal information management 174–175
platform as a service (PaaS) 63, *64*
platform organizations 25
platform strategy 30
playmaker 85, *85*
predictive analytics 189
prescriptive analytics 189
printing, 3D 240–243, *241*
privacy 148–149
processes: in information systems *11*, 11–12
process expert: accountant as 84

professional delegation 169
proof of work, in blockchain 269
public trust stewards, accountants as 80

RaaS *see* robots as a service (RaaS)
receivables management 53
research 5–6, **6**
risk landscape 159–160
risks: with artificial intelligence 218; with blockchain 275; data 186; with internet of things 207
robotic process automation (RPA) 43, 47, **48,** *53*, 60, 68–69, **69,** 236
robotics: business value of 234–236; defined 232; innovation and 235–236; use cases of 234–236
robots: building blocks of 233; defined 232–233; drones 236–240, *237*, *239*; fixed 234; industrial 234; inputs in 233; mobile 234; outputs in 234; processing in 233–234; risk reduction with 235; service 234; types of 234; workings of 233–234
robots as a service (RaaS) 236
roles: of information systems 12–13
Ross, Jeanne 112, 113
RPA *see* robotic process automation (RPA)

SaaS *see* software as a service (SaaS)
Samuels, Mark 34
satellite networks 252, *252*
satellites, low earth orbit 255, *255*, **256**
Schatz, Daniel 145
search engines 174
Sebastian, Ina 112, 113
smart buildings 203–204
smart cities 206, **206**
smart contracts 272
smart government 207
smart homes 204–205
smart infrastructure 205
smart workplaces 204
social media 174
social networks 173–174
software: in information systems 11, *11*
software as a service (SaaS) 63, *64*
speech recognition 216–217
STaaS *see* storage as a service (STaaS)
startup, volunteering for 177
storage as a service (STaaS) 63, *64*
storyteller: accountant as 83
strategic digital technology competencies 98
strategic information systems 15
strategy-making processes 94–95, *95*
sustainability trailblazer 85, *85*, 87

tax accounting: digital disruption and 56–57
technological knowledge renewal effectiveness 168
technology competencies 96–100, *97*

technology learning competencies 95–96
technology sourcing: accounting roles for 138–139; competencies 138–139; defined 138; unpacking 138
thought leaders 173–174
threats, existential 23–24
tolerance for ambiguity 169
transaction processing systems 13, *14*
transcription: in personal information management strategy 175
transformation, digital business 33
transformation methods 91–92

video analytics 221–223, *222*, *223*
virtual reality (VR) 224–225, 226–228

vision, computer 217, *217*, 221–223, *222*, *223*
volunteering, for startup 177
VR *see* virtual reality (VR)

Wade, Michael 33
Wall, Julie 145
workplaces, smart 204

XBRL (Extensible Business Reporting Language) 8, 43, 45, 48, 51, 53, 54, 65–66
XML (Extensible Markup Language) 65

YouTube: in personal information management strategy 175